THE BOOK OF
DANIEL

With Introduction and Notes

by

The Rev. S. R. DRIVER, D.D.

WIPF & STOCK · Eugene, Oregon

Wipf and Stock Publishers
199 W 8th Ave, Suite 3
Eugene, OR 97401

The Book of Daniel
With Introduction and Notes
By Driver, Samuel R.
Softcover ISBN-13: 978-1-7252-7706-9
Publication date 4/10/2020
Previously published by Cambridge University Press, 1900

CONTENTS.

	PAGES
CHRONOLOGICAL TABLE	viii

INTRODUCTION:

§ 1.	The person of Daniel and the contents of the Book	ix
§ 2.	History embraced by the Book of Daniel	xxiii
§ 3.	Authorship and Date	xlvii
§ 4.	Some characteristic features of the Book of Daniel	lxxvi
§ 5.	Versions, Commentaries, &c.	xcviii

| TEXT AND NOTES | 1 |

ADDITIONAL NOTES:—

On the term 'Chaldaeans'	12
On the terms 'Excellent' and 'Excellency' in A.V., R.V., and P.B.V. of the Psalms	32
On Nebuchadnezzar's madness	58
On the Four Empires of Daniel II., VII.	94
On the Expression 'one like unto a son of man' in Dan. vii. 13	102
On the Ruins of Susa	125
On the Prophecy of the Seventy Weeks	143
On the Expression 'The abomination of desolation'	150

APPENDIX:—

| The Inscription recording the vote of thanks to Eumenes and Attalus passed by the Council and people of Antioch | 207 |
| INDEX | 209 |

Principal Abbreviations employed.

*KAT.*²...Eb. Schrader, *Die Keilinschriften und das A. T.*, ed. 2, 1883 (translated under the title *The Cuneiform Inscriptions and the O.T.* 1885, 1888). The references are to the pagination of the original, which is given on the margin of the English translation. (*KAT.*³, 1902, by Zimmern and Winckler, is a new work altogether.)

KB....Eb. Schrader, *Keilinschriftliche Bibliothek* (transliterations and translations of Assyrian and Babylonian inscriptions), 1889—1900.

*L.O.T.*⁶...S. R. Driver, *Introduction to the Literature of the Old Testament*, ed. 6, 1897 (ed. 8, revised, 1909).

NHWB....M. Levy, *Neuhebräisches und Chaldäisches Wörterbuch*, 1876—89.

*OTJC.*²...W. Robertson Smith, *The Old Testament in the Jewish Church*, ed. 2, 1892.

P.S. (or Payne Smith)...R. Payne Smith, *Thesaurus Syriacus*.

*RP.*¹ or *RP.*²...*Records of the Past*, first and second series, respectively.

Schürer²...E. Schürer, *Gesch. des Jüdischen Volkes im Zeitalter Jesu Christi*, ed. 2, 1886, 1890 (translated, Edinb. 1890—3); Vol. 2, also, in ed. 3 (2 vols.), 1898. Ed. 4, considerably enlarged (1901—1909), in three volumes, has not at present (May 1911) been translated into English.

ZATW....*Zeitschrift für die Alttestamentliche Wissenschaft*, 1881 ff.

For the names of Commentators, &c., see pp. cii—civ.

It has been found difficult to preserve entire consistency in the transliteration of foreign words, especially Babylonian and Assyrian names; but it is hoped that the reader will not be seriously misled in consequence. Familiar names have usually been left unchanged. In other words *ḥ* (or sometimes *ch*) = ח; *ḳ* = ק; *ṣ* (or *ẓ*) = צ; *ṭ* = ט.

CHRONOLOGICAL TABLE.

B.C.

605.	Defeat of Egyptians by Nebuchadnezzar at Carchemish.
604.	NEBUCHADNEZZAR.
586.	Fall of Jerusalem.
561.	AMÊL-MARDUK (Evil-Merodach).
559.	NERGAL-SHAR-UZUR (Neriglissar).
555 (9 months).	LÂBASHI-MARDUK (Laborisoarchod).
555.	NABU-NA'ID (Nabonnēdus, Nabonidus).
538.	CYRUS. Return of Jews under Zerubbabel.
529–522.	CAMBYSES. 522 (7 months). GAUMÂTA (Pseudo-Smerdis).
522–485.	DARIUS HYSTASPIS. 485–465. XERXES.
333.	Persian empire overthrown by ALEXANDER THE GREAT.
323.	Death of Alexander.

Kings of Syria.		*Kings of Egypt.*
312. SELEUCUS I (Nicator).	322.	PTOLEMY I (Lagi), satrap.
	305.	PTOLEMY I (Lagi), king.
	285.	PTOLEMY II (Philadelphus).
280. ANTIOCHUS I (Soter).		
261. ANTIOCHUS II (Theos).		
249. ANTIOCHUS II receives in marriage Berenice, daughter of Ptolemy Philadelphus.		
246. SELEUCUS II (Callinicus).	247.	PTOLEMY III (Euergetes I).
226. SELEUCUS III (Ceraunos).		
223. ANTIOCHUS III (the Great).	222.	PTOLEMY IV (Philopator).
	205.	PTOLEMY V (Epiphanes).

198.	Antiochus the Great defeats Ptolemy Epiphanes at Paneion, and obtains possession of Palestine.
194–3.	Antiochus the Great marries his daughter, Cleopatra, to Ptolemy Epiphanes.

187.	SELEUCUS IV (Philopator).	182.	PTOLEMY VI (Eupator).
175–164.	ANTIOCHUS IV (Epiphanes).	182–146.	PTOLEMY VII (Philometor).

175.	Jason purchases the high-priesthood from Antiochus, expelling his brother Onias III.
172.	Menelaus, outbidding Jason, becomes high-priest.
170.	Antiochus' *first* expedition into Egypt. On his return he enters the Temple, and carries off the sacred vessels.
168.	Antiochus' *third* (or *second*?) expedition into Egypt.
168.	Apollonius surprises Jerusalem on the Sabbath-day.
168.	Antiochus' measures against the Jews. Desecration of the Temple (25 Chisleu).
167.	Rise of the Maccabees.
166–5.	Victories over the generals of Antiochus.
165.	Re-dedication of the Temple (25 Chisleu).
164.	Death of Antiochus.

DANIEL.

INTRODUCTION.

§ 1. *The person of Daniel and the contents of the Book.*

ALL that is known of Daniel is contained substantially in the book which bears his name. The Book consists essentially of two parts : (1) a series of *narratives* (ch. i.—vi.), describing the experiences of Daniel and his companions, in the three reigns of Nebuchadnezzar (ch. i.—iv.), Belshazzar (ch. v.), and Darius the Mede (ch. vi.); and (2) a series of *visions* (ch. vii.—xii.), with introductions describing the circumstances attending them, purporting to have been seen by Daniel during the reigns of Belshazzar (ch. vii., viii.), Darius the Mede (ch. ix.), and Cyrus (ch. x.—xii.). The principal link connecting the two parts of the book is afforded by chaps. ii. and vii.—the four empires symbolized by the image in Nebuchadnezzar's dream in ch. ii. being the same as the four empires symbolized by the four beasts seen by Daniel in his vision described in ch. vii. The following is an outline of the contents of the Book.

Nebuchadnezzar, having in the third year of Jehoiakim, king of Judah (B.C. 605), laid siege to Jerusalem, and carried away to Babylon several Jewish prisoners, determined shortly afterwards to have a number of noble and promising youths educated in the language and learning of the 'Chaldaeans,'—i.e. of the professors of divination, magic, and astrology in Babylon,—with a

INTRODUCTION.

view to their entering the king's service. Among the youths selected for the purpose were four of the Jewish captives, viz. Daniel, who received now the name of Belteshazzar, and Hananiah, Mishael, and Azariah, who received similarly the new names of Shadrach, Meshach, and Abed-nego, respectively[1]. The four youths, while content to pursue the studies prescribed by Nebuchadnezzar, determined, if possible, not to compromise their religious principles, by partaking of the special food provided for them from the royal table; and succeeded in obtaining permission to confine themselves to vegetable diet. At the end of three years, being found to excel all the others who had been educated with them, they are promoted to a place among the king's personal attendants, and prove themselves, when tested, to be superior in knowledge and ability even to the 'wise men' of Babylon themselves (ch. i.).

An opportunity soon arrives for Daniel to give proof of his abilities. Nebuchadnezzar, in his second year, being disquieted by a dream, demands of the 'wise men' of Babylon that they should repeat and interpret it to him: being unable to do this, they are condemned by him to death. Daniel and his companions, being, in virtue of their education, regarded as belonging to the class of 'wise men,' and finding consequently their lives to be in danger, betake themselves to prayer; and in answer to their supplication the secret of the dream is revealed to Daniel. Being now, at his own request, brought before the king, Daniel declares and interprets to him his dream. The dream was of a colossal image, the head consisting of gold, the breast and arms of silver, and the rest of the body of various inferior materials: as the king beheld it, a stone 'cut out without hands' suddenly fell, and struck the feet of the image, which thereupon broke up, while the stone grew into a mountain, which filled the whole earth. The image was interpreted by Daniel as signifying four empires—the head of gold being Nebuchadnezzar himself, representing the empire of the Chal-

---

[1] According to Josephus (*Ant.* XI. x. 1)—though this may be only an inference, which does not necessarily follow, from the terms of Dan. i. 3 *b*—the four youths were all related to King Zedekiah.

daeans, the other parts of the body symbolizing three other empires, which are not named explicitly, but which (see the notes on ii. 39, 40) are in all probability the Median, Persian, and Greek (the empire of Alexander and his successors, the Seleucidae and the Ptolemies). The stone 'cut out without hands' denoted the kingdom of God, before which all earthly powers were to succumb, and which was itself ultimately to embrace the entire world. The king was profoundly impressed by Daniel's skill, and not only rewarded him with numerous gifts, but also made him administrator of 'the whole province of Babylon,' and President of all the 'wise men' (cf. v. 11). At Daniel's request, his three friends also received promotion— probably to act as deputies or assistants to himself (ch. ii.).

Ch. iii. describes the wonderful deliverance of Daniel's three companions, Shadrach, Meshach, and Abed-nego. Nebuchadnezzar had erected, in the plain of Dura, near Babylon, a colossal golden image, and assembled for its dedication the high officials of his kingdom, all being commanded, under penalty of being cast into a burning fiery furnace, to fall down at a given signal and worship it. Shadrach, Meshach, and Abed-nego, refusing to do this, are cast into the furnace; but, to the king's astonishment, are rescued miraculously from the power of the flames. Thereupon Nebuchadnezzar solemnly acknowledges the power of their God, issues a decree threatening death to all who presume to blaspheme Him, and bestows upon the three men various marks of his favour.

Afterwards (chap. iv.) Nebuchadnezzar had another dream, which Daniel was likewise called in to interpret. This time, the dream was of a mighty tree, the head of which towered to heaven, while its branches sheltered and nourished the beasts and fowls of the earth: as the king watched it, he heard the command given that it should be hewn down to the ground, and only its stump be left standing, and that 'seven times' should then 'pass over' it. Daniel explained that the tree symbolized Nebuchadnezzar himself; and that the dream was an indication that a great humiliation would ere long befall him: for seven years he would be bereft of his reason; he would imagine himself an ox, and live in the open fields; nor would he recover, and be restored to his kingdom, till he was ready to acknowledge that the Most High was supreme over the kingdoms of the earth, and that he owed all his greatness to Him. At the end of twelve months, as the king was contemplating from the roof of his palace the city which he had built, Daniel's prediction was suddenly verified, and Nebuchadnezzar remained bereft of his reason for seven years. At the end of that time his reason returned to him; and in gratitude for his recovery, and his restoration to his kingdom, he issued a proclamation, addressed to all the world, in which he publicly acknowledged God's power and goodness towards him.

The scene of ch. v. is Belshazzar's palace, on the eve of Cyrus' conquest of Babylon (B.C. 538), 23 years after the end of Nebuchadnezzar's reign (B.C. 561), when Daniel, supposing him to have been 16 or 17 at the time of his captivity (B.C. 605), would be 83 or 84 years old. Belshazzar and his lords are at a feast, impiously drinking their wine out of the golden vessels which had once belonged to the Temple of Jehovah in Jerusalem. Suddenly there appears on the white plaister of the wall, almost directly above where the king is sitting, the palm of a hand, with fingers writing on the wall. The 'wise men,' being summoned to interpret what is written, are unable to do so. At the suggestion of the queen-mother, Daniel is called. He reads the king a lesson on his impiety and pride, and on his neglect to take warning by the example of Nebuchadnezzar; and having done this, interprets the writing. Its import is that Belshazzar is no more worthy to enjoy his kingdom: its days are numbered, and it is about to be given to the Medes and Persians. Daniel thereupon receives from Belshazzar the rewards which he had promised to any one who should interpret the writing; and is made one of the three chief Ministers in his kingdom. In the same night Belshazzar is slain, and 'Darius the Mede' 'receives' the kingdom.

Darius the Mede appointed over his kingdom 120 satraps, with three Presidents at their head, to whom they were to be accountable. One of these presidents was Daniel, whom, as he distinguished himself remarkably in his office, Darius contemplated making his chief minister. Upon this, the satraps, and other presidents, were filled with envy, and hoping to ruin him, sought to convict him of some act of disloyalty. They accordingly induced Darius to issue an interdict, forbidding any one, under penalty of being cast into a den of lions, to ask a petition of either God or man, except the king, for 30 days. The aged Daniel nevertheless continued, as before, to pray at his open window towards Jerusalem. The king, upon learning that Daniel had thus incurred the penalty, was greatly vexed; but feeling nevertheless that the law must be obeyed, reluctantly gave directions for him to be cast into the den of lions. Next morning, hastening to the spot, he is over-joyed to find him uninjured; and publishes a decree, enjoining men, in all parts of his dominion, to honour and revere the God of Daniel, who had given such wonderful evidence of His power (ch. vi.).

The second, or 'apocalyptic,' part of the book, describing Daniel's *visions*, now begins (ch. vii.—xii.).

In the first year of Belshazzar, Daniel had a dream, in which he saw four beasts emerging from the sea, a lion with eagle's wings, a bear, a leopard with four wings and four heads, and a fourth beast, with powerful iron teeth destroying all things, and with ten horns: as Daniel was contemplating it, another 'little horn' sprang up among the ten horns, 'speaking proud things,' before which three of the other horns were rooted up. The scene then suddenly changed: the Almighty appeared, seated on a throne of flame, and surrounded by myriads of attendants; the books, recording the deeds of men, were opened, and the beast whose horn spake proud things was judged and slain. After this, a figure in human form, coming with the clouds of heaven, was ushered into the presence of the Judge, and received from Him a universal and never-ending dominion. The meaning of the vision was explained to Daniel by one of the angels that stood by: the four beasts represented four kingdoms,—in all probability, as in ch. ii., the Babylonian, Median, Persian, and Greek; the 'little horn' was a king (Antiochus Epiphanes), who would persecute, and seek to exter-

b 2

minate, the holy people; but he would be judged, and have his power taken from him, before he had accomplished his purpose: the people of God would then receive a universal and never-ending dominion (ch. vii.).

Chap. viii. describes a vision seen by Daniel, in the third year of Belshazzar,—in the view of the author, therefore, two years after the vision described in ch. vii.,—in the citadel of Shushan (Susa). A ram with two horns appeared, pushing towards the west, the north, and the south, until a he-goat, with a conspicuous horn between its eyes, emerging from the west attacked the ram, and broke its two horns. After this, the he-goat gained further successes; but ere long its horn was broken; and in place of it there rose up four other horns, looking towards the four quarters of the earth. Out of one of these there came forth a little horn which, waxing great towards the land of Judah, exalted itself against the host of heaven, and against its Prince (i.e. God), struck and hurled down to the earth many of the stars, desecrated the sanctuary, and interrupted the daily sacrifice for 2300 'evenings mornings.' The meaning of this vision was explained to Daniel by the angel Gabriel. The ram with two horns was the Medo-Persian empire; the he-goat was the empire of the Greeks, the conspicuous horn being its 'first king' (i.e. Alexander the Great); and the four horns which rose up after this had been broken, were the four kingdoms,—viz. those of Macedonia, Thrace, Syria, and Egypt,—into which, after Alexander's death, his empire was ultimately resolved. The little horn, which arose out of one of these, and magnified itself against the host of heaven and the sanctuary, represented a king who, though not named, is shewn by the description of his character and doings (*vv.* 23—25) to be Antiochus Epiphanes (B.C. 175—164).

Chapter ix. is assigned to the first year of 'Darius the Mede.' In that year, Daniel, considering that the seventy years of desolation prophesied by Jeremiah for the Holy City were drawing to their close, made an earnest appeal to God on behalf of his people, confessing his nation's sin and the justice of the punishment which had overtaken it, and entreating Him now to pardon Israel's transgression, and no longer to defer its promised restoration. In answer to his entreaty, Gabriel appears, and explains to Daniel that it would be not 70 years, but 70 weeks of years (i.e. 490 years), before Israel's transgression would be forgiven and its redemption would be complete; that though Jerusalem would indeed before this be rebuilt and re-inhabited, it would be in 'strait of times'; and that during the last 'week' of the 490 years great troubles would fall upon the city and the sanctuary, a heathen abomination would desecrate the Temple, and the regular sacrifices in it would be suspended for 'half of the week,' until the destined judgement overtook the persecutor.

The last section of the book (chaps. x.—xii.) describes a vision seen by Daniel in the third year of Cyrus by the Ḥiddeḳel (the Tigris), and the revelations respecting the future communicated to him in it by an angel. Daniel, grieving for his people's sin, and anxious about its future, had been fasting for 21 days, when he fell into a state of trance, in which he had a vision of a shining being standing before him, who told him that he had been sent in answer to his prayers, but that he had been prevented from reaching him before by the opposition of the 'prince,' or patron-angel, of Persia: with the help of Michael, the 'prince,' or patron-angel, of the Jews, he had at length been able to start on his mission, and he was now with Daniel for the purpose of giving him a revelation concerning the future of his nation (x. 1—xi. 1). The contents of the revelation may be summarized briefly as follows. First, there would be four Persian kings, one of whom (Xerxes) would 'stir up all' in conflict with Greece; then would follow the empire of a 'warrior-king' (Alexander the Great), which, however, would soon be broken, and divided into four (Macedonia, under Cassander; Thrace, under Lysimachus; Syria and the East, under Seleucus; and Egypt, under Ptolemy); the leagues and conflicts, with varying fortunes, between the kings of the 'north' (Antioch) and of the 'south' (Egypt) during the following century and a half are next outlined (xi. 5—20); afterwards, in greater detail, is described the reign of Antiochus Epiphanes (B.C. 175—164), including his conflicts with Egypt, his persecution of the Jews, and the doom which should suddenly cut short his career (xi. 21—45). The death of Antiochus would be followed by the resurrection (of Israelites), and the advent of the kingdom of God (xii. 1—3). The revelation is to be 'sealed up' by Daniel until the time of the end (xii. 4), i.e. the time of Antiochus' persecution (see on viii. 17); for it is intended for the encouragement of the Israelites suffering then for their faith. Daniel asks how long the period of trial is to continue. He is told in reply, with solemn emphasis, that it will last for 3½ years (cf. vii. 25, viii. 14, ix. 27); there will be 1290 days from the time when the daily burnt-offering was interrupted, and the 'abomination that appalleth' (a small heathen altar, on the altar of burnt-offering) set up; but 45 days more, or 1335 in all, before complete happiness will have been attained. Daniel himself is commanded meanwhile to depart, and rest (in the grave) till then.

The Book, as will be apparent from this outline of its contents, is very different from those of most of the canonical prophets, even from those which, like the books of Amos, Isaiah, and Jeremiah, contain biographical particulars respecting their authors. It resembles most the Book of Jonah. The canonical prophets shew themselves immersed in the history and circumstances of their own time, in the political, moral, and spiritual condition of their nation, in its relations to its neighbours, especially to the great powers of Assyria, Egypt, or Babylon, and in its prospects in the immediate future,—the discourses, relating primarily and in the main to these various subjects, ever and again dissolving into visions of the future ideal glories of the people of God. In the Book of Daniel, on the contrary, hardly any interest is shewn in the condition or prospects of Israel in the age of Daniel himself: the *narratives* (ch. i.—vi.) have an essentially *didactic* import, their object being to shew how religious constancy and fortitude are, in various ways, rewarded by God, and how one heathen monarch after another is obliged to own the power of Daniel's God, while Daniel himself and his companions are not only delivered from peril or death, but rise to fresh honours[1]; and in the *visions* (ch. vii.—xii.), the writer, filling in the great historical picture sketched in outline in Nebuchadnezzar's dream (ch. ii.), depicts with particular and increasing distinctness the age of Antiochus Epiphanes, which he plainly regards as immediately preceding the advent of Israel's final glory. The thoughts and interests of the author thus centre not in the age of the captivity, in which Daniel himself lived, but in the *future*; and they are directed especially upon a period some four centuries distant from that of Daniel's lifetime, viz. the reign of Antiochus Epiphanes. The one chapter in the book which might seem to contradict what has been said, does so only in appearance: in ch. ix., it is true, Daniel is represented as bewailing the continued exile of his people; but in the answer to his complaint which follows (*vv.* 25—27), he is referred to the same far-distant age which is ever foremost in the writer's thoughts: Jeremiah's 70 years are to be understood as 70 weeks of years; and 63 'weeks' (i.e. 441 years) have still to run their course before the redemption which it was expected (see Is. xliv. 28, xlv. 13) would follow immediately upon Cyrus' conquest of Babylon, could yet be consummated.

With regard to Daniel himself, there is little to be added from other sources to what is stated in the Book. In Ezekiel mention is made of a 'Daniel' as a pattern of righteousness (xiv. 14, 'Though these three men, Noah, Daniel, and Job, were in it, they should deliver but their own souls by their righteousness'; similarly *v.* 20) and wisdom (xxviii. 3, addressed to the king of Tyre, 'Behold, thou art wiser than Daniel; there is no secret that they can hide from thee'); but it is doubted by many whether the reference is to the Daniel of the present book. Ez. xiv. and xxviii. date from about B.C. 594 and 588 respectively; and, as Prof. Davidson remarks[2], it is scarcely natural that the prophet should mention Daniel in such terms, grouping him at the same time with two patriarchs of antiquity, if he were really a younger con-

---

[1] See, more particularly, the introductions to chaps. i.—vi.
[2] Note on Ezek. xiv. 4 in the *Cambridge Bible*: cf. also Farrar, *The Book of Daniel* (in the 'Expositor's Bible'), pp. 9, 10.

temporary of his own. The association with Noah and Job, and the nature of the allusion, imply rather that, in the mind of the prophet, the Daniel whom he referred to was some ancient patriarch, renowned in the traditions of Israel for his piety and wisdom, as Enoch, for instance, was on account of his 'walking' with God. The tradition respecting Job was utilized, as we know, by the author of the book which bears his name, for the purpose of teaching a great moral lesson; and it is at least possible, if this view of the 'Daniel' of Ezekiel be correct, that there are features in the narrative of the Book of Daniel, which owe their origin, or at all events their form, to traditions of piety and wisdom associated with the name of the ancient patriarch (cf. Davidson, *l.c.*)[1].

The Greek translations of Daniel (LXX. and Theodotion), and following them the Vulgate, and some of the other derived versions, contain, like the LXX. of Esther, several passages not in the original text, the longer of which are contained, in a separate form, in the Apocrypha of the English Bible, under the titles of *The Song of the Three Holy Children*, *The History of Susanna*, and *The History of the Destruction of Bel and the Dragon*. The first of these additions follows iii. 23 of the Aramaic text, and contains a confession and prayer represented as having been uttered by Azariah in the midst of the flames (*vv.* 25—45), and a doxology (*vv.* 52—56) leading on into the hymn known familiarly as the *Benedicite* (*vv.* 57—90), which has been used in the public services of the Church since the fourth century. The *History of Susanna* is found in MSS. of Theod. at the beginning of the book[2]. Susanna was the wife of

---

[1] 'Daniel' is also the name of two other persons mentioned in the O. T.: (1) David's second son, 1 Ch. iii. 1 (called in 2 Sam. iii. 3, Chileab: the text in both places is uncertain; cf. the versions); (2) a priest of the line of Ithamar, who in 458 B.C. returned with Ezra to Judah, Ezr. viii. 2, Neh. x. 6. Among the contemporaries of the latter, it has been observed, there occur a Hananiah (Neh. x. 23), a Mishael (Neh. viii. 4), and an Azariah (Neh. x. 2); but the coincidence is probably accidental.

[2] In the LXX., the Syriac translation of the LXX. (the Syro-Hexaplar), and the Vulg., it follows at the end of the book (as chap. xiii.), before Bel and the Dragon (chap. xiv.). Perhaps this was its

a wealthy Jew, named Joakim (Jehoiakim), resident in Babylon. Two elders, becoming enamoured of her, but finding their advances repelled, accused her falsely of adultery, declaring that she had been detected by them in the act. The tribunal before which she was arraigned, accepting without inquiry the testimony of the two elders, condemned her to death. She protested loudly her innocence; and God, it is said, in answer to her appeal, 'stirred up the spirit[1]' of a youth among the bystanders, named Daniel, who, as she was being led forth to execution, proclaimed aloud that he would be no partner in the wrong that was about to be perpetrated, and remonstrated with the people upon what they were permitting. Being invited to conduct the inquiry himself, Daniel examined the two pretended witnesses separately, and quickly proved their testimony to be self-contradictory. Thereupon, in accordance with the law of Deut. xix. 19, the punishment which they had designed against the innocent Susanna was put in force against themselves; and Daniel 'became great in the sight of the people from that day onwards.' It is this apocryphal incident in Daniel's life that gives its point to Shylock's famous line (*Merch. of Venice*, IV. I. 223):—

    A Daniel come to judgement! yea, a Daniel!

and to Gratiano's hardly less famous retort (*ibid.* 333):—

    A second Daniel, a Daniel, Jew!

and (*ibid.* 340):—

    A Daniel, still say I, a second Daniel!

The narrative of Susanna is evidently designed to illustrate the truth that Providence watches over the innocent, and does not allow them to become the prey of the wicked. It is difficult not to connect the part taken in it by Daniel with the meaning

---

original place: the fact that it narrates an anecdote of Daniel's youth, might readily have led to its subsequent transference to the beginning of the book. (On the Greek versions of Dan., see further p. xcviii ff.)

[1] So Theod. In LXX. an *angel* is mentioned, who gives Daniel a 'spirit of understanding.'

of the name (which is transparent in the Hebrew), 'God is my *judge.*'

The *History of Bel and the Dragon* stands in Greek MSS. at the end of the Book of Daniel: in the LXX. it bears the curious title 'From the prophecy of Habakkuk, son of Joshua, of the tribe of Levi,' which would seem to imply that it was an extract from a pseudepigraphic writing, attributed to the prophet Habakkuk. Whether that be the case or not, the scene of the story is laid in Babylon, shortly after the accession of Cyrus[1], with whom, it is said (*v.* 2), Daniel lived on familiar terms (ἦν συμβιωτὴς τοῦ βασιλέως), and was honoured by him above all his friends. The Babylonians had an idol called Bel (cf. on v. 1), before whom were placed daily large offerings of flour, sheep, and wine, which the god was supposed to consume during the night. Daniel, being asked by Cyrus why he did not worship this idol, answered that he could worship only the living God, and not idols made with hands. The king replied that Bel was a living god, pointing, in proof of his assertion, to the amount of food regularly consumed by him. Daniel thereupon undertook to prove the contrary. The food was placed, as usual, before Bel; but, before the door of the temple was finally locked, Daniel strewed the floor within with ashes. Next morning, when the door was opened, the food was, of course, found to be gone. The king was triumphant: but, upon Daniel's pointing out to him the marks of footsteps on the floor, he saw that he had been duped: the priests were discredited and put to death, and Daniel was allowed to overthrow the temple. There was also a dragon in Babylon, which was believed to be a god, and worshipped as such. Daniel, being challenged by Cyrus, gave it a food which caused it to die. The people, enraged with Daniel, terrified the king into delivering him into their hands, and he was cast into a lions' den. Whilst he was there, the prophet Habakkuk, while carrying food to his reapers, at his home in Judah, was taken up by a lock of his hair (cf.

---

[1] So, at least, according to the text of Theodotion. *V.* 1, which alone gives the name of the king, is not in the LXX.

Ezek. viii. 3), and transported by an angel to Babylon, to provide Daniel with a repast. Upon the seventh day the king proceeded to the den to bewail Daniel; but, finding him still alive, he confessed aloud the power of his God: and, like 'Darius the Mede' (Dan. vi. 24), delivered those who would have destroyed Daniel to the same fate[1].

It is not possible to speak with certainty as to the date of these additions to Daniel; but they may be assigned without improbability to the first cent. B.C.[2]

Later Jewish writings contain various anecdotes relating to Daniel[3]; but they are destitute of historical value. Naturally, he is often referred to honourably on account of his wisdom, his opposition to idolatry, and his good deeds[4]. It was sometimes said that he returned to Judah and died there: but in the Middle Ages there was a persistent tradition that he was buried in Susa[5]. An early Arab historian describes how what was supposed to be Daniel's body was discovered at Susa about 640 A.D., and buried by King Sangar's orders under the river. Benjamin of Tudela, who visited Susa about 1160, found there a community of 7000 Jews, with 14 synagogues, in front of one of which there was, he says, the tomb of Daniel: the bones of the prophet were, however, elsewhere; for, as they were supposed to bring prosperity with them, there had been a dispute between the two quarters of the town for the possession of them, which had been settled by King Sangar ordering them to be suspended in a glass coffin exactly above the middle of the river, where, he adds, they still were. What purports to be the tomb of Daniel is shewn to the present day, a little W. of the mounds which mark the site of the ancient acropolis of Susa (cf. on viii. 1), on the opposite side of the Shaour[6].

---

[1] For various allusions in Rabbinical literature to these two stories of Bel and the Dragon, see the extracts quoted by Mr Ball in the *Speaker's Commentary on the Apocrypha*, ii. 344 f.
[2] Cf. Schürer, *Realencyklop. für Prot. Theol.*[3] i. (1896), p. 640.
[3] See *e.g.* the *Midrash on the Song of Songs*, on iii. 4, v. 5, vii. 8, 9.
[4] Cf. Farrar, p. 6 f.
[5] See Loftus, *Chaldaea and Susiana* (1857), pp. 317—323.
[6] See the Frontispiece to the present volume.

The Book of Daniel is written in two languages, i. 1—ii. 4*a* and viii.—xii. being in Hebrew, and ii. 4*b* (from 'O king')—vii. 26 being in Aramaic (cf. on ii. 4). It cannot be said that this change of language has been altogether satisfactorily explained. The principal explanations that have been offered are the following. (1) Diversity of origin, ii. 4*b*—vi. being supposed (Meinhold) to be a narrative written in Aramaic c. 300 B.C., which was afterwards accommodated to the needs of the Maccabaean age by a writer living then, who prefixed i.—ii. 4*a* as an introduction, and added chs. vii.—xii., with special regard to the persecutions of Antiochus. But, though the Aramaic sections of the Book of Ezra (iv. 8—vi. 18; vii. 12—26) are due no doubt to the fact that the compiler incorporated in his work extracts from a pre-existing Aramaic source, the supposition of dual authorship is not probable in the case of the Book of Daniel: not only are there links of subject-matter connecting together the Heb. and the Aram. portions, but i. 1—ii. 4*a* forms an introduction without which the sequel (ii. 4*b* ff.) would not be intelligible; and ch. vii., relating as it does chiefly to Antiochus, ought by the hypothesis to be in Hebrew (which it is not). (2) That the book was written originally in Hebrew, but translated early into Aramaic: a portion of the Hebrew text was accidentally lost, and it was then replaced by the Aramaic translation (Lenormant, Bevan, Prince). This explanation does not account for the two facts (which can hardly both be accidental) that the Aramaic part begins in ch. ii. just where the Aramaic language is mentioned, and breaks off just at the end of a chapter. (3) The explanation which seems to be relatively the best is that of Behrmann and Kamphausen, who suppose that in ch. ii. 'the author introduced the "Chaldaeans" as speaking the language which he believed to be customary with them: afterwards he continues to use the same language on account of its greater convenience, both for himself and for his original readers, alike in the narrative portions, and in the following (seventh) chapter, which in many respects is a counterpart to ch. ii.; for the last three visions (chs. viii., ix., x.—xii.) a return to Hebrew was suggested by

BILINGUAL CHARACTER OF THE BOOK. xxlii

the consideration that this had from of old been the usual sacred language for prophetic subjects[1].'

§ 2. *History embraced by the Book of Daniel.*

The Book of Daniel covers a wide period of history; and a survey of it, with more particular reference to such portions of it as bear especially upon the book, will probably be of service to the reader.

The Book opens in the third year of king Jehoiakim (B.C. 605), in which, it is said, Daniel and his companions were carried captive by Nebuchadnezzar to Babylon. The bulk of the nation went into exile subsequently, in two detachments, in 597 and 586 respectively. Upon the condition of the Jews generally during the years of exile, it is not necessary for our present purpose to dwell: for the only Jews who figure in the book are Daniel and his three companions; their compatriots being, for all practical purposes, non-existent. Something must, however, be said on the history of Babylon itself, and on the kings who successively occupied its throne. Babylon was at this time under the rule of a dynasty of Chaldaean kings. Originally (see p. 12) resident in the S.E. of Babylonia, near the seacoast, the Chaldaeans had gradually advanced inland until, under Nabopolassar (B.C. 625—605), they became the ruling caste in Babylon itself. Nabopolassar was at first, it seems, the viceroy in Babylon of the last king of Assyria, Sin-shar-ishkun (Saracus): but, as soon as circumstances appeared favourable, he declared his independence; and the Medes, invading Assyria soon afterwards, at his invitation, razed Nineveh to the ground (B.C. 607)[2]. Pharaoh Necho, taking advantage of this disaster to Assyria, proceeded to lay hands on Western Asia as far as the Euphrates (2 Ki. xxiii. 29; cf. *vv.* 33—35, xxiv. 7 *end*); and it was as Nabopolassar's general, sent on behalf of his

---

[1] Comp. Kamphausen in the *Encyclopaedia Biblica*, col. 1005.
[2] See further particulars in Maspero, *The Passing of the Nations* (1900), p. 483 ff.; and cf. Davidson's *Nahum* (in the *Cambridge Bible*), p. 137 f.

infirm and aged father, to oppose his further advance, that Nebuchadnezzar in 605 gained his victory at Carchemish (Jer. xlvi. 2; cf. on i. 1). Shortly afterwards Nabopolassar died; and Nebuchadnezzar hastened home (see Berosus, as quoted in the note on i. 1) to receive the crown.

Nebuchadnezzar reigned for 43 years (B.C. 604—561). So far as our information goes, he had no pleasure in warlike expeditions; his campaign against Pharaoh Necho, his two expeditions against Jehoiachin and Zedekiah, his siege of Tyre (Ezek. xxix. 17, 18)[1], which lasted, according to Josephus (*c. Ap.* i. 21), for 13 years (B.C. 585—572), and an invasion of Egypt in his 37th year (B.C. 568)[2], being all that we hear of. Nebuchadnezzar was emphatically a *builder*; and 'nearly every cuneiform document now extant dating from his reign treats, not of conquest and warfare, like those of his Assyrian predecessors, but of the building and restoration of the walls, temples, and palaces of his beloved city of Babylon' (Prince, p. 31)[3]. The celebrated 'India House Inscription[4],' now preserved in the India Office, gives an eloquent and detailed description of his principal architectural and defensive works. In this inscription, after an exordium, in which he pays homage to Marduk (the supreme God of Babylon), who had 'created' him, and entrusted him with the sovereignty over a great empire, Nebuchadnezzar describes first how he renovated, on a sumptuous scale, the two ancient and famous temples of Marduk in Babylon, called E-sagil, and of Nebo in Borsippa (a city 8—9 miles S.W. of Babylon), called E-zida, panelling their roofs with cedar brought from Lebanon, and decorating their walls, till they 'glistened like suns,' with gold and precious stones; then, how he restored fifteen other temples in Babylon; after this, how he completed the two great walls of Babylon, which, with a broad moat between them, had been begun by his father,

---

[1] Cf. Maspero, *op. cit.* pp. 543 (the Wady Brissa Inscriptions), 549.
[2] Schrader, *KAT.*[2] p. 364.
[3] See the inscriptions translated in *KB.* iii. 2, pp. 1—71.
[4] *RP.*[2] iii. 104—123; *KB.* iii. 2, pp. 11—31: cf. Tiele, *Bab.-Ass. Gesch.* (1886), ii. 441 ff., Maspero, *op. cit.* pp. 561—6.

Nabopolassar, adding, at the same time, at some distance from the city on the E., a new and enormous rampart, 'mountain-high,' together with another protecting moat; and lastly, how he not only rebuilt the palace of Nabopolassar, but also constructed in fifteen days[1] a yet more magnificent palace, surrounding it with lofty walls, and so making it into a kind of fortress. 'That house, for admiration I made it, for the beholding of the hosts of men I filled it with magnificence. Awe-inspiring glory, and dread of the splendour of my sovereignty, encompass it round about; the evil, unrighteous man cometh not within it. I kept far from the wall of Babylon the hostile approach of the foe; the city of Babylon I made strong as the wooded hills' (ix. 29—44). And he ends with a prayer to Marduk, his 'lord,' beseeching him, as he loves and has adorned his abode, to grant him long and prosperous life in the palace which he has built, and to permit his descendants to rule in it for ever (ix. 45—x. 18).

In addition to the works here described, Nebuchadnezzar also constructed many others: for instance, a huge wall, with outside moats, called the 'Median wall,' for protection against invaders from the north, and quays, dykes, and canals for the commerce or irrigation of the country.

Secondly, Nebuchadnezzar, judged by the standard of his age and country, was pre-eminently a *religious* king. It is true, his treatment of Zedekiah was cruel; but it must be remembered that Zedekiah, even in the judgement of Ezekiel (xvii. 18, 19), had broken faith with him, and acts which would not be tolerated among civilized belligerents now, were not proscribed then by the manners of the age. As Prof. Hommel[2] says, 'In his inscriptions we see on the one hand the fatherly care of a prince zealously considerate for the welfare of his land, on the other a genuine and heart-felt piety, which does not at all

---

[1] So also Berosus, *ap.* Jos. *c. Ap.* i. 19. The famous 'hanging garden' (κρεμαστὸς παράδεισος, *ibid.*), or park with trees arranged on rising terraces (not mentioned in the Inscription), was connected with this palace. See Maspero, *op. cit.* p. 782.

[2] *Gesch. Bab. und Ass.* (1885), p. 764.

produce the impression of consisting simply of empty phrases.' His longer inscriptions invariably begin with an acknowledgement of what he owes to Marduk and Nebo, and end with a prayer for further blessings. In the introduction of the India House Inscription, Nebuchadnezzar quotes a prayer which he had addressed to Marduk, perhaps at the time of his accession, for help and guidance in his rule:—

> O Eternal Ruler! Lord of all that is!
> Grant that the name of the king whom thou lovest,
> Whose name thou hast mentioned (i.e. whom thou hast called to the throne), may flourish as seems good to thee.
> Guide him on the right path.
> I am the ruler who obeys thee, the creation of thy hand.
> It is thou who hast created me,
> And thou hast entrusted to me sovereignty over mankind.
> According to thy mercy, O lord, which thou extendest over all,
> Cause me to love thy supreme rule.
> Implant the fear of thy divinity in my heart.
> Grant to me whatsoever may seem good before thee,
> Since it is thou that dost control my life[1].

And here is a prayer addressed by him to Shamash, the sun-god (whom the Assyrians called 'the judge of heaven and earth'), upon occasion of his restoring his temple in Sippar—

> Shamash, great lord, look graciously with gladness upon my deeds;
> Length of days, enjoyment of life, security of throne, and permanence of rule, grant me as thy gift;
> Accept favourably in thy faithfulness the lifting up of my hands[2].

Elsewhere also Nebuchadnezzar describes himself as one into whose hands Nebo, 'overseer of the hosts of heaven and earth, has committed a righteous sceptre for the government of men,' and as 'the king of righteousness, the humble, the submissive, who loves justice and righteousness,' and who 'places in the mouth of men the fear of the great gods[3].'

---

[1] Jastrow, *Religion of Bab. and Ass.* (1898), p. 296; *KB.* iii. 2, p. 13.
[2] *KB.* iii. 2, pp. 61, 63.
[3] *Ib.* pp. 13, 63.

SUCCESSORS OF NEBUCHADNEZZAR. xxvii

Nebuchadnezzar was succeeded by his son Amêl-Marduk ('man of Marduk'), the Ĕvīl-Merodach of 2 Ki. xxv. 27 ff. (B.C. 561—559). The only inscriptions of this reign, which we at present possess, are contract-tablets. Amêl-Marduk, after a 'lawless and dissolute' reign of two years[1], was assassinated by his brother-in-law, Nergal-shar-uẓur (Neriglissar), who then seized the throne. Nergal-shar-uẓur, like Nebuchadnezzar, was a devoted worshipper of Marduk, and restored temples and other buildings[2]. After reigning for four years (B.C. 559—555) he was succeeded by his youthful son Lâbashi-marduk, who, on account of the evil qualities which he displayed (διὰ τὸ πολλὰ ἐμφαίνειν κακοήθη), was after nine months beaten to death (ἀπετυμπανίσθη) by his friends[3]. The conspirators then placed one of their own number, Nabonnēdus (Nabu-na'id), on the throne: in the king's own words, which here supplement the brief narrative of Berosus by some graphic details[4]—

They all conducted me to the palace, cast themselves at my feet, and did homage to my royalty. At the command of Marduk, my lord, I was exalted to the sovereignty of the land, while they cried out, 'Father of the country! there is none his equal!'

Nabu-na'id, as Abydenus says[5], was 'no relation' to his predecessor: he was not, like Nebuchadnezzar, a Chaldaean, but a native Babylonian, the son of one Nabu-balâṭsu-iḳbi, as the inscription on a brick from Babylon testifies[6]—

Nabu-na'id, king of Babylon, the chosen of Nebo and Marduk, the son of Nabu-balâṭsu-iḳbi, the wise prince, am I.

Nabu-na'id was the last native king of Babylon: he was still on the throne when the city was taken by Cyrus, B.C. 538. As

---

[1] Berosus, in an extract *ap.* Joseph. *c. Ap.* i. 20.
[2] *KB.* iii. 2, pp. 71—79.
[3] Berosus, *l.c.* His successor speaks of him as one who 'knew not how to rule, and placed himself on the throne against the will of the gods' (Messerschmidt, *Die Inschr. der Stele Nabuna'ids*, 1896, p. 29).
[4] Messerschmidt, p. 29 (col. V. ll. 1—13).
[5] *Ap.* Euseb. *Praep. Ev.* ix. 41, 3 (προσήκοντά οἱ οὐδέν).
[6] *KB.* iii. 2, p. 119, No. I (similarly No. II, and pp. 97, 121).

DANIEL   *c*

his inscriptions shew[1], he devoted himself to restoring the ancient shrines and temples of the country, and excavated the substructures of such ancient sanctuaries as those at Larsa, Uruk, Ur, Sippar, and Nippur, until he reached the foundation-stones of the kings who had either originally built or subsequently restored them. The dates given by him for several of the kings thus mentioned by him have been of importance to modern scholars in fixing the chronology of ancient Babylonia. Belshazzar (Bêl-shar-uẓur) was Nabu-na'id's son: he is named on several contract-tablets[2], in all except one, with the adjunct, 'the king's son,'—a title something like that of 'Crown Prince.' There are also two of Nabu-na'id's own inscriptions in which, after describing his restoration of different temples, he closes with a prayer on his son's behalf—

And as to Bêl-shar-uẓur, the chief son, the offspring of my body, the fear of thy great divinity do thou set in his heart; may he not give way to sin; with life's abundance may he be satisfied[3].

Other references to Belshazzar are contained in the 'Annalistic Tablet' of Cyrus, found by Mr Pinches in 1879 among the collections in the British Museum, which also throws valuable light upon the political events of Nabu-na'id's reign, and upon the manner in which ultimately Cyrus gained possession of Babylon. The top of the tablet is broken off or mutilated; but the most important parts are, happily, intact. Thus, in Nabu-na'id's 6th year (B.C. 549) it is stated that Kurâsh (Cyrus), 'king of Anshan' (a district E. of the Tigris, in the S. or S. W. of Elam), was engaged in war with Ishtuvegu (the Astyages of Herodotus, king of Media); the troops of Ishtuvegu, however, revolted, and delivered their king into the hands of Cyrus (cf. Hdt. i. 127), who then attacked and took his capital Agamtânu (Ecbatana). In his 7th year Nabu-

---

[1] *KB*. iii. 2, pp. 81—113.
[2] Eight are referred to by Prince, p. 263 f.; three of these are translated in *RP*.[2] iii. 125—7. The notices are all incidental; e.g. a house is let for three years to 'Nabo-kin-akhi, the secretary of *Bêl-shar-uẓur*, *the king's son*.'
[3] *KB*. iii. 2, p. 97; similarly pp. 83, 89.

na'id was in Tevâ,—probably some favourite residence in the country,—and did not come to Babylon, so that the great annual procession of Bel and Nebo on New Year's Day could not take place: '*the king's son*,—i.e. Belshazzar,—the nobles, and his soldiers were in the country of Akkad' (north Babylonia). The 8th year is without incident. In the 9th year the statements respecting the king and 'the king's son' are repeated: it is also added that in Nisan (March) Cyrus, 'king of Persia,' collected his troops, and crossed the Tigris below Arbēla (a little E. of Nineveh), and in Iyyar (April) attacked and conquered a country, the name of which is now lost. In the 10th and 11th years the statements respecting the king and 'the king's son' are again repeated. The part of the tablet relating to the 12th to the 16th years is lost: under the 17th year (B.C. 538) we have the account of Cyrus' conquest of Babylon:—

¹²In[1] the month of Tammuz[2] [July], when Cyrus, in the city of Upê (Opis),[3] on the banks of ¹³the river Zalzallat, had delivered battle against the troops of Akkad, he subdued the inhabitants of Akkad. ¹⁴Wherever they gathered themselves together, he smote them. On the 14th day of the month, Sippar[4] was taken without fighting. ¹⁵Nabu-na'id fled. On the 16th, Gubaru[5], governor [*piḫu*,—whence the Heb. *peḥāh*] of the country of Guti[6], and the soldiers of Cyrus, without fighting ¹⁶entered Babylon. In consequence of delaying, Nabu-na'id

---

[1] The translation is based on that of Hagen in Delitzsch and Haupt's *Beiträge zur Assyriologie*, ii. (1894), pp. 205 ff. The translation in *RP*.², v. 158 ff., is in many respects antiquated. See further on the inscription Whitehouse, *Expos. Times*, June, 1893, p. 396 ff.

[2] Probably (Meyer, *ZATW*. 1898, p. 340 f.) an error of the engraver for *Tishri* (October); for Elul (September) has been already reached in l. 10.

[3] On the Tigris, about 110 miles N. of Babylon.

[4] Near the Euphrates, about 70 miles N.W. of Babylon.

[5] Evidently the prototype of the 'Assyrian' Gobryas, who, according to Xenophon, having a grudge against the King of Babylon for the murder of his only son, joined Cyrus (*Cyrop.* IV. vi, v. ii); and is mentioned by him in his (unhistorical) account of the capture of Babylon, as a principal leader of those who first entered the city, while the inhabitants were feasting, and made their way into the palace (VII. v. 8, 24—32).

[6] A part of the mountainous region W. of Media, and N. of Babylonia.

was taken prisoner in Babylon. To the end of the month the shield (-bearer)s [17] of the country of Guti guarded the gates of E-sagil[1]: no one's spear approached E-sagil, or came within the sanctuaries, [18] nor was any standard brought therein. On the 3rd day of Marcheshvan [November], Cyrus entered Babylon. [19] Dissensions (?) were allayed (?) before him. Peace for the city he established: peace to all Babylon [20] did Cyrus proclaim. Gubaru, his governor, appointed governors in Babylon. [21] From the month of Kislev [December] to the month of Adar [March—*viz.* in the following year, 537], the gods of the country of Akkad, whom Nabu-na'id had brought down to Babylon, [22] returned to their own cities. On the 11th day of Marcheshvan, during the night, Gubaru made an assault (?), and slew [23] the king's son (?)[2]. From the 27th of Adar [March] to the 3rd of Nisan [April] there was lamentation in Akkad: all the people smote their heads, etc.

The stages in the conquests of Cyrus are here traced by a contemporary hand. First, in 549, he appears as king of Anshan (or Anzan)—evidently his native home—in the S. of Elam[3]: in that capacity, the troops of Astyages desert to him, and he gains possession of Ecbatana. In 546 he is called 'king of Persia': it is reasonable therefore to infer that in the interval since 549 he had effected the conquest of this country. We thus learn incidentally that though Cyrus and his successors are commonly spoken of as 'Persian' kings, he was not a Persian by origin; he and his ancestors were kings of 'Anshan,' a district of Elam, and he only became king of Persia by right of conquest. In 538 his attack upon Babylon begins. His approach is made from the North. First, he secures Opis and the surrounding parts of N. Babylonia; then he advances to Sippar, which he takes without striking a blow: two days afterwards his general, Gubaru, enters Babylon, which likewise offers no resistance; Nabu-na'id is taken prisoner, but otherwise everything proceeds peaceably; the victors respect the property of

---

[1] The great temple of Marduk in Babylon.
[2] The tablet is injured at this point; but 'the king's son' is the reading which those who have most carefully examined the tablet consider the most probable.
[3] See the Map in Maspero's *Struggle of the Nations*, p. 31.

the citizens and of the temples, and a strong guard is placed round the temple E-sagil to protect it from plunder. Shortly afterwards, Cyrus himself enters Babylon, and proclaims peace to the city. He entrusts the government of the city to Gubaru, who in his turn appoints subordinate governors. Belshazzar, however, more energetic—or successful—than his father, still held out,—perhaps in a fortified palace,—but is slain by Gubaru in a night assault. After this, Cyrus formally assumed the title of 'king of Babylon' as well as the other grandiloquent titles borne by the Babylonian kings; and (as contract-tablets of the time shew) was at once recognized as the legitimate sovereign.

The story told by Herodotus (i. 191), and Xenophon (*Cyrop*. VII. v. 15—31), of the stratagem by which Babylon was taken by Cyrus, the waters of the Euphrates being diverted, and the city entered during the night—according to Xenophon, by Gobryas and Gadates—from the river-bed, while the people were all celebrating a festival,—which has been supposed to fall in with the representation in Dan. v. and with Is. xxi. 5 (cf. xliv. 27; Jer. li. 36),—is shewn by the inscription to be unhistorical: Babylon, it is clear, offered no resistance to the conqueror. At the same time, it is worth observing, Xenophon and the inscription both agree in assigning a prominent part to Gubaru (Gobryas) in gaining possession of the city.

The ease with which the transference of power from Nabu-na'id to Cyrus was effected, was no doubt due largely to the unpopularity of Nabu-na'id, who not only year after year lived in retirement at Tevâ, and neglected to discharge the public duties devolving upon him, but also gave great offence by removing arbitrarily the images of many local deities from their shrines and transferring them to Babylon. It is probable that the priests, who were both numerous and influential, were in particular adverse to the ruling dynasty. Cyrus, in a proclamation (the so-called 'Cylinder Inscription') issued by him shortly after his entry into the city, shewed that he understood how to utilize the popular disaffection; he represented himself as the favoured servant of Marduk, specially chosen by him to become sovereign of Babylon, in order to undo the evil deeds of Nabuna'id, and to redress the grievances of its people[1].

It may be of interest to the reader to compare the account given by Berosus (who had access to native records), preserved by Josephus (*c. Ap.* i. 20):—

In the 17th year of his reign Cyrus, advancing out of Persia with a great army, and having already subdued all the rest of Asia, advanced against Babylonia. Nabonnēdus, hearing of his approach, met him with his forces, but joining battle, was defeated, and fleeing with only a few companions was shut up in the city of Borsippa [the suburb of Babylon, on the S.W.]. Cyrus having taken Babylon, gave directions for the walls outside the city to be destroyed, because the city appeared to him to be very strong, and difficult to take; after which he marched against Borsippa, intending to force Nabonnēdus to surrender. As Nabonnēdus, however, did not await the siege, but delivered himself up beforehand, Cyrus treated him kindly, and giving him Carmania [the country E. of Persia] as a residence, sent him out of Babylonia. Nabonnēdus accordingly spent the rest of his life in that country, and there ended his days.

The two centuries of subjection to Persia (B.C. 538—333), which now followed, may be passed over rapidly. Cyrus continued to reign till B.C. 529,—for the first year or so after his accession in conjunction with his son Cambyses[2]. In his first year (Ezr. i. 1) he gave permission to the Jewish exiles to return to Palestine; and a considerable number under Zerubbabel availed themselves of the permission. The nucleus of a restored community was thus formed, which, though it did not realize the ideal glories promised by the great prophet of the exile, the author of Is. xl.—lxvi., nevertheless gave vitality again, in their

---

[1] The inscription is translated in Ball's *Light from the East*, pp. 224 f.; the principal parts of it may be found also in Hogarth's *Authority and Archaeology*, p. 128; cf. Prince, pp. 92—104.

[2] Maspero, *Passing of the Empires*, p. 636. Contract-tablets exist dated 'in the first year of Cyrus king of countries, and of Cambyses king of Babylon,' or 'of Cambyses, king of Babylon, in the days of Cyrus, his father, king of countries': see *KB*. iv. 261—3, or more fully Prášek, *Forschungen zur Gesch. des Alterthumes* (1897), i. 25—29, 34—5.

ancient home, to the institutions and traditions of the past. Judah became part of a province of the Persian empire, under the authority of the governor (peḥāh) of what, spoken from the Babylonian standpoint, was called 'the other side of the river' (עֲבַר נַהֲרָא); and its people, provided they paid their appointed taxes, and did nothing calculated to arouse suspicion upon political grounds, enjoyed full social and religious freedom. The restoration of the Temple under Darius, son of Hystaspes (522 —485), the return of a second body of exiles under Ezra in 458, the re-building of the city-walls by Nehemiah in 444, and the reforms introduced by these two leaders, need only be alluded to in passing. The reign of Artaxerxes I (465—425) is followed by a period which, so far as the recorded history of the Jews is concerned, is almost without incident; but under Artaxerxes Ochus (359—339) a revolt of Jews is reported (c. 350), followed by reprisals on the part of the Persians, and the transportation of many captives into Hyrcania and Babylonia, which have been supposed by some recent scholars to have been the occasion of certain prophecies and psalms[1]. In the fourth year of Darius Codomannus (336—333), the Persian empire was brought to its close by the conquests of Alexander the Great[2].

It was Alexander's ambition to build up a world-wide empire, which should be permeated in every part by the spirit and civilization of Greece. Struck down by fever in Babylon, in 323, when even the conquests that he was meditating were still incomplete, he necessarily left this design unrealized: nevertheless, the impulses which he set in motion did not cease to operate with his death, and under his successors, especially those who ruled at Antioch and Alexandria, the diffusion of Greek culture and manners was steadily maintained, and affected Palestine as well as other parts[3]. For the present, however, we may confine ourselves to the political history of Judah during the century and a half which now begins.

Alexander, after his seven months' siege of Tyre (332), had

[1] See *L. O. T.*[6] pp. 222, 246, 321, 389.
[2] See a summary of these conquests in the note on viii. 5.
[3] Cf. Ewald, *Hist.* v. 235—249; Schürer[2], ii. 9—50 (§ 22).

marched through Palestine, on his way to Egypt, but did not come into hostile collision with the Jews: in fact, though the story of his having offered sacrifice in the Temple is doubtless apocryphal[1], he treated them with favour, and, according to Josephus (*c. Ap.* ii. 4), settled many of them as colonists in his new city of Alexandria. The Jews formed an industrious, peace-loving community, which, except when religious fervour stirred them up into rebellion, there was no motive to assail.

After Alexander's death, the fiction of a united empire was still for a while maintained, the generals who ultimately became his heirs being at first administrators of particular provinces under Perdikkas, who acted as regent on behalf of Alexander's feeble brother, Aridaeus. As it happened, an ambiguous position was taken, almost from the beginning, by Coele-Syria, Phoenicia, and Palestine; and this, coupled with the fact that these provinces lay on the debateable border-land between the two powerful kingdoms of Syria and Egypt, caused Judah repeatedly to change hands during the century and a half which followed. On the whole, however, except during some brief intervals, Palestine remained subject to Egypt till Antiochus the Great, in 198, defeated the forces of Ptolemy Epiphanes at Paneion (under the foot of Hermon); after this date it passed permanently into the power of Syria. In the preliminary distribution of provinces arranged between Alexander's generals on the day after his death, Syria was assigned to Laomedon, and Egypt to Ptolemy Lagi. In 321 Perdikkas, having quarrelled with Ptolemy, led an army against him through Palestine, and advanced as far as Pelusium, where, however, he met with a repulse and was defeated. At the convention of Triparadisus, held shortly afterwards in the same year, Laomedon's title to Syria was confirmed. Ptolemy, however, in direct contravention of this agreement, sent in 320 an expedition through Palestine, and annexed Syria by force of arms. But Ptolemy did not hold it long. Antigonus, the general who had obtained Phrygia, Syria, and Pamphylia, cherished ambitious projects, and in 315

---

[1] Ewald, v. 214 f.

UNDER ALEXANDER'S SUCCESSORS.

invaded Syria. Ptolemy's garrisons had to withdraw; and Syria and Palestine remained for the greater part of the next 14 years in the hands of Antigonus, Ptolemy only recovering them for a few months after his victory at Gaza in 312. In the course of the following years a coalition was formed between Seleucus (the satrap of Babylonia), Lysimachus, Cassander, and Ptolemy, for the purpose of checking the advances of Antigonus; and in 302 Ptolemy took possession of Coele-Syria. In the next year (301) Antigonus met his antagonists at Ipsus (in Phrygia), where he was totally defeated and slain. As a result of the victory, Seleucus became master of Syria; but upon his proceeding to occupy Coele-Syria, Ptolemy remonstrated, averring that he had only joined the coalition on the understanding that Coele-Syria was to be his. Seleucus denied this, declaring that not only had he contributed to the victory far more than Ptolemy (who had not been present at the battle at all), but that after the battle it had been agreed by his colleagues, Lysimachus and Cassander, that he should have the whole of Syria. He consented, however, for the present to waive his claim[1]. The dispute thus remained an open one; but, for the time, the rights of possession remained with Ptolemy.

These repeated occupations of Palestine by foreign armies seem to have been not unaccompanied by hardships for the Jews. On one occasion Ptolemy captured Jerusalem by a sudden attack on the Sabbath, because the Jews refused to fight on that day: he also transported numbers, either as slaves or as compulsory settlers, to Egypt, where, however, recognizing their honesty and fidelity, he employed many in his garrisons, giving them equal rights with the Macedonians in Egypt: after the battle of Gaza, also, many Jews migrated to Egypt voluntarily, attracted partly by the advantages which the country offered them, partly by the kindliness shewn towards them by Ptolemy[2]. These settlements of Jews in Egypt (which, as we have seen, appear to have begun under Alexander) were the nucleus of

[1] See Mahaffy, *Empire of the Ptolemies*, p. 66 (an extract from Diod. xxi. 5), p. 254 f. (from Polyb. v. 67).
[2] Jos. *Ant.* XII. i.; *c. Ap.* i. 22, ii. 4; cf. Mahaffy, pp. 85—90.

what ultimately became an extensive and important Jewish colony[1].

The successors of Ptolemy Lagi were Ptolemy Philadelphus (285—247) and Ptolemy Euergetes I (247—222). Ptolemy Euergetes I, an active, enterprising ruler, in revenge for his sister Berenice's murder (see on xi. 6), began his reign with a war against Syria, attacking it, however, from the sea, and not by land. Among his successes (cf. Dan. xi. 7, 8), he took in 246 Seleukeia, the port of Antioch, which remained in the possession of Egypt for some 26 years. Under both these Ptolemies Coele-Syria and Palestine appear to have continued provinces of Egypt[2]. The same two rulers were also favourably disposed towards the Jews: Philadelphus figured in Jewish tradition—rightly or wrongly—as the royal patron, at whose instance the Law was translated into Greek; and Euergetes, after a successful campaign in Syria, was reported to have offered sacrifices of thanksgiving in the Temple at Jerusalem[3].

Under Ptolemy (IV) Philopator (222—205), the prosperity of Egypt began to decline. Philopator, who was aged only 24 at his accession, was a dissolute and indolent king, who thought solely of his own pleasures, and was the prey of intriguing courtiers. His great rival was Antiochus (III), the Great (223—187), who almost as soon as he came to the throne, began taking steps to secure Coele-Syria and Palestine (cf. Dan. xi. 10). First, he recovered Seleukeia, which since 246 had been held by an Egyptian garrison. Next Theodotus, the Aetolian, governor of Coele-Syria, 'despising Ptolemy Philopator for his vices, and mistrusting his court,' betrayed Coele-Syria and Phoenicia to Antiochus (219). An army sent by

---

[1] Cf. Schürer[2], ii. 499 ff. (§ 31); more fully ed. 3, iii. 19 ff.
[2] For Philadelphus cf. the lines of Theocritus (xviii. 86 f.).

Ναὶ μὴν Φοινίκας ἀποτέμνεται Ἀραβίας τε,
Καὶ Συρίας Λιβύας τε κελαινῶν τ' Αἰθιοπήων.

Cf. Mahaffy, p. 130 f.
[3] Ewald, *Hist.* v. 283 ff.; Jos. *c. Ap.* ii. 4. 5. Philo, in a passage (*Vit. Mos.* § 5) quoted by Cheyne, *Origin of the Psalter*, p. 146, passes a warm encomium on Ptolemy Philadelphus.

Ptolemy in 218 for their recovery was defeated by Antiochus near Lebanon. Antiochus now occupied Palestine; but advancing with a large army to meet Ptolemy, was defeated by him with great loss at Raphia, on the border of Egypt, and obliged to retire to Antioch (217; cf. Dan. xi. 11—12). Philopator, in consequence, recovered Coele-Syria and Palestine; and Antiochus, being engaged in wars elsewhere, made no attempt for the time to retrieve his disaster. In 205, however, Philopator died, leaving the throne to his son Ptolemy Epiphanes (205—182), a child four or five years old. Antiochus now formed a league with Philip, king of Macedonia, for the partition of the dominions of Egypt between them (Dan. xi. 13—14). In 202 he occupied Coele-Syria and Palestine, and took possession of Jerusalem. An Egyptian army was sent under Scopas, an Aetolian *condottiere*, to recover these provinces; but though successful at first he was in 198 defeated at Paneion (Bâniâs), near the sources of the Jordan, and afterwards, when he had withdrawn to Sidon, obliged to surrender (Dan. xi. 15, 16). From this time onwards, until the Romans interfered, Palestine remained in the undisturbed possession of the kings of Syria. The sufferings of the Jews during these years were considerable: as Josephus says (*Ant.* XII. iii. 3), whichever side prevailed for the time, their country was burdened by the presence in it of an invading army; and many in addition were either carried off as slaves, or took refuge in flight. In the end, however, the Jews gave their support to Antiochus, welcomed his troops into Jerusalem, and assisted in the ejection of the Egyptian garrison which had been left in the citadel by Scopas. In return for this support, Antiochus, in a letter written to his general Ptolemy, directed many privileges to be granted to them: contributions were to be made, on a liberal scale, towards defraying the expenses both of the regular sacrifices, and of the repair of the Temple, till the country should have recovered its losses (cf. on Dan. xi. 14).

In 193 Antiochus gave the taxes of Coele-Syria and Palestine as a dowry to his daughter, Cleopatra, on her marriage to Ptolemy Epiphanes (Dan. xi. 17). This grant of Antiochus

INTRODUCTION.

became before long the occasion of serious disputes between Egypt and Syria, but it made no difference in the position of the two subject provinces: they continued to be held by Syria. Three years afterwards, in 190, Antiochus was utterly defeated at Magnesia by the Romans (Dan. xi. 18): humiliating conditions of peace were imposed; and Antiochus was bound to pay for 12 years an annual fine of 1000 talents, his son Antiochus and other hostages being sent to Rome as security for his observance of the terms of the treaty. In 187 Antiochus was succeeded by his son Seleucus (IV) Philopator (187—175). The reign of this prince was uneventful; the only incident in it which need be here mentioned is the attempt made by him to replenish his empty treasuries by sending his chief minister, Heliodorus, on an abortive mission to pillage the Temple (see on Dan. xi. 20).

Seleucus Philopator was murdered in 175 in consequence of a conspiracy headed by Heliodorus, who aspired to the throne. Heliodorus did not, however, attain his ambition: Antiochus, the brother of Seleucus, after having been for 14 years a hostage in Rome, had just been exchanged for Seleucus' son, Demetrius, and was at Athens on his way home when he heard of his brother's fate: hastening back at once to Antioch, he succeeded, with the help of Eumenes, King of Pergamum, and his brother Attalus, in expelling Heliodorus and securing the throne for himself (cf. Dan. xi. 21, and p. 207 f.).

Antiochus, who afterwards assumed the title Epiphanes[1], is, in the later chapters of the Book of Daniel, the principal figure. He was a strange character,—a man of ability, though with a taint of folly and madness in his veins. On the one hand he was ambitious, arbitrary, and determined. He laid deep designs, and had a remarkable power of concealing them. During the years spent by him as hostage at Rome, he was well received[2], and

---

[1] This title does not mean 'illustrious,' but 'manifest'; and implies that the bearer of it claimed to be a visible god. There was a Ptolemy 'Epiphanes' in Egypt (205—182 B.C.), who was also called θεὸς ἐπιφανής (Mahaffy, pp. 290, 315, 316, 317, &c.). See below (p. 193) the titles of Antiochus, as borne by him on his coins.

[2] Cf. p. 177, *note*.

moved in the best circles of Roman society; the consequence was that he contracted a taste for Western habits and ideas, and also for Western luxuries. He was munificent, and even lavish: he shewed, in Livy's words, a truly 'regal mind' in the gifts made by him to Greek cities and temples[1]: he also greatly improved his capital, Antioch: he added a new quarter to it; he adorned it with numerous copies of the principal masterpieces of Greek sculpture: he erected magnificent temples both in Antioch, and in its suburb Daphne; and even introduced gladiatorial shows (Livy xli. 20). But he courted popularity to an excessive degree. Polybius, in a well-known passage[2], describes how, putting off his royal robes, he would wander alone through the streets of Antioch, now discussing questions of art in the gold-smiths' shops, now offering himself as a candidate for some public office, and entreating people to vote for him, while at other times, again, he might be seen making unexpected presents to utter strangers, startling a party of boon companions by rushing in upon them with a band of music, or bathing with the townspeople in the public bath. His behaviour was at times so undignified and extraordinary that men doubted even whether he was altogether sane, and instead of 'Epiphanes' he was called 'Epimanes' (Madcap). To the Jews, on account of the determined effort made by him to denationalize them and heathenize their religion, he appeared simply as a persecuting tyrant and monster of iniquity; and though other features of his character are alluded to (Dan. viii. 23; xi. 21—30 a, 39), it is this aspect of it which is chiefly delineated in the Book of Daniel (vii. 8, 21, 25; viii. 9—12, 23—25; ix. 26, 27; xi. 28, 30 b—38; xii. 7 b, 11).

The principal public events in Antiochus's reign referred to in Daniel are (1) his expeditions against Egypt; and (2) his treatment of the Jews. The former may be dealt with briefly here: fuller particulars will be found in the note on xi. 21.

---

[1] Cf. p. 183, *note*.
[2] XXVI. x. 3 ff. (preserved in Athen. v. 21, p. 193 f.); cf. Athen. x. 52, Diod. xxix. 32. It is translated in Montefiore's *Bible for Home Reading*, ii. 660 f.

INTRODUCTION.

Ptolemy Epiphanes had died in 182, and his widow, Cleopatra (Antiochus's sister), in 173, leaving as heir to the throne Ptolemy Philometor, a boy 14 or 15 years old, who was, of course, nephew to Antiochus Epiphanes. The youthful king having been induced by his ministers to take steps for the recovery of Coele-Syria, Antiochus determined to forestall him: in 170 he led an army into Egypt, defeated Ptolemy's forces at Pelusium, and obtaining possession of his nephew's person, occupied the country,—ostensibly, on his nephew's behalf, in reality with the view of securing it for himself. In spite, however, of the presence in Egypt of Antiochus's troops, Philometor's younger brother, Ptolemy Physcon (afterwards Ptolemy Euergetes II), was proclaimed king in Alexandria. This gave Antiochus an excuse for resuming military operations[1], under the pretence of restoring Philometor to his lawful rights: he accordingly laid siege to Alexandria, but finding himself unable to take it, returned home to Syria, leaving Philometor nominal king at Memphis, and stationing a large garrison at Pelusium (cf. Dan. xi. 25—28). The garrison left at Pelusium opened Philometor's eyes: a reconciliation between the two brothers was soon effected, and Philometor was received into Alexandria. This led to Antiochus's 'third' campaign in Egypt (168), which was brought to an abrupt termination by the intervention of the Romans; Antiochus, when within four miles of Alexandria, being met by the Roman legate, Q. Popilius Laenas, and peremptorily commanded to leave the country (Dan. xi. 29—30 a).

The policy of Antiochus towards the Jews was not, at least in its origin, the outcome of any particular hostility towards their religion: it was simply a corollary of the plan which he had conceived of unifying the various peoples of his empire by bringing them all under the influence of Hellenic civilization. 'His reign, his political *rôle*, and even the types of his coins, cannot be properly understood, unless account is taken of the fact that this prince was profoundly Hellenized, and that he

---

[1] On the question whether or not this was a *second* invasion of Egypt, see the note on xi. 27 (p. 185).

exerted himself, without intermission and without scruple, to transplant Hellenic culture into Syria[1].' His plan was not entirely out of harmony with feeling in Judah. For some time past,—probably indeed from the peaceful years of the earlier Ptolemies,—Greek influences had been making their way into Judah, and had found a home among the educated classes. Alexander himself, in furtherance of his scheme alluded to above, of creating a Hellenic world-empire, had founded Greek cities in several of the countries conquered by him; and under his successors Greek colonies were established in Palestine, and Greek colonists found their way thither. Many Jews also, as we have seen (p. xxxv), settled in Egypt; and the intercourse which was kept up in consequence between the two countries formed another channel by which Western influences would find entrance into Judah. Under Ptolemy Philadelphus (285—247) parts of the O. T. were (in Egypt) translated into Greek: the Greek language became known in Judah—the grandson of Ben-Sira, who translated his grandfather's gnomic work into Greek, was a native of Palestine; and Greek ideas and Greek customs were no longer unfamiliar in Jewish circles[2].

The effect of this influx of new ideas into Judah was to emphasize parties there. On the one hand, since the return from Babylon, attention had more and more been concentrated by the Jews on their sacred books, especially on the Law, which had been made into an absolute rule of conduct, and the principles of which had been,—or at least, were being,—gradually systematized into a code governing every department of life. Though this devotion to the Law had its dangers, and in fact (as allusions in the N. T., and the Mishna, shew) degenerated ultimately into a barren ceremonialism, this was not its effect upon the more spiritually-minded Israelites; and the Psalms, many of which (especially those in the later books) certainly date from this period, shew what a real and profound piety prevailed among the religious section of the people. On the other hand, among the more worldly-minded, it became a

[1] Babelon, *Les Rois de Syrie*, p. xcii.
[2] Cf. Ewald, *Hist.* v. 244—267.

fashion to adopt ostentatiously Greek customs: Hebrew names were exchanged for Greek, Joshua or Jesus became Jason, Eliakim became Alkimos; an influential and growing Hellenizing party sprang up, who made it their aim to obliterate the distinctive characteristics of their nation. Naturally innovations such as these intensified the rigour of the opposite or conservative party, and led them to cling together the more closely for the purpose of maintaining the integrity of their national institutions; and the crisis was precipitated by the accession of Antiochus Epiphanes.

Jesus, or, as he preferred to call himself, Jason, brother of the high-priest, Onias III, was the principal leader of the Hellenizing party; and by means of a large bribe, induced Antiochus not only to depose his brother and confer the vacant office upon himself, but also to grant permission for a 'gymnasium,' or exercise-ground, to be constructed in Jerusalem, in which the Jewish youths might emulate the Greeks in athletic contests, and to bestow the citizenship of Antioch upon the inhabitants of Jerusalem (175 or 174 B.C.). 'And when the king had given assent, and he had gotten possession of the office, he forthwith brought over them of his own race to the Greek fashion. And setting aside the royal ordinances of special favour to the Jews..., he brought in new customs forbidden by the Law: for he eagerly established an exercise-ground under the citadel itself, and caused the noblest of the young men to wear the (Greek) cap [the *petasus*, a broad-brimmed hat, such as appeared on statues of Hermes, the patron-god of the palaestra]. And thus there was an extreme of Greek fashions, and an advance of an alien religion, by reason of the exceeding profaneness of Jason, that ungodly man and no high-priest,' so that even the priests, it is said, leaving their sacrificial duties unfinished, hastened down from the Temple-court to take part in the spectacle, as soon as they heard the signal for throwing the discus, with which the games were opened (2 Macc. iv. 7—14; cf. 1 Macc. i. 11—15).

Jason continued high-priest for three years (till 172 or 171); and under his patronage, the Hellenizing Jews naturally became

ANTIOCHUS EPIPHANES.

bolder. At the end of this time, one Menelaus, an unscrupulous adventurer, whom Jason had employed as his agent to carry the promised money to Antiochus, outbid his master, got him expelled from the high-priesthood, and secured the office for himself. Jason fled across the Jordan, and took refuge with the Ammonites: Menelaus, who is described as 'having the passion of a cruel tyrant, and the rage of a savage beast' (2 Macc. iv. 25), stole some of the vessels of the Temple for the purpose of meeting his obligations to Antiochus, and when rebuked by the late high-priest for sacrilege was said to have procured his murder (see on ix. 26). The sacrileges of Menelaus occasioned riots in Jerusalem: he was arraigned before Antiochus at Tyre, but managed by judicious bribery to get himself liberated, and his accusers condemned. Menelaus consequently remained for the time in power (2 Macc. iv. 43—50). Soon afterwards a rumour reached Palestine that Antiochus had been killed in Egypt; and Jason, thinking that now his opportunity had come for recovering his position in Jerusalem, attacked the city with 1000 men, shut up Menelaus in the citadel, and slew many of the citizens, but was obliged before long to retire. Antiochus, thinking Judaea to be in revolt (2 Macc. v. 11), and (Jos. *B. J.* I. 1) invited also by Menelaus and his friends, on his return from Egypt in 170 made a *détour* by way of Jerusalem: the gates of the city were opened to him by Hellenizing sympathisers within (Jos. *Ant.* XII. v. 3); he led his army in, slew many of the inhabitants, under the guidance of Menelaus 'entered presumptuously into the sanctuary,' and carried away most of its golden vessels, as well as whatever other valuables he found in it: having done this, he proceeded home to Antioch, leaving, as governors in Jerusalem, Menelaus, and a Phrygian, named Philip, described as being 'more barbarous than him that set him there' (1 Macc. i. 20—28; 2 Macc. v. 11—16, 21—23: cf. Jos. *ll. cc.*; Dan. xi. 28 *b*).

Two years afterwards, in 168, after his final withdrawal from Egypt, partly perhaps through disappointment at his failure to secure that country, partly on account of reports received from his Hellenizing friends in Jerusalem (cf. Dan. xi. 30), Antiochus

INTRODUCTION.

sent Apollonius, a 'chief collector of tribute,' who, pretending that his intentions were peaceable, surprised the city on a sabbath-day: a massacre took place in the streets: numbers of women and children were sold into slavery; many of the houses and fortifications were demolished; and a Syrian garrison was established in the citadel overlooking the Temple, for the purpose of controlling and overawing the city. The immediate result was that many of those who had escaped massacre or servitude took to flight, and their places were filled by strangers (1 Macc. i. 29—40). In the pathetic, semi-poetical words of 1 Macc., 'And the inhabitants of Jerusalem fled because of them; and she became a habitation of strangers; and she became strange to them that were born in her, and her own children forsook her. Her sanctuary was laid waste like a wilderness, her feasts were turned into mourning, her sabbaths into reproach, her honour into contempt' (*vv.* 38, 39).

Soon after this, Antiochus adopted energetic measures to give effect to his scheme for the religious unification of his empire, 'that all should be one people, and that each should forsake his own laws' (*ib. v.* 41). Jerusalem, and the Jewish people, were to be completely Hellenized. All practices of the Jewish religion were to be prohibited under pain of death; the Temple was to be transformed into a sanctuary of Zeus Olympios (2 Macc. vi. 2); altars dedicated to heathen gods were to be set up, not only in Jerusalem, but also in the country towns of Judah; the Jews were to be compelled to sacrifice upon them, and also to eat of food ceremonially 'unclean'; and officers were appointed to see that all these injunctions were duly carried out (1 Macc. i. 41—53). On the 15th of Chisleu (Dec.) B.C. 168, an 'abomination of desolation,' i.e. a small heathen altar, was erected upon the altar of burnt-offering, and on the 25th of the same month the first sacrifices were offered upon it (1 Macc. i. 54, 59; see further the notes on Dan. xi. 31). Books of the Law were burnt; and women who had their children circumcised were put to death. Many of the Jews, it is added, conformed to the requirements of Antiochus (1 Macc. i. 43—61; cf. Dan. xi. 30 *b*—32 *a*).

ANTIOCHUS EPIPHANES.

The distress among the loyal Jews was naturally intense. Many, as has been already mentioned, had abandoned their homes in the city, when Apollonius took possession of it: others now followed their example, taking refuge in hiding-places in the country (1 Macc. i. 53; cf. ii. 29—31). The dirge over the desolation of Jerusalem, placed in the mouth of Mattathias (1 Macc. ii. 7—13), no doubt represents truly the feelings of faithful Jews at the time. Nevertheless, they were quite determined, even at the risk of their lives, not to yield to the demands of Antiochus. The consequence was that there were numerous martyrdoms (1 Macc. i. 62, 63; ii. 31—38, etc.: Dan. xi. 32 b, 33, 35). But the 'little help' (Dan. xi. 34) before long appeared (167). The brave Mattathias, a priest, resident at Modin, a town about 18 miles N.W. of Jerusalem, when ordered by the king's commissioner to do sacrifice, stoutly refused, and slew both an apostate Jew who came forward to do it in his stead, and the king's officer as well. The flame of revolt soon spread. The national party, who were now known as the *ḥasīdīm* or 'godly' (1 Macc. ii. 42, vii. 13; 2 Macc. xiv. 6)[1], rallied round Mattathias and his five sons, and organized themselves for concerted action. At first they remained on the defensive, fleeing to the mountains, and taking refuge in inaccessible hiding-places. In one case, a party of 1000 allowed themselves to be cut off without resistance, rather than profane the sabbath by fighting. But as their numbers increased they grew bolder, and began soon to assume the aggressive. Traversing the country, they destroyed heathen altars, enforced circumcision, and hunted down apostates. In 167 Mattathias died, after exhorting his sons, in a parting charge, to continue the struggle bravely (1 Macc. ii.).

His son Judas, the 'Maccabee,' a man of singular ability and strength of character, assumed now the leadership of the

[1] The word is a frequent one in the Psalms (as Ps. iv. 3, xii. 1; A.V., R.V. often 'saints'); and in some of the later ones (as cxvi. 15, cxlix. 1, 5, 9) may denote the same party. It is the party which developed ultimately into that of the 'Pharisees' (פְּרוּשִׁים, 'separated ones,' or, as we should say, 'separatists'): see Schürer[2], ii. 334 f. (§ 26).

patriotic party. His enterprises were almost uniformly successful. Within a year, he defeated and slew the two Syrian generals, Apollonius and Seron, who had successively invaded Judah (1 Macc. iii. 10—24). Exasperated by these disasters, Antiochus (166) entrusted his general, Lysias, with half of his entire army, commissioning him to extirpate entirely the Jewish nation, and to people their land with strangers (1 Macc. iii. 34—36). But his efforts were of no avail: though Lysias despatched against Judah an army of 4000 infantry, and 7000 cavalry, under three generals, they were discomfited by Judas, with great loss, at Emmaus (15 m. W.N.W. of Jerusalem); and when, in the following year (165), he took the command in person with an army of 65,000 men, he met with no better fortune, but was defeated at Beth-zur (16 m. S.S.W. of Jerusalem), and returned to Antioch (1 Macc. iv. 1—35). As a consequence of these successes, the Jews were in a position to restore the 'desolated' sanctuary,—the gates, it is said, were burnt, the priests' chambers pulled down, and shrubs were growing in the courts,—and to re-dedicate the altar. 1 Macc. iv. 36—60 describes how this was done, amid great rejoicings, on the 25th of Chisleu (Dec.), 165, exactly three years after the first heathen sacrifices had been offered upon it. The heathen neighbours of Judah, Idumaeans, Ammonites, and others, were jealous of these successes, and 'took counsel to destroy the race of Jacob': but Judas and his brother Simon took the field against them (164), and gained important victories in Galilee and Gilead, and smaller successes in Idumaea and Philistia (1 Macc. v.). In the same year (164), Antiochus, who had made an expedition into the far East for the purpose of replenishing his exchequer (1 Macc. iii. 28—31, 37), died, somewhat suddenly, at Tabae (a little S.E. of Ecbatana), after a futile attempt to rob a temple in Elymais (1 Macc. vi. 1—16; see also the note on p. 197). Lysias made another determined effort to stamp out the rebellion in Judah, and succeeded in capturing the fortress of Beth-zur; but being anxious, for political reasons, to get back to Antioch, he agreed to sign a treaty with the Jews, granting them complete religious freedom

(1 Macc. vi. 55—61). The war did not indeed end yet; but it was henceforth a war for merely civil independence: the religious liberties of the Jews were now secure.

§ 3. *Authorship and Date*[1].

It used formerly to be assumed as a matter of course that the Book of Daniel was written by Daniel himself,—and there are still scholars who, upon apologetic grounds, defend this opinion. A careful survey, however, of the facts presented by the book, in the light of the larger knowledge which recent years have brought, shews that this position is not really a tenable one. Internal evidence demonstrates, with a cogency that cannot be resisted, that the Book of Daniel must have been written not earlier than *c.* 300 B.C., and in Palestine; and there are considerations which make it highly probable that it was, in fact, composed during the persecution of Antiochus Epiphanes, between B.C. 168 and 165.

i. The following are facts of a historical nature which point, more or less decisively, to an author later than Daniel himself:—

1. The position of the Book in the Jewish Canon, not among the prophets, but in the miscellaneous collection of writings, called the *Kethūbīm*, or 'Hagiographa.' The Jewish Canon consists of three distinct parts: (1) the *Tōrāh* or Pentateuch; (2) the *Prophets* (consisting of the 'Former Prophets,' i.e. Josh., Judg., Sam., Kings, and the 'Latter Prophets,' i.e. Is., Jer., Ezek., and the 12 Minor Prophets); and (3) the *Kethūbīm*, or 'Hagiographa,' comprising (according to the order adopted in ordinary Hebrew Bibles) Psalms, Proverbs, Job, the five *Megilloth* (Song of Songs, Ruth, Lamentations, Ecclesiastes, Esther), Daniel, Ezra-Nehemiah, and Chronicles. This is the manner in which the books of the O. T. are arranged

---

[1] The following pages are adapted, with some additions and modifications of form, from the writer's *Introduction to the Literature of the Old Testament*, chap. xi.

in both MSS. and printed editions[1]; and though little definite is known respecting the formation of the Canon, there are strong reasons for thinking that the threefold division represents three stages in the collection and canonization of the sacred books of the O. T.,—the Pent. being canonized first, then the 'Prophets' (in the Jewish sense of the expression), and lastly the *Kethūbīm*. The collection of the 'Prophets' could hardly have been completed before the third century B.C.[2]; and had the Book of Daniel existed at the time, and been believed to be the work of a prophet, it is difficult not to think that it would have ranked accordingly, and been included with the writings of the other prophets.

2. Jesus, the son of Sirach (writing *c.* 200 B.C.), in his enumeration of famous Israelites, Ecclus. xliv.—l., though he mentions Isaiah, Jeremiah, Ezekiel, and (collectively) the Twelve Minor Prophets, is silent as to Daniel. In view of the remarkable distinctions attained by Daniel, and the faculties displayed by him, according to the Book, the statement in Ecclus. xlix. 15 that no man had ever been born 'like unto Joseph,' seems certainly to suggest that the writer was unacquainted with the narratives respecting Daniel.

3. That Nebuchadnezzar besieged Jerusalem, and carried away some of the sacred vessels in 'the *third* year of Jehoiakim' (Dan. i. 1, 2), though it cannot, strictly speaking, be disproved, is at least doubtful: not only is the Book of Kings silent, but Jeremiah, *in the following year* (xxv. 9 ff., see *v.* 1), as also in Jehoiakim's fifth year (xxxvi. 29, see *v.* 9), speaks of the Chal-

---

[1] There are slight differences in Heb. MSS. in the order in which the books comprising both the Latter Prophets and the Hagiographa are arranged (see *L.O.T.*[6] p. ii; or more fully Ryle, *Canon of the O. T.* pp. 219—234, 281 f., ed. 2, pp. 230—246, 292 ff.); but no book belonging to one division of the Canon is ever found in another.

The Canon of Melito (Euseb. iv. 26) does not bear witness to a different arrangement of the Heb. Bible: as (amongst other things) the Septuagint titles shew, it merely enumerates the Hebrew books in the order in which they were current in the Greek O. T. (Ryle, pp. 214, 218 f., ed. 2, pp. 225, 229 f.).

[2] Ryle, *l. c.* pp. 106—113 (ed. 2, pp. 117—124); cf. p. 120 f. (131 f.).

daeans in terms which seem to imply that their arms had not yet been seen in Judah (see further the note on i. 1).

The following table exhibits the chronology of the period:—

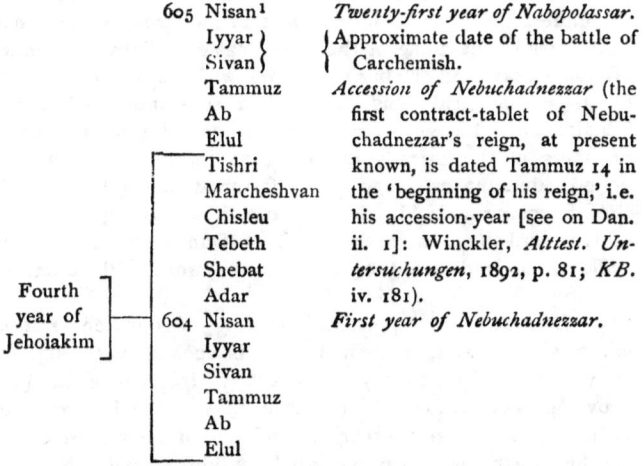

	605 Nisan[1]	*Twenty-first year of Nabopolassar.*
	Iyyar } Sivan }	*Approximate date of the battle of Carchemish.*
	Tammuz	*Accession of Nebuchadnezzar* (the
	Ab	first contract-tablet of Nebu-
	Elul	chadnezzar's reign, at present
	Tishri	known, is dated Tammuz 14 in
	Marcheshvan	the 'beginning of his reign,' i.e.
	Chisleu	his accession-year [see on Dan.
	Tebeth	ii. 1]: Winckler, *Alttest. Un-*
	Shebat	*tersuchungen*, 1892, p. 81; *KB.*
Fourth year of Jehoiakim	Adar	iv. 181).
	604 Nisan	*First year of Nebuchadnezzar.*
	Iyyar	
	Sivan	
	Tammuz	
	Ab	
	Elul	

The Babylonian year began in spring (with Nisan), the Jewish year (probably) in autumn (with the month called by the Babylonians Tishri)[2]. The fourth year of Jehoiakim would be most naturally equated with the first year of Nebuchadnezzar (Jer. xxv. 1) in the manner suggested. It is consequently doubtful whether the date in Jer. xlvi. 2 is correct: it may be a gloss, added to the text of Jeremiah upon the assumption that Nebuchadnezzar was already king when he won the battle of Carchemish. If the scheme given above is correct, the battle of Carchemish will have taken place in Jehoiakim's third year; but there remains the doubt (see below, p. 2 f.) whether, following it in the same year, there was really any 'siege' of Jerusalem.

4. The 'Chaldaeans' (*Kasdim*) are synonymous in Dan.

[1] The names of the months are given in their Hebraized forms.
[2] Nowack, *Hebr. Archäologie* (1894), i. 219. Cf. also Tiele, *Bab.-Ass. Gesch.* (1886), pp. 439—41; Hommel, *Gesch. Bab. u. Ass.* (1885), pp. 752—5.

INTRODUCTION.

(i. 4, ii. 2, 4, 5, etc.) with the class of wise men. This sense 'is unknown in the Ass.-Bab. language, and, wherever it occurs, has formed itself after the end of the Babylonian empire; it is thus an indication of the post-exilic composition of the book' (Schrader, *KAT.*[2], p. 429). It dates in fact from a time when 'Chaldaean' (the name of the ruling caste in Babylonia under Nabopolassar and Nebuchadnezzar) was no longer current in its ethnological sense, and when substantially the only 'Chaldaeans' known were either, as in Herodotus's time, members of the priestly class, or, as in the later classical period, itinerant astrologers and fortune-tellers (cf. p. 12 ff.). Prof. Sayce writes[1]: 'In the eyes of the Assyriologist the use of the word Kasdim in the Book of Daniel would alone be sufficient to indicate the date of the work with unerring certainty.'

5. Belshazzar is represented as *king* of Babylon (v. 1 ff., vii. 1, viii. 1), and Nebuchadnezzar is spoken of throughout ch. v. (*vv.* 2, 11, 13, 18, 22) as his *father*. In point of fact (see above, p. xxx) Nabu-na'id (p. xxvii ff.) was the last king of Babylon; he was a usurper, not related to Nebuchadnezzar; and his father's name was Nabu-balāṭsu-iḳbi (p. xxvii). Bêl-shar-uẓur (i.e. Belshazzar) is mentioned in the inscriptions as his son, the title regularly appended to his name being 'the king's son.' In the 'Annalistic Tablet' of Cyrus (see p. xxix) the 'king's son' is mentioned during a series of years as being 'with the nobles and his soldiers in the country of Akkad' (North Babylonia): it may thus be supposed that he acted as his father's general. When at last the troops of Cyrus gained possession of Babylon, Nabu-na'id was taken prisoner: not long afterwards[2], on the 3rd of Marcheshvan (Oct.), Cyrus himself entered Babylon, and eight days later, on the 11th of Marcheshvan, during the night, the 'king's son' was slain. The inscriptions thus lend no support to the supposition that Bêl-shar-uẓur was his father's viceroy, or was entitled to be

---

[1] *Monuments*, p. 535.
[2] 17 or 18 days, if the correction in l. 12 (p. xxix) is right.

AUTHORSHIP AND DATE.

spoken of as 'king[1]': according to the best accredited reading of the passage just quoted (p. xxx, *note*), he was called the 'king's son' to the day of his death. Further, when the Persians (as the same inscription shews) were already in peaceable possession of Babylon, and governors had been appointed in it (ll. 19, 20), it is difficult to understand how Belshazzar, even supposing (what is not in itself inconceivable) that he still held out in the palace, and was slain afterwards in attempting to defend it, could promise and dispense (Dan. v. 7, 16, 29) honours in his kingdom; or what need there could be for the solemn announcement (v. 25—28), as of something new and unexpected, that his (or his father's) kingdom was to be given to the Medes and Persians, when it must have been patent to every one that they were already in possession of it. As regards Belshazzar's relationship to Nebuchadnezzar, there remains the *possibility* that Nabu-na'id may have sought to strengthen his position by marrying a daughter of Nebuchadnezzar, in which case the latter might be spoken of as Belshazzar's father (=grandfather, by Heb. usage). None of Nabu-na'id's inscriptions, however, imply any kind of relationship to Nebuchadnezzar, or trace his descent beyond his father Nabu-balāṭsu-iḳbi[2]; and the terms of ch. v. produce certainly the impression that in the view of the writer Belshazzar was actually Nebuchadnezzar's son. The historical situation presupposed by Dan. v. is not consistent

---

[1] The supposition, sometimes made, that he was 'co-regent' with his father is also destitute of foundation in the inscriptions.

[2] Dr Green's statement (*The Canon*, p. 63) that Nabu-na'id calls himself 'descendant' of Nebuchadnezzar and Neriglissar, is incorrect. The passage referred to follows the one quoted, p. xxvii, and runs, 'I am the mighty legate (*nasparu*) of Nebuchadnezzar and Nergal-shar-uẓur, the kings who walked before me. Their people are committed to my hand, their command I transgress not, their mind I obey. Amêl-Marduk, and Lâbashi-Marduk... broke their commands' (Messerschmidt, p. 29 f.). The passage is in fact evidence that Nabu-na'id could not call himself son (or descendant) of the famous kings whom he names: he was, as Abydenus says (p. xxvii, *n.* 5), no relation to them; but he claims nevertheless to be in a sense their representative, and to be ruling as their lawful successor, on the ground that he follows out their policy and principles of government, which Amêl-Marduk and Lâbashi-Marduk (see p. xxvii) had deserted (cf. Messerschmidt, p. 22).

with the testimony of the contemporary monuments. Belshazzar may have distinguished himself, perhaps more than his father Nabu-na'id, at the time when Babylon passed into the hands of the Persians; and hence in the recollections of a later age he may have been pictured as its last king: but he was not styled 'king' by his contemporaries (cf. Schrader, *KAT.*² on Dan. v. 1—2).

6. Darius, son of Ahasuerus—*Ăḥashwērōsh*, elsewhere the Hebrew form of *Xerxes* (Pers. *Khshayârshâ*)—a *Mede*, after the death of Belshazzar, 'receives the kingdom,' and is 'made king over the realm of the Chaldaeans' (v. 31, ix. 1; cf. vi. 1 ff., xi. 1).

It has been disputed what sense is to be attached to these expressions, and whether Darius the Mede, according to the representation of the Book, is an independent sovereign (Bevan, p. 20; *al.*), or merely a viceroy with 'delegated royalty' (Hengst., Keil, Pusey, p. 122 f.). Certainly, if v. 31 and ix. 1 be read under the presupposition that Cyrus was conqueror of Babylon, it is natural to suppose that it was he from whom Darius 'received the kingdom,' and by whom he was 'made king'; but Cyrus is not mentioned in this connexion in the Book itself: the Medes are mentioned regularly (v. 28, vi. &c.) before the Persians, as though in the view of the writer they were the more important people; and according to the representation of the Book (see on ii. 39 and v. 31), the Persian empire (of Cyrus) was preceded by a Median empire: hence it is more natural to suppose that, in the view of the writer, Darius 'received the kingdom' from the victors jointly, and was 'made king,' either by them, or by God (cf. v. 28 'is given,' *sc.* by God)[1]. This interpretation agrees with ch. vi., in which Darius unquestionably acts as an independent sovereign, organising (*v.* 1) the whole kingdom into satrapies, and (*v.* 25) addressing the entire world as his subjects, exactly as Nebuchadnezzar had done (iv. 1); while (*v.* 28) his 'reign' is succeeded by the 'reign' of Cyrus the Persian. At all events, if the 'kingdom,' received by him in v. 28, was conferred upon him by Cyrus, he must have been 'made king' by him in as full a sense

---

[1] Prof. Bevan (p. 20) points to an example in Syriac, in which the same words, 'received the kingdom,' are used of the accession of the Emperor Julian.

AUTHORSHIP AND DATE.   liii

as Jehoiakim, for instance, was 'made king' by Pharaoh Necho, or Zedekiah by Nebuchadnezzar (2 Ki. xxiii. 34, xxiv. 17).

There seems, however, to be no room for such a ruler: for according to all other authorities, Cyrus is the immediate successor of Nabu-na'id, and the ruler of the entire Persian empire.

The following are the principal identifications that have been proposed of 'Darius the Mede.' Four kings of the Medes are known to us from Herodotus (i. 96—130), viz. Deioces (699—646), Phraortes (646—624), Cyaxares (624—584), and Astyages (584—549), whose reign was brought to a close, as described above (p. xxx), by Cyrus. 'Darius the Mede,' now, has been supposed to be (1) Cyaxares (II),—according to Xenophon's *Cyropaedia*, a son of Astyages, and his successor on the throne of Media (Joseph. *Ant.* x. xi. 4; Häv., Hengst., Keil., *al.*). According to Xenophon this Cyaxares assisted Cyrus in his military preparations, and after his conquest of Babylon was assigned a palace in the city; at the same time he also made Cyrus his heir, by giving him his daughter in marriage. 'It appears to be a fatal objection to this hypothesis that the only direct evidence for the existence of a second Cyaxares is that of Xenophon's romance. Herodotus, on the other hand, expressly states that Astyages was the last king of the Medes, and that he died without leaving any male issue (i. 109, 127—130)' (Westcott, in Smith, *DB*.[1] s.v. 1 DARIUS). (2) Another opinion is that 'Darius the Mede' may have been Astyages (Niebuhr, Westcott): it is pointed out that it would have been quite in accordance with Cyrus's usual magnanimity to treat his vanquished foe with respect, and it would have been good policy on his part to gratify his Median subjects by making the son of Cyaxares viceroy in Babylon. A younger brother, or a nephew, of Astyages, or an otherwise unknown Median prince, whom Cyrus may have appointed under-king in Babylon, while he himself was completing his conquests elsewhere, have also been suggested (cf. Pusey, pp. 126, 128)[1].

It is, however, far from apparent why Astyages (who is regularly known by this name) should, especially by a contemporary (as is supposed by those who adopt this view), be called 'Darius'; and in point of fact, if Cyrus made any one 'king' in Babylon, it was his son Cambyses, who, in certain

---

[1] See further, on these hypotheses, Kuenen, *Einl.* ii. § 90. 3.

inscriptions of his first year (p. xxxii), is named conjointly with himself. And Cambyses was neither 'Darius,' nor a 'Mede.' Contemporary monuments, though they do not indeed shew that a Median, named 'Darius,' did not exist, shew that, if he existed, he could not have occupied the position assigned to him in the Book of Daniel; he could not have acted as 'king' in Babylon. If it be supposed that he was merely a governor, this is inconsistent with the representation of the Book of Daniel: if he was a 'king,' this is inconsistent with the testimony of the inscriptions, which allow no room for such a 'king' at this time[1].

How the figure of 'Darius the Mede' arose, must remain matter of conjecture; it seems, however, clearly to be connected with the unhistorical idea of a 'Median' empire, intervening between the Chaldaean and the Persian, implied elsewhere in the Book of Daniel (see on ii. 39). In vi. 1 the temptation to suspect a confusion with Darius *Hystaspis* (the successor of Cambyses), B.C. 522—485, who actually organized the Persian empire into 'satrapies,' though much fewer than 120[2],—is strong. Tradition, it can hardly be doubted, has here confused persons and events in reality distinct (Behrmann, p. xix): 'Darius the Mede' must be a 'reflection into the past' of Darius Hystaspis, father—not *son*—of Xerxes ('Ahasuerus,' ix. 1), who had twice to reconquer Babylon from the hands of rebels[3], and who established the system of satrapies, combined, not impossibly, with indistinct recollections of Gubaru, who first occupied Babylon on Cyrus's behalf, and who, in appointing governors there (p. xxx), appears to have acted as Cyrus's deputy[4].

---

[1] This is particularly clear from the contract-tablets, which have been discovered recently in such numbers (see *KB.* iv. *passim*), and which, bearing date at this period almost continuously, pass from the 10th of Marcheshvan, in the 17th year of Nabu-na'id, to the 24th of the same month in the accession-year of Cyrus: comp. Sayce, *Monuments*, pp. 522 f., 528; Strassmaier, *Babyl. Texte*, i. (1887), p. 25, vii. (1890), p. 1; and the translations in *KB.* iv. 255 (No. LVIII), and 259 (No. II).

[2] See the note on vi. 1.

[3] Behistun Inscr. (*RP.*[1] i. 111 ff.), i. 16—ii. 1 (cf. Hdt. iii. 150—9); iii. 13, 14; see also Rawlinson, *Anc. Mon.*[4] iii. 410 f., 414.

[4] Comp. Sayce, *Monuments*, pp. 524—537. The statement of

AUTHORSHIP AND DATE.

7. In ix. 2 it is stated that Daniel 'understood by *the books* (בַּסְּפָרִים)' the number of years, during which, according to Jeremiah, Jerusalem should lie waste. The expression used implies that Jeremiah's prophecies formed part of a *collection* of sacred books, which, nevertheless, it may be safely affirmed, was not the case in 538 B.C.[1]

8. The incorrect explanation of the name Belteshazzar in iv. 8 is often quoted as evidence that the writer, if not the speaker (Nebuchadnezzar), was ignorant of the Babylonian language; but possibly it is only an *assonance*, not an etymology (in our sense of the word), which is implied by the king's words: see the note *ad loc.*

9. Other indications adduced to shew that the Book of Daniel is not the work of a contemporary, are such as the following:—The improbability that Daniel and his companions, all strict Jews, should have suffered themselves to be initiated into the superstitious arts of the 'wise men' (p. 14 ff.), or that he should have been accepted as their president by the 'wise men' themselves (ch. i.; cf. ii. 13, 48)[2]; the improbability that Nebuchadnezzar should hold *all* the wise men of Babylon, including Daniel and his three companions, responsible for the failure of some, and condemn them to death even before their skill had been tried (ii. 12, 13); Nebuchadnezzar's seven years' insanity ('lycanthropy'), with his public proclamation respecting it (iv. 1—3, 34—37); the absolute terms in which both he and Darius, while retaining, so far as appears, their idolatry, recognize the eternal and universal sovereignty of the God of Israel

---

Harpocration and Suidas (Prince, p. 49 *n.*) that the name of the coin 'darik' ($\delta\alpha\rho\epsilon\iota\kappa\acute{o}s$) was derived from a king 'Darius,' though not Darius Hystaspis, but an earlier king of that name, has been supposed to be indirect testimony to the historical character of Darius the Mede; but its correctness is, upon philological grounds, extremely questionable (see Prince, p. 265).

[1] Cf. Ryle, *Canon of the O. T.*, p. 104 ff.

[2] Lenormant felt the latter difficulty so strongly that he regarded the words, or clauses, in ii. 48, iv. 9, v. 11, 12, which attributed this position to Daniel, as interpolated (*La Divination chez les Chaldéens*, 1875, p. 219 f.). This, however, is an expedient of very questionable legitimacy.

INTRODUCTION.

(iv. 1—3, 34—37; vi. 25—27: cf. ii. 47, iii. 29). On these and some other similar considerations our knowledge is hardly such as to give us an objective criterion for estimating their cogency. The circumstances alleged will appear improbable, or not improbable, according as the critic, upon *independent* grounds, has satisfied himself that the Book is the work of a later author, or written by Daniel himself. It might be hazardous to use the statements in question in *proof* of the late date of the Book; though, if its late date were established on other grounds, it is certainly true that they would be more naturally explained as due to the manner in which the past was viewed by a writer living at some distance from it, than as statements of actual fact authenticated by a contemporary.

Of the arguments that have been here stated, while 8 is doubtful, and 9 should be used with reserve, the rest all possess weight,—particularly 4, 5, and 6. They do not, however, except 2 (which, standing alone, it would be hazardous to press), shew positively that the Book is a work of the second cent. B.C.; but they point with some cogency to the conclusion that it reflects the traditions, and historical impressions, of an age considerably later than that of Daniel himself.

ii. The evidence of the *language* of Daniel must next be considered.

(1) The number of *Persian* words in the Book, especially in the Aramaic part, is remarkable.

The number is at least 15, if not more: viz.[1] פרתמים *nobles* (i. 3; also Est. i. 3, vi. 6), פתבג *choice food, delicacy* (i. 5, 8, 13, 15, 16, xi. 26), אזדא *certain* (ii. 5, 8), הדם *limb* (ii. 5, iii. 29), דת *law* (ii. 9, 13, 15, vi. 5, 8, 12, 15, vii. 25; also Ezr. viii. 36, and often in Est.), רז *secret* (ii. 18, 19, 27, 28, 29, 30, 47, iv. 9), אחשדרפן *satrap* (iii. 2, 3, 27, vi. 1, 2, 3, 4, 6, 7; also Ezr. viii. 36, Est. iii. 12, viii. 9, ix. 3), אדרגזר *counsel-giver* (iii. 2, 3), דתבר *law-bearer, justice* (iii. 2, 3), זן *kind* (iii. 5, 7, 10, 15; also 2 Ch. xvi. 14, Ps. cxliv. 13, Ecclus. xxxvii. 28, xlix. 8 [Heb.]), פתגם *message, order, decree* (properly *something going* [i.e. *sent*] *to*), even in the weakened sense of *word*, or *thing* (iii. 16,

---

[1] For further particulars on most of the following words, see the note on the first occurrence of each.

AUTHORSHIP AND DATE.   lvii

iv. 17; also Ezr. iv. 17, v. 7, 11, vi. 11, Est. i. 20, Eccl. viii. 11), הדבר *minister* (iii. 24, 27, iv. 36, vi. 7), סרך *president* (vi. 2, 3, 4, 6, 7), נדן *receptacle, sheath* (vii. 15—if the reading be correct; also 1 Ch. xxi. 27); אפדן *palace, throne-room* (xi. 45); probably also נבזבה *present* (ii. 6, v. 17), סרבל *mantle* (iii. 21, 27), and המניך *necklace* (v. 7, 16, 29). נדבריא (iii. 2, 3), and תפתיא (iii. 2, 3), are both uncertain.

These words are not Assyrian or Babylonian (as *peḥāh*, ii. 8, and *sāgān*, iii. 2, for example, are): they are distinctively Persian[1]. Some of them describe offices or institutions, and are not found elsewhere in the O. T., or occur only in Ezra, Esther, and other late parts of the O. T., written after the establishment of the Persian rule: the mention of 'satraps' under Nebuchadnezzar (iii. 2, 3, 27) is alone a remarkable anachronism. Others (as those for *law, limb, secret, kind, word*) are used exactly as in the later Aramaic, and are of a kind that would not be borrowed by one people from another unless intercourse between them had subsisted for a considerable time. That words such as these should be found in books written after the Persian empire was organised, and when Persian influences prevailed, is not more than would be expected; Persian words (both some of those noted here, and also others) occur in Ezra, Nehemiah, Esther, and the Chronicles[2], and many were permanently naturalised in Aramaic (both Syriac and the Aramaic of the Targums); but that they should be used as a matter of course by Daniel under the Babylonian supremacy, or in the description of Babylonian institutions *before* the conquest of Cyrus, is in the last degree improbable. The argument is confirmed by the testimony of the Inscriptions. The numerous contract-tablets which have come down to us from the age of Nebuchadnezzar and his successors, and which represent the every-day language of commercial life, shew no traces of Persian influence; and if the language of Babylonia

[1] The attempt made in the *Speaker's Commentary* to shew some of these words to be Semitic, is a resort of desperation.

[2] These books, it will be recollected, contain nothing earlier than *c.* 450 B.C. (the reign of Artaxerxes); and they are mostly considerably later.

lviii   INTRODUCTION.

was uninfluenced by Persia, that of Israel would be far less likely to be so influenced¹.

(2) Not only, however, does Daniel contain Persian words, it contains at least three *Greek* words: קיתרס *kītharos*, iii. 5, 7, 10, 15 = κίθαρις; פסנתרין (פסנטרין), *psantērīn*, iii. 5, 7, 10, 15 = ψαλτήριον²; סומפניה *sûmpōnyāh*, iii. 5, 15 (A.V. dulcimer) = συμφωνία³. Whatever might conceivably be the case with κίθαρις, it is incredible that ψαλτήριον and συμφωνία can have reached Babylon *c.* 550 B.C. Anyone who has studied Greek history knows what the condition of the Greek world was in the sixth century B.C., and is aware that the arts and inventions of civilised life streamed then into Greece from the East, not from Greece eastwards⁴. Still, if the instruments named were of a primitive kind, such as the κίθαρις (in Homer), it is *just* possible—though, in view of the fact that the Semitic languages have their own name for the 'lyre,' by no means probable—that it might be an exception to the rule, and that the Babylonians might have been indebted for their knowledge of it to the Greeks; so that, had קיתרס stood alone, it could not, perhaps, have been pressed. But no such exception can be made in the case of ψαλτήριον and συμφωνία, both *derived* forms, the former found first in Aristotle, the latter first in

¹ Cf. Sayce, *Monuments*, p. 493 f.
² With ין- for -ιον, as in סנהדרין = συνέδριον, מסטירין = μυστήριον, &c.; and with ת and ט interchanging, as in פיתם and פיטם (πιττάκιον), and other words.
³ Cf. סומפניה in the sense of *double flute* in the Mishna. The form סיפוניה in iii. 10 is remarkably illustrated by ספון = σύμφωνοι, in the sense *agreed*, in the great bilingual inscription from Palmyra of A.D. 137 (Cooke, *North-Sem. Inscr.*, 1903, pp. 328, l. 46, 329, l. 14, 331, l. 45).
⁴ Cf. Sayce in the *Contemporary Review*, Dec. 1878, p. 60 ff. Such facts as that a Mytilenaean, the brother of the poet Alcaeus, fought in the ranks of the Babylonians, *c.* 600 B.C. (Strabo, XIII, ii. 3), or that Psammitichus (B.C. 664—610) introduced Greek settlers and mercenaries into Egypt, are altogether insufficient to make it probable that Greek words could have found their way to Babylon in the sixth cent. B.C.: cf. Whitehouse in the *Expos. Times*, 1894, March, p. 284 ff., July, p. 474 f. Orr (*Probl. of the O.T.* 428 f.) and Petrie (cited *ib.*) signally omit to shew that, even though Jews may have met Greeks in Daphnae in 607—587 B.C., ψαλτήριον and συμφωνία (see above) are words likely to have been heard by them there (cf. also Cheyne, *Origin of Psalter*, p. 10).

AUTHORSHIP AND DATE.

Plato, and in the sense of concerted music (or, perhaps, of a specific musical instrument) first in Polybius[1]. These words, it may be confidently affirmed, could not have been used in the Book of Daniel unless it had been written *after the dissemination of Greek influences in Asia through the conquests of Alexander the Great* (cf. pp. xxxiii ff.)[2].

(3) The *Aramaic* of Daniel (which is all but identical with that of Ezra) is a *Western* Aramaic dialect, of the type spoken in and about *Palestine*[3]. It is nearly allied to the Aramaic of the Targums of Onkelos and Jonathan; and still more so to the Aramaic dialects spoken E. and S.E. of Palestine, in Palmyra and Nabataea, and known from inscriptions dating from the 1st cent. B.C. to the 3rd cent. A.D. In some respects it is of an earlier type than the Aramaic of Onkelos and Jonathan; and this fact was formerly supposed to be a ground for the antiquity of the Book. But the argument is not conclusive. For (1) the differences are not considerable[4], and

---

[1] And, singularly enough, in his account of the festivities in which *Antiochus Epiphanes* indulged (xxvi. 10. 5; xxxi. 4. 8); see p. 39 *n*. In Plato and Aristotle συμφωνία means only *harmony*.

[2] The *Speaker's Commentary* makes the vain endeavour to prove these three words to be Semitic!

[3] Nöldeke in the *Encyclopaedia Britannica*[11], xxiv. 624*a*—624*b* (=*Die Semitischen Sprachen*, 1899, pp. 35, 37); Kautzsch, *Gramm. des Bibl.-Aram.* §§ 1, 2, 6. The idea that the Jews forgot their Hebrew in Babylonia, and spoke in 'Chaldee' when they returned to Palestine, is unfounded. Haggai and Zechariah and other post-exilic writers use Hebrew: Aramaic is exceptional. Hebrew was still normally spoken *c.* 430 B.C. in Jerusalem (Neh. xiii. 24). The Hebrews, after the Captivity, acquired gradually the use of Aramaic *from their neighbours* in and about Palestine. See, for example, Wright, *Compar. Gramm. of the Semitic Languages* (1890), p. 16: 'Now do not for a moment suppose that the Jews lost the use of Hebrew in the Babylonian Captivity, and brought back with them into Palestine this so-called Chaldee. The Aramean dialect, which gradually got the upper hand since 4–5 cent. B.C., did not come that long journey across the Syrian desert; it was *there*, on the spot; and it ended by taking possession of the field, side by side with the kindred dialect of the Samaritans.' The term 'Chaldee' for the Aramaic of either the Bible or the Targums is a misnomer (due originally to a misunderstanding of Dan. ii. 4), the use of which is only a source of confusion. The proper term for the Aramaic of Ezra and Daniel is 'Biblical Aramaic.'

[4] They are carefully collected (on the basis, largely, of M'Gill's

largely orthographical: the Targums of Onkelos and Jonathan did not probably receive their present form before the 4th cent. A.D.[1]: and we are not in a position to affirm that the transition from the Aramaic of Daniel and Ezra to that of the Targums must have required eight or nine centuries, and could not have been accomplished in four or five; (2) recently discovered inscriptions have shewn that many of the forms in which it differs from the Aramaic of the Targums were in use in neighbouring countries, especially in Palmyra and Nabataea, *down to the 1st cent.* A.D.[2]

A particularly clear indication that the Aramaic of Daniel was not that spoken in Babylon in the 6th cent. B.C. is afforded by the fact that in the numerous, if brief, Aramaic inscriptions from Nineveh and Babylon which we possess, dating from *c.* 725 B.C. to the 5th cent., the relative is regularly זי, not, as uniformly in Dan. (and Ezra), די (see the *Corpus Inscr. Sem.* II. i. Nos. 1, 2, 3 מנן ווו זי ארקא 'three m'nas of the country' [Jer. x. 11; *L.O.T.*[6] p. 255], 4, 5, 17, 28, 30, &c., esp. No. 65, B.C. 504, Nos. 69—71, B.C. 418, 407, 408, all contract-tablets from Babylon)[3].

(4) The *Hebrew* of Daniel is also that of a much later age than the sixth cent. B.C. The type of Hebrew which it mostly resembles is not that of Ezekiel, or of Isaiah xl.—lxvi., or even

---

investigations) by Dr Pusey, *Daniel*, ed. 2, pp. 45 ff., 602 ff. (an interesting lexical point is that the vocabulary agrees sometimes with Syriac against the Targums). But when all are told, the differences are far outweighed by the *resemblances*; so that relatively they cannot be termed important or considerable. (The amount of difference is much exaggerated in the *Speaker's Commentary*, p. 228. The statement in the text agrees with the judgment of Nöldeke, *l.c.* p. 624 *b*.)

[1] Deutsch in Smith's *D. B.* iii. 1644, 1652; cf. Dalman, *Gramm. des Jüd.-Pal. Aramäisch*, pp. 9, 11 (5th cent. A.D.).

[2] See particulars in the writer's *Introduction*, p. 472 f. (edd. 6—8, p. 504). Numerous specimens of the inscriptions there referred to may be seen in Cooke's *North-Semitic Inscriptions*, p. 214 ff., 263 ff.

[3] Cf. זנה and זא, for the demonstr. pron., in the inscriptions from Zinjirli, Cilicia, Têma, and Egypt, not, as in Ezr., Dan., Palmyrene, and Nabataean, דנה, דא (S. A. Cook, *Glossary of Aramaic Inscriptions*, 1898, pp. 46, 49); G. A. Cooke, Index, p. 367. See further *L.O.T.*[8] p. 504 (second paragr.); and p. 514 f. (where fuller particulars are given of the relation of Biblical to Egyptian Aramaic, as known now from the Papyri recently discovered at Elephantine).

of Haggai and Zechariah, but that of Esther, Ecclesiastes (to a certain extent), and especially the Chronicles (c. B.C. 300). The Hebrew of the three last-named books differs in a marked degree from that of all earlier writers, even including those who lived in the early post-exilic period. In vocabulary many new words appear, often of Aramaic origin, occasionally Persian, and frequently such as continued in use afterwards in the 'New Hebrew' of the Mishna (200 A.D.), &c.; old words also are sometimes used with new meanings or applications. In syntax, the ease and grace and fluency of the earlier writers (down to at least Zech. xii.—xiv.) have passed away; the style is often laboured and inelegant; and new and uncouth constructions make their appearance. The beginnings of these peculiarities are observable in the 'memoirs' of Ezra and Nehemiah (i.e. the parts of Ezra and Neh. which are the work of these reformers themselves)[1]; but they become much more numerous afterwards. The three books mentioned above do not, however, exhibit them in equal proportions: Ecclesiastes[2] has the most striking *Mishnic* idioms: the Chronicler[3] has many peculiarities of his own, and may be said to shew the greatest uncouthness of style; but they agree in the possession of many common (or similar) features, which differentiate them from all previous Hebrew writers (including Zech., Hagg., Mal.), and which recur in them with decidedly greater frequency and prominence than in the memoirs of Ezra and Neh. And the Hebrew of Daniel is of the type just characterised: in all distinctive features it resembles, not the Hebrew of Ezekiel, or even of Haggai and Zechariah, but that of the age *subsequent to Nehemiah.*

In the writer's *Introduction* p. 474 f. (506 f.) will be found a list of upwards of thirty expressions, some found otherwise only in post-Biblical Hebrew, or in Aramaic, others common to the Hebrew of Daniel and that of Chronicles and other late writings, but occurring never, or (in the case of one or two) very rarely, in the earlier literature. For instances of sentences constructed in the later, uncouth style, see

---

[1] See the writer's *Introduction*, p. 511 ff. (edd. 6—8, p. 544 ff.).
[2] *Ibid.* p. 444 ff. (474 f.).
[3] *Ibid.* p. 502 ff. (535 ff.).

viii. 12 ff., 24 ff., ix. 25 ff., x. 9 *b*, xii. 11, and the greater part of ch. xi. The only part of the Book in which a better style prevails is the prayer of ch. ix.; but here the thought expresses itself almost entirely in phrases borrowed from earlier writings (esp. Deut. and Jer.).

The supposition that Daniel may have unlearnt in exile the language of his youth does not satisfy the requirements of the case: it does not explain, viz., how the new idioms which he acquired should have so exactly agreed with those which appeared in Palestine independently 250 years afterwards. Daniel himself, also, it is probable, would not (unlike both Jer. and Ezek.) have uniformly written the name Nebuchad*n*ezzar incorrectly (see the note on i. 1).

It is evident that the author is more at home in Aramaic than in Hebrew, and writes it much more idiomatically and fluently. No doubt it was the language which was spoken around him, and which he would use naturally himself (cf. p. lix, *note*). 'The recently discovered fragments of the original Hebrew of Ecclesiasticus shew,' however, 'that a very fair imitation of classical Hebrew was written in the Greek period' (W. H. Bennett in *A Biblical Introduction*, 1899, p. 226). The Heb. style of Daniel is not, however, *identical* with that of Ben-Sira, any more than it is *identical* with that of Ecclesiastes. The age was a transitional one; and different writers adopted different styles, according to choice. The author of Ecclesiastes yielded himself largely to the 'New Hebrew,' which had already developed considerably, especially in the schools. The author of the book of Daniel wrote sometimes in Hebrew, sometimes in Aramaic: in his Hebrew, like the Chronicler, he writes in imitation of the older Biblical style, though constantly, in idiom and vocabulary, betraying his later date. Ben-Sira did the same, and in some respects with better success than either of these other writers: his general style is decidedly more flowing and idiomatic than theirs, but his vocabulary is marked by a greater proportion of Aramaic and New Hebrew words.

It may interest the reader to see Delitzsch's judgement on this subject (Herzog's *Real-Encyklopädie*², s.v. DANIEL, p. 470); 'The Hebrew of Daniel attaches itself here and there to Ezekiel (cf. עת קץ *time of the end*, xi. 35, 40, xii. 4, viii. 17, with עת עון קץ *time of the iniquity of the end*, Ez. xxi. 30, 34, xxxv. 5; בן אדם *son of man* in the address to the seer, viii. 17, as regularly in Ezekiel)[1]; and also to

---

[1] Delitzsch means that the writer borrows particular expressions from Ezek. He might have added one or two more: as הצבי *the*

Habakkuk (cf. xi. 27, 29, 35, with Hab. ii. 3); in general character it resembles the Hebrew of the Chronicler, who wrote shortly before the beginning of the Greek period [B.C. 333], and, as compared either with the ancient Hebrew or with the Hebrew of the Mishnah, is full of singularities (*Sonderbarkeiten*) and harshnesses of style[1].'

The verdict of the language of Daniel is thus clear. The *Persian* words presuppose a period after the Persian empire had been well established: the Greek words *demand*, the Hebrew *supports*, and the Aramaic *permits*, a date *after the conquest of Palestine by Alexander the Great* (B.C. 332). The Aramaic is also that which was spoken *in or near Palestine*. With our present knowledge, this is as much as the language authorizes us definitely to affirm; though συμφωνία, as the name of an instrument (considering the history of the term in Greek), would seem to point to a date somewhat advanced in the Greek period.

(iii) The *theology* of the Book (in so far as it has a distinctive character) points to a later age than that of the Exile. It is true, this argument has sometimes been stated in an exaggerated form, as when, for instance, it is said that the doctrine of the resurrection, or that of distinctions of rank and office among the angels, is derived from Parseeism, or that the asceticism of Daniel and his companions, and the frequency of their prayers, &c., are traits peculiar to the later Judaism. For exaggerations such as these there is no adequate foundation: nevertheless it is undeniable that the conception of the future kingdom of God, and the doctrines of angels, of the resurrection, and of a judgement on the world, appear in Daniel in a more developed form than elsewhere in the O.T., and exhibit features

---

beauty, viii. 9, and ארץ הצבי, *the land of beauty*, xi. 16, 41 (cf. *v.* 45), of Canaan (comp. Jer. iii. 19, Ezek. xx. 6, 15); נחשת קלל, *burnished brass*, x. 6, Ezek. i. 7; לבוש הבדים, *clothed in linen*, xii. 6 f., Ezek. ix. 3. The statement in Smith's *Dict. of the Bible* (ed. 1) and the *Speaker's Comm.* (p. 227), that the language of Daniel bears 'the closest affinity' to that of Ezek. is altogether incorrect, and seems indeed to be due merely to a misunderstanding of Delitzsch's expression in Herzog (ed. 1).

[1] Comp. Breasted, *Hebraica*, vii. (1891), p. 246.

approximating to (though not identical with) those met with in the Book of Enoch (which was written probably, for the most part, during the century following the rise of the Maccabees). Whether the 'one like unto a son of man' in vii. 13 symbolizes the Messiah or the ideal people of Israel (see p. 104 f.), the representation of the judgement upon heathen powers, and of the manner in which the Divine kingdom is inaugurated upon earth (vii. 9—14, 26, 27), is unlike any other representation of the same facts contained in the Old Testament: let the reader study, for example, successively Am. ix. 9—15; Hos. i. 10—ii. 1, xiv. 4—8; Is. ii. 2—4, iv. 2—6, ix. 1—7, xi., xxviii. 18—24, xxix. 18—24, xxxii. 1—8; Jer. xxiii. 1—8, xxxi., xxxiii.; Ez. xxxiv. 11—31, xxxvi.; Is. liv., lv., lx.; and he can hardly fail to feel that when he comes to Dan. vii. he is in a different circle of ideas: on the other hand, the representation in Daniel (as shewn on pp. 85 f., 106 f.) has many traits resembling those appearing shortly afterwards in the Book of Enoch. Angels, again, have in Daniel 'special personal names (viii. 16, ix. 21, x. 13, 21, xii. 1), special ranks (x. 13, 20, xii. 1), and the guardianship of different countries (x. 13, 20, 21)[1]. These representations go far beyond those of Ezek., and Zech., and are relatively identical with those of Tobit, and other Jewish writings of the first cent. B.C. Daniel plainly teaches a personal resurrection of both the righteous and the wicked (xii. 2). This also is a decided advance upon the doctrine taught elsewhere in the O.T.[2]...... Thus while the determination of the date of an O.T. writing from its religious doctrines is always a delicate procedure, yet, as far as a doctrinal development can be found in the O.T., the Book of Daniel comes after all other O.T. writings, and approximates most closely to the Jewish literature of the first cent. B.C.'[3]

Even though there should be no truth in the opinion that these developments have been even partially moulded by foreign

---

[1] See further the notes on iv. 13, viii. 16, x. 13.
[2] Comp. p. xc ff.
[3] Curtis in Hastings' *Dict. of the Bible*, i. 554.

influences[1], they undoubtedly mark a later phase of revelation than that which is set before us in other books of the O.T. And the conclusion to which these *special* features in the Book point is confirmed by the *general* atmosphere which breathes in it, and the tone that prevails in it. This atmosphere and tone are not those of any other writings belonging to the period of the Exile: they are those of a stage intermediate between that of the early post-exilic and that of the early post-Biblical Jewish literature.

A number of independent considerations, including some of great cogency, thus combine in favour of the conclusion that the Book of Daniel was not written earlier than *c.* 300 B.C. And there are certainly grounds, which though they may not be regarded as *demonstrative*, except on the part of those who deny all predictive prophecy, nevertheless make the opinion a highly *probable* one, that the Book is a work of the age of Antiochus Epiphanes. The interest of the Book manifestly *culminates* in the relations subsisting between the Jews and Antiochus. Antiochus, it is admitted on all hands, is the subject of viii. 9—14, 23—25; and, as pointed out on pp. 99 f., there are cogent exegetical reasons for supposing that he is likewise the 'little horn' of vii. 8, 21, 24—26, and that events of his reign are described in ix. 25—27. The survey of Syrian and Egyptian history in ch. xi. leads up to a detailed description of his reign (*vv.* 21—45[2]): xii. 6, 7, 10—12 revert again to the persecution which the Jews experienced at his hands. This being so, it is certainly remarkable that the revelations respecting him should be given to Daniel, in *Babylon*, nearly four centuries previously: it is consonant with God's general methods of providence to raise up teachers, for the instruction or encouragement of His people, *at the time when the need arises.* It is remarkable also that Daniel—so unlike the prophets generally—should display, as remarked above (p. viii), so little interest in the welfare, or prospects, of his contemporaries; that his hopes and Messianic visions should attach themselves, not

---

[1] Comp. below, p. xciv ff. [2] Cf. p. 193.

(as is the case with Jer., Ezek., Isa. xl.—lxvi.) to the approaching return of the exiles to the land of their fathers, but to the deliverance of his people in a remote future. The minuteness of the predictions, embracing even special events in the distant future, is also out of harmony with the analogy of prophecy. Isaiah, Jeremiah, and other prophets unquestionably uttered predictions of the future; but their predictions, when definite[1], relate to events of the proximate future only; when (as in the case of Jeremiah's prediction of 70 years' Babylonian supremacy) they concern a more distant future, they are general and indefinite in their terms. And while down to the period of Antiochus's persecution the *actual* events are described with surprising distinctness, after this point *the distinctness ceases:* the closing events of Antiochus's own life are, to all appearance, not described as they actually occurred (see on xi. 40—45); and when the end of his life has been reached, the prophecy either breaks off altogether (viii. 25, ix. 27), or merges in an *ideal* representation of the Messianic future (vii. 27, xii. 1—3). Judged by the analogy of other prophecies (e.g. Is. viii. 1—ix. 7; x. 5—xi. 16), these facts would imply that the author wrote *during the period of Antiochus's persecution itself.*

As a matter of fact, this supposition explains consistently all the features of the Book. The author lives in the age in which he manifests an interest, and which needs the consolations which he has to address to it. He does not write *after* the persecutions are ended (in which case his prophecies would be pointless), but while they are in progress, when his message of encouragement would have a value for the godly Jews in the season of their trial.

It is hardly possible to fix the actual year in which the book was written; but the inexactness respecting the closing events of Antiochus' life renders it almost certain that these were still in the future when the author wrote: the general tenor of chs. ix., xi., and xii. makes it

---

[1] As Is. viii. 4; Jer. xxviii. 16. See more fully the writer's *Sermons on the Old Testament*, pp. 107—113. Prophecies relating to the future kingdom of God stand upon a different footing: comp. p. lxxxvii ff.

AUTHORSHIP AND DATE. lxvii

improbable that the re-dedication of the Temple had yet taken place (Bevan, p. 129; Kamphausen in the *Encycl. Bibl.* col. 1013): from the Maccabees being alluded to as a 'little help' (xi. 34), it is probable further (Kuenen, *Einl.* §§ 88. 12; 89. 20) that it was written before Judas' defeat of Lysias in 165[1] (1 Macc. iv. 28—35), perhaps (Kuen.) in 166, during the time described in 1 Macc. iii. 1—iv. 27. Cf. Ewald, *Hist.* v. 303, *Proph.* iii. 301, 308 [E.T. v. 155 f., 163], 'B.C. 168—167'; Wellh. *Isr. u. Jüd. Gesch.* p. 252 (ed. 3, p. 246), 'before B.C. 165.'

The author thus utters genuine predictions[2]: at a moment when the national peril was great, and the very existence of Israel as a nation was threatened (1 Macc. iii. 35, 36), he comes forward with words of consolation and hope, assuring his faithful compatriots that the future, like the past and the present, is part of God's predetermined plan, and that within less than $3\frac{1}{2}$ years of the time at which he speaks, their persecutor will be no more, and the period of their trial will be past. This prediction is exactly on a footing with those of the earlier prophets—of Isaiah, for instance, who says (viii. 4) that before a child just born can cry Father, and Mother, Damascus will be taken by the king of Assyria; who declares (xvi. 14, xxi. 16) that within three years the glory of Moab, and within one year the glory of Kedar, will both be humbled; and who announces (xxix. 1—5) Jerusalem's deliverance, within a year, from the siege and distress, which he sees impending; or of the great prophet of the Exile, who, as Cyrus is advancing on his career of conquest (Is. xli. 2, 3, 25), bids his people not be in alarm (xli. 8—11, &c.), the successes of Cyrus are part of God's providential plan (xli. 2, 4, 25), and will issue in the deliverance of Israel from exile (xliv. 28, xlv. 4, 13)[3].

The *historical* features of the Book are also explained consistently by means of the same supposition. In some respects

---

[1] N.B. Kuenen's dates for this period are consistently lower by a unit than those commonly adopted; so that by B.C. 164, for instance, he means the same year which is commonly called B.C. 165.

[2] Comp. especially viii. 25 *end* with the event.

[3] On the manner in which the Book of Daniel, like the earlier prophets, represents the kingdom of God as beginning immediately after the coming deliverance, see below, p. lxxxix.

it preserves the memory of genuine historical facts: in other respects, it exhibits confused and inaccurate traditions, such as might easily be current in an age later than that of Daniel himself. Nebuchadnezzar was actually the builder of Babylon, and the words placed in his mouth in iv. 30 are, as Prince observes, in entire accordance with historical fact; Belshazzar was a real person, whose lifetime is correctly placed at the close of the Babylonian empire[1]; there was in all probability an actual plain of Dura; and the learned men of Babylon were actually versed in the interpretation of dreams. But there were no 'satraps' (iii. 2) under Nebuchadnezzar; the learned men of Babylon were not then known distinctively as 'Chaldeans'; Belshazzar was not either 'son' of Nebuchadnezzar, or 'king' of Babylon; Darius the Mede, son of Aḥashwerosh, and 'king' over the realm of the Chaldeans (ix. 1), is a figure for whom history has no room: in other representations of the Book,—as, for example, the attitude assumed by the different heathen kings towards the God of Daniel, and the madness of Nebuchadnezzar,—there are also in all probability elements of exaggeration or distortion. This double character of the narrative is exactly what would be expected, supposing the Book to be what critics hold it to be, a work not of Daniel's own age, but written some four centuries subsequently.

It by no means follows, however, from this view of the Book that the narrative is throughout a pure work of the imagination. That is not probable. Delitzsch, Meinhold, and others—most recently Behrmann—insist rightly that the Book rests upon a *traditional basis*. How much of its contents is, in our sense of the word, historical, it is, indeed, impossible to say: but it is probable that Daniel was one of the Jewish exiles in Babylon, who, with his three companions, was noted for his staunch adherence to the principles of his religion, who attained a

---

[1] As Josephus (*Ant.* x. xi. 2) identifies Belshazzar with Nabonidus, it is probable that Berosus (whom Jos. quotes for this period of the history) did not mention him; and hence it may perhaps be inferred that his name was preserved by Jewish tradition, and handed down by it in conjunction with that of Daniel.

position of influence at the court, and who perhaps also foretold something of the future fate of the Chaldaean and Persian empires. The traditions relating to him were combined with those which reached the author respecting the public events of Daniel's time, and developed by him into the existing narratives, with a special view to the circumstances of his own age. The motive underlying chs. i.—vi. is manifest. The primary aim of these chapters is not historical, but *didactic*: the incidents of Daniel's life are not narrated for their own sakes, but for the sake of inculcating certain lessons, to magnify the God of Daniel, and to shew how He, by His providence, frustrates the purposes of the proudest of earthly monarchs, while He defends and rewards His servants, who in time of danger or temptation cleave to Him faithfully. The narratives in chs. i.—vi. are thus adapted to supply motives for the encouragement, and models for the imitation, of the loyal Israelites, at the time when Antiochus was making his assaults upon their religion,—when (1 Macc. i. 62, 63) the question of eating meat was made a test of faith (cf. Dan. i.), when (1 Macc. i. 41—50) the worship of foreign deities was commanded and that of Jehovah proscribed, under pain of death (cf. Dan. iii., vi.), and when men might well need to be reminded that it was not God's purpose to allow the powers of heathenism to prevail against Him (cf. Dan. ii., iv., v.). The general aim of the visions attributed to Daniel in chs. vii.—xii. is to shew, with increasing detail and distinctness, that as the course of history, so far as it has hitherto gone, has been in accordance with God's predetermined plan, so it is not less part of His plan that the trial of the saints should not continue indefinitely, but that within three years and a half of the time when the persecuting measures of Antiochus first began it should reach its appointed term. God, in other words, was guiding the whole course of history towards the salvation of His people. And the standpoint from which the survey of the future is represented as being made is an appropriate one: from the very centre and stronghold of heathendom, and in the age in which Israel first becomes permanently dependent upon foreign rulers, Daniel views the centuries, and in weird, impressive imagery portrays the growing deterioration and final impotence of the one, and the ultimate triumph of the other.

It is sometimes objected that this view of the Book of Daniel not only destroys its religious value, but makes it into a forgery: the Book, it has been said, is either Divine or an imposture; if the writer be not Daniel himself, describing events which actually occurred, he must be an impostor, manufacturing falsehoods deliberately in the name of God. In estimating this argument it is necessary in the first place to consider carefully whether the dilemma suggested is a real one. There are circumstances under which no doubt this would be the case: the dilemma would, for instance, be a real one, if we were assured that the object for which the Book was written was to *prove the reality of the supernatural* by an appeal to miracles, or fulfilled predictions; a writer who alleged unreal miracles or predictions, for such a purpose, would unquestionably be guilty of gross and unpardonable imposture. The assumption, however, that this was the purpose for which the Book of Daniel was written is a gratuitous one: there is nothing in the Book either stating or suggesting it; and if the Book was written for another purpose, this may have been one for which the use of imaginative narratives would be perfectly innocent and harmless: all depends upon the *motive* actuating the writer, and the *purpose* with which he wrote. According to critics, the purpose for which the Book of Daniel was written was the consolation and encouragement of the afflicted Jews in the time of Antiochus Epiphanes. For this purpose imaginative narratives might be employed with perfect propriety, and without the smallest intention to deceive. Fiction, even fiction without any foundation of fact whatever, has played an important part in the education of humanity; and religious fiction, written with a didactic purpose, has in both ancient and modern times, been valued by teachers as a powerful instrument of edification, and has won a remarkable amount of popular appreciation. The Old Testament abounds with instances in which poetry and oratory have been employed by the Spirit of God for the purpose of giving expression to moral and religious truth, and

AUTHORSHIP AND DATE.   lxxi

of stirring the moral and religious emotions of those who either listened in the first instance to the words of the poet or the prophet, or who have since read them; and if the imagination be a faculty granted by God to man, and capable of being employed in instruction and edification, there is no intelligible reason why, where no fact conditioning a theological verity is concerned, it may not have been made subservient to religious ends. The idea that the Bible can contain nothing but matter-of-fact descriptions of actual occurrences is supported by nothing said in the Bible itself, and is in reality a survival of an extreme Puritanical conception of its contents. The opening words of the Epistle to the Hebrews authorize us to expect diversity in the literary forms in which 'God spake unto the fathers' in the Old Testament[1]. The Jews are moreover a nation highly gifted with powers of imagination: many passages of the prophets owe the magic of their charm to a chastened use of the imagination; and in post-Biblical times, imaginative narratives, or anecdotes, with a didactic purpose ('haggādāhs,' or 'midrāshīm')[2], have formed a large and important part of their religious literature. There is thus the less reason, especially when examples of this kind of literature appear among the earliest of the non-canonical books (for instance, in Tobit and Judith), that it should be unrepresented in the Old Testament.

But it may be said, 'If we have no assurance that God really helped and delivered His servants in the manner described in the Book, what value could the narratives have had for the encouragement and consolation of the Jews persecuted by Antiochus? To encourage them by the narrative of deliver-

---
[1] πολυμερῶς καὶ πολυτρόπως. Cf. the writer's *Sermons on the O.T.*, p. 143 ff., esp. p. 155 f. Jonah is another book of the same character.

[2] I.e. edifying religious narratives, longer or shorter as the case might be, and sometimes developed out of a text, or even a word, of Scripture, sometimes constructed independently. See further, on these two terms, the author's *Literature of the Old Testament*, p. 497 (ed. 6 or 7, pp. 484, 487, 529). The term 'midrash' occurs twice in the O.T., of two of the sources used by the Chronicler, 2 Ch. xiii. 22, xxiv. 27 [A.V. *story*]; and many of the narratives peculiar to the Chronicles have a 'midrashic' character.

ances which never happened is nothing but cruel mockery.' The answer to this objection lies in the distinction which must be drawn between a truth or doctrine in itself, and the form,—where there are independent reasons for supposing this to be figurative,—in which the truth or doctrine is presented. This distinction is so aptly explained by the Rev. C. J. Ball, in his Introduction to the 'Song of the Three Children' in the *Speaker's Commentary on the Apocrypha* (ii. 307), that the passage is worth transcribing in full:—

'The above passages [quotations from the Talmud, including a reference to the story of Abraham's deliverance from the fire, mentioned below, p. 35] not only illustrate the tendency to put appropriate thanksgivings into the mouth of the Three Martyrs, which we find exemplified at length in our Apocryphon: they also shew that the conception of a deliverance from a fiery furnace was traditional among the Jews, in all probability from very ancient times. And we have to bear in mind a fact familiar enough to students of the Talmudic and Midrashic literature, though apparently unknown to many expositors of Scripture, whose minds conspicuously lack that *orientation* which is an indispensable preliminary to a right understanding of the treasures of Eastern thought; I mean the inveterate tendency of Jewish teachers to convey their doctrine not in the form of abstract discourse, but in a mode appealing directly to the imagination, and seeking to arouse the interest and sympathy of the man rather than of the philosopher. The Rabbi embodies his lesson in a story, whether parable, or allegory, or seeming historical narrative; and the last thing he or his disciples would think of is to ask whether the selected persons, events, and circumstances which so vividly suggest the doctrine are in themselves real or fictitious. The doctrine is everything; the mode of presentation has no independent value. To make the story the first consideration, and the doctrine it was intended to convey an after-thought, as we, with our dry Western literalness, are predisposed to do, is to reverse the Jewish order of thinking, and to do unconscious injustice to the authors of many edifying narratives of antiquity.'

AUTHORSHIP AND DATE.

The Book of Daniel, like the Book of Jonah, is in its narrative parts (chs. i.—vi.) a vivid presentation of real and important religious truths, even though the events described in it did not in all cases occur in actual fact as the narrative recounts.

Mutatis mutandis, the dream in ch. ii., and the visions in chs. vii.—xii. are to be explained upon the same principles. They are (for the most part) indirect, and to our minds artificial, modes of presenting the truth that the movements of history are in God's hands, and are determined by Him beforehand. At the same time, in what relates to the close of the persecution, and the period of happiness which they represent as then beginning, they contain, as has been already remarked, genuine predictions, and genuine delineations of the future kingdom of God, quite in the manner of the older prophets (comp. also the notes on ix. 24, p. 136 f.).

The following are the earliest extant references, or allusions, to the Book of Daniel. (1) The prophecy vii. 7 *end*, 8 seems to be alluded to in the so-called 'Sibylline Oracles' (p. lxxxiii), iii. 397—400 (*c.* 140 B.C.): see p. 98. (2) In 1 Macc. i. 54 (cf. vi. 7)—written, probably, during the early decades of the first cent. B.C.[1]—the heathen altar erected by Antiochus on the altar of burnt-offering is called an 'abomination of desolation,' being the same expression which is used in the LXX. of Dan. xi. 31, xii. 11 (see more fully p. 150). This, however, does not prove necessarily the use of the Book of Daniel by the author of 1 Macc.: the author of 1 Macc. may have known independently that the Jews of the Maccabee period called the heathen altar a שִׁקּוּץ שֹׁמֵם (מְשֹׁמֵם); and the identity of the Greek rendering ($\beta\delta\acute{\epsilon}\lambda\nu\gamma\mu\alpha$ $\dot{\epsilon}\rho\eta\mu\dot{\omega}\sigma\epsilon\omega\varsigma$) may be accounted for in more ways than one: it may have been the conventional Greek rendering of the Heb. expression in question, or the translator of either book may have adopted it from the translation of the other. (3) In 1 Macc. ii. 59 f., in the speech put into the mouth of the dying Mattathias, after the mention of Abraham, Joseph, and other Israelitish worthies, who had been examples

---

[1] Schürer, ii. 581 (§ 32); 1 *Maccabees* in the *Cambridge Bible*, p. 43.

of constancy and faith, there occur the words, 'Hananiah, Azariah, Mishael believed, and were saved out of the flame. Daniel in his guilelessness [ἐν τῇ ἁπλότητι αὐτοῦ = בְּתֻמּוֹ; cf. *v*. 37] was delivered from the mouth of lions,' with evident allusion to the narratives contained in Dan. iii. and vi. (4) The prayer in Baruch i. 15—iii. 8 contains (in i. 15—ii. 19) many nearly verbal similarities of expression with Dan. ix. 4—19, which shew incontestably either that the author of the one derived many of his expressions from the other, or that both were dependent upon a common source: it can scarcely, however, be said to be clear, beyond the reach of doubt, that it is the prayer in Daniel which is the original (see p. lxxv). (5) In the N.T. Daniel is mentioned by name in Mt. xxiv. 15 (but in the || Mk. xiii. 14 not in the best MSS.); and the narratives of the book are not improbably alluded to in Heb. xi. 33, 34 (Dan. vi., iii.). For instances in which the imagery or expression of the N.T. appears to have been suggested by the book see p. lxxxv.

The external evidence which has been sometimes appealed to as tending to shew that the Book of Daniel was in existence before B.C. 168—165, is slight and inconclusive.

(i) The allusion, just noted, in 1 Macc. ii. 59, 60 does not prove more than that the narratives of Dan. iii. and vi. were known to the author of 1 Macc., who wrote pretty clearly (see xvi. 23, 24) after the close of the reign of John Hyrcanus, B.C. 135—105, probably about B.C. 90.

(ii) The parallels between Dan. ix. 4—19 and Baruch i. 15—ii. 19 are numerous and striking: see Bar. i. 15 (Dan. ix. 7 *a*, 8 *a*), 16 (ix. 8 *b*). 17 (ix. 8 *end*), 18 (ix. 9 *b*, 10), 20 *a*[1] (ix. 11 *b*), 21 (ix. 10), ii. 1 *a* (ix. 12), 2[1] (ix. 12 *b*, 13 *a*) 4 *b* (ix. 16 *b*), 6 (ix. 7 *a*, 8 *a*), 7[1] (ix. 13 *a*), 8 (ix. 13 *b*), 9[1] (ix. 14), 10 (ix. 10), 11 *a, c*, 12 *a* (ix. 15), 12 *b*, 13 *a* (ix. 16 *a*), 14 *a* (ix. 17 *a*), 14 'for thine own sake' (ix. 17), 15 *b* (ix. 18 *middle*, 19 *end*), 16 *b*, 17 *a* (ix. 18 to 'eyes'), 19 (ix. 18 *b*); in other parts of the prayer in Baruch, there are reminiscences principally from Deut. and Jer. The Book of Baruch is manifestly of composite authorship; and i. 1—iii. 8 (if i. 1—14 is the real introduction to the sequel) purports to be a

---

[1] N.B. 'Plagues' in A.V., R.V. of i. 20, ii. 2, 7, 9, iii. 4 = κακά = the 'evil' of Dan. ix. 12 (Gk. κακά), 13, 14.

AUTHORSHIP AND DATE. lxxv

confession and prayer sent by the exiles in Babylon, in the fifth year of the captivity of Jehoiachin, to their brethren in Jerusalem, to be used by them on their (the exiles') behalf[1]. The real date of the Book of Baruch is disputed. The second part (iii. 9—v. 9) is generally allowed to have been written shortly after the destruction of Jerusalem by Titus (A.D. 70): the first part is assigned by Schürer (ii. 723[2]) to the same date, though others think it to be a good deal earlier, Ewald, and Reuss, for instance, assigning it to the period of the earlier Ptolemies (c. 300 B.C.)[3]. It is, however, seldom possible, given simply two parallel texts, to determine, without assuming the question in dispute, which is the older, and which it is that contains reminiscences of the other: the prayer in Baruch might, no doubt, be an expansion (with, at the same time, some omissions) of that in Daniel[4], but the prayer in Daniel might also be an abridgement and adaptation of that in Baruch; or both might also be based upon an ancient traditional form of confession, preserved in its most original form in Daniel[5]. The Book of Baruch cannot be regarded as having any bearing on the date of the Book of Daniel until it has been shewn more clearly than has yet been done, not only that the prayer in Baruch is older than c. 165 B.C., but also *if* this is really the case, that the passages common to it and Dan. cannot have been borrowed in the latter from the former.

[1] The *rôle* assumed is not however consistently maintained, ii. 13, 14, iii. 7, 8, being evidently spoken from the standpoint of the exiles themselves. See BARUCH, BOOK OF, in Hastings' *Dict. of the Bible*.

[2] And in his art. on Baruch in Herzog, ed. 2, i. 500 f., ed. 3, i. 641 f. So also Kneucker, in his excellent edition of Baruch (1879), pp. 57—60, cf. 68—70.

[3] The positive grounds favouring this early date are, however, slight: cf. Kneucker, p. 39 f. The arguments in Hastings against Schürer's date do not seem to be conclusive.

[4] The principal additions in *Baruch* are in i. 16 b, 19 a, 20 b—22, ii. 1 b, 3—7 a, 8 b, 11 *middle*, 13 b, 14 b—16 a, 17 b—18, 19 a ('of our fathers and of our kings'), and all from ii. 20 to iii. 8. The principal additions in *Daniel* are in ix. 4—6, 7 b—8 a, 9 a, 10 *end*, 11 b (partly), 13 *end*, 16 (from 'and thy fury'), 17 b, 18 (from ' our desolations' to ' thy name,' and ' but for thy great mercies '), 19. (The references, both here and in the text, are to the *Greek*, which should be compared throughout: let the reader underline, in his two texts (Daniel in Theod.), the passages which are (substantially) the same in both. In Bar. ii. 12 b observe that δικαιώματα = צְדָקוֹת (see vv. 17, 19), while in Dan. ix. 16 ἐλεημοσύνη in Theod., and δικαιοσύνη in LXX., both = צְדָקָה: see below, p. 54; Kneucker, pp. 235, 353.)

[5] Marshall, *ap*. Hastings, p. 252a, towards the bottom.

(iii) No conclusion of any value as to the date of Daniel can be drawn from the LXX. translation. (1) The date of the translation is quite uncertain; the grounds that have been adduced for the purpose of shewing that it was made in the time of Antiochus Epiphanes himself (e.g. the renderings of ix. 24—27, xi. 30, 33) being altogether insufficient. (2) The errors in the LXX. translation of the book have been supposed to shew that many Hebrew words used in it were unfamiliar to the translators, and consequently that it must have been written at a much earlier date than that assigned to it by critics. It is, however, remarkable that throughout O.T. the LXX. translators (who, as is well known, were not the same for all the books) stand singularly aloof from the Palestinian tradition—often, for instance, not only missing the general sense of a passage, but shewing themselves to be unacquainted with the meaning even of common Hebrew words. Thus the errors in the LXX. translation of Daniel merely shew that the meaning of particular words was unknown in *Alexandria* at the time, whatever it may have been, at which the translation was made: they do not afford evidence that the words were unknown in *Palestine* in the second cent. B.C., and would not have been used by an author writing there then. The Greek translator of the Proverbs of Jesus, the son of Sirach (Ecclesiasticus), though a grandson of the author himself, nevertheless often misunderstood the Hebrew in which they were written.

§ 4. *Some characteristic features of the Book of Daniel.*

As has been pointed out in § 1, the first part of the Book of Daniel (chs. i.—vi.) consists essentially of a series of *didactic narratives*; the second part of the Book (chs. vii.—xii.),—as also ch. ii., in so far as a succession of world-empires forms the subject of Nebuchadnezzar's dream,—deals with what, viewed from Daniel's standpoint, is future, and is *apocalyptic* in its character. It will not be necessary to dwell further upon the narrative portions of the Book; but something remains to be said with regard to its apocalyptic parts, and also on some of the more characteristic doctrines which find expression in it. And firstly, as regards the symbolism and the veiled predictions, which form such conspicuous features in these parts of the Book. Symbolism is employed already by the later prophets to a

APOCALYPTIC LITERATURE. lxxvii

greater extent than is the case with the earlier prophets. Thus in Ezekiel we have the allegories of the vine-tree (ch. xv.), the abandoned infant (ch. xvi.), the two eagles and the vine (ch. xvii.), the lion's whelps (ch. xix.), the two harlots (ch. xxiii.), the flourishing tree (ch. xxxi.), the shepherds and their flock (ch. xxxiv.); and in Zech. we find a series of visions, in which the prophet sees, for instance, the Divine horses, symbolizing the ubiquity of Jehovah's presence upon the earth (i. 8—17), four horns symbolizing the powers of the world arrayed against Israel (i. 18—21), a golden candlestick, representing the restored community (ch. iv.), and chariots proceeding to the different quarters of the earth, symbolizing the fulfilment of Jehovah's judgements (vi. 1—8). But, as applied in Daniel, both the symbolism and the veiled predictions are characteristic of a species of literature which was now beginning to spring up, and which is known commonly by modern writers as *Apocalyptic Literature*.

The word 'apocalypse' means *disclosure, revelation*; and though ordinary prophecy contains 'disclosures,' whether respecting the will of God in general, or respecting the future, the term is applied in particular to writings in which the 'disclosure,' or 'revelation,' is of a specially marked and distinctive character. The beginnings of this type of writing are to be found in those post-exilic prophecies of the O. T. relating to the future, which are less closely attached to the existing order of things than is usually the case, and which, though they cannot be said actually to describe it, may nevertheless be regarded as prophetic anticipations of the final judgement, and consummation of all things, as Is. xxiv.—xxvii., Zech. xiv., Joel iii. 9—17[1]. But at a later date, apocalyptic prophecy assumed a special form, and became the expression of particular feelings and ideas.

Apocalyptic prophecy arose in an age in which there were no longer any prophets of the older type, addressing themselves directly to the needs of the times, and speaking in person to the people in the name of God: and it consists essentially of a

---

[1] Cf. Kirkpatrick, *Doctrine of the Prophets*, pp. 475 f., 481, 488 f.; and the present writer's *Joel and Amos* (in the *Cambridge Bible*), p. 33.

development and adaptation of the ideas and promises expressed by the older prophets, designed especially with the object of affording encouragement and consolation to faithful Israelites in a period of national distress. The call to repentance, and rebuke for sin, which formed the primary and central element in the teaching of the older prophets, assumed in the age now under consideration a secondary place: Israel was subject to the heathen, and the crying question was, When would its long and humiliating servitude be at an end? When would the older prophecies of future glory and triumph over the heathen be fulfilled? How much longer would Jehovah's promised redemption be deferred? Hence, in the form of prophecy which now arose, a much more prominent place was taken than had formerly been the case by visions of the future: older, but hitherto unfulfilled, promises of Israel's destined glory were reaffirmed, and were made the basis of larger and broader outlooks into the future. Its mode of representation was artificial. The disclosures which were the most characteristic element of apocalyptic prophecy were not made by the author in his own person, they were placed in the mouth of some pious and famous man of old—an Enoch, a Moses, a Baruch, an Ezra: from the standpoint of the assumed speaker the future was unrolled, usually under symbolic imagery, down to the time in which the actual author lived: the heavens were thrown open, glimpses were given of the offices and operation of the celestial hierarchy: God's final judgement both upon His own people and upon the powers opposed to it was described: the approaching deliverance of the afflicted Israelites was declared: the resurrection and future lot alike of the righteous and of the wicked were portrayed in vivid imagery. The seer who is represented as the author of the book, sometimes beholds these things himself in a vision or dream, but often he holds discourse with an angel, who either explains to him what he does not fully understand, or communicates to him the revelations in their entirety. Naturally there are variations in detail: the subjects enumerated do not appear uniformly with precisely the same prominence; hortatory or didactic matter is also often present as well: but speaking generally some at least of them are present in every 'apocalypse,' and constitute its most conspicuous and distinctive feature. A brief account of two or three of the more important apocalypses may help to give substance to what has been said.

The *Book of Enoch* is the longest known work of the kind; and in its earliest parts (for it is evidently of composite authorship) is certainly the nearest in date to the Book of Daniel. It is said of Enoch in Gen. v. 24 that he 'walked with God'; and the expression was taken in later times to mean not only that he led a godly life, but also that he was the recipient of supernatural knowledge. The 'Book of Enoch' gives an account of the knowledge which he was supposed in this way to have attained. The oldest sections of the book are chs. i.—xxxvi., lxxii.—cviii., probably (Dillmann, Schürer) *c.* 120 B.C., and chs. lxxxiii.—xc. may even, according to Charles, be almost contemporary with Daniel (B.C. 166—161). In chs. i.—xxxvi. Enoch first (ch. i.) tells how he had had a vision of future judgement: God would appear, 'with ten thousands of His holy ones' (Jude 14, 15) on Mount Sinai, to punish the fallen angels, and wicked men, and to reward the righteous with peace and felicity. In chs. xvii.—xxxvi. he relates how he had been led in vision through different parts of the earth; and had been shewn by an angel, Uriel or Raphael, the fiery abyss prepared for the rebellious angels, Sheol, with four divisions set apart for different classes of the departed (xxii.), Jerusalem (xxv.—xxvi.), Gehenna (the valley of Hinnom) close by (xxvii.), and Paradise, with the tree of life, in the far East (xxxii.). The ultimate lot of the righteous, as depicted here, is not, however, eternal life in heaven, but long, untroubled life in an ideal Paradise on earth. In chs. lxxxiii.—xc.—perhaps, as just said, the oldest part of the book,—Enoch recounts to his son Methuselah two visions which he has seen. The first vision (lxxxiii.—lxxxiv.) describes the approaching Deluge; the second (lxxxv.—xc.) unfolds, in a symbolical form,—the leaders of the chosen race being represented by domestic animals, bulls or sheep, and the Gentiles by different wild beasts and birds of prey,—the entire history of the patriarchs and Israel, from Adam to the author's own time; after that (xc. 18 ff.) God Himself appears to judge the world, Israel's oppressors are destroyed, and the Messianic kingdom is established. The events indicated by the symbolism are usually sufficiently clear; but sometimes (as in Daniel) there is ambiguity:

indeed, the date of this part of the book depends upon whether the 'great horn' which grows upon one of the 'sheep' in xc. 9 is to be interpreted (with Dillm., Schürer, and others) of John Hyrcanus (B.C. 135—105), or (with Charles) of Judas Maccabaeus (B.C. 165—161). As illustrating Dan. x. 13, 20, 21, xii. 1, it is worth noticing that Israel, after its apostasy, is committed to the charge of 70 'shepherds' (i.e. *angels*), who are held responsible for what happens to it, and are afterwards called up before God for judgement (lxxxix. 54—xc. 17, 22—25).

Chs. xci.—xciii., also addressed to Methuselah, contain another historical apocalypse: the history of the patriarchs and of Israel is divided into seven weeks, in the first of which lives Enoch, in the second Noah, &c. (but without any names being actually mentioned); at the end of the seventh week, which is described as an age of apostasy, the writer lives himself: the eighth week, that of 'righteousness,' sees the kingdom of God established in the land of Israel: in the ninth week it is spread over all the earth: in the tenth week will be the 'eternal judgement' upon the fallen angels; there will then follow 'weeks without number in goodness and righteousness, and sin will no more be mentioned for ever' (xciii. 1—10, xci. 12—17). Chs. xciv.—cv., addressed to Enoch's sons, consist of a series of woes pronounced upon sinners, intermixed with exhortations to follow righteousness and avoid the ways of sin and death.

In all the preceding sections of the book there is either no Messiah, or, at most (xc. 37), a Messiah who is merely a superior man, mentioned only in passing, very different from the glorious super-human Messiah of chs. xxxvii.—lxxi.

Chs. xxxvii.—lxxi., commonly known as the 'Similitudes,' date, according to Dillm., Charles, and others, from shortly before B.C. 64, according to Schürer, from the time of Herod. In these chapters the Messiah is a much more prominent and also a much more exalted figure than in the other parts of the book. The chapters consist of three 'similitudes,' or visions. In the first (xxxviii.—xliv.) Enoch sees the abodes of the righteous, and the 'Elect One' (the Messiah), the Almighty surrounded by myriads of angels, and with the four 'presences,' Michael, Raphael, Gabriel, and Phanuel, ever praying before Him, and is admitted also to the 'secrets of the heavens' (including the explanation of different natural phenomena, as lightnings, wind, dew, &c.). In the second vision (xlv.—lvii.) he beholds the Messianic judgement, the 'Elect One,' or the 'Son of Man,' beside the 'Head of

Days' (the Almighty), and afterwards sitting on the 'throne of his glory,' for the purpose of judging the world; after the judgement, the fallen angels and wicked kings are cast into a furnace of fire; a resurrection of Israelites takes place (li. 1), the righteous 'become angels' (li. 4), and enjoy everlasting felicity. In the third vision (lviii.—lxix., but with many interpolations, interrupting the connexion) Enoch describes more fully the ultimate felicity of the righteous (lviii.) in the light of eternal life (lviii. 3), and in the immediate presence of the 'Son of Man' (lxii. 14), and the judgement of the Messiah upon angels and men (lxi.—lxiii., lxix. 26—29). The imagery of the 'Similitudes' is fine: and the thought is often an expansion of parts of Daniel (see the notes on vii. 9, 10, and p. 106 f.).

The *Apocalypse of Baruch* was written probably shortly after the destruction of Jerusalem by Titus (A.D. 70), at a time when the problem which seemed to the Jews so difficult of solution was, how God could have permitted such a disaster to fall upon His people. Baruch, after the Chaldaeans have carried off the mass of the people, having fasted (cf. Dan. x. 3) for seven days, is told to remain in Jerusalem in order to receive disclosures respecting the future; and, after a second fast (xii. 5), hears a voice telling him that the heathen also will receive their punishment in due time (xiii. 5): he debates at some length with God respecting the prosperity of the wicked and the sufferings of the righteous, but is given to understand that these anomalies will be adjusted in a future life. After a third fast, and prayer (ch. xxi.), Baruch sees the heavens opened (Ezek. i. 1), and is assured, in answer to his further questionings, that the time of redemption is not now far distant: 'Behold, the days come, and the books will be opened in which are written the sins of all those who have sinned, and the treasuries in which the righteousness of all those who have been righteous in creation is gathered' (xxiv. 1): the period of coming tribulation is divided into 12 times, each marked by its own woe (xxvi.—xxvii.); at the end of the twelfth time, the Messiah will be revealed, those who have 'fallen asleep in hope' will rise again, and a reign of happiness will begin upon earth (xxix.—xxx.). Soon afterwards Baruch has a vision of a great forest, with a vine growing opposite to it: the forest was laid low till only a single cedar remained standing; this, after being rebuked by the vine for its iniquities, was destroyed by fire, while the vine spread, and the plain around blossomed into flowers. The forest is explained to signify the four empires which oppressed Israel: the vine was the Messiah, who should destroy the last empire (the Roman) for its impieties, and establish a rule of peace (xxxvi.—xl.). On the strength of this revelation, Baruch exhorts the elders of the people to obedience and patience (xliv.—xlvi.). In a fourth vision Baruch sees a great cloud rising up from the sea, and pouring down upon the earth black and bright waters alternately, twelve times in succession, the last bright waters being followed by waters blacker than any which had preceded, and these being followed by lightnings, and twelve rivers ascending from the sea (liii.). After a prayer (liv.), the interpretation of the vision is disclosed to him by the angel Ramiel: the twelve black and bright waters symbolize twelve evil and good periods in the history of the world: the eleventh dark waters symbolizing the Chaldaean disaster, the twelfth bright waters the restoration of Jerusalem, the blacker waters which followed, the future consummation of troubles, the lightning and the twelve rivers, the Messiah, and the felicity which he would bring (lvi.—lxxiv.).

A third apocalypse is the *Fourth Book of Esdras* (2 Esdras of the English Apocrypha), written most probably under Domitian (A.D. 81—96). Chs. i.—ii., xv.—xvi., are Christian additions: the Apocalypse itself consists only of chs. iii.—xiv. It contains seven visions, purporting to have been seen by Ezra whilst in captivity. In the first of these Ezra, having unfolded to God in prayer his perplexity at the sight of Israel suffering at the hand of a nation more wicked than itself, is told, in the course of a colloquy with the angel Uriel, that he is not in a position to judge of the dealings of Providence (iii. 1—v. 13). In a second and third vision (v. 20—vi. 34, vi. 36—ix. 25), the same subject being continued, Ezra is taught (among other things) that the events of history must run their appointed course, and that in a future state the righteous and the wicked will each be rewarded according to their due: there will be 'seven ways' of punishment for the one, and 'seven orders' of blessedness for the other (vii. 79—99, R.V.). In the fifth vision Ezra sees in a dream an eagle rising up out of the sea, with 12 wings and three heads: as he watched her spreading her wings over the earth, he perceived eight smaller wings growing up out of them: the 20 wings and the three heads bare rule over the earth in succession until a lion appeared, and in a loud voice rebuked the eagle for its tyranny and cruelty, and bade it disappear (xi.). The interpretation follows. The eagle is the fourth kingdom which appeared to Daniel, i.e. according to the interpretation adopted by the author (p. 95, 99 *n.*), the Roman empire: the wings and heads are different Roman rulers[1]: the lion is the 'anointed one' (the Messiah), who should arise in the end of the days out of the seed of David, and reprove and overthrow these rulers, and give rest and peace unto his people, for 400 years (xii. 24; see vii. 28 ff.), until the final judgement. The sixth vision (xiii.), of the one 'in the likeness of a man,' is summarized below, p. 107 f. In the seventh and last vision (xiv.), we have the curious story of the manner in which, the law having been burnt, the 24 books of the O.T., as well as 70 other 'apocryphal' books, were written, in the course of 40 days, by five scribes, at Ezra's dictation.

The *Assumption of Moses*,—written, as vi. 2—9 shews, within a very few years of the death of Herod, B.C. 4,—contains an 'apocalypse' of the history of Israel from their entry into Canaan till the days of Herod (chs. ii.—v.). Ch. vii. describes the rule of impious and scornful men, preceding the time of the end. Chs. viii.—ix., as the text at present stands, foretell a 'second visitation' destined then to befall the nation, which reads like a repetition of the persecution of Antiochus: indeed, it is possible that Dr Charles is right in supposing that it is really a description of that persecution, and that the two chapters have become displaced from their proper position after ch. v. Ch. x. is a Psalm of triumph over the approaching judgement. From the death of Moses till the final judgement there are assigned (x. 12) 250 'times,' or weeks of years, i.e. (cf. i. 2) it is placed A.M. 4250.

The so-called *Sibylline Oracles*,—a heterogeneous compilation, in Greek hexameters, of materials of very different origin and dates, partly Jewish and partly Christian,—contain in Book III. (ll. 162—807) a long 'apocalypse,' in which the seventh Ptolemy (Physcon, B.C. 145—117) is more than once referred to (ll. 191—193, 316—318, 608—610), and which is considered by the best authorities to have been written *c.* 140 B.C. This apocalypse contains a survey of the history of Israel from the age of Solomon: Antiochus Epiphanes is referred to in all probability in ll. 388—400 (see p. 98), and certainly in ll. 612—615; the Sibyl also foretells the advent of the Messianic king, his vengeance on his adversaries, the prosperity which will prevail under him (652

---

[1] The names are not given; and very different opinions have been held as to what rulers are meant. See Schürer, ii. 650 ff. (ed. 3, 1898, iii. 236 ff.).

—731), and the signs which are to herald the end of all things (795—807)[1].

These examples will illustrate sufficiently the general character of the Jewish 'Apocalypses.' While including an element of exhortation, and theological reflexion, they are in their most distinctive parts imaginative developments, varying in detail, but with many common features, partly of the thought (which is usually placed as a 'revelation' in the mouth of an ancient seer) that the movements of history, including the course and end of the distress out of which the apocalypse itself arose, are predetermined by God; partly of the eschatological hopes which the writer expects to see realized as soon as the period of present distress is past, but which vary in character—being for instance more or less material, and being with or without a Messiah—according to the individual writer. And these are just the features which appear in the Book of Daniel. It is of course not for a moment denied that the Book of Daniel is greatly superior to the other 'apocalypses' that have been referred to,—not only for example is its teaching more spiritual, but it is entirely free from the fantastic and sometimes indeed absurd representations in which the non-canonical apocalyptic writers often indulge: nevertheless, just as there are Psalms both canonical and non-canonical (the so-called 'Psalms of Solomon'), Proverbs both canonical and non-canonical (Ecclesiasticus), histories both canonical and non-canonical (1 Macc.), 'midrashim' both canonical (Jonah) and non-canonical (Tobit, Judith), so there are analogously apocalypses both canonical and non-canonical; the superiority, in each case, from a theological

---

[1] See further, on both these and other 'Apocalypses,' Charles' translations of the *Book of Enoch*, the *Book of the Secrets of Enoch*, the *Apocalypse of Baruch*, and the *Assumption of Moses*; the introductions and translations in Kautzsch's *Pseudepigraphen des A T.s* (1899); the art. APOCALYPTIC LITERATURE in the *Encyclopaedia Biblica*; the arts. BARUCH, ENOCH, &c. in Hastings' *Dict. of the Bible*; Schürer, ii. 616—691, 790—807, § 32 (ed. 3, iii. 190—294, 420—450); Dillmann in Herzog², xii. 342 ff.; W. J. Deane, *Pseudepigrapha* (1891); and comp. the remarks of Wellhausen in his *Skizzen und Vorarbeiten*, vi. (1899), pp. 226—234.

point of view, of the canonical work does not place it in a different literary category from the corresponding non-canonical work or works. Probably, indeed, the Book of Daniel formed the model, especially in chs. vii.—xii., upon which the non-canonical apocalypses were constructed: it is at all events undoubted that there are many passages in the book which furnished in germ the thought or imagery which was expanded or embellished by subsequent apocalyptic writers.

Comp., for instance, not merely the general mode of representation by means of symbolism and visions, the latter being often explained to the seer by the intervention of an angel; but also, more particularly, in Enoch, the titles 'Most High' (see on Dan. iii. 26), and 'watcher,' or wakeful one (see on iv. 13), the representation of the Almighty as an aged man, seated as judge on His throne, surrounded by myriads of angels (vii. 9, and p. 106 f.), the books in which the deeds of men are recorded (vii. 10), and those in which the citizens of the Messianic kingdom are registered (xii. 1), the resurrection and 'eternal life' (xii. 2), the 'son of man' (vii. 13, and p. 106 f.), the saints compared to stars (viii. 10, and xii. 3), the fear at the sight of the vision, and the restoration by an angelic touch (viii. 17, 18, x. 8 ff.), the revelation designed for the future, not for the present (viii. 26 b, xii. 4), the 10 'weeks' into which the history of the world is divided (En. xciii., xci. 12—15), the names and ranks of angels (more fully developed than in Dan.), with Michael appointed guardian over Israel (Dan. viii. 16, x. 13); comp. in Baruch and 2 Esdras, also, the fast, predisposing to a vision (Dan. x. 3; see on vv. 5—9).

The Book of Daniel is also one of the sources of the imagery, or the expression, of the Book of Revelation: see on iii. 4, vii. 3, 7 ('ten horns': Rev. xii. 3, xiii. 1, xvii. 3, 7, 12, 16), 8, 9 ('white as snow'), 10 (thrice), 13 (Rev. i. 7, 13, xiv. 14), 21 (Rev. xiii. 7), 25 (Rev. xii. 14; cf. also the 42 months of tribulation in xi. 2, xiii. 5 (see v. 7), and the 1260 days of xi. 3 and xii. 6—each being equal to $3\frac{1}{2}$ years), 27, viii. 10 (Rev. xii. 4), x. 6 (Rev. i. 14 b, 15), xii. 1, 7 (Rev. x. 5, 6, xii. 14). Comp. also p. xcvii f.

It remains to consider briefly certain doctrines and representations, which are characteristic of the Book of Daniel.

1. *The kingdom of God.* One of the most fundamental ideas in the Book of Daniel is the triumph of the kingdom of God

over the kingdoms of the world. This is the thought expressed already in Nebuchadnezzar's dream in ch. ii., where the stone 'cut out without hands,' falling upon the feet of the colossal image, and causing it to break up, and afterwards itself filling the entire earth, represents the triumph of the kingdom of God over the anti-theocratic powers of the world. It is the same ultimate triumph of the kingdom of God over the kingdoms of the world, which, with increasing distinctness of detail, and with more special reference to the climax of heathen hostility to the truth in the person of Antiochus Epiphanes, is depicted in chs. vii.—xii.: upon a divinely appointed succession of world-empires follows at last the universal and eternal kingdom of the holy people of God, a kingdom which (ch. vii.) contrasts with all previous kingdoms, as man contrasts with beasts of prey. The book is thus dominated, 'not only by an unshaken confidence in the ultimate triumph of truth, but also by an over-mastering sense of a universal divine purpose which overrules all the vicissitudes of human history, the rise and fall of dynasties, the conflicts of nations, and the calamities that overtake the faithful[1].'

According to the Book of Daniel, when the need of the saints is the greatest, through the exterminating measures of Antiochus Epiphanes (vii. 21, 25, viii. 24, 25, xi. 31—39, xii. 7b), the Almighty will interpose: His throne of judgement will be set up, and the powers hostile to Israel will be overthrown (ii. 35, 44, vii. 9—12, 22a, 26, viii. 25 *end*, xi. 45 *end*); everlasting dominion will be given to the people of the saints, and all surviving nations will serve them (vii. 14, 22b, 27); sin will be abolished and forgiven, and everlasting righteousness be brought in (ix. 24). The righteous dead of Israel will rise to an eternal life of glory; the apostate Jews will rise likewise, but only to be visited with contumely and shame (xii. 2, 3). The inauguration of the kingdom of God will follow immediately upon the overthrow of the 'fourth empire' in the person of Antiochus Epiphanes.

This representation of the future kingdom of God, though it differs in details, and displays traits marking the later age to

---

[1] Ottley, *Bampton Lectures*, 1897, p. 332.

which it belongs, is, in all essential features the same as that which is found repeatedly in the earlier prophets. The earlier prophets, as Amos, Hosea, Isaiah, Jeremiah, Ezekiel, the Second Isaiah, all pictured the advent of an age, when the trials and disappointments of the present would be no more, when human infirmity and human sin would cease to mar the happiness of earth, when Israel, freed from foreign oppressors without and purified from unworthy and ungodly members within, would realize its ideal character, and live an idyllic life of righteousness and peace upon its own soil (see e.g. Hos. xiv. 4—8; Is. i. 26, iv. 2—4, xxix. 18—24, xxxii. 1—8, xxxiii. 24, &c.), and when the nations of the world would either be themselves incorporated in the kingdom of God (Is. ii. 2, xix. 18—25; Jer. iii. 17; Is. li. 4, 5, lvi. 7), or would be held in more or less willing subjection by the restored and invigorated people of Israel (Am. ix. 12; Is. xi. 14, xiv. 2, xlv. 14, lx. 10, 14, lxi. 5), or,—which is more particularly the representation of the later prophets,—in so far as they remained irreconcilably hostile, would be destroyed (Zeph. iii. 8 [but contrast iii. 9]; Ez. xxxviii.—xxxix.; Is. lx. 12, lxiii. 3—6, lxvi. 15, 16; Joel iii. 9—17; Zech. xiv. 12—13)[1].

In comparing these representations with that contained in the Book of Daniel, there are two important points which ought to be borne in mind, one a point of difference, the other a point of resemblance. The point of *difference* is that the representation in Daniel is more distinctly *eschatological* than are those of the earlier prophets. The change did not take place at once; it was brought about gradually. At first the future contemplated by the prophets consisted of little more than a continuance of the existing state of society, only purged by a judgement from sin, and freed from trouble; but gradually it was severed more and more widely from the present order of things: whereas for long the prophets had been content to look at the destinies of the nation as a unity, without distinctly facing the question of the ultimate fate of individuals, in course of time

---

[1] On the prophetic pictures of the future kingdom of God, see more fully Kirkpatrick's *Doctrine of the Prophets*; the present writer's *Isaiah, his life and times*, or the third of his *Sermons on the Old Testament*.

the destinies of individuals began to claim consideration[1]; the judgement which was to introduce God's kingdom assumed more and more the character of a *final* judgement, which, as soon as the idea of a resurrection began to be current, was regarded as held by God over the dead as well as over the living; and the expectation of a glorified *earthly* life of righteous Israelites, which was the prevalent ideal of the Old Testament, became gradually transformed into the belief in a spiritual or *heavenly* life of all righteous men in general, which is the ideal revealed in the New Testament. Some of the later prophets, the Book of Daniel, and the Apocalyptic writers spring from the transition-period, in which the former of these ideals was gradually merging into the other, and in which the line of demarcation between the earthly and the heavenly ideal was not always clearly or consistently drawn, so that it is not always easy to be confident in particular passages which of the two ideals the writer means to express. The passages from the prophets in which the character of the representation is such as to suggest that it is beginning to be eschatological, are Is. xxvi. 18—19; Joel iii. 9—17; Mal. iv. 2—3. The representation in Daniel is of the same intermediate character; it is more distinctly eschatological than the passages just quoted, but less so than, for instance, parts of the Book of Enoch. The scene of judgement in vii. 9—14 belongs far more to the other world than any other representation of God's judgement to be found in the Old Testament; and in xii. 2 the doctrine of a resurrection is taught more distinctly and definitely than is the case in any other Old Testament writing (see below, p. xcii).

The characteristic point of *resemblance* between the representation of the kingdom of God contained in the Book of Daniel and that found in earlier prophets is this. It was a great and ennobling ideal which the prophets, as described briefly above, projected upon the future, and it was one which was portrayed by many of them in brilliant colours. But it was an

---

[1] Comp. A. B. Davidson, art. ESCHATOLOGY in Hastings' *Dict. of the Bible*, p. 738*b*.

THE KINGDOM OF GOD.

ideal which was not destined to be realized in the manner in which they anticipated. The prophets almost uniformly foreshortened the future: they did not stop to ask themselves *how* national character was to be regenerated and transformed: and consequently they did not realize the length of period which must necessarily elapse,—for God does not in such cases interpose by miracle,—before corrupt human nature could be so transformed as to produce a perfect or ideal society. Isaiah and Micah pictured the Messianic age as commencing immediately after the troubles were past, to which their nation was exposed at the hands of the Assyrians (Is. xi. 1—10, see x. 28—34; xxix. 19—26, see *v*. 31; xxxi. 7, xxxii. 1—8, see xxxi. 8; Mic. v. 4—7); the prophets of the exile pictured it as beginning with the restoration of Israel to Palestine. Neither of these anticipations corresponded to the event: in each case the sombre reality contrasted strongly with the glowing delineations of the prophets. The same foreshortening of the future is characteristic of the prophecies in the Book of Daniel. A careful study of Dan. vii.—xii. makes it evident that the reign of righteousness, and the everlasting dominion of the saints, are represented as beginning immediately after the fall of Antiochus: as in the case of the other prophets, the ideal consummation of history is thus conceived by the writer as being much closer at hand than actually proved to be the case.

The facts just referred to meet an objection which might otherwise perhaps be felt against the interpretation of the visions adopted in the present commentary, on the ground that the age of righteousness (vii. 27, ix. 24), or the resurrection (xii. 2), did not actually follow immediately after the fall of Antiochus: the ideal glories promised by Isaiah and other earlier prophets were not realized, as these prophets in many cases plainly shew that they expect them to be realized, in the immediate future; the Book of Daniel, regarded from this point of view, is consequently in exact analogy with the writings of the earlier prophets. The non-agreement (as it seems) of the particulars contained in xi. 40—45 *a* with the event (see the notes) is also in exact accordance with the same analogies: the earlier prophets often foretell correctly a future event,—e.g. the failure of Sennacherib's expedition against Jerusalem, or the capture of Babylon by Cyrus,—though the *details* by which they imaginatively represent these events as accompanied do not form part of the fulfilment, but merely constitute the drapery in which the prophet clothes what is to him the important and central idea (see, for example, Is. x. 28—34, xxiii. 15—18, xxx. 32, 33, xlvi. 1, 2)[1]. In the same way, Antiochus did actually meet his doom shortly, as foretold in Dan. xi. 45 *b* (cf. viii. 25 *end*, ix. 27 *end*), though the circumstances under which the writer pictures him as advancing towards it (xi. 40—45 *a*) do not correspond to what we know of the historical reality[2].

2. *The Resurrection.* The ordinary belief of the ancient Hebrews on the subject of a future life, was that the spirit after death passed into the underworld, Sheol, the 'meeting-place,' as Job (xxx. 23) calls it, 'for all living,' good and evil alike (Gen. xxxvii. 35; Is. xiv. 8, 9, 15), where it entered upon a shadowy, half-conscious, joyless existence, not worthy of the name of 'life,' where communion with God was at an end, and where God's mercies could be neither apprehended nor acknowledged (Is. xxxviii. 18; Ps. vi. 5, xxx. 9, lxxxviii. 10—12, cxv. 17, &c.). But the darkness which thus shrouded man's hereafter did not remain in the O.T. without gleams of light; and there are *three* lines along which the way is prepared for the fuller revelation brought by the Gospel. There is, firstly, the limitation of the power of death set forth by the prophets, in their visions of a glorified, but yet earthly, Zion of the future: 'For as the days of a tree shall be the days of my people, and the work of their hands shall my chosen ones wear out' (Is. lxv. 22; cf. *v.* 20, where it is said that death at the age of 100 years will be regarded then as premature); or even its abolition altogether,

---

[1] Comp. the writer's *Isaiah*, pp. 61, 73, 94, 106, 111—114, 146 *n*.
[2] The idea that prophecy is 'history written beforehand' is radically false: it is a survival from an age in which the prophets were not studied in the light of history, and it is a source of many and serious misunderstandings of their meaning (comp. Kirkpatrick, *Doctrine of the Prophets*, pp. 15—17, 194—6, 402—6, 524 f.)

DOCTRINE OF THE RESURRECTION. xci

'He hath swallowed up death for ever' (Is. xxv. 8). There is, secondly, the conviction uttered by particular Psalmists that their close fellowship with God implies and demands that they will themselves be personally superior to death: 'Therefore my heart is glad and my glory [i.e. my spirit] rejoiceth: my flesh also dwelleth securely. For thou wilt not leave my soul to Sheol[1]; thou wilt not suffer thy godly one to see the pit' (Ps. xvi. 9, 10; cf. xvii. 15, xlix. 15, lxxiii. 26; Job xix. 26)[2]. And, thirdly, we meet with the idea of a *resurrection*, which, however, only takes shape gradually, and is at first a hope and not a dogma, national and not individual, and in the Old Testament, even to the end, is *limited to Israel*. The hope is expressed first, though dimly, in Hos. vi. 2, where it is evidently national: 'After two days he will revive us : in the third day he will raise us up, and we shall live before him': and the promise in Hos. xiii. 14 is national likewise[3]. The passage which comes next chronologically is Ezek. xxxvii., the vision of the valley of dry bones, where, by the express terms of *v*. 11 ('Son of man, these bones are *the whole house of Israel*'), the promise is limited to Israel, and where also, as Prof. Davidson points out[4], what the prophet contemplates is a resurrection, not of individuals, but of the *nation*,—'it is a prophecy of the resurrection of the nation, whose condition is figuratively expressed by the people when they represent its bones as long scattered and dry.' In the next prophecy in which the idea occurs, the (post-exilic) apocalyptic prophecy, Is. xxiv.—xxvii., there is, however, an advance, and the resurrection of *individual* Israelites is certainly contemplated, though rather as the object of a hope or prayer than as a fixed doctrine: the people confess that they could not effect any true deliverance themselves: 'We were with child, we writhed in pain, when we bare, it was wind, we

---

[1] Not '*in* Sheol': the hope expressed by the Psalmist is not that he will rise again, but that he *will not die*.
[2] See further the notes on these passages in the *Cambridge Bible*; and the Introduction to the *Psalms*, pp. lxxv.—lxxviii.
[3] Cf. Oehler, *Theol. of the O.T.*, § 225.
[4] In his notes on the chapter in the *Cambridge Bible*.

made not the land salvation, neither were inhabitants of the world brought forth'; they turned therefore to God: 'May Thy dead live! may my dead bodies arise!' and the prophet breaks in with the words of jubilant assurance: 'Awake, and sing aloud, ye that dwell in the dust; for a dew of lights [a dew charged with the light of life] is Thy dew, and the earth shall bring forth the Shades!' The dwindled and suffering nation is thus represented as replenished and strengthened by the resurrection of its deceased members. 'The doctrine of the resurrection here presented is reached through the conviction, gradually produced by the long process of revelation, that the final redemption of Israel could not be accomplished within the limits of nature. It became clear that the hopes and aspirations engendered by the Spirit in believing minds pointed forward to the great miracle here described, and thus the belief in the resurrection was firmly bound up with the indestructible hopes of the future of Israel. The idea is represented in a form which is immature in the light of the New Testament[1],' but it marks almost the highest development of O.T. revelation on the subject. That the hope is limited to *Israel*, appears both from the words of the passage itself, and also from *v.* 14, where it is denied of Israel's foes ('The dead live not (again), the Shades arise not').

The last passage in the O.T. in which the idea is expressed is Dan. xii. 2, 'And many of them that sleep in the dusty ground shall awake, some to everlasting life, and some to reproaches and everlasting abhorrence.' Here a resurrection of the *wicked* is taught for the first time, as also a doctrine of future rewards and punishments: both doctrines are, however, still applied only to Israelites, and (as the word 'many' shews) not even to all of these; the writer, it seems, having in view not individuals as such, but those individuals who had in an extraordinary degree helped or hindered the advent of God's kingdom, i.e. the Jewish martyrs and apostates respectively, the great majority of the nation, who were of average character,

---

[1] Skinner, in the *Cambridge Bible, ad loc.*

DOCTRINE OF THE RESURRECTION.

neither overmuch righteous nor overmuch wicked, remaining still in Sheol[1]. The nature of the future reward and retribution is also left indefinite, the expressions used being quite general[2].

It does not fall within the scope of a Commentary on Daniel to trace the development of the doctrine in subsequent times; it must suffice to point out generally how, in the century or so following the age of the Maccabees, the religious imagination of pious Jews, meditating upon the intimations of a future life contained in the Old Testament, and combining them with different prophetic representations of the future triumph of the kingdom of God, arrived at fairly definite, though not always perfectly consistent, conceptions of a resurrection, a final judgement, a place of punishment (Gehenna), Paradise, and a future life (which is more or less spiritually conceived, according to the point of view adopted by the particular writer); and how, further, by this means currency was given to certain figures and expressions, in which even our Lord and His Apostles could clothe appropriately the truths enunciated by them[3].

3. *Angels.* The angelology of the Book of Daniel has been sufficiently explained, and compared with that of other Jewish writings of 2—1 cent. B.C., in the notes on viii. 16 and x. 13. It has there been shewn that it is only in the later books of the

---

[1] Cf. the note *ad loc.*, and Charles, *Eschatology*, p. 180. The idea that the resurrection was to be limited to Israel appears also among the later Jews; indeed, it became ultimately the accepted doctrine that it was to be limited to *righteous* Israelites, the wicked being either annihilated, or confined in prison-houses of perpetual torment: cf. e.g. 2 Macc. vii. 9, 14, 36; Psalms of Sol. iii. 13, 16, xiii. 9, 10, xiv. 6, 7, xv. 13—15; Apoc. of Baruch xxx.; Joseph. *Ant.* XVIII. i. 3 (the creed of the Pharisees); and see Charles on Enoch li. 1, Weber, *Altsynag. Theol.* p. 372 ff.

[2] See further, on the subject of the two preceding paragraphs, Salmond's *Christian Doctrine of Immortality*, ed. 3 (1897), pp. 233—267.

[3] The writer has sketched the growth of belief in a future state, with special reference to the Book of Enoch and the Targums, in the fourth of his *Sermons on subjects connected with the Old Testament* (pp. 72—98); for more detailed particulars see Charles' *Eschatology, Hebrew, Jewish, and Christian* (1899), chaps. v.—viii.

O.T. that angels begin to receive names, and that differences of grade and function are recognized among them; in particular, also, it has been pointed out that the 'chief princes' mentioned in x. 13 are very probably the seven superior angels (or 'archangels') referred to in Tob. xii. 15 and in different parts of the Book of Enoch, and that the doctrine of patron or tutelary angels of nations, though alluded to probably in Is. xxiv. 21, appears for the first time distinctly in Daniel (x. 13, 20, 21, xi. 1, xii. 1). A few words must however be said here on the opinion that the angelology of Daniel was derived from, or at least influenced by, the religion of the ancient Persians, commonly called either (from the name of its traditional founder) Zoroastrianism, or (from the name of its supreme deity) Mazdeism. There are undoubtedly affinities between some of the doctrines of Zoroastrianism and those of Israel,—its supreme god, Ahuramazda (mentioned repeatedly by Darius Hystaspis in his inscriptions), 'the Lord, the great knower,' was, for instance, a purer and more spiritual being than many of the gods of the heathen,—so that it is not difficult to imagine elements from the system being borrowed by the Jews; but in the case of angels, the influence, if it was exerted at all, must have been slight. The facts are these. Ahura-mazda is in the sacred canon of Zoroastrianism,—known generally as the *Zend-Avesta*,—the Creator of all things, but 'he is assisted in his administration of the universe by legions of beings, who are all subject to him. The most powerful among his ministers were originally nature-gods, such as the sun, moon, earth, winds, water,' &c.; but there were an immense number besides. At the head of all these subordinate beings are 'six genii of a superior order, six ever-active energies, who preside under his guidance over the kingdoms and forces of nature.' These genii are called 'Amesha-spentas' (Mod. Pers. 'Amshaspands'), or 'Beneficent (lit. 'increase-giving') immortals'; and their names are Vohumanô ('good thought') presiding over cattle, Asha-vahista ('perfect holiness') presiding over fire, Khshathra-vairya ('good government') over metals, Spenta-armaiti ('meek piety') over the earth, Haurvatât ('health') over vegetation, and Ameretât

DOCTRINE OF ANGELS.

('immortality') over water. Sometimes, also, Ahura-mazda is himself included among the Amesha-spentas, thus bringing their number up to seven. There is also an evil principle, Angrô-mainyus (Ahriman), co-eternal with Ahura-mazda, who is ever endeavouring to thwart the purposes, and mar the work, of Ahura-mazda, who against the six Amesha-spentas sets in array six evil spirits of equal power, and who also has under him a multitude of other evil beings (Daêvas), who never cease to do what they can to vex and seduce mankind[1].

The Amesha-Spentas are alluded to frequently in the sacred writings of Mazdeism: we meet for instance constantly with such invocations as these:—'We sacrifice to Ahura-Mazda, bright and glorious: we sacrifice to the Amesha-Spentas, the all-ruling, the all-beneficent' (invocations to the individual Amesha-Spentas, and to other subordinate spirits, or deities, follow)[2].

In Daniel, now, two angels, Gabriel and Michael, are mentioned by name; and Michael is said (x. 13) to be one of 'the chief princes,' i.e. probably (see on x. 13) one of the 'seven holy angels' mentioned in Tob. xii. 15 as presenting the prayers of the saints before God; seven principal angels are also mentioned in Enoch xx. 1—7, lxxxi. 5, xc. 21, 22 (elsewhere four are particularized, viz. in ix. 1[3], xl. 2—10, lxxxvii. 2, 3, lxxxviii. 1, lxxxix. 1). In order to estimate properly the bearing of Tobit upon the question, it should be added that Asmodeus, the name of the evil spirit in Tob. iii. 8, 17, is almost certainly of Mazdean origin, viz. *Aêshmô daêvô*, the 'raving demon[4].' It must however be owned that the resemblance between this system and the angelology of Daniel is exceedingly slight. Even supposing that seven principal angels are certainly implied in

---

[1] Maspero, *The Passing of the Empires*, pp. 577—586 (who quotes further authorities).
[2] Darmesteter in the *Sacred Books of the East*, XXIII. (the Zend-Avesta, Part ii.) pp. 13, 15, 17, 37, &c. (see the Index).
[3] Where, in the Greek text of Syncellus (Charles, p. 67), but not in the Gizeh text (*ib.* p. 333), they are called 'the four great archangels.'
[4] Maspero, *l.c.* p. 585. Aêshma is one of the leaders of the evil demons created by Ahriman.

Dan. x. 13, they differ from the Amesha-spentas not only in the names (which bear no resemblance whatever), but also in the fact that the seven Amesha-spentas *include* the supreme god of Zoroaster, Ahura-mazda, whereas the seven angels are of course *exclusive* of Jehovah. Seven, also, though it may be a mystical or sacred number among the Iranians[1], was also, independently, regarded similarly by the Hebrews; so that, as the idea of angels generally is unquestionably a native Hebrew one, the idea of seven principal angels might readily have arisen upon purely Hebrew ground. The utmost that can be granted,—and that not as certain, but only as possible,—is that the idea of *seven* superior angels—in so far as this is rightly regarded as involved in Dan. x. 13—may have been suggested by the vague knowledge that the religion of Zoroaster knew of seven good spirits, holding supremacy over the rest[2].

4. *Antiochus Epiphanes and Antichrist.* The Jews had suffered often at the hands of foreign rulers; but Antiochus Epiphanes was the first foreign king who persecuted them expressly on account of their religion, and not only forbade them, under pain of death, to practise any of its observances, but when they resisted him, avowed openly his determination to extirpate their nation (1 Macc. iii. 35, 36). By all loyal Jews he was regarded in consequence with far greater aversion than any of their previous conquerors or oppressors; and his hostility to their religion, combined with his ostentatious admiration of Hellenic deities, and the assumption by himself of Divine honours (see p. 191), caused him to be viewed by them as the impersonation of presumptuous and defiant impiety. These are the traits which appear prominently in the descriptions of vii. 8 *b*, 20 *b*, 21, 25, viii. 10—12, 25, xi. 36—38. Many of the older interpreters supposed the description in ch. vii., and also that in

---

[1] Darmesteter, *u. s.* IV. p. lix. § 7: cf. also the seven Persian counsellors or princes of Ezr. vii. 14, Est. i. 14, and the seven principal Persian families in Hdt. iii. 84.

[2] In the later angelology of the Talmud, however, Mazdean influences are unquestionably traceable. Cf. further Pusey, pp. 463, 526—539; Cheyne, *Origin of the Psalter*, p. 335.

vv. 36—45 of ch. xi., to refer not to Antiochus Epiphanes, but to the future 'Antichrist.' The figure of 'Antichrist,' the future ideal arch-enemy of the Messiah and of Israel, is ultimately of Jewish origin[1]; but it was appropriated at an early date by the Christian Church, and received a Christian colouring. St John, though he spiritualizes the idea, applying it to tendencies already at work, attests its currency even in the Apostolic age (1 John ii. 18, 23, iv. 3; 2 John 7); and St Paul (2 Thess. ii. 3—10) developes it with fuller details. This interpretation of the passages of Daniel is indeed, upon exegetical grounds, untenable[2]: nevertheless, it is true that Antiochus, as described in Daniel, is to a certain degree a prototype of the future Antichrist, and that traits in St Paul's description have their origin in the Book of Daniel. In 2 Thess. it is said that the coming of Christ is to be preceded by a great falling away ('apostasy'—$\dot{\eta}$ $\dot{a}\pi o\sigma\tau a\sigma i a$), in which the 'man of sin' (or, according to what is probably the better reading, 'the man of lawlessness') will be revealed, who 'opposeth and exalteth himself against all that is called God or that is worshipped, so that he sitteth in the temple of God, setting himself forth as God' (cf. Dan. xi. 36, 37): there is something (*vv.* 6, 7) which for the time prevents his appearance, though, when he does appear, he will be slain by the Lord Jesus, with the 'breath of his mouth' (cf. Is. xi. 4[3]). The beast having seven heads and ten horns, who in Rev. xiii. 1—8 rises out of the sea, and has given him 'a mouth speaking great things and blasphemies,' who receives authority 'to do (his pleasure) [$\pi o\iota\hat{\eta}$-$\sigma a\iota$] during forty and two months' ($=3\frac{1}{2}$ years), and 'to make war with the saints and overcome them,' and whom all inhabitants of the earth (except those whose names are written in the 'book of life') 'will worship' (cf. *vv.* 12—15, xix. 20), is in all probability 'Nero redivivus'; but traits of the representation, as

[1] Cf. 2 Esdr. v. 6; Apoc. of Baruch xl. 1, 2. If chaps. viii.—ix. of the Assumption of Moses are not displaced (p. lxxxiii), the writer expected the time of the end to be preceded by a period of persecution almost exactly resembling that of Antiochus.

[2] Cf. pp. lxv, 99 f., 193.

[3] Where, according to an old, though of course incorrect, Jewish exegesis, the 'wicked' is the future arch-enemy of the Jews.

xcviii INTRODUCTION.

will be evident from the words quoted, are suggested by the descriptions in Dan. vii. 8, 20, 21, 25, viii. 24 [LXX. Theod. ποιή-σει], xi. 28 and 30 [ποιήσει], 36, of Antiochus Epiphanes[1]. Many of the Fathers, also, drew afterwards pictures of Antichrist, formed by a combination of the representations in Dan. vii. and xi. 36—45 (according to the interpretation mentioned above) with those contained in the New Testament[2]; but it lies beyond the scope of the present introduction to pursue the history of the subject further.

§ 5. *Versions, Commentaries, &c.*

A detailed consideration of the Versions of Daniel does not fall within the scope of the present Commentary: but some general remarks must be made with reference to the *Greek* Versions. The Septuagint Version of the O.T., as is well known, was completed gradually, and is the work of different hands, the translations of the different books, or groups of books, varying in style, and exhibiting very different degrees of excellence and accuracy. The translation of Daniel is one of the most paraphrastic and unsatisfactory; and upon this ground, as it seems,—intensified perhaps by the difficulty which was practically experienced in appealing to it in controversy,—it was viewed with disfavour by the early Christian Church, and the more literal version of Theodotion took its place. Jerome mentions the fact, and though he owns that he does not know the precise explanation of it, he is evidently inclined to believe that it was that which has been just stated:—

'Danielem prophetam, iuxta LXX interpretes, Domini Salvatoris Ecclesiae non legunt, utentes Theodotionis editione; et hoc cur acciderit, nescio. Sive enim quia sermo Chaldaicus est, et quibusdam proprietatibus a nostro eloquio discrepat, noluerunt LXX interpretes

---

[1] See further the article MAN OF SIN in Hastings' *Dict. of the Bible*, and (with fuller details) ANTICHRIST in the *Encyclopaedia Biblica*.
[2] See e.g. Iren. v. 25; Hippolytus (*c.* 220 A.D.), ed. Lagarde, pp. 101—114, &c.

easdem linguae lineas in translatione servare; sive sub nomine eorum ab alio nescio quo non satis Chaldaeam linguam sciente editus est liber; sive aliud quid causae extiterit ignorans: hoc unum affirmare possum, quod multum a veritate discordet, et recto iudicio repudiatus sit[1].'

Cf. *Contra Ruff.* ii. 33 (ed. Bened. iv. 431; ed. Vallarsi, ii. 527): '...ecclesias Christi hunc prophetam iuxta Theodotionem legere, et non iuxta LXX translatores. Quorum si in isto libro editionem dixi multum a veritate distare et recto ecclesiarum Christi iudicio reprobatam, non est meae culpae qui dixi, sed eorum qui legunt.'

And in his *Commentary* on iv. 5 [A.V. 8] (ed. Bened. iii. 1088; ed. Vallarsi, v. 645, 646): '*donec collega ingressus est in conspectu meo Daniel, cui nomen Balthasar secundum nomen Dei mei* [as in the Vulg.]. Exceptis LXX translatoribus, qui haec omnia [viz. *vv.* 3—6 (A.V. 6—9)] nescio qua ratione praeterierunt, tres reliqui [Aq. Theod. and Symm.] *collegam*[2] interpretati sunt. Unde iudicio magistrorum Ecclesiae editio eorum in hoc volumine repudiata est; et Theodotionis legitur, quae et Hebraeo, et ceteris translationibus, congruit.'

Theodotion lived probably in the second century: he is mentioned by Irenaeus (iii. 21), who wrote about A.D. 180. The age was one in which a desire was felt to have a Greek version of the Old Testament more faithful than that of the LXX.: and three scholars, Aquila, Theodotion, and Symmachus, came forward to supply the want. The principles upon which they worked were not entirely the same; while Aquila's ideal was, for example, a translation of extreme literalness, Theodotion sought merely to revise the LXX. version, by correcting its more serious deviations from the Hebrew[3]. None of these

---

[1] Preface to Daniel, printed at the beginning of ordinary editions of the Vulgate (cf. in the Prologue to his *Commentary on Daniel*, ed. Bened. iii. 1074, ed. Vallarsi, v. 619 f.). There follows a curious passage, in which Jerome speaks of the 'anhelantia stridentiaque verba' of the 'Chaldee' language, and of the difficulty which he experienced in acquiring it.

[2] This is an error, due apparently to ἕτερος, in the MS. used by Jerome, being written ἑταῖρος.

[3] See particulars in Dr Field's edition of the *Hexapla*, I. pp. xxi ff., xxx ff., xxxix ff.; or the art. HEXAPLA in the *Dict. of Christian Biography*. It is remarkable that renderings differing from those of the

three 'revised versions' of the O.T. has, however, been preserved in its integrity: in most cases, they have been transmitted only in the form of glosses on the text of the LXX., which was placed by Origen (3rd cent. A.D.) in the fifth column of his 'Hexapla[1],' and transcribed thence into other MSS. But in the case of Daniel, the version of Theodotion displaced the true Septuagintal version in MSS. of the LXX.; and the latter version remained actually unknown to scholars till the middle of the last century, when a MS. containing it, was published at Rome in 1772[2]. This MS. belongs to the Library of the Chigi family, and is known as the *Codex Chisianus*. It contains Jer., Baruch, Lam., Ep. of Jeremiah, Daniel according to the LXX., Hippolytus on Daniel, Daniel according to Theodotion, Ezekiel, and Isaiah. It has been supposed to date from the ninth century, though it is very possibly later. In Tischendorf's edition of the LXX., the version of Daniel contained in the body of the work (ii. 480 ff.) is, in accordance with what has been just stated, that of Theodotion: the genuine 'Septuagint' version, as found in the Chisian MS., is given at the end of the volume (p. 589 ff.). In Dr Swete's edition of the LXX., to the great convenience of the reader, the two versions are printed side by side on opposite pages (vol. iii. p. 498 ff.).

The recension of the LXX. exhibited by the Chisian MS.,

LXX., but agreeing largely with those of Theod., occur in the N.T. (see esp. 1 Cor. xv. 54; John xix. 37, cf. Rev. i. 7), and writers of the early part of the second cent. A.D.; hence it has been conjectured that there was a 'Theodotion' before Theodotion, or in other words, that a revision of the LXX. had been begun before Theodotion, though Theodotion was the first to carry it through systematically (cf. Salmon, *Introd. to the N.T.*[3], p. 586 ff.; Schürer[3], iii. 323 f.).

[1] The five remaining columns contained, respectively, the Hebrew, the Hebrew in Greek characters, and the versions of Aquila, Theodotion, and Symmachus.

[2] Cf. Dr Field's *Hexapla*, II. 904 ff. There are also other, more recent editions, the best being that of Cozza in his *Sacrorum Bibliorum vetustissima fragmenta*, vol. iii. (1877). It is true, in the colophon at the end of Dan. xii., the text of this MS. is said to have been taken from a copy based on the *Tetrapla* of Origen; but the Tetrapla was simply a subsequent edition of the Hexapla, with the first two columns omitted.

being based upon the text adopted by Origen for his Hexapla, is known as the 'Hexaplar' text; and it contains (though with many misplacements and omissions) the obelisks and asterisks by which this learned Father indicated, respectively, the passages which had nothing corresponding to them in the current Hebrew text, and those which, having something corresponding to them in the Hebrew, but being not represented in the genuine LXX., were supplied by him from some other version (usually that of Theod.). Of the 'Hexaplar' text of the LXX., now, a very literal Syriac translation was made at Alexandria in 616—7 by Paul, Bishop of Tella (in Mesopotamia); and a great part of this Syriac version of the LXX. has been preserved in a MS., now in the Ambrosian Library at Milan, which was edited in *facsimile* by Ceriani in 1874[1]. The text which formed the basis of this 'Syro-hexaplar' version of the LXX. (as it is commonly called) was in a purer state than that found in the Chisian MS.: it exhibits more completely the obelisks and asterisks, and it is not disfigured by the omissions, additions, and other clerical errors, which are manifest blots in the Chisian text. It is thus of importance for assisting scholars to restore the LXX. text of Daniel, at least approximately, to the state in which it was when it left Origen's hands; and the readings which it presupposes, when they differ from those of the Chisian MS., are accordingly appended at the foot of the LXX. text in Tischendorf's edition, and (after the more thorough collation of Dr Field in his *Hexapla*, II. 908 ff.) in that of Dr Swete (e.g. ii. 28, 29, a long passage which has dropped out of the Chisian text by inadvertence; vii. 27 ὑψίστου for the erroneous ὑψίστῳ)[2].

For further particulars respecting the character of the LXX., and illustrations of its renderings, reference must be made to

---

[1] The Book of Daniel in this version was published first by Bugati in 1788. See further Field, *Hexapla*, I. lxvii ff.; and cf. Swete, *The Old Testament in Greek*, III. p. xiii.

[2] The *longer* additions in the Greek versions of Dan. (both LXX. and Theod.), *The Song of the Three Children*, *Susanna*, and *Bel and the Dragon*, have been referred to above, p. xviii ff.

the Commentaries of Bevan, pp. 42—54, and Behrmann, pp. xxviii—xxx, xxxiv—xxxvii, and to the monograph of A. Bludau, *De Alex. Interpr. Libri Danielis indole critica et hermeneutica* (1881)[1]. Behrmann, also, describes briefly (p. xxxii f., cf. pp. xxxiv—xxxvi) the characteristics of Theodotion's version, of the Peshiṭtā, and of that of Jerome (the Vulgate). There is no Targum to Daniel, just as there is none to Ezra-Nehemiah.

As regards the Massoretic text of Daniel, though it contains, no doubt, a few corrupt or suspicious passages, there are no reasons for questioning that we possess it, on the whole, in a correct form. The LXX., though in isolated passages it may preserve a more original reading, as a whole has no claim whatever to consideration beside it: the liberties which the translator has manifestly taken with his text being such as to deprive the different readings which, if it were a reasonably faithful translation, it might be regarded as presupposing, of all pretensions to originality,—except, indeed, in a comparatively small number of instances, in which they are supported by strong grounds of intrinsic probability. The other versions (which deviate very much less widely from the Heb. and Aram. than the LXX. does) also occasionally preserve a reading better than that of the Massoretic text. The principal cases in which the existing text of Daniel may be corrected from the versions are mentioned in the notes; but it must not be inferred that there are no suspicious or doubtful passages beyond those on which corrections have been noted.

The principal commentaries on Daniel in modern times are those of Hävernick (1832), von Lengerke (1835), Hitzig (1850), Auberlen (1857), Ewald (in vol. iii. of his *Propheten*, ed. 2, 1868: in the translation, vol. v. 152 ff.), Keil (1869), Zöckler, in Lange's 'Bibelwerk' (1870), Reuss in *La Bible, Traduction nouvelle, avec introductions et commentaires*, O.T., Part vii. (1879), p. 205 ff., Meinhold, in Strack and

---

[1] On the *text* of the LXX., both in itself, and in the light of the renderings of the Syro-Hex., see also Löhr's study in the *ZATW*. 1895, p. 75 ff., 1896, p. 33 ff. A synopsis of the very numerous variations from the Heb. is given (in English) by Dr Pusey, p. 606 ff. (ed. 2, p. 624 ff.).

Zöckler's 'Kurzgef. Komm.' 8th div. p. 257 ff. (1889), Bevan (1892), and Behrmann (1894): the older commentaries, however, including that of Keil (who identifies, for instance, Belshazzar with Evil-merodach), contain much that has been superseded, or shewn to be untenable, by the progress of archaeology. There are also Kamphausen's edition of the Heb. and Aram. text, with critical annotations, in Haupt's 'Sacred Books of the O.T.' (1896: the part containing the English translation, and exegetical notes, has not at present [May, 1911] appeared); and Marti's translation, with critical and exegetical notes, in Kautzsch's *Die Heilige Schrift des AT.s*, ed. 3, vol. ii. (1910), p. 416 ff. Dean Farrar's Commentary, in the 'Expositor's Bible' (1895), contains much that is helpful and suggestive. J. D. Prince's Commentary (London and New York, 1899) is especially rich in Assyriological information.

Among ancient commentaries, a special value attaches to that of Jerome. Porphyry, a learned and able neo-Platonist, the most distinguished pupil of Plotinus (see the art. PORPHYRY in the *Dict. of Christian Biography*), had written a treatise (not now extant) in which he sought to shew that the historical survey in Dan. xi. must have been written after the events referred to had taken place; and the information collected by him from Greek historians, whose works are now lost, and preserved to us by Jerome, often throws a welcome light on passages of this chapter, which must otherwise have remained obscure[1]. There are also many other points on which this, like the other commentaries of the same most learned and industrious Biblical scholar, contains much that is still valuable, and should not be neglected by the student.

On the question of the *date* of the Book of Daniel, the chief advocates of the traditional view have been Hengstenberg in vol. i. of his *Beiträge zur Einl. ins alte Test.*, 1831 (cf. the discussion of ix. 24—27 in his *Christologie des AT.s*, 1854—7, iii. 83—235 in Clark's translation); Hävernick in his *Comm.* (1832), his *Neue kritische Untersuchungen*, 1838 (a reply to von Lengerke), and his *Einleitung*, II. ii. (1844), p. 435 ff.; Auberlen; Keil in his *Comm.* (1869), and his *Einleitung*, ed. 3, 1873, §§ 131—7; E. B. Pusey in the volume of lectures entitled *Daniel the Prophet*, 1864 (extremely learned and

---

[1] Jerome, though he upheld himself the interpretation of Dan. xi. 36—45 current at the time (see below, p. 193), added, however, the notable and far-sighted words, 'Pone haec dici de Antiocho, *quid nocet religioni nostrae?*'

thorough)¹: the same view is also adopted by J. M. Fuller in the 'Speaker's Commentary,' and by J. E. H. Thomson in the 'Pulpit Commentary' (1897),—who, however, like Zöckler (pp. v, 16ᵇ, 17ᵇ, 199 f.), rejects most, if not all, of ch. xi. as an interpolation (pp. iv, vii, xviii, 287), and evades many other difficulties which the book presents by the hypothesis that 'the text is in a very bad state, and has been subjected to various interpolations and alterations' (p. 40ᵇ); see also H. Deane, *Daniel, his life and times*, in the 'Men of the Bible' series (1888)². The most complete treatment of the question from the opposite standpoint is that of Kuenen in his *Hist.-crit. Onderzoek*, Part ii. (1889), §§ 87—92 (in the German translation, the *Einleitung*, ii. p. 430 ff.): see also Bleek's classical exegetical study, 'The Messianic prophecies in the Book of Daniel,' in the *Jahrb. für Deutsche Theologie*, 1860, pp. 47—101 (discusses ix. 24—27 very fully; and shews in particular that the acknowledged fact that ch. viii. and xi. 21—35 refer to Ant. Ep., involves, on exegetical grounds, the conclusion that chs. ii., vii., ix., xi. 36—xii., culminate in references to the same age); and Kamphausen's *brochure, Das Buch Daniel und die neuere Geschichtsforschung* (1893).

Books or monographs dealing with special points are referred to, as occasion requires, in the notes. The most thorough grammar of the Biblical Aramaic is Kautzsch's *Gramm. des Bibl.-Aram.* (1884); there are shorter grammars by Marti (*Kurzgefasste Grammatik der Bibl.-Aram. Sprache*, 1896), and Strack (*Grammatik des Bibl.-Aram.*, ed. 5, 1911). The Commentaries most useful philologically are those of Bevan, Behrmann, Prince, Marti, 1901 (in his *Hand-Comm. zum A.T.*), and C. H. H. Wright, *Daniel and its Critics*, 1906 (a philol. Comm.).

The view of the date of the Book of Daniel adopted in the present volume is that accepted by the most moderate and reasonable of recent critics, as Delitzsch (in Herzog's *Real-Encyklopädie²*, vol. iii. (1878), s.v.), Riehm, *Einleitung* (1890), ii. 292 ff., König, *Einleitung* (1893), §§ 78—9, Kamphausen, *op. cit.*, and in the *Encyclopaedia Biblica*, Strack, *Einleitung*⁴ (1895), § 63, Schürer², ii. 613 ff. (Engl. tr. II. iii. p. 49 ff.), C. A. Briggs, *Messianic Prophecy* (1886), p. 411 f., Sanday, *Bampton Lectures*, 1893, p. 215 ff., Dillmann, *A.T. Theol.* (1895), p. 522 f., Ottley, *Bampton Lectures*, 1897, p. 331 f., *Hebrew Prophets* (1898), pp. 15, 103 ff., E. L. Curtis in Hastings' *Dict. of the Bible*, s.v.,

---

¹ The references are to ed. 1: in ed. 2 (1868), after p. 44, the pagination gradually rises till p. 564 in ed. 1 = p. 568 in ed. 2.
² See also C. H. H. Wright, *Daniel and his Prophecies*, 1906.

&c. The position is one of those which are sometimes yielded with reluctance, especially by those who have been brought up in the older view, and who can recollect the strenuousness and firm conviction with which that view was contended for by the apologists of a former generation. But the wider knowledge of antiquity which we now possess has shewn that many opinions relating to the Old Testament, not less than to the literature and history of other ancient nations, which were once generally accepted, can no longer be maintained; and the apologist, where, in a matter affecting him, he finds this to be the case, must change his ground. The traditional view of the authorship of the Book of Daniel, it must be remembered, is no article of the Christian faith; and the impossibility of defending it by arguments which will carry general conviction, deprives it of the apologetic value which it was once regarded as possessing.

As stated above (p. xxii), it is argued by Meinhold that the Book of Daniel is of composite authorship, ii. 4^b—vi. being earlier in origin than the rest of the Book; and Torrey (*Ezra Studies*, 1910, 48 f., 162) holds this view of ii. 4^b—vii. Another theory of the composite character of the book is developed by G. A. Barton in the *Journ. of Biblical Literature*, 1898, p. 62 ff. The unity of the Book has also been doubted, on the conservative side, and with the object, at the same time, of explaining its bilingual character, by Mr Thomson: the Book, he supposes (p. vii), 'originally floated about in separate little tractates, some relating incidents, others visions; some in Aramaic, some in Hebrew; and in a somewhat later age an editor collected them together, and added a prologue.' It is true, there are features in the Book which might seem to suggest that the author was not throughout the same; but the question is, whether they are decisive, especially in view of the many marks of unity which link the different parts of the Book together. The reader who is interested in the subject may consult further Budde's criticism of Meinhold in the *Theol. Lit.-zeitung*, 29 Dec. 1888; and von Gall, *Die Einheitlichkeit des Buches Daniel* (1895), with J. W. Rothstein's reviews of Behrmann's Comm. and of this work in the *Deutsche Litt.-zeitung*, 28 Nov. and 26 Dec. 1896: comp. also Kamphausen in the *Encycl. Biblica*, s.v., § 4.

It is possible that, as Gunkel has argued (*Schöpfung und Chaos in Urzeit und Endzeit*, 1895, pp. 323—335), the imagery of the four beasts in Dan. vii. is in part suggested by traditional reminiscences of the old Babylonian cosmogonic epic: but the fact, in so far as it is true (for it is certainly overstated by Gunkel), possesses only an antiquarian

INTRODUCTION.

interest; it has no bearing upon the sense in which the author applied his materials, or upon the exegesis of the vision (cf. Wellhausen, *Skizzen*, vi. 232—5). Some verbal parallels between Dan. i.—vi. and the 'Story of Aḥiḳar[1],' have suggested also the inference that the author of Dan. was perhaps acquainted with the last-named work: see J. Rendel Harris, *The Story of Aḥiḳar* (Camb. 1898), pp. lvii—lx, lxxxiii, 25, 72, 73, 87, 101, and Barton, *Amer. Journ. of Sem. Lang.*, July 1900, p. 242 ff.

For the history of the Seleucidae, the English reader will now turn naturally to the elaborate and masterly work of E. R. Bevan, in two vols. (published since the first edition of the present Commentary appeared), called *The House of Seleucus*; and for that of the Jews (during the period referred to in the Book of Daniel) to the same writer's briefer and more popular, but brilliantly written volume, *Jerusalem under the High-Priests. Five lectures on the period between Nehemiah and the New Testament* (1904).

[1] The 'Achiacharus' of Tob. i. 21, 22, ii. 10, xi. 18, xiv. 10 (cf. Harris, p. xxviii). The story is a 'midrash,' or moralizing narrative, describing how Aḥiḳar, a vizier of Sennacherib, being accused falsely of treason, was cast into a dungeon, and how afterwards he was delivered, and his accuser consigned to the dungeon in his stead (cf. Tob. xiv. 10).

ADDENDA.

P. lx, n. 3. Sachau's *Aramäische Papyrus und Ostraka aus einer Jüdischen Militär-Kolonie zu Elephantine* (5th cent. B.C.) has just (Sept. 1911) appeared. The documents are written in the same Egyptian Aramaic previously known; and confirm the conclusions expressed in *L.O.T.*[8], p. 515. Though highly interesting in other respects, they do not, however, throw any materially fresh light upon the language of Daniel, or elucidate the obscure terms sometimes occurring in it.

P. 138 *bottom*, 139 (ix. 25—6). It is, however, quite possible that we should read, with Grätz: 'it shall be built again, with broad place and street. (26) And *at the end* [so LXX. (in *v.* 27), Pesh., Bevan, von Gall, Marti] of the times, after the threescore' &c.

P. 140—1 (ix. 26). Marti reads, with von Gall and partly Bevan: 'and the city and the sanctuary *shall be destroyed, together with* [עִם for עַם: so LXX. Theod. Pesh.] a prince [*viz.* Onias III]; and *the end* [viii. 17] *shall come* with a flood' &c.

P. 174 (xi. 18). It should have been stated that the Heb. rendered 'nay,...even' is very strange. Perhaps Marti is right in developing a clever suggestion of Bevan's (based on the LXX.), and reading (for the whole second part of the verse): 'but a commander shall turn back (*i.e.* requite) his reproach to him *seven-fold*' (see Ps. lxxix. 12 Heb.).

P. 193. On the cult of the Seleucidae see further Bevan, *Journ. Hell. Stud.* 1900, 26—30; *House of Seleucus*, i. 125, 177, ii. 154—6.

DANIEL.

IN the third year of the reign of Jehoiakim king of Judah 1 came Nebuchadnezzar king of Babylon *unto* Jerusalem,

CHAPTERS I.—VI.

The *first* part of the book, describing the experiences of Daniel and his three companions under Nebuchadnezzar (chs. i.—iv.), Belshazzar (ch. v.), and Darius the Mede (ch. vi.).

CHAP. I. INTRODUCTION.

Chap. i. describes how Daniel and his three companions, Hananiah, Mishael, and Azariah, came to be in Babylon, at the court of Nebuchadnezzar, the scene of the events narrated in the following chapters (ii.—iv.). Nebuchadnezzar, in the third year of Jehoiakim, king of Judah (B.C. 605), laid siege to Jerusalem: part of the vessels of the Temple and some Jewish captives fall into his hands and are carried by him to Babylon (*vv.* 1, 2). He there gives directions for a number of youths of noble blood, including some of the Jewish captives, to be instructed in the language and learning of the sacred caste, and educated for the king's service (*vv.* 3—7). Among these youths are Daniel and his three companions, who, while content to pursue the studies prescribed by Nebuchadnezzar, crave and obtain permission to be allowed not to defile themselves in any way by partaking of the special delicacies provided for them from the king's table (*vv.* 8—16). At the expiration of three years, when the education of the selected youths is completed, the four Jewish youths are found to be distinguished beyond all the others in wisdom and knowledge, Daniel being skilled in particular in the interpretation of visions and dreams; they are accordingly admitted to the rank of the king's personal attendants (*vv.* 17—21).

The chapter serves a double purpose. It both serves as an introduction to the Book generally; and also teaches the practical lessons of the value, in God's eyes, of obedience to principle, and of abstinence from self-indulgence. The rule which the four Jewish youths felt called upon to obey was indeed a ceremonial rule, of no permanent obligation; but it was one which, to Jews living amongst heathen, acquired sometimes a supreme importance (cf. on *vv.* 8—10), so that obedience to it became a most sacred duty.

1. *In the third year* &c.] Whether this is historically correct is doubtful. Jehoiakim's reign lasted eleven years (B.C. 608—597); and the Book of Jeremiah (xxv. 1) equates his *fourth* year with the first year of Nebuchadnezzar. Early in the same year (if the date in Jer. xlvi. 2 is correct[1]) there had taken place the great defeat of the Egyptians by Nebuchadnezzar at Carchemish on the Upper Euphrates, the effect of which was to transfer the whole (virtually) of Western Asia from the power of Egypt to that of Babylon (cf. Jer. xxv. 9—11, 18—26, xlvi. 25 f.; 2 Ki. xxiv. 7). We learn, now, from Berosus (*ap.* Josephus, *Ant.* x. xi. 1) that in this campaign Nebuchadnezzar was acting on behalf of his father, Nabopolassar, who was too infirm to conduct the war himself: 'hearing soon afterwards of his father's death, and having arranged the affairs of Egypt and the remaining country (i.e. Coele-Syria and Phoenicia, mentioned just before), and committed the Judaean, Phoenician, and Syrian prisoners, as well as those of the nations in Egypt, to some of his friends to convoy to Babylon with the heavy part of his army, he himself hastened home across the desert accompanied only by a few attendants.' Although Judahite captives are here mentioned, nothing is said of any siege of Jerusalem; and the terms in which Jeremiah speaks, not only in the fourth year of Jehoiakim (xxv. 9 ff.), but also in his fifth year (xxxvi. 29, see *v.* 9), seem to imply that a Chaldaean invasion of Judah was still in the future (Ewald, *Hist.*, iv. 257, *n.* 5, Keil), and that Jehoiakim had not already, in his third year, fallen into Neb.'s hands[2].

On the other hand, in the summary of Jehoiakim's reign which, in 2 Chr. xxxvi. 6, 7, *takes the place of* 2 Ki. xxiv. 1—4, we read, 'Against him came up Nebuchadnezzar, king of Babylon, and bound him in fetters to carry him to Babylon. And some of the vessels of the house of Jehovah brought Nebuchadnezzar to Babylon; and he put them in his palace in Babylon': but the year in which this invasion took place is not specified; and a statement which rests on the authority of the Chronicler alone, and is not supported by contemporary testimony, is of slight value. It bears witness, however, to the existence, at about 300 B.C., of a tradition respecting an attack upon Jerusalem, and the carrying away of a part of the sacred vessels of the Temple, during Jehoiakim's reign, which is also no doubt the basis of Dan. i. 1, 2. The tradition, it must be owned, wears the appearance of being a Haggadic development of 2 Ki. xxiv. 1. Those who defend the accuracy of the statement of Daniel sometimes (Hengst., Keil, Zöckler) understand בָּא ('came'), with reference to the starting-point, virtually as equivalent to *set out*, sometimes suppose that Nebuchadnezzar made an attack upon Jerusalem either (Hävernick, Pusey, p. 401) the year before the battle of Carchemish, or (Behrmann, p. xvii) after it, but that more serious consequences were for the time averted by Jehoiakim's timely submission, and the surrender of some of the valuable vessels of the Temple. The

---

[1] See the Introduction, p. xlix.

[2] The invasion of Judah by Neb., and the three years' submission of Jehoiakim, mentioned in 2 Ki. xxiv. 1, 2, are also certainly to be placed after Jehoiakim's fourth year—most probably, indeed, towards the close of his reign (cf. Ewald, *l. c.*).

According to Josephus (*Ant.* x. vi. 1) Neb., after the battle of Carchemish, 'acquired possession of the whole of Syria, as far as Pelusium, *except Judah*'; and only made Jehoiakim tributary four years afterwards (2 Ki. xxiv. 1).

and besieged it. And the Lord gave Jehoiakim king of 2 Judah into his hand, with part of the vessels of the house of God: which he carried *into* the land of Shinar *to* the

first of these explanations is opposed to Heb. usage; the second, though possible in the abstract, is not strategically probable; the third, though it cannot be categorically rejected, seems scarcely consistent with what appears, from other indications, to have been the historical situation at the time. Cf. Ewald, iv. 264, *n.* 2.

Nebuchadnezzar] So *v.* 18, and uniformly in this book. The more correct form of the name is Nebuchad*r*ezzar (properly *Nabû-kudurri-uṣur*, i.e. (probably) 'Nebo, protect [Heb. נְצֹר] the boundary!'), which is the one usually found in contemporary writers, as Jer. xxi. 2, 7 (and generally in Jer.); Ezek. xxvi. 7, xxix. 18, 19, 30[1].

king of Babylon] Nebuchadnezzar did not become 'king of Babylon' until after the battle of Carchemish, in Jehoiakim's fourth year (Jer. xxv. 1, xlvi. 2), so that the title must be used here (as in Jer. xlvi. 2) proleptically. There is no authority in either Berosus or the Inscriptions for the supposition sometimes made that Nebuchadnezzar was associated on the throne by his father, Nabopolassar.

2. *gave* **into his hand Jehoiakim,** *king of Judah,* **and** *part,* &c.] To 'give into the hand,' as Jud. iii. 10; Jer. xx. 4, xxi. 7, xxii. 25, and frequently. The expression is a strong one, and seems to imply that the writer had in view a defeat, and not merely a timely submission.

the house of God] A frequent expression in late writers for the Temple (e.g. 2 Chr. iii. 3, iv. 19, v. 1, 14, vii. 5): earlier writers say nearly always 'the house of *Jehovah*' (e.g. 1 Ki. vii. 40, 45, 48, 51).

which he carried] **and** *he* **brought them.** The pron. (as the text stands: see below, p. 4) refers to the vessels.

Shinar] properly *Shin'ar*, a Hebrew name for Babylonia (Gen. x. 10, xi. 2, xiv. 1, 7; Josh. vii. 21; Isa. xi. 11; Zech. v. 11), here, no doubt, an old expression revived. The explanation of the name is uncertain, as nothing directly parallel has been found hitherto in the Inscriptions. According to some Assyriologists there are grounds for supposing it to be a dialectic variation of *Shumer*, the name given in the Inscriptions to South Babylonia[2]; but this explanation is not accepted by all scholars[3].

to the house (i.e. temple) *of his god*] If any stress is to be laid upon the particular deity intended, it would be Marduk (the Merodach of Jer. l. 2), the patron-god of Babylon. According to 2 Chr. xxxvi. 7, the vessels which Nebuchadnezzar brought to Babylon in the reign of Jehoiakim were placed by him in his palace[4]. But see the next note.

---

[1] The incorrect form with ***n*** is found in Jer. xxvii—xxix. (except xxix. 21: see Baer's note on xxi. 2); in 2 Ki. xxiv—xxv.; and in Chr., Ezr., Neh., Est.

[2] As in the common title of the Assyrian kings, 'King of Shumer and Akkad' (Akkad being North Babylonia): so Delitzsch, *Paradies* (1881), p. 198, *Assyr. Gramm.* (1889), § 49*a*, Rem.; Schrader, *KAT.*[2], p. 118 f.; Prince, p. 58.

[3] Cf. Dillmann on Gen. x. 10. Sayce, *Patriarchal Palestine*, p. 67 f., connects the name with Sangar, a district a little W. of Nineveh.

[4] See, however, Ezr. i. 7, v. 14, though the gold and silver vessels mentioned here may be those carried away by Nebuchadnezzar with Jehoiachin (Jer. xxvii. 16 [see *v.* 20, and cf. 2 Ki. xxiv. 13], xxviii. 3), or Zedekiah (2 Ki. xxv. 14, 15).

house of his god; and he brought the vessels *into* the treasure house of his god.

3 And the king spake unto Ashpenaz the master of his

and the vessels he brought, &c.] In the Heb. 'the vessels' is emphatic by its position, and would naturally imply that something different had been mentioned before. As the verse stands, the clause is almost tautologous with the preceding one: at all events, if the 'treasure house of his god' be really a place distinct from the 'house of his god,' the correction is attached very awkwardly. Ewald supposed that some words had fallen out, and proposed to read 'Jehoiakim, king of Judah, *with the noblest of the land*, and part,' &c. Certainly the transportation of captives is presupposed in v. 3; but the insertion of these words does not relieve the awkwardness of v. 2. It is better, with Marti, to reject the preceding words, '(in) the house of his god,' as a gloss, intended originally to define the position of the 'treasure house' of clause *b*, which has found its way into the text in a wrong place[1]. Still, the author's Hebrew is often far from elegant, and the anomalous wording of the verse is possibly original.

3—5. Nebuchadnezzar's purpose to have certain noble and promising youths educated for the king's service.

3. *Ashpenaz*] No satisfactory explanation of this name has yet been found. *Açp* in old Persian means a *horse* (Sansk. *açpa*); but the name as a whole, in its present form, is not explicable from either Persian or Babylonian. LXX. has Αβιεσδρι. The word is not improbably a corrupt form (like 'Holophernes,' in Judith; or 'Osnappar,' Ezra iv. 10).

the master of his eunuchs] Eunuchs were, and still are, common in Oriental Courts; they sometimes attained to great influence with the monarch, and were treated by him as confidential servants. Eunuchs are often represented on the Assyrian monuments, where they are readily recognizable by their bloated and beardless faces (cf. Smith, *D. B.*[2] s. v.; Rawlinson, *Ancient Monarchies*[4], I. 496—8, III. 221—223). The 'master,' or superintendent, of the eunuchs would have the control of the eunuchs employed in the palace, and would naturally hold an important position at court. The principal eunuch, with other eunuchs under him, would have the care of the royal harem; and the training of youths for the service of the king was a duty which would be naturally entrusted to him[2]. Cf. the prophecy, 2 Ki. xx. 18 (=Is. xxxix. 7); though it is not said that Daniel and his companions were made eunuchs, and it is too much to infer this (as has been done) from the statement that they were put in charge of the 'master of the king's eunuchs': in Persia eunuchs superintended the education of the young princes (Rawl. *Anc. Mon.*[4], III. 221); and in Turkey, Rycaut states (see the note below), a eunuch had charge of the royal pages.

[1] The words were not, it seems, in the original LXX. (see Swete, footnote).
[2] In Turkey, as described by Rycaut in 1668 (*The Ottoman Empire*, p. 35 ff.), the office was divided, the women being under the charge of a black eunuch, called *Kuzlir Agasi*, and the selected youths who were being educated in the Seraglio as pages for the royal service (together with the white eunuchs employed about the Court) being under the superintendence of a white eunuch, the *Capi Aga* (p. 25 ff.).

eunuchs, that *he* should bring *certain* of the children of Israel, and of the king's seed, and of the princes; children in whom 4 *was* no blemish, but well favoured, and skilful in all wisdom, and cunning in knowledge, and understanding science, and

bring] bring **in** (R.V.), viz. into the palace (*v.* 18).
children of Israel] The expression would include, at the time here referred to, men of Benjamin and Levi, as well as of Judah (cf. Ezra i. 5, iv. 1, x. 9), perhaps also men of other tribes who had migrated into the territory of Judah.
and of the **seed royal**, *and of the* **nobles**] If the first ו ('and') is to be taken in its obvious sense, the reference must be to members of the royal family and nobility of Babylon (so Prof. Bevan). Most commentators render *both* (cf. viii. 13; Jer. xxxii. 20; Ps. lxxvi. 7 [A.V. 6]), though that is hardly a sense which it would naturally convey in the present sentence. Perhaps it is best to understand it in the sense of *and in particular* (cf. viii. 10).
of the seed **royal**] Lit. *seed of royalty*, or *of the kingdom*: so Jer. xli. 1 (=2 K. xxv. 25); Ezek. xvii. 13. Not necessarily the descendants of the reigning 'king.' LXX. 'of the royal race.'
nobles] Heb. *partĕmim*, elsewhere only in Est. i. 3, vi. 9: the Pers. *fratama*, Sansk. *fratama*, akin etymologically to πρότ-ερος, πρῶτ-ος. "The phrase *martiyā fratamā*, 'foremost men,' occurs several times in the Achaemenian inscriptions" (Bevan).

4. *children*] **youths** (R.V.).
blemish] here of physical imperfection, as Lev. xxi. 17, 18, &c.
well favoured] An archaistic English expression for *good-looking*: so Gen. xxix. 17, xxxix. 6, xli. 2 *al.* As Mr Wright (*Bible Word-Book*, s. v. FAVOUR) shews, 'favour' in old English meant *face*[1], so that 'well favoured' means having a handsome face. The Heb. (lit. *good in looks*) is the same as in Gen. xxiv. 16, xxvi. 7. An Oriental monarch would attach importance to the personal appearance of his attendants.
intelligent *in all wisdom, and* **knowing** *knowledge, and understanding science*] i.e. men of sagacity and intelligence, the combination of synonyms merely serving to emphasize the idea. 'Cunning' (i.e. *kenning*) in A.V., R.V., is simply an archaism for *knowing*, *skilful*, though the word is used generally where the reference is to some kind of technical knowledge (Gen. xxv. 27; Ex. xxxviii. 23 [where, for 'cunning workman,' read 'designer']; 1 Sam. xvi. 16; 1 Chr. xxv. 7 [not R.V.]; 2 Chr. ii. 7, 13, 14; Jer. ix. 17, x. 9 *al.*). The modern associations of the word prevent it, however, from being now a good rendering of the Hebrew.
science] In the Heb. a (late) synonym of 'knowledge' (as it is rendered *v.* 17; 2 Chr. i. 10, 11, 12), and derived from the same root: the word is not to be understood here in a technical sense, but simply

---

[1] Bacon, *Essays*, XXVII. p. 113, 'As S. James saith, they are as men, that looke sometimes into a glass, and presently forget their owne shape, and *favour*'; *Cymbeline*, v. 5, 93, 'His *favour* is familiar to me.'

such as *had* ability in them to stand in the king's palace, and whom *they* might teach the learning and the tongue of 5 the Chaldeans. And the king appointed them a daily provision of the king's meat, and of the wine which he drank:

as a Latinism for 'knowledge,' used in default of any more colourless synonym.

ability] Properly, *power*; i.e. capacity, both physical and mental.

to stand] to take their place—with a suggestion of the idea of *serving*, which, with 'before' (see on *v.* 5), the word regularly denotes.

learning] literature: lit. *book*(*s*), *writing*(*s*), cf. Is. xxix. 11, 12.

and the tongue of the Chaldeans] 'Chaldeans' is used here, not in the ethnic sense, which the word has in other books of the O. T., but to denote the learned class among the Babylonians, i.e. the priests, a large part of whose functions consisted in the study and practice of magic, divination, and astrology, and in whose hands there was an extensive traditional lore relating to these subjects (see more fully below, p. 12 ff.). The word has the same sense elsewhere in the Book of Daniel (ii. 2, 4, 5, 10, iii. 8 (prob.), iv. 7, v. 7, 11). The literature on the subjects named is what is referred to in the present verse. The 'tongue of the Chaldeans' would be Babylonian, a Semitic language, but very different from Hebrew, so that it would have to be specially studied by a Jew. Many of the magical texts preserved in the cuneiform script are also written in the non-Semitic Sumerian (or 'Accadian'); but it is hardly likely that the distinction between these two languages was present to the author.

5. *a daily* **portion** *of the king's* **delicacies**] Superior food, such as was served at the table of the king himself, was to be provided for the selected youths. It was a compliment to send anyone a portion of food from the table of a king or great man (Gen. xliii. 34, in Egypt; 2 Sam. xi. 8, in Israel: 2 Ki. xxv. 30, in Babylon, *may* be similar); and at least in Persia the principal attendants of the king, especially his military ones, seem to have had their provision from the royal table (Plut. *Quaest. Conv.* VII. iv. 5; Athen. iv. 26, p. 145 e, f.). The word rendered 'delicacies' (*pathbāg*) is a peculiar one, found in the O.T. only in Dan.: it is of Persian origin, and passed (like many other Persian words) into Syriac (Payne Smith, *Thes. Syr.* col. 3086 f.), as well as into late Hebrew. The Persian original would be *patibāga*, 'offering,' 'tribute' (from *pati*, Sanskr. *prati*, Greek ποτί, προτί, to, and *bâg*, tribute, Sk. *bhâga*, portion). The Sansk. *pratibhâga* actually occurs, and means 'a share of small articles, as fruit, flowers, &c., paid daily to the Rája for household expenditure[1].' The Pers. *patibāga* originally, no doubt, denoted similarly choice food offered to the king[2], though in Heb. and Syriac *pathbāg* was used more widely of

[1] Gildemeister, as quoted by Max Müller, *ap.* Pusey, p. 565.
[2] Dinon in his *Persica*, writing c. 340 B.C., says (*ap.* Athen. xi. 503) that ποτίβαζις (which must be the same word) denoted a repast of cakes and wine, such as was prepared for the kings of Persia (ἔστι δὲ ποτίβαζις ἄρτος κρίθινος καὶ πύρινος ὀπτὸς καὶ κυπαρίσσου στέφανος καὶ οἶνος κεκραμένος ἐν ᾠῷ χρυσῷ οὗ αὐτὸς βασιλεὺς πίνει).

so nourishing them three years, that at the end thereof they might stand before the king. Now among these were of the children of Judah, Daniel, Hananiah, Mishael, and Azariah: unto whom the prince of the eunuchs gave names: for he gave unto Daniel *the name of* Belteshazzar; and to Hananiah, of Shadrach; and to Mishael, of Meshach; and to Azariah, of Abed-nego.

choice food, or *delicacies*, in general. The word recurs in *vv.* 8, 13, 15, 16, xi. 26.

and that they should be nourished] or brought up: lit. *made great*: so Is. i. 2, xxiii. 4 *al.*

stand before the king] as his attendants, to wait upon him: Deut. i. 38; 1 Ki. x. 8, xii. 8.

6, 7. Among the noble youths thus selected were four belonging to the tribe of Judah, who are named specially as forming the subject of the following narratives.

6. *Mishael*] 'Who is what God is?' (cf. Michael, 'Who is like God?'), a name found also in Ex. vi. 22, Lev. x. 4 (of a cousin of Moses'); and in Neh. viii. 4.

7. And *the prince of the eunuchs* **gave names unto them: unto Daniel he gave,** &c.] as R.V. 'Prince' (Heb. *sar*, i.e. here, governor, superintendent, 1 Ki. ix. 22 ['rulers'], xxii. 26) is a synonym of the *rab* of *v.* 3 (cf. Gen. xxxvii. 36 with Jer. xxxix. 9). The practice of giving a person a new name, when admitted into the public service of a foreign country, is well attested in the case of Egypt (see not only Gen. xli. 45, but also Erman, *Life in Ancient Egypt*, p. 517 f.), and was probably usual elsewhere. There is an example, though it is not quite parallel, quoted from the reign of the Assyrian king, Esarhaddon, when Neco's son was made viceroy of Athribis under the Assyrian name of Nabu-ušêzib-anni ('Nebo saves me'). In the present instance the change has the effect in each case of obliterating the name of God: Daniel, 'God is my judge'; Ḥananiah, 'Yah is gracious'; Mishael, 'Who is what God is?'; Azariah, 'Yah hath holpen.'

Belteshazzar] i.e. *balâṭsu-uṣur*, 'protect his life!'; probably elliptical for *Bêl-balâṭsu-uṣur*, 'Bel, protect his life!' The name (which recurs ii. 26, iv. 8, 9, 18, 19, v. 12) is quite distinct from *Belshazzar* (see on **v. 1**).

Shadrach] Of uncertain meaning, but explained plausibly by Friedr. Delitzsch as *Shudur-Aku*, 'the command of Aku' (*Aku* being the Sumerian equivalent of *Sin*, the Semitic name of the Moon-god); cf. the proper name *Ḳibit-Ishtar*, 'the word, or command, of Ishtar.'

Meshach] Explained by Delitzsch, somewhat less satisfactorily, as a hybrid word, partly Hebrew and partly Babylonian, properly *Mî-sha-Aku*, 'Who is what Aku is?', cf. Mishael above, and the Babylonian names *Mannu-ki-Rammân*, 'Who is like Rammân (Rimmon)?', and *Mannu-ki-ilu*, 'Who is like God?'

Abed-nego] generally recognized as a corruption of 'Abed-ne*b*o, 'ser-

8   But Daniel purposed in his heart that he would not
defile himself with the portion of the king's meat, nor with
the wine which he drank: therefore he requested of the
9 prince of the eunuchs that he might not defile himself. Now
God had brought Daniel into favour and tender love with

vant of Nebo' (Is. xlvi. 1). Proper names, compounded with '*Abd* (or
'*Ebed*), 'servant,' are common in most Semitic languages; and, though
it is not the usual word for *servant* in Babylonian, Babylonian names
compounded with it occur. Indeed, the name Abed-nebo itself has
been found in a bilingual (Assyr. and Aram.) inscription (Schrader,
KAT.² *ad loc.*); it is also, as Prof. Bevan remarks, met with as that
of a heathen Syrian long after the Christian era (Cureton's *Ancient
Syriac Documents*, p. 14).

8—16. The loyalty to their faith shewn by the four Jewish youths.

8—10. Daniel and his companions crave to be allowed not to use
the provision supplied from the royal table. The meat might be that
of animals not slaughtered in the proper manner (Deut. xii. 23, 24),
or of animals prohibited to the Jews as food (Lev. xi. 4—7, 10—12,
13—19, 20); while both the meat and the wine might have been consecrated to the Babylonian gods by portions having been offered to
them in sacrifice, so that to partake of either would be tantamount to
the recognition of a heathen deity (cf. 1 Cor. x. 20, 27—29). The
Jews, especially in later times, attached great importance to the dietary
laws, and were also very scrupulous in avoiding acts which, even indirectly, might seem to imply the recognition of a heathen deity.
Antiochus Epiphanes, in his endeavour (B.C. 168) to Hellenize the
Jews, sought to compel them both to sacrifice to heathen deities and
to partake of unclean food; and resistance to his edict was a point on
which the utmost stress was laid by the loyal Jews (1 Macc. i. 47, 48,
62, 63; cf. 2 Macc. vi. 18 ff., vii. 1). Comp. also 2 Macc. v. 27; Add.
to Esther xiv. 17; Judith xii. 1, 2 (see x. 5); Tobit i. 10, 11 (where
Tobit says that when he and his companions were taken captive to
Nineveh, 'all my brethren and those that were of my kindred did eat
of the bread of the Gentiles, but I *kept myself from eating*'). Josephus
(*Vita* 3) speaks of certain priests who, being sent to Rome, partook
on religious grounds of nothing but figs and nuts. For the abrogation
of the principle, in the new dispensation, see Mark vii. 19 (R.V.),
Acts x. 9—16,—comparing, however, also, 1 Cor. viii. 4—13.

with the king's delicacies] as *v.* 5.

purposed in his heart] lit. *laid* (it) *on his heart*, i.e. gave heed (Is.
xlvii. 7, lvii. 11, Mal. ii. 2). 'Purposed' is too strong.

9. And *God* made *Daniel* to find kindness *and* compassion in
the sight *of*, &c.] lit. '*gave* Daniel *to* kindness and compassion *before*':
exactly the same idiom which occurs (without 'kindness and') in
1 Ki. viii. 50 (whence Ps. cvi. 46). The pluperfect ('had brought')
is grammatically incorrect: the meaning is that the kindness was experienced immediately after the request. Cf., though the expressions are
different, the similar case of Joseph, Gen. xxxix. 21.

the prince of the eunuchs. And the prince of the eunuchs 10
said unto Daniel, I fear my lord the king, who hath appointed
your meat and your drink: for why should he see your
faces worse liking than the children which *are* of your sort?
then shall ye make *me* endanger my head to the king. Then 11
said Daniel to Melzar, whom the prince of the eunuchs had
set over Daniel, Hananiah, Mishael, and Azariah, Prove thy 12
servants, I beseech thee, ten days; and let them give us

10. *for why should*] i.e. 'lest,' which would in fact be the better rendering. The expression is the translation into Hebrew of the ordinary Aramaic idiom for 'lest' (cf. Theod. μή ποτε).

worse liking] An old English expression for 'in worse condition.' Cf. 'well-liking' in Ps. xcii. 13, P. B. V.; properly 'well-pleasing,' i.e. in good condition; and 2 *Hen. IV.* iii. 2, 92, 'You *like well*, and bear your years very well.' The Heb. is *zō'ăphîm*, 'gloomy,' 'sad,'—in Gen. xl. 6 used of Pharaoh's butler and baker, who were troubled mentally, here of the dejected appearance produced by insufficient nutriment. Theod. σκυθρωπά; cf. Matth. vi. 16.

than the youths (*v.* 4) *which are of your own* age (R.V.); **so should ye** (Bevan) **make my head a forfeit** (lit. *make my head guilty*) *to the king*] The two sentences might be rendered more concisely, '**lest** he see..., **and ye** make my head a forfeit,' &c. The officer who had charge of the Hebrew youths dreaded his master's displeasure if he should see them thriving badly under his care.

age] The word (*gîl*), which occurs only here in the O. T., is found in the same sense in the Talmud (Levy, *NHWB.* i. 324); and in Samaritan, as Gen. vi. 9, xv. 16, xvii. 12, and often (not always), for the Heb. *dôr* ('generation').

11—16. From the answer given by the chief of the eunuchs, Daniel gathers that he does not view his request unfavourably, though he declines the responsibility of acceding to it himself. He therefore applies to the subordinate officer who has the immediate charge of himself and his companions, and induces him to try them temporarily with vegetable diet. The result of the experiment being satisfactory, the royal food is withdrawn from the Jewish youths.

11. *Melzar*] the melẓar,—'melẓar' being the title of some officer, or attendant, of the court. What officer is intended is, however, uncertain, as the word has not hitherto been satisfactorily explained. Friedr. Delitzsch thinks that *Melzar* may be the Ass. *maẓẓaru*, 'keeper' (as in *maẓẓar bâbi*, 'keeper of the gate'), the *l* taking the place of the doubled *ẓ* (cf. βάλσαμον from *bassām*); and Schrader agrees that this explanation is possible. The term evidently denotes some subordinate official, appointed by the chief of the eunuchs to be in personal charge of Daniel and his companions.

12. *ten days*] a round number of days (cf. Gen. xxiv. 55, xxxi. 7), sufficiently long to test the effects of the proposed diet.

let them] i.e. the people appointed for the purpose. A Hebrew

13 pulse to eat, and water to drink. Then let our countenances be looked upon before thee, and the countenance of the children that eat *of* the portion of the king's meat: and as 14 thou seest, deal with thy servants. So he consented to them 15 in this matter, and proved them ten days. And at the end of ten days their countenances appeared fairer and fatter in flesh than all the children which did eat the portion of the 16 king's meat. Thus Melzar took away the portion of their meat, and the wine that they should drink; and gave them pulse.

17 As for these four children, God gave them knowledge and skill in all learning and wisdom: and Daniel had under-

idiom, the force of which would here be better expressed in English by the passive, 'let there be given us' (cf. Job vii. 3*b*, lit. 'they have appointed,' Ps. lxiii. 11*a* [A.V. 10*a*], lxiv. 9*a* [A.V. 8*a*]; and on ch. iv. 25).

pulse] rather **vegetable food** in general; there is no reason for restricting the Heb. word used to leguminous fruits, such as beans and peas, which is what the term 'pulse' properly denotes. Cf. Is. lxi. 11, where almost the same word is rendered 'the things that are sown,' i.e. vegetable products.

13. *of the* **youths that eat** *the king's* **delicacies**] as *vv.* 5, 8.

14. *consented*] **hearkened** (R.V.),—the expression exactly as 1 Sam. xxx. 24.

15. *and* (they were) *fatter in flesh*, &c.] the expression as Gen. xli. 2, 18 (of the kine) 'fat-fleshed.'

the children, &c.] *the* **youths** *which did eat the king's* **delicacies.**

16. And the melzar continued taking *away their* **delicacies,**......*and* **giving them vegetable food**] The Heb. idiom employed implies that the treatment which they received was now continuous.

17—19. At the end of the three years (*v.* 5), Daniel and his three companions are brought before the king; and being found by him to be the most proficient of all whom he had directed to be educated, are promoted to a place among his personal attendants.

17. Now *as for these four* **youths,** *God gave them knowledge* (the word rendered *science* in *v.* 4), *and* **intelligence** (cf. *intelligent, v.* 4) *in all* **literature** (*v.* 4) *and wisdom*] 'Wisdom' is used here, in a concrete sense, of an intelligently arranged body of principles, or, as we should now say, *science.* The term must be understood as representing the popular estimate of the subjects referred to: for the 'wisdom' of the Chaldaean priests, except in so far as it took cognizance of the actual facts of astronomy, was in reality nothing but a systematized superstition.

and Daniel had understanding in all visions and dreams] or, 'in *every kind* of vision and dreams.' This was a point in which Daniel excelled the rest. The words are intended as introductory to the narrative following.

standing in all visions and dreams. Now at the end of the 18 days that the king had said *he* should bring them in, then the prince of the eunuchs brought them in before Nebuchadnezzar. And the king communed with them; and among 19 them all was found none like Daniel, Hananiah, Mishael, and Azariah: therefore stood they before the king. And *in* 20 all matters of wisdom *and* understanding, that the king inquired of them, he found them ten times better than all the magicians *and* astrologers that *were* in all his realm.

18. And *at the end of the days that the king had* **appointed** (*v.* 5) **for bringing** *them in* (R.V.)] viz. to attend upon the king. 'Appointed' is lit. *said*, i.e. commanded, decreed, a common use in late Hebrew: cf. *v.* 3. As *v.* 19 ('among them all,' &c.) shews, the pron. *them* refers, not as the connexion with *v.* 17 might suggest, to the four Hebrew lads alone, but to the whole number of youths mentioned in *vv.* 3, 4.

19. *communed*] **talked**. The Heb. word is the usual one for 'speak,' or 'talk'; and nothing different from ordinary conversation is meant. 'Commune' occurs elsewhere in A.V., R.V., for the same Heb. word, and with exactly the same meaning; as Gen. xviii. 33, xxiii. 8, xxxiv. 6; Ex. xxv. 22, xxxi. 18; 1 Sam. ix. 25, xix. 3, &c.

and (i.e. *and so*) **they stood** *before the king*] i.e. became his personal attendants (*v.* 5).

20. The king found further, upon putting to them difficult questions, that in a knowledge of the technicalities of their science the four Jewish youths excelled even the wise men of Babylon themselves.

and in **every particular** *of* **reasoned wisdom**] lit. *wisdom of understanding*, i.e. wisdom determined or regulated by understanding, 'wisdom' having the same concrete sense of 'science' which it has in *v.* 17. Marti, however, following Theod., reads 'wisdom *and* understanding.'

magicians] *ḥarṭummim*, recurring in ii. 2, 10, 27, iv. 7, 9, v. 7, probably of Egyptian origin (though not at present known to occur in Egyptian inscriptions), used otherwise only of the 'magicians' of Egypt (Gen. xli. 8, 24; Ex. vii. 11, 22, viii. 7, 18, 19, ix. 11), and no doubt borrowed from the Pent. by the author of Daniel. The precise sense of the term is difficult to fix. It is not improbable that originally it denoted the *sacred scribes* (ἱερογραμματεῖς)[1] of Egypt; but, even if this opinion be accepted, it is doubtful how far the idea was consciously present to the Hebrews who in later times used the word. In Gen. the *ḥarṭummim* appear as interpreters of dreams (LXX. ἐξηγηταί), in Ex. as men able to work magic (LXX. ἐπαοιδοί, in ix. 11 φαρμακοί): Theod. in Dan. renders by ἐπαοιδοί. Probably the word was used by the author

---

[1] Clem. Alex. *Strom.* vi. 36; cf. Ebers, *Aeg. u. die Bb. Mose's*, pp. 343, 347. On the functions of these sacred scribes, and the nature of the literature with which they had to deal (which included a knowledge of magic and charms), see Brugsch, *Aegyptologie* (1891), pp. 77, 85, 149—159.

21 And Daniel continued *even* unto the first year of king Cyrus.

of Daniel in the sense of men acquainted with occult arts in general, so that the rendering 'magician' may be allowed to stand.

astrologers] **enchanters**, Heb. *'ashshāph*, Aram. *'āshaph*, found only in the Book of Daniel (ii. 2, 10, 27, iv. 4, v. 7, 11, 15), the Assyrian *ashipu* (Schrader, *KAT.*² *ad loc.*), which passed also into Syriac, where it is used specially of the charmers of serpents.

21. A remark on the long continuance of Daniel—with the reputation, it is understood, implied in *v.* 20—in Babylon. The first year of Cyrus (B.C. 538) would be nearly 70 years after the date of Daniel's captivity (*v.* 1), so that he would then be quite an aged man.

continued **even unto**] lit. *was until*. The expression is an unusual one; but the meaning, it seems, is that Daniel survived the fall of the empire of Nebuchadnezzar and his successors, and remained, unaffected by the change of dynasty, till the first year of Cyrus, the year in which (Ezr. i. 1, v. 13, vi. 3) the Jews received permission to return to Palestine. He is mentioned indeed as still alive in the third year of Cyrus (x. 1); but that fact is here left out of consideration.

Cyrus] Heb. *Kōresh*, as regularly. The Persian form is *Kuru*(*sh*), the Babylonian *Kurâsh*.

Additional Note on the term 'Chaldaeans.'

The term 'Chaldaeans' (Heb. *Kasdîm*) is used in the Book of Daniel in a sense different from that which it has in any other part of the Old Testament. In other parts of the Old Testament (e.g. in Jeremiah, *passim*) it has an *ethnic* sense: it denotes a people which (in the inscriptions at present known) is thought to be first alluded to about 1100 B.C., and is certainly named repeatedly from 880 B.C.: they lived then in the S.E. of Babylonia, towards the sea-coast; afterwards, as they increased in power, they gradually advanced inland; in 721 B.C. Merodach-baladan, 'king of the land of the *Kaldu*,' made himself king of Babylon; and ultimately, under Nabopolassar and Nebuchadnezzar, they became the ruling caste in Babylonia. In the Book of Daniel (except in v. 30, ix. 1, where the term plainly has its ethnic sense), 'Chaldaean' is the designation not of the ruling caste at large, but of the class—or one of the classes—of *wise men* (i. 4, ii. 2, 4, 5, 10, iii. 8 (prob.), iv. 7, v. 7, 11). Of this sense of the word there is no trace in the inscriptions; it is first found in Herodotus (*c.* 440 B.C.), and is common afterwards in the classical writers; and it dates really from a time when 'Chaldaean' was no longer used in its ethnological sense, and when virtually the only 'Chaldaeans' known were members of the priestly or learned class. The following passages will shew how the classical writers understood the term.

Hdt. i. 181 (in the description of the 'ziggurat' of Bel, i.e. [Tiele] Merodach, in Babylon): 'as the *Chaldaeans*, being priests of this god, say.'

i. 183: 'On the greater altar [in the precincts of the temple at the foot of the 'ziggurat'] the *Chaldaeans* burn also 1000 talents of frankincense every year, when they celebrate the festival of this god.'

Also, in the same chapter, 'as the *Chaldaeans* said,' and 'I did not see it, but I say what is said by the *Chaldaeans*.'

Strabo (1 cent. B.C.) XVI. 1 § 6: 'There is also a quarter reserved in Babylon for the native philosophers called "Chaldaeans," who pursue principally the study of astronomy. Some claim also to cast nativities; but these are not recognized by the others. There is moreover a tribe of the Chaldaeans, and a district of Babylonia, inhabited by them, near the Arabian and the Persian Gulf[1]. There are also several classes (γένη) of the astronomical Chaldaeans, some being called Orcheni [i.e. belonging to Orchoe, or Uruk], others Borsippans, and others having other names according to the different doctrines held by their various schools.'

Diodorus Siculus (1 cent. B.C.) describes them at greater length. The 'Chaldaeans,' he says (ii. 29), 'form a caste, possessing a fixed traditional lore, in which successive generations are brought up, and which they transmit unchanged to their successors. They are among the most ancient of the Babylonians, and hold in the state a position similar to that of the priests in Egypt. Appointed primarily to attend to the worship of the gods, they devote their lives to philosophy, enjoying especially a reputation for astrology. They are also much occupied with divination (μαντική), uttering predictions about the future; and by means partly of purifications, partly of sacrifices, and partly of incantations (ἐπῳδαί), endeavour to avert evil [cf. Is. xlvii. 9, 11—13] and to complete happiness. They are moreover experienced in divination by means of birds, and interpret dreams and omens (τέρατα); they are also practised in the inspection of sacrificial animals (ἱεροσκοπία), and have a character for divining accurately by their means.' And he proceeds (*cc.* 30, 31) to give some account of the astronomical doctrines of the 'Chaldaeans,' and to speak of their remarkable skill in predicting the destinies of men from observation of the planets[2].

In the view of the classical writers, the 'Chaldaeans' were thus a caste of priests, who were also diviners, magicians, and (especially) astrologers. Except in what concerns the name 'Chaldaeans,' the statements of Diodorus, as far as they go, are correct, and substantiated by what is now known from the inscriptions. Here is what is said in the most recent and best work upon the subject[3]:

"The general name for priests was *shangû*, which by a plausible etymology suggested by Jensen, indicates the function of the priest as the one who presides over the sacrifices. But this function represents only one phase of the priestly office in Babylonia, and not the most important one, by any means. For the people, the priest was primarily the one who could drive evil demons out of the body of the person smitten with disease, who could thwart the power of wizards and witches, who could ward off the attacks of mischievous spirits, or who

---

[1] This sentence (cf. § 8 and 3 § 6) is interesting, as it shews that 'Chaldaeans,' in the original ethnic sense of the name, were still resident in their ancient homes.
[2] Cf. also Cic. *Divin.* I. i., xli., II. xli—xliii., xlvii.; *Tusc.* I. xl.; *de Fato* viii. (a criticism of their astrological claims); Juv. x. 94, xiv. 248, with Mayor's notes.
[3] Jastrow's *Religion of Babylonia and Assyria* (Boston, U.S.A. 1898), p. 656 f.

could prognosticate the future and determine the intention or will of the gods. The offering of sacrifices was one of the means to accomplish this end, but it is significant that many of the names used to designate the priestly classes have reference to the priest's position as the exorciser of evil spirits, or his power to secure a divine oracle or to foretell the future, and not to his function as sacrificer. Such names are *mashmashu*, the general term for 'the charmer'; *kalû*, so called, perhaps, as the 'restrainer' of the demons, the one who keeps them in check; *lagaru*, a synonym of *kalû*; *makhkhû*[1], 'soothsayer'; *surrû*, a term which is still obscure; *shâilu*, the 'inquirer,' who obtains an oracle through the dead or through the gods[2]; *mushêlu*[3], 'necromancer'; *âshipu*[4] or *ishippu*, 'sorcerer'."

The antiquity, if not of the 'Chaldaeans' under this name, yet of the priests in whose hands the traditional lore mentioned by Diodorus was, is also well established: "the magical texts formed the earliest sacred literature" of Babylonia[5]; and the great astrological work, called *Nûr-Bel*, 'the Light of Bel,' is earlier than B.C. 2000.

Babylonia was the land of magic (cf. Is. xlvii. 9—13); and a very extensive literature, dealing with different branches of the subject, has been brought to light during recent years. Demons, or evil spirits, were supposed to be active upon earth, bringing to mankind diseases, misfortunes, and every kind of ill; the heavens were supposed to exercise an influence over the destinies of men and nations; all kinds of natural occurrences which we should describe as accidental, such as an animal entering a building, were supposed to be declarations of the will of the gods; and methods had to be devised for the purpose of dealing with the occult agencies concerned, of interpreting all significant phenomena, and of averting, where this was held to be possible, the evils which they portended. The demons were ever present and ever active: so sorcerers and sorceresses sprang up, who, by means of various magical devices, could invoke the demons at their will, and bring such persons as they chose within their power. On the other hand, the priests were ready with means for protecting people who were thus assailed; and many collections of 'incantations' have come down to us, each dealing with some particular kind of demonic evil, or providing some particular method of protection against demons. In particular, every kind of disease was attributed to the action of some malignant spirit, either attacking a person spontaneously, or induced to do so by bewitchment; and the cure was effected by exorcising the demon through prescribed formulae of supposed power, accompanied by symbolical acts (e.g. burning the image of the witch)[6]. Omens were also carefully observed, and tables were drawn up describing the significance of all kinds of occurrences, including the most trifling, in heaven and earth. "Fully one-fourth of the portion of Asshurbanabal's library

---

[1] Whence, probably, the 'Rab-*mag*,' i.e. 'chief of the soothsayers,' of Jer. xxxix. 3, 13.
[2] Cf. the Heb. שָׁאַל in Deut. xviii. 11; Jud. i. 1; 1 Sam. xxiii. 2, xxviii. 6, &c.
[3] Lit. the 'bringer up,' from *elû* = עָלָה: comp. 1 Sam. xxviii. 11.
[4] Comp. on Dan. i. 20.
[5] Sayce, *Hibbert Lectures*, p. 327.
[6] Jastrow, pp. 253—293.

that has been discovered consists of omen-tablets of various sizes in which explanations are afforded of all physical peculiarities to be observed in animals and men, of natural phenomena, of the positions and movements of the planets and stars, of the incidents and accidents of public and private life—in short, of all possible occurrences and situations[1]."

The principles upon which the explanations of all these phenomena were drawn up were, no doubt, partly the association of ideas (as when the sight of a lion symbolized strength, or success), and partly the extension of a single coincidence between a given phenomenon and a particular subsequent occurrence, into a general law. It is, however, evident to what long and elaborate treatises the systematization of rules for dealing with, and explaining, such an immense variety of phenomena would ultimately lead.

There are six terms used in the Book of Daniel as designations of diviners or magicians, viz. (1) wise men (חכמים), (2) enchanters (אשפים), (3) magicians (חרטמים), (4) 'Chaldeans' (כשדים), (5) determiners (of fates) (גזרין), (6) sorcerers (מכשפים), which are distributed as follows:—

i. 20 the magicians and the enchanters.
ii. 2 the magicians, the enchanters, the sorcerers, and the Chaldeans.
ii. 10 *b* any magician, enchanter, or Chaldean.
ii. 27 wise men, enchanters, magicians, (or) determiners (of fates).
iv. 7 the magicians, the enchanters, the Chaldeans, and the determiners (of fates).
v. 7 the enchanters, the Chaldeans, and the determiners (of fates).
v. 11 (of Daniel) 'master of magicians, enchanters, Chaldeans, (and) determiners (of fates).'
v. 15 the wise men, (even) the enchanters.

Wise men occurs besides, alone, in the expression '(all) the wise men of Babylon,' in ii. 12, 13 ('the wise men'), 14, 18, 24, 48, iv. 6, 18 ('all the wise men of my kingdom'), v. 7, 8 ('the wise men of the king'): 'Chaldeans' also occurs alone in i. 4 'the literature and language of the Chaldeans' (seemingly in a general sense); in ii. 4, 5, 10 *a* (as speaking on behalf of the 'wise men' generally); and in iii. 8: and *ḥarṭummim* is used in a generic sense in iv. 9 (where Daniel is called 'master of the *ḥarṭummim*'; cf. ii. 48 and v. 11).

A comparison of the passages shews that the terms in question are used with some vagueness. The generic term appears certainly to be 'wise men'; but in ii. 27 even this appears to be coordinated with three of the special classes. In Diodorus Siculus 'Chaldaeans' is the generic term; but in Daniel that, except once, appears as the name of one class beside others: in i. 4, however (unless, which is improbable, there was no special 'literature' connected with any of the other classes), it is used in a generic sense. In iv. 7 and v. 11 'determiners (of fates)' appears to take the place of 'sorcerers' in ii. 2, although the two terms do not seem to be by any means synonymous. Nor are the several classes of wise men named in Daniel known to correspond to any division or classification indicated by the inscriptions. The attempts

---

[1] Jastrow, pp. 352—406. See further Lenormant, *La Magie chez les Chaldéens* (1874), and *La Divination et la Science des Présages chez les Chaldéens* (1875); the translations of magical texts in Sayce's *Hibbert Lectures* for 1887, p. 441 ff. ('to be accepted with caution,' Jastrow, p. 713); and the literature cited by Jastrow, p. 717 ff. Minuter details would here be out of place, as they would not really illustrate anything in the Book of Daniel.

which have been made to prove the contrary cannot be pronounced successful. Lenormant, for example[1], observing that the great work on magic preserved in Asshurbanabal's library consists of three parts, dealing respectively with incantations against evil spirits, incantations against diseases, and magical hymns, argued that these three divisions corresponded exactly to the three classes, *ḥarṭummim* or 'conjurateurs,' *wise men* or 'médecins,' and *'ashshāphim* or 'théosophes,' mentioned in Daniel by the side of the astrologers and diviners (*kasdim* and *gāzerin*): but the parallel drawn is an arbitrary one; there is no reason whatever for supposing that 'wise men' in Heb. or Aramaic denoted 'médecins,' or *'ashshāphim* 'théosophes.' It seems evident that the author simply took such terms denoting diviners or magicians, as were traditionally connected with Babylon, or seemed to him on other grounds to be suitable, and combined them together, for the purpose of presenting a general picture of the manner in which the arts of divination and magic were systematically studied in Babylon.

CHAP. II. NEBUCHADNEZZAR'S DREAM.

Nebuchadnezzar, in his second year, being disquieted by a dream, demands of the wise men of Babylon that they should repeat and interpret it to him: as they are unable to do this, they are condemned by him to death (*vv.* 1—12). Daniel, and his companions, being involved in the condemnation, and finding consequently their lives in jeopardy, betake themselves to prayer; their supplication is answered by the secret of the dream being revealed to Daniel in a vision of the night (*vv.* 13—23). Being now, at his own request, brought before the king, Daniel describes and interprets his dream to him (*vv.* 24—45), and is rewarded by him with high honours (*vv.* 46—49).

The dream was of a colossal image, the head consisting of gold, the breast and arms of silver, the body of brass, the legs of iron, the feet of iron and clay mixed: as Nebuchadnezzar was contemplating it, a stone 'cut out without hands' suddenly fell, smiting the feet of the image, which thereupon broke up, while the stone became a mountain, filling the whole earth. The image symbolizes the anti-theocratic power of the world; and its principal parts are interpreted to signify four empires, the head of gold being Nebuchadnezzar himself, representing the first empire. With the exception of the first, the empires intended are not expressly indicated; and it has been much disputed what the three following the first are. It is, however, generally admitted that the four kingdoms symbolized in Nebuchadnezzar's dream are the same as the four represented by the four beasts in Daniel's vision in Chap. VII.; so that the discussion of the question will come more suitably at the end of the notes on Chap. VII. The conclusion there reached, it may be premised, is that the second, third, and fourth empires are, respectively, the Median, the Persian, and the Macedonian. But whatever may be the case with the three disputed empires, the 'stone cut out without hands' clearly represents the kingdom of God, before which all earthly powers are destined ultimately to fall.

---

[1] *La Magie*, p. 13 f.

And in the second year of the reign of Nebuchadnezzar, 2
Nebuchadnezzar dreamed dreams, wherewith his spirit was

The main object of the chapter is to shew—(1) how the heathen king is brought (v. 47) to acknowledge the supremacy of Daniel's God; (2) how the sequence of empires is in the hands of God; and (3) how a Divine kingdom is destined ultimately to be established upon earth. The representation of the magnificent but hollow splendour of earthly empire in the form of a 'huge, gleaming, terrible colossus, of many colours and different metals,' brilliant at its summit, but gradually deteriorating, both in material and appearance, towards its base, and, when struck by the falling rock, instantly collapsing into atoms, is fine and striking.

The narrative seems to a certain extent to be modelled on that of Joseph in Gen. xli., there being parallels in both idea and expression. In both narratives a heathen monarch is troubled by a dream which he cannot understand; in both he sends for his own wise men, who fail to remove his perplexity; in both a young Jewish captive, relying on the help of his God, is successful, and is rewarded by the king with high honours, and a life-long position of influence in his kingdom. For similarities of expression, see the notes on *vv*. 1, 2, 12, 28, 30.

1—6. Nebuchadnezzar, being troubled by a dream, summons the wise men of Babylon before him, and bids them both tell him what his dream had been, and also interpret it to him.

1. *in the second year*] There is not, perhaps, necessarily a contradiction here with the 'three years' of i. 5, 18. By Heb. usage, fractions of time were reckoned as full units: thus Samaria, which was besieged from the fourth to the sixth year of Hezekiah, is said to have been taken 'at the end' of three years (2 Ki. xvii. 9, 10); and in Jer. xxxiv. 14 'at the end of seven years' means evidently when the seventh year has arrived (see also Mark viii. 31, &c.). If, now, the author, following a custom which was certainly sometimes adopted by Jewish writers, and which was general in Assyria and Babylonia, 'post-dated' the regnal years of a king, i.e. counted as his first year not the year of his accession but the first full year afterwards[1], and if further Nebuchadnezzar gave orders for the education of the Jewish youths in his accession-year, the end of the 'three years' of i. 5, 18 might be reckoned as falling within the king's second year. Ewald, Kamphausen, and Prince, however, suppose that 'ten' has fallen out of the text; and would read 'in the *twelfth* year.'

dreamed dreams] In Assyria and Babylonia, as in Egypt[2], and other countries of the ancient world, dreams were regarded as significant, and as portending future events. The Assyrian inscriptions furnish several instances of deities appearing in dreams with words of encouragement or advice. Thus Asshur appears to Gugu (Gyges), king of Lydia, in a dream, and tells him that, if he 'grasps the feet' (i.e. owns the sovereignty) of Asshurbanapal, he will overcome his foes (*KB*. ii.

---

[1] See art. CHRONOLOGY, in Hastings' *Dict. of the Bible*, p. 400.
[2] See Hastings' *Dict. of the Bible*, ii. p. 772 *b*.

18   DANIEL, II.   [v. 2.

2 troubled, and his sleep brake from him. Then the king
commanded to call the magicians, and the astrologers, and
the sorcerers, and the Chaldeans, for to shew the king his

173, 175). During Asshurbanapal's war with his 'false' brother,
Shamash-shum-ukin, a professional dreamer saw written on the moon,
'Whoso plans evil against Asshurbanapal, an evil death will I prepare
against him' (*ib.* p. 187). When the same king was warring against
Ummanaldashi, king of Elam, Ishtar sent his army a dream, in which she
said to them, 'I march before Asshurbanapal, the king whom my hands
have made' (*ib.* p. 201); and in another war she appeared to a professional dreamer, standing before the king, armed, and assuring him that,
wherever he went, she went likewise (*ib.* p. 251). Nabu-na'id, the last
king of Babylon (B.C. 555—538), was commanded, or encouraged, to
restore temples by deities appearing to him in dreams (*ib.* iii. 2, pp. 85,
97, 99). On another occasion, Nabu-na'id saw in a dream a great star
in heaven, the significance of which Nebuchadnezzar (also in the
dream) explained to him[1]. These, however, are mostly cases of the
apparitions of deities; for instances of *symbolical* dreams, such as the
one of Nebuchadnezzar, we may compare rather, though they are much
briefer, the dreams in Herodotus, i. 107, 108, 209, iii. 30, 124, vii. 19
(cited below, on iv. 10).

**and *his spirit was troubled*] More exactly, was agitated, dis-
turbed; so *v.* 3.** The expression is borrowed from Gen. xli. 8: cf.
Ps. lxxvii. 5 'I am *agitated* and cannot speak.'

***brake from him*] More lit. *was come to pass,*—i.e. *was completed* or
done with (something like the Latin *actum est*; cf. viii. 27),—upon
him,—'upon' being used idiomatically to emphasize the person who is
the subject of an experience, or (more often) of an emotion, and who,
as it were, is sensible of it as acting or operating *upon* himself. Cf.
Ps. xlii. 4 'I will pour out my soul *upon* me,' 5 'why moanest thou
upon me?' 6 'my soul *upon* me is cast down,' cxlii. 3 'when my spirit
fainteth *upon* me,' cxliii. 4, Jer. viii. 18 'my heart *upon* me is sick,' Job
xxx. 16 (R.V. *marg.*), Lam. iii. 20 'my soul is bowed down *upon* me':
within, in all these passages, does not express the idea of the Hebrew.
Cf. the writer's *Parallel Psalter*, Glossary I, s. v. *upon* (p. 464); and see
also Dan. v. 9.

2. *the magicians, and the* enchanters] See on i. 20. As in Egypt
(Gen. xli. 8), the 'magicians' and 'wise men' (*v.* 12) would be the
natural persons for the king to consult on the interpretation of a dream.

***and the sorcerers*]** This is a word which is well known in the
earlier literature: e.g. Ex. vii. 11, xxii. 18 (in the *fem.*); Deut. xviii. 10;
cf. the subst. *sorceries* Mic. v. 11, and (in Babylon) Is. xlvii. 9, 12.

***Chaldeans*]** Here, as in **i. 4**, used in the sense of the priestly or
learned class (see p. 12 ff.). So *vv.* 4, 5, 10.

***for to shew*] *for to* tell (R.V.).** To 'shew' is used often in A.V., and
sometimes in R.V., not in the modern sense of *pointing out*, but in
that of *telling* or *declaring*; and it stands here for the Heb. word

[1] Messerschmidt, *Die Inschrift der Stele Nabuna'ids*, 1896, p. 30 f.

dreams. So they came and stood before the king. And 3
the king said unto them, I have dreamed a dream, and my
spirit was troubled to know the dream. Then spake the 4
Chaldeans to the king in Syriack, O king, live for ever: tell
thy servants the dream, and we will shew the interpretation.
The king answered and said to the Chaldeans, The thing is 5

usually rendered *tell* or *declare*. So Gen. xlvi. 31 (R.V. *tell*); Jud.
xiii. 10; 1 Sam xi. 9 (R.V. *told*), xix. 7, xxv. 8 (R.V. *told*); 2 Ki. vi. 11;
Is. xli. 22, 26 (R.V. *declare*), &c.; cf. the *Parallel Psalter*, p. 481.

3. was disturbed] or **is disturbed**. It is not perfectly clear whether
the intention of the writer is to represent the king as having really
forgotten the dream and desiring to have it recalled to him; or as still
remembering it, and merely making this demand for the purpose of
testing the magicians' skill.

4. *in Syriack*] *in* **Aramaic**, i.e. the language of the Aramaeans, an
important branch of the Semitic stock, inhabiting chiefly Mesopotamia,
Syria, and part of Arabia. There were numerous 'Aramaic' dialects—
as the Aramaic spoken in Assyria, at Zinjirli (near Aleppo), in Palmyra,
in Têma, by the Nabataeans at 'el'Ōla, that of the books of Daniel
and Ezra, that of the Targums of Onkelos and Jonathan, that of the
Babylonian, that of the Palestinian Talmud—which, while similar in
their general features, differed in details, somewhat in the manner in
which the Greek dialects differed from one another: but the language
which is now known distinctively as 'Syriac,'—i.e. the language in
which the 'Peshiṭtā' version of the Bible (2nd cent. A.D.) was made,
and in which an extensive Christian literature exists,—differs markedly
from the Aramaic of Daniel and Ezra: and hence the rendering 'Syriack'
suggests an entirely false idea of the language here meant. R.V., 'in
the Syrian language' (cf. Is. xxxvi. 11) is some improvement; but the
term which ought to be employed is 'Aramaic.'

The Aramaic part of the book begins with the words *O king;* and
if '(in) Aramaic' forms an integral part of the sentence, the author, it
seems, must mean to indicate that in his opinion Aramaic was used at
the court for communications of an official nature. That, however,
does not explain why the use of Aramaic continues to the end of
ch. vii.; and it is besides quite certain that Aramaic, such as that of
the Book of Daniel, was *not* spoken in Babylon. Very probably
Oppert, Lenormant, Nestle, and others are right in regarding 'Aramaic'
as originally a marginal note, indicating that that language begins to be
used here; in this case the word will in English be naturally enclosed
in brackets, 'And they spake to the king, [*Aramaic*] O king, &c.'
The second '(in) Aramaic' in Ezra iv. 7 is probably to be explained
similarly ('was written in Aramaic, and interpreted. [*Aramaic*]').

O king, live for ever] The standing formula, with which, in Dan.,
the king is addressed (iii. 9, v. 10, vi. 6, 21); elsewhere (in the 3rd
person) only on somewhat exceptional occasions, 1 Ki. i. 31; Neh. ii. 3.

we will shew] **declare**.

5. *The thing is gone from me*] The thing (or word) on my part

gone from me: if ye will not make known unto me the dream, with the interpretation thereof, ye shall be cut in
6 pieces, and your houses shall be made a dunghill. But if ye shew the dream, and the interpretation thereof, ye shall receive of me gifts and rewards and great honour: therefore
7 shew me the dream, and the interpretation thereof. They answered again and said, Let the king tell his servants the
8 dream, and we will shew the interpretation of it. The king answered and said, I know of certainty that ye would gain

(מן nearly as in iii. 29) **is sure**. The king means that the threat which follows is fully resolved upon by him. *Azda* is a Persian word, meaning *sure, certain* (see Schrader, *KAT*.², p. 617); the rendering 'gone' is philologically indefensible.

if ye will not make known] *if ye* **make not** *known* (R.V.). '*Will* not,' in this sentence would (in modern English) mean '*are* not *willing to*,' which is not in the Aramaic at all.

cut in pieces] more exactly, *dismembered*; lit. *made into* (separate) *limbs*; so iii. 29 (cf. 2 Macc. i. 16 μέλη ποιήσαντες). The word for 'limb' (*haddām*,—common in Syriac, but in the O.T. found only here and iii. 29) is Persian (Zend *handāma*, Mod. Pers. *andām*). The violence and peremptoriness of the threatened punishment is in accordance with what might be expected at the hands of an Eastern despot: the Assyrians and Persians, especially, were notorious for the barbarity of their punishments.

be made a dunghill] Cf. iii. 29 and Ezra vi. 11 (where Darius decrees the same punishment for any one altering the terms of his edict).

6. *shew* (twice)] declare. So *vv*. 7, 9, 10, 11, 16, 24, 27, iv. 2, v. 7, 12, 15.

rewards] A rare word, probably of Persian origin (according to Andreas, in the Glossary in Marti's *Gramm. der Bibl.-Aram. Sprache*, properly, *tribute, present*), found otherwise only in v. 17, where it stands in a similar context.

7—12. The wise men profess their willingness to interpret the king's dream: but protest that his demand that they should tell him what his dream was is an extravagant one. Nebuchadnezzar, however, adheres to his original demand: and as they are unable to comply with it, commands them to be put to death.

7. *again*] **the second time** (R.V.).

8. *of certainty*] We should say now, 'of *a* certainty.' Murray quotes from North's *Plutarch* (1580), 'It is *of certainty* that her proper name was Nicostrata.'

would **gain time** (R.V.)] lit. *are buying the time*. Their repeated request to the king to tell them his dream is proof to him that they have no power to reveal secrets, and that they could not therefore interpret his dream, even though he were to describe it to them: hence he charges them with *buying the time*, i.e. with endeavouring to defer

DANIEL, II.

the time, because ye see the thing is gone from me. But if ye will not make known unto me the dream, *there is but* one decree for you: for ye have prepared lying and corrupt words to speak before me, till the time be changed: therefore tell me the dream, and I shall know that ye can shew me the interpretation thereof. The Chaldeans answered before the king, and said, There is not a man upon the earth that can shew the king's matter: therefore *there is* no king, lord, nor ruler, *that* asked such things at any magician, or astrologer, or Chaldean. And *it is* a rare thing that the king requireth, and there is none other that can

the fatal moment when the truth must appear, and when their inability to interpret his dream must be exposed.

because ye see **that** *the* **thing on my part is sure, (9) That,** *if,* **&c.**] Because you see that I am resolved to punish you, if you do not fulfil the conditions I lay down (*v.* 5).

9. That, *if ye* **make not** *known unto me the dream,* there is but *one* **law** *for you*] you can expect nothing else but punishment. Lit. *your law* (i.e. the law or sentence against you) *is one,* implying that it is unalterable and inevitable; cf. Est. iv. 11. The word for 'law' (*dāth*) is Persian, Zend *dāta,* Mod. Pers. *dād* (see the Introduction, p. lvi).

and (also) *lying and corrupt words ye have* **agreed** *to speak before me*] pretending falsely that you will be able to explain the dream, if it is only told you.

prepared] So the Kt.; but the Qrê, '**ye have** *prepared yourselves,* or **agreed together** ' (cf. Am. iii. 3 Targ.), is more in accordance with usage (see Levy, *Chald. W. B.,* s.v.).

before me] to speak 'before,' rather than 'to,' a king, is the language of respect: so *vv.* 10, 11, 27, 36, v. 17, vi. 12; Est. i. 16, vii. 9, viii. 3. Cp. on vi. 10.

till the time be changed] till circumstances take a favourable turn, and the king, for instance, has his attention diverted to something else.

therefore tell me, &c.] if they are able to tell him the dream, it will be a guarantee to him that their explanation will be trustworthy.

10. *shew*] **declare.**

therefore, &c.] forasmuch as (R.V.) *no* **great and powerful** *king* (cf. R.V. *marg.*) hath *asked such* a thing of *any magician or* **enchanter** *or Chaldean.* As no king has ever thought of making such a demand, it may be fairly concluded to be one which it is impossible to satisfy.

11. *rare*] **difficult**: properly *heavy*. The word has the same sense sometimes in Syriac, as Ex. xviii. 18, in the Peshiṭtā.

requireth] **asketh** (as *v.* 10), which indeed is all that the translators of 1611 meant by their rendering: for *require* formerly did not express the idea now attaching to the word of demanding as a right. So elsewhere in A.V., as 2 Sam. xii. 20; Prov. xxx. 7 (R.V. *asked*); Ezr. viii. 22 (R.V. *ask*); and in P.B.V. of the Psalms, as Ps. xxvii. 4, xxxviii. 16, xl. 9, li. 6, cxxxvii. 3.

shew it before the king, except the gods, whose dwelling is
12 not with flesh. For this cause the king was angry and
very furious, and commanded to destroy all the wise *men*
13 of Babylon. And the decree went forth that the wise
men should be slain; and they sought Daniel and his
fellows to be slain.
14 Then Daniel answered with counsel and wisdom to Arioch
the captain of the king's guard, which was gone forth to slay

shew] declare.
whose dwelling is not with flesh] i.e. who are superhuman, supramundane beings.
12. *wise* men] of those versed in occult arts, as Gen. xli. 8; Jer. l. 35 (of Babylon), and several times in the sequel (cf. p. 15). Similarly *wisdom*, Is. xlvii. 10 (of Babylon), and ch. i. 17, 20.
13—16. Daniel and his three companions, being regarded now (cf. i. 17—20) as belonging to the class of 'wise men,' and being consequently involved in the condemnation, are in danger of their lives; but Daniel, through Arioch's intervention, obtains an audience of the king, and promising to tell him his dream, gets execution of the sentence deferred.
13. *the decree went forth*] Cf. Luke ii. 2, where the Greek is exactly the same as that of Theodotion's rendering here (τὸ δόγμα ἐξῆλθε).
that the wise men, &c.] **and** *the wise men* **were to be slain** (R.V.). See Kautzsch, *Gramm.* § 76. 3.
fellows] **companions** (R.V.), as *v.* 17. So *v.* 18.
14. *answered with counsel and* **discretion**] lit. *returned counsel and* **discretion** (or **tact**) : lit. *taste*, and so figuratively of the faculty which discriminates and selects what is suitable for a given occasion. Cf. 1 Sam. xxv. 33, 'And blessed be thy *discretion*' (R.V. *marg.*), of the tact displayed by Abigail in averting David's vengeance from Nabal; Job xii. 20, 'and taketh away the *discretion* of the elders;' Prov. xxvi. 16 (the same phrase as here), 'than seven men *answering with discretion*' (lit. *returning discretion*).
Arioch] The name, in Gen. xiv. 1, of an ancient king of Ellasar (Larsa, in S. Babylonia); and, no doubt, borrowed thence, both here and in Judith i. 6 (where it is the name of a 'king of the Elymaeans '). " The name was Sumerian and not used at that period [Nebuchadnezzar's] of Babylonian history" (Sayce, in Hastings' *Dict. of the Bible, s.v.*).
captain of the king's guard] 'Captain of the guard' is the same expression which occurs in 2 Ki. xxv. 8 ff., Jer. xxxix. 9 ff., of an officer of Nebuchadnezzar, and (with *sar* for *rab*) in Gen. (xxxvii. 36, xxxix. 1, *al.*) of an officer of Pharaoh. It is lit. 'captain (or superintendent, chief) of the slaughterers' (viz. of animals [*not* executioners]) : the royal butchers came in some way to form the royal body-guard (cf. W. R. Smith, $OTJC.^2$, p. 262 f.). The use of the same term in reference to two such different countries as Egypt and Babylon, shews that, though

the wise *men* of Babylon: he answered and said to Arioch 15
the king's captain, Why *is* the decree *so* hasty from the
king? Then Arioch made the thing known to Daniel.
Then Daniel went in, and desired of the king that he would 16
give him time, and that *he* would shew the king the interpretation. Then Daniel went to his house, and made the 17
thing known to Hananiah, Mishael, and Azariah, his companions: that *they* would desire mercies of the God of 18
heaven concerning this secret; that Daniel and his fellows
should not perish with the rest of the wise *men* of Babylon.

Then *was* the secret revealed unto Daniel in a night 19
vision. Then Daniel blessed the God of heaven. Daniel 20
answered and said,

it happens only to be applied to foreigners, it was really a native
Hebrew title.

15. so *hasty*] **harsh** (Bevan). R.V. *urgent*, as A.V. itself has in
iii. 22. This is not, however, strong enough: in Syriac and the Targums the word and its cognates express the idea of *bold, shameless,
insolent.* Cf. Theod. here, ἀναιδής (LXX. πικρῶς).

16. *give him time*] or (R.V.) *appoint him a time.*

and that he would shew] **that he might** (R.V. *marg.*) **declare.**
Daniel only asked for time; and such a request would be the more
readily granted, as Nebuchadnezzar had already (i. 20) been favourably
impressed by his superior skill.

17—19. In answer to the supplication of Daniel and his three
friends, the secret of Nebuchadnezzar's dream is revealed to him in a
dream.

18. *that they would*] '*that they might*' would be clearer, as it
would include more easily a reference to Daniel (see *v.* 23 'me').

mercies] **compassion**, as the corresponding Heb. word is rendered in
Lam. iii. 22, Zech. vii. 9 in A.V., and in Dan. i. 9 in R.V.

the God of heaven] So *vv.* 19, 37, 44. A favourite expression
among the post-exilic Jews[1]: see Ezr. i. 2 (=2 Chr. xxxvi. 23),
v. 11, 12, vi. 9, 10, vii. 12, 21, 23, Neh. i. 4, 5, ii. 4, 20, Jon. i. 9,
Ps. cxxxvi. 26 (אֵל): also Enoch xiii. 6, Tob. x. 11, Judith v. 8, vi. 19,
xi. 17, Rev. xi. 13, xvi. 11.

fellows] **companions** (R.V.), as *v.* 17.

19. *in a* **vision of the night**] For the expression, comp. Is. xxix. 7
('like a dream, a *vision of the night*'), Job iv. 13, vii. 14, xx. 8,
xxxiii. 15, Gen. xlvi. 2.

20—23. Daniel's thanksgiving for the great mercy vouchsafed to
him.

20. *answered*] In the sense of commencing to speak: so iii. 9, 14,

---

[1] In Gen. xxiv. 7 it is probable that 'and earth' (so LXX) has accidentally fallen
out: see *v.* 3.

Blessed be the name of God for ever and ever:
For wisdom and might are his:
21 And he changeth the times and the seasons:
He removeth kings, and setteth up kings:
He giveth wisdom unto the wise,
And knowledge to them that know understanding:
22 He revealeth the deep and secret *things*:
He knoweth what *is* in the darkness,
And the light dwelleth with him.
23 I thank thee, and praise thee, O thou God of my fathers,
Who hast given me wisdom and might,
And hast made known unto me now what we desired of thee:
For thou hast *now* made known unto us the king's matter.

19, 24, *al.*; and ἀποκριθεὶς εἶπε in the N.T., Matt. xi. 25, xvii. 4, xxviii. 5, *al.*: cf. Dalman, *Die Worte Jesu* (1898), p. 19.

Blessed, &c.] Cf. Ps. cxiii. 2; also Job i. 21.

for ever and ever] **from eternity and to eternity**, as Ps. xli. 13, cvi. 48, cf. Neh. ix. 5; also (without the art. in the Heb.) Jer. vii. 7, Ps. xc. 2, ciii. 17, *al.*

wisdom, &c.] Job xii. 13 'With him are wisdom and might.'

21. *the times and the seasons*] more exactly **seasons and times**; cf. vii. 12; Acts i. 7; 1 Thess. v. 1. The meaning is, History does not move with the regularity of a clock: the order of things established at a given time is not necessarily permanent; it frequently happens that kings are overthrown and a new *régime* is established.

he giveth wisdom, &c.] The doxology now assumes special reference to Daniel's own case. As Joseph ascribed his skill in interpreting dreams to God (Gen. xl. 8, xli. 16), so Daniel acknowledges that He is the source of wisdom to those who possess it.

know understanding] Cf. Prov. iv. 1.

22. *He revealeth*, &c.] Cf. Job xii. 22, 'Who revealeth deep things out of darkness.'

light] physical light (cf. 1 Tim. vi. 16), but suggesting and implying fulness of intellectual light; cf. 1 John i. 7 (of spiritual light).

23. **Thee, O God** *of my fathers*, **do I thank** *and* **praise**] 'God of my fathers,' i.e., the same as of old, unchanged among the changes of human generations, and still able to help and defend His servants. Cf. 'God of thy (Israel's) fathers,' Deut. i. 21, vi. 3, xii. 1, *al.*

wisdom and might] a share of His own attributes (*v.* 20): 'might,' however, rather in the special sense of moral strength, enabling Daniel, for instance, to remain firm in his religion (i. 8).

24—30. Daniel, brought by Arioch into Nebuchadnezzar's presence, professes his readiness to declare and interpret to him his dream.

Therefore Daniel went in unto Arioch, whom the king 24
had ordained to destroy the wise *men* of Babylon: he went
and said thus unto him; Destroy not the wise *men* of
Babylon: bring me in before the king, and I will shew unto
the king the interpretation. Then Arioch brought in Daniel 25
before the king in haste, and said thus unto him, I have
found a man of the captives of Judah, that will make known
unto the king the interpretation. The king answered and 26
said to Daniel, whose name *was* Belteshazzar, Art thou able
to make known unto me the dream which I have seen, and
the interpretation thereof? Daniel answered in the presence 27
of the king, and said, The secret which the king hath demanded cannot the wise *men*, the astrologians, the magicians,
the soothsayers, shew unto the king; but there is a God in 28
heaven that revealeth secrets, and maketh known to the

24. *ordained*] i.e. **appointed** (R.V.; cf. *v.* 49, iii. 12), though (in the general application which the word has here) the meaning is now obsolete: see 1 Chr. xvii. 9 (R.V. *appoint*); Is. xxx. 33; Ps. cxxxii. 17.
shew] **declare.**

25. *captives*] lit. *children of the captivity* (or, better[1], *of the exile*), as A.V. itself renders in v. 13, vi. 13; Ezr. vi. 16: cf. Ezr. iv. 1, vi. 19, 20, viii. 35, x. 7, 16.

27. *in the presence of*] **before** (R.V.), as *v.* 9.
demanded] simply **asked,** which is all that 'demand' formerly expressed. 'Like Fr. *demander*, to ask, simply; not as now in the stronger sense of "to ask with authority, or as a right,"' (W. A. Wright, *Bible Word-book*, *s.v.*). So Ex. v. 14; 2 Sam. xi. 7; Job xxxviii. 3. 'Demand' in the modern sense would suit these passages; but the Hebrew word used is the one that ordinarily means 'ask.'

can neither *wise men*, **enchanters** (*v.* 2), *magicians*, **nor determiners** (of fates) **declare** *unto the king*] The terms are all indefinite in the original. 'Determiners' (also iv. 4, v. 7, 11), viz. of future destinies, whether by observation of the heavens (Is. xlvii. 13), or by other means. The Babylonians were famed for their astrology, and in classical times the idea of astrologer was that which was almost entirely associated with the term 'Chaldaean' (cf. above, p. 13). The verb (strictly, *to cut*), in the general sense of *decide, decree*, occurs in the Targums and in Syriac, and once also in the Aramaizing idiom of Job (xxii. 28); cf. the cognate subst., Dan. iv. 14, 21. In this particular appli-cation, however, it is at present known only in the Biblical Aramaic.

28. But, though human skill is unable to satisfy the king, there is a God in heaven, the revealer of secrets, who has in reality by means of this dream disclosed to him the future. Cf. Gen. xli. 28.
and maketh known] **and he hath** *made known.*

[1] See on Am. i. 5, 6, in the *Cambridge Bible.*

king Nebuchadnezzar what shall be in the latter days. Thy dream, and the visions of thy head upon thy bed, *are* these; 29 *As for* thee, O king, thy thoughts came *into thy mind* upon thy bed, what should come to pass hereafter: and he that revealeth secrets maketh known to thee what shall come to 30 pass. But *as for* me, this secret *is* not revealed to me for *any* wisdom that I have more than any living, but for *their*

in the latter days] lit. *in the end* (*closing-part*[1]) *of the days*. An expression which occurs fourteen times in the O.T., and which always denotes the *closing period* of the future so far as it falls within the range of view of the writer using it. The sense expressed by it is thus relative, not absolute, varying with the context. In Gen. xlix. 1 (spoken from Jacob's standpoint) it is used of the period of Israel's occupation of Canaan; in Numb. xxiv. 14 of the period of Israel's future conquest of Moab and Edom (see *vv.* 17, 18); in Deut. xxxi. 29 and iv. 30, of the periods, respectively, of Israel's future apostasy and return to God; in Ez. xxxviii. 16 (cf. *v.* 8—with *years* for *days*) of the imagined period of Gog's attack upon restored Israel; in Dan. x. 14 of the age of Antiochus Epiphanes. Elsewhere it is used of the ideal, or Messianic age, conceived as following at the close of the existing order of things: Hos. iii. 5; Is. ii. 2 (=Mic. iv. 1); Jer. xlviii. 47, xlix. 39; comp. xxiii. 20 (=xxx. 24)[2]. Here, as the sequel shews, it is similarly the period of the establishment of the Divine Kingdom which is principally denoted by it (*vv.* 34, 35; 44, 45); but the closing years of the fourth kingdom (*vv.* 40—43) may also well be included in it.

visions of thy head] iv. 5, 10, 13, vii. 1, 15.

29. *came* into thy mind] lit. *came* up,—the corresponding Heb. word followed by 'upon the heart,' being a Heb. idiom for *occur to*, *be thought of by:* cf. 2 Esdr. iii. 1; and see Is. lxv. 17; Jer. iii. 16, vii. 31, xix. 5, xxxii. 35, xliv. 21, li. 50; Acts vii. 23. The king, as he lay awake at night, was meditating on the future, speculating, it may be, upon the future destinies of his kingdom, or the success of his projects for the beautification of his capital; and the dream, it seems to be implied, was the form into which, under Providence, his thoughts gradually shaped themselves. In a dream, the images and impressions, which the mind, while in a waking state, has received, are recombined into new, and often fantastic forms; in the present case, a colossal and strangely constructed statue was the form which the recombination ultimately produced.

30. Like Joseph (Gen. xl. 8, xli. 16), Daniel disclaims the power of interpreting dreams by his own wisdom.

but for their *sakes that shall make known*, &c.] *but* **to the intent that** *the interpretation* **may be made** *known to the king, and that thou* **mayest** *know*, &c. (R.V.).

---

[1] For the sense of אַחֲרִית see Job viii. 7, xlii. 12 (where it denotes clearly the *latter part* of a man's life).

[2] Cf. in the N.T. Acts ii. 17 (for the 'afterward' of Joel ii. 28), Heb. i. 2, 2 Tim. iii. 1, 2 Pet. iii. 3.

sakes that shall make known the interpretation to the king, and *that* thou mightest know the thoughts of thy heart.

31 Thou, O king, sawest, and behold a great image. This great image, whose brightness *was* excellent, stood before thee; and the form thereof *was* terrible. 32 This image's head *was* of fine gold, his breast and his arms of silver, his belly and his thighs of brass, his legs of iron, his feet part of iron 33 and part of clay. 34 Thou sawest till that a stone was cut out without hands, which smote the image upon his feet *that were* of iron and clay, and brake them in pieces. 35 Then was the iron, the clay, the brass, the silver, and the gold, broken to pieces together, and became like the chaff of the summer threshingfloors; and the wind carried them away, that no

31—35. Daniel tells Nebuchadnezzar his dream.

31. *sawest*] more exactly, *wast seeing*. So *v.* 34.

This image, which was mighty, and whose brightness was surpassing] 'Excellent' in Old English (from *excello*, to rise up out of, to surpass) had the distinctive meaning, which it has now lost, of *surpassing, preeminent;* and it is regularly to be understood with this force, wherever it occurs in P.B.V. of the Psalms, in A.V., and (usually) even in R.V. See the passages cited in the Note at the end of the Chapter; and cf. Blundeville, *Exercises*, fol. 156 a (ed. 1594), stars are not seen by day "because they are darkened by the *excellent* brightness of the sun" (W. A. Wright, *Bible Word-book*, s.v.).

form] aspect (R.V.), or appearance. Cf. Gen. xii. 11, 2 Sam. xiv. 27 (and elsewhere), where the Hebrew is lit. ' fair of *aspect*.'

32, 33. The head of the image was of gold; but its substance deteriorated more and more until the feet were reached, which were of mingled iron and clay.

32. *This image's head* was, &c.] more forcibly, and also in better agreement with the original, **As for that** *image*, **its** *head was*, &c.

brass] i.e. copper (or bronze): see Wright's *Bible Word-book*.

34. *was cut out*] viz. from a neighbouring mountain (see *v.* 45).

without hands] without human cooperation; it seemed to fall away of itself. But of course the implicit thought is that its secret mover was God: cf. the similar expressions in viii. 25 *end* ('shall be broken without hand,' of the death of Antiochus Epiphanes); Job xxxiv. 20; Lam. iv. 6: also (in a different connexion) 2 Cor. v. 1, Heb. ix. 24.

35. The absolute dissipation of the image. The feet being broken, the entire image fell to pieces; and the fragments were dispersed by the wind. A fall would not naturally break masses of metal into fragments small enough to be scattered by the wind; but in a dream physical impossibilities or improbabilities occasion no difficulty.

threshingfloors] which were generally on exposed or elevated spots, where the chaff might readily be cleared away by the wind. Cf. Hos. xiii. 3, Is. xli. 16, Ps. i. 4; and with *no place*, &c., Rev. xx. 11.

place was found for them: and the stone that smote the image became a great mountain, and filled the whole earth.
36 This *is* the dream; and we will tell the interpretation
37 thereof before the king. Thou, O king, *art* a king of kings: for the God of heaven hath given thee a kingdom, power,
38 and strength, and glory. And wheresoever the children of men dwell, the beasts of the field and the fowls of the heaven hath he given into thine hand, and hath made thee
39 ruler over them all. Thou *art* this head of gold. And

became a great mountain, and filled the whole earth] another figure, the incongruity of which would not be perceived in a dream, implying the irresistible expansive force, and also the ultimate universality, of the kingdom of God (*v.* 44).

36—45. The interpretation of the dream. The four parts of the image signify four kingdoms,—the first being represented by its present and greatest ruler, Nebuchadnezzar.

37. *a king of kings*] king of kings,—a title applied to Nebuchadnezzar in Ez. xxvi. 7, though (Prince) not the customary Babylonian form of address. It is, however, one that was borne constantly by the Persian kings: cf. Ezr. vii. 12; and see the series of inscriptions of Persian kings, published in *Records of the Past*, 1st ser., i. 111 ff., v. 151 ff., ix. 65 ff. An Aramaic inscription found at Saqqarah, near Cairo, is dated in the 4th year of "Xerxes, *king of kings*."

for, &c.] **unto whom** *the God of heaven* (v. 19) *hath given* **the** *kingdom*, **the** *power*, **the** *strength, and* **the** *glory*. Daniel ascribes Nebuchadnezzar's dominion to the Providence of God, exactly as is done (in other terms) by Jeremiah (xxv. 9, xxvii. 6, xxviii. 14).

38. *the beasts of the field*] i.e. wild animals (cf. in Heb. e.g. Ex. xxiii. 11, 29). These and the birds are mentioned in order to represent Nebuchadnezzar's rule as being as absolute as possible; the former are borrowed, no doubt, from Jer. xxvii. 6, xxviii. 14.

art *this*] *art* **the**. The pronoun in the Aramaic has here no demonstrative force; see Kautzsch, *Gramm. des Bibl. Aram.*, § 87. 3. The four parts of the image symbolize four kingdoms; but Nebuchadnezzar, both in reality and in the memory of posterity, so eclipsed all other rulers of the first monarchy, that he is identified with it as a whole.

39. The second and third kingdoms are, in all probability, the Median and the Persian. The home of the Medes was in the mountainous country N. and N.E. of Babylon, and S.W. of the Caspian Sea; they are often mentioned in the Assyrian inscriptions from the 8th cent. B.C.; but they were first consolidated into an important power by Cyaxares, B.C. 624—584, during whose reign, in 607, they were the chief instruments in bringing about the destruction of Nineveh. Cyaxares was succeeded by Astyages, whose soldiers deserted *en masse* to Cyrus (B.C. 549); and the empire of the Medes thus passed into the hands of the Persians. Their name was however long remembered; for the Greeks regularly spoke of the Persians as *Medes* (οἱ Μῆδοι, τὰ Μηδικά).

after thee shall arise another kingdom inferior to thee, and another third kingdom of brass, which shall bear rule over all the earth. And the fourth kingdom shall be strong as iron: forasmuch as iron breaketh in pieces and subdueth all *things*: and as iron that breaketh all these, shall it break in pieces and bruise. And whereas thou sawest the feet and toes, part of potter's clay, and part of iron, the kingdom shall be divided; but there shall be in it of the strength of the iron, forasmuch as thou sawest the iron mixed with miry clay. And *as* the toes of the feet *were* part of iron, and

In the book of Daniel the 'Medes and Persians' are, it is true, sometimes represented as united (v. 28, vi. 8, 12, 15, cf. viii. 20): but elsewhere they are represented as distinct; after the fall of Babylon, Darius 'the Mede' 'receives the kingdom' (v. 31), and acts in it as king (vi. 1, 2, 15, 25, 26); he reigns for a time—it is not said how long—and is succeeded by Cyrus, who is called pointedly 'the Persian' (vi. 28; cf. x. 1, and contrast ix. 1, xi. 1); the two horns of the ram in viii. 3 are distinguished from each other, one (representing the Persian empire) being higher (i.e. more powerful) than the other (the Median empire), and coming up after it. Thus in the view of the author of the book, the more powerful rule of Persia is preceded by a 'kingdom' of the Medes, beginning immediately after the death of Belshazzar. It is possible that this representation is based upon the prediction in Is. xiii. 17, Jer. li. 11, 28, that the Medes would be the conquerors of Babylon. If the second kingdom be the Median, the third will be that of Persia; it is described as ruling 'over all the earth,' with allusion to the wide empire of Cyrus and his successors, which embraced virtually the whole of Western Asia (including Asia Minor) and Egypt (cf. the note on iv. 1, at the end). Compare in the O.T. Ezr. i. 2, Est. i. 1, x. 1.

inferior to thee] lit. *lower than thou*.

40. The fourth kingdom, the formidable crushing power of which is compared to iron. The allusion is to the Macedonian empire, founded by Alexander the Great.

subdueth] or **beateth down**: in Syr. the word used means to *forge* a metal.

breaketh all these...and bruise] **crusheth** *all these...and* **crush** (R.V.).

41. The kingdom which began by being of iron, ended in being partly of iron and partly of clay, symbolizing its division, one part being stronger than the other.

it *shall be* **a divided kingdom**] alluding to the manner in which Alexander's empire, immediately after his death (B.C. 332) was partitioned between his generals, the two who, in the end, divided it substantially between them being Seleucus and Ptolemy Lagi, who founded, respectively, dynasties which continued long in power at Antioch in Syria and in Egypt (see fuller particulars on xi. 5 ff.). The stronger kingdom, represented by the iron, is that of the Seleucidae.

strength] an unusual word, more exactly **firmness**.

part of clay, *so* the kingdom shall be partly strong, and partly
43 broken. And whereas thou sawest iron mixt with miry clay,
they shall mingle themselves with the seed of men: but they
shall not cleave one to another, even as iron is not mixed
44 with clay. And in the days of these kings shall the God of
heaven set up a kingdom, which shall never be destroyed:
and the kingdom shall not be left to other people, *but* it
shall break in pieces and consume all these kingdoms, and
45 it shall stand for ever. Forasmuch as thou sawest that the
stone was cut out of the mountain without hands, and *that*
it brake in pieces the iron, the brass, the clay, the silver,
and the gold; the great God hath made known to the king
what shall come to pass hereafter: and the dream *is* certain,
and the interpretation thereof sure.

42. so *the kingdom*, &c.] so **part of** *the kingdom shall be strong, and* **part of it** *shall be broken*.

43. *shall* **be mingling** *themselves* **by** *the seed of men*] i.e. will contract matrimonial alliances. By 'seed of men' are meant probably children of the monarchs ruling at the time.

is not mixed with clay] **doth not mingle** *with clay*. The allusion in this verse is to matrimonial alliances contracted between the Ptolemies and the Seleucidae (cf. xi. 6, 17), which did not, however, succeed in producing permanent harmony or union between them.

44, 45. The kingdom of God, to succeed these kingdoms.

44. *in the days of these kings*] i.e. of the Seleucidae and Ptolemies, as is implied by the part of the image on which the stone falls (*v*. 34). The period in the history of these monarchies which is more particularly referred to is the reign of Antiochus Epiphanes (B.C. 175—164), whose fall, according to the representation of the book of Daniel (cf. vii. 25—27, xi. 45—xii. 3), was to be succeeded immediately by the establishment of the kingdom of God.

shall never be destroyed] in contrast to the previous kingdoms, which, from different causes, had all perished. Cf. vii. 14.

and the kingdom, &c.] **nor shall the sovereignty thereof** *be left to* **another** *people*. It will endure for ever; and its power will never be transferred to another people. The expression implies that the Divine kingdom itself is in the hands of a people, viz. Israel.

break in pieces] cf. *vv*. 34, 35.

and it shall stand for ever] the *it* is emphatic.

45. *Forasmuch as* thou hast seen in thy dream this colossal image preternaturally destroyed (*vv*. 34, 35), **a** *great God hath* let thee see behind the veil of the future, and *made known to thee what will come to pass hereafter* (cf. Gen. xli. 28).

a *great God*] the original is indefinite, not definite: Daniel speaks from the standpoint of the heathen king.

the dream is certain, &c.] an asseveration of the truth of what has

Then the king Nebuchadnezzar fell upon his face, and 46 worshipped Daniel, and commanded that *they* should offer an oblation and sweet odours unto him. The king answered 47 unto Daniel, and said, Of a truth *it is*, that your God *is* a God of gods, and a Lord of kings, and a revealer of secrets,

been stated, in the apocalyptic style: cf. viii. 26, x. 1, xi. 2; Rev. xxi. 5, xxii. 6.

46—48. Nebuchadnezzar is profoundly impressed by Daniel's skill, and bestows upon him high honour and rewards (cf. the promise of *v.* 6).

46. *fell upon his face*] a mark of respect—whether to God, as Gen. xvii. 3, or to men, 2 Sam. ix. 6, xiv. 4.

and worshipped Daniel] **bowed down to** Daniel,—the word used in iii. 5, 6, 7 &c. of adoration paid to a deity. In the Targums, however, the same word is used (for the Heb. *to prostrate oneself to*) of obeisance done to a human superior (as 2 Sam. xiv. 33, xviii. 21, 28, xxiv. 20); so that it does not necessarily imply the payment of divine honour.

that they *should offer*] lit. *pour out*,—the word used of pouring out a libation or drink-offering (2 Ki. xvi. 13, and elsewhere), though here employed evidently in a more general sense.

an oblation] The word means properly *a present*, especially one offered as a mark of homage or respect (Gen. xxxii. 13, xliii. 11); it is also used generally in the sense of an *oblation* presented to God (Gen. iv. 3, 4, 5; 1 Sam. ii. 17), as well as technically, in the priestly terminology, of the 'meal-offering' (Lev. iii. &c.). The second of these three senses is the most probable here.

sweet odours] lit. *rests* or *contentments*. The word is that which occurs in the sacrificial expression '*sweet* savour' (Gen. viii. Lev. i. 2, &c.), lit. 'savour of *rest* or *contentment*': it is used (exceptionally) without 'savour,' exactly as here, in Ezr. vi. 10, 'that they may offer *rests* (or *contentments*) to the God of heaven.' 'Bowed down to' is ambiguous; but the subsequent parts of the verse certainly represent Daniel as receiving the homage due to a god. Daniel does not refuse the homage (contrast Acts xiv. 13—18): in the view of the writer, he is (cf. *v.* 47) the representative of the God of gods to Nebuchadnezzar. Compare the story in Jos. *Ant.* XI. viii. 5, according to which Alexander the Great prostrated himself before the Jewish high-priest, and when asked by his astonished general, Parmenio, why he did so, replied, "I do not worship the high-priest, but the God with whose high-priesthood he has been honoured."

47. *a God...a Lord*] **the** *God*...**the** *Lord*. Nebuchadnezzar acknowledges the supremacy of Daniel's God over all other gods, and His sovereignty over all kings. 'Lord of lords' (bêl bêlê), and 'Lord of gods' (bêl ilâni), are titles often given by the Babylonian kings (including Nebuchadnezzar) to Marduk, the supreme god of Babylon; but it is doubtful whether the terms here used were chosen with allusion to the fact. 'God of gods,' as Deut. x. 17; Ps. cxxxvi. 2; ch. xi. 36.

a revealer of secrets] as Daniel had averred, *v.* 28; cf. *v.* 22.

48 seeing thou couldest reveal this secret. Then the king made Daniel a great man, and gave him many great gifts, and made him ruler over the whole province of Babylon, and chief of the governors over all the wise *men* of Babylon.
49 Then Daniel requested of the king, and he set Shadrach, Meshach, and Abed-nego, over the affairs of the province of Babylon: but Daniel *sat* in the gate of the king.

couldest] better, **hast been able to**.
48. *made Daniel a great man*] *made Daniel* **great**, i.e. advanced, promoted him.
made him **to rule**, &c.] i.e., probably, made him administrator of the principal province of the empire, in which the capital was; opp. to the local 'provinces,' iii. 2.
and (appointed him) *chief of the* **praefects** *over*, &c.] The idea appears to be (Hitz., Keil, Pusey, p. 20) that each division, or class (*v.* 2), of the 'wise men' had its own head; and Daniel was promoted to have the supervision of them all. Cf. iv. 9, v. 11 ('made him chief of the magicians, enchanters, Chaldeans, and determiners of fates'). 'Praefect' (*s^egan*, Heb. *sāgān*) recurs iii. 2, 3, 27, vi. 7; and is found also in Jer. li. 23, 28, 57; Ez. xxiii. 6, 12, 23; Is. xli. 25 (A.V. in Jer., Ez. *rulers*, in Is. *princes*; R.V. always *deputy* or *ruler*). It is a Hebraized form of the Assyrian *shaknu* (from *shakânu*, to appoint), a word used constantly in the inscriptions of the 'praefect' appointed by the Assyrian king to govern a conquered district, or a city. Here the term is used more generally, as it is also in Ezr. ix. 2, Neh. ii. 16, iv. 14, 19, v. 7, 17, vii. 5, xii. 40, xiii. 11, of certain civic officials in Jerusalem (A.V., R.V., 'ruler').
On the historical difficulty arising out of this statement respecting Daniel, see the Introd. p. lv, *note*.
49. At Daniel's request, his three companions are transferred from the ranks of those who 'stood before the king' (i. 19) to positions of authority over the 'business of the province of Babylon,'—i.e., probably, to act as deputies or assistants to Daniel himself. Daniel's motive in making this request may have been either simply the promotion of his three friends, or (Hitz., Keil, Meinh.) that he himself might be relieved of duties necessitating his absence from Nebuchadnezzar's court.
but Daniel was *in the gate of the king*] at the main entrance to the palace; fig. for, he remained at court (Sept. ἐν τῇ βασιλικῇ αὐλῇ). Cf. Est. ii. 19, 21, where it is said that Mordecai 'sat in the king's gate' (cf. iii. 2, 3; iv. 2, 6, v. 9, 13, vi. 10, 12); and Xen. *Cyrop.* VIII. i. 6 (cf. Hdt. iii. 120), where this is said to have been the usual custom with the officials of the Persian court. The verse is apparently written in view of chap. iii. (see *vv.* 3 *end*, 12).

Additional Note on '*Excellent*' and '*Excellency*.'

The following synopsis of the occurrences of these words in A.V., R.V., and in the P.B. Version of the Psalms, may illustrate and support what is said above with regard to their meaning in these versions.

Excellency stands for

יֶתֶר *superiority*: A.V., R.V. Gen. xlix. 3; A.V. Job iv. 21; and in 'have the excellency' for הוֹתִיר *to shew superiority*, Gen. xlix. 4 R.V.

יִתְרוֹן *superiority*: A.V., R.V. Eccl. vii. 12.

גָּאוֹן *majesty*, fig. *glory, pride*: A.V., R.V. Ex. xv. 7, Ps. xlvii. 4, Is. lx. 15, Am. vi. 8 (R.V. *marg.* pride), viii. 7, Nah. ii. 2; A.V. Job xxxvii. 4 (R.V. majesty), Is. xiii. 19 (R.V. glory), Ez. xxiv. 21 (R.V. pride); R.V. Job xl. 10.

גֵּאוּה *majesty*: A.V., R.V. Deut. xxxiii. 26, 29, Ps. lxviii. 34.

שְׂאֵת *uprising, loftiness, dignity*: A.V., R.V. Job xiii. 11, Ps. lxii. 4; R.V. Job xxxi. 23.

שִׂיא *loftiness, dignity*: A.V., R.V. Job xx. 6.

גֹּבַהּ *height*, fig. *loftiness*: A.V. Job xl. 10 (R.V. dignity).

יֶקֶר *preciousness*, fig. *beauty*: R.V. Ps. xxxvii. 20[1].

הָדָר *glory, splendour*: A.V., R.V. Is. xxxv. 2 (*bis*).

ὑπεροχή *superiority*: A.V., R.V. 1 Cor. ii. 1.

ὑπερβολή *excess*: A.V. 2 Cor. iv. 7 (R.V. exceeding greatness).

τὸ ὑπερέχον *the surpassingness*: A.V., R.V. Phil. iii. 8.

ἀρετή *virtue*: R.V. 1 Pet. ii. 9[1].

And *excellent* is used for

גְּדוּלָּה *greatness*: A.V., R.V. Est. i. 4 (lit. the majesty of his *greatness*).

שַׂגִּיא *great*: A.V., R.V. Job xxxvii. 23.

אַדִּיר *grand, glorious* (Is. xxxiii. 21), *noble* (Judg. v. 13): P.B.V., A.V., R.V. Ps. viii. 1, 9; A.V., R.V. Ps. xvi. 3, lxxvi. 4.

יָקָר *precious*: P.B.V., A.V. Ps. xxxvi. 7 (R.V. precious); A.V. Prov. xvii. 27 (following the Qrê: R.V. follows the K'tib).

לְמַעְלָה *upwards* (paraphrased): P.B.V. Ps. lxxiv. 6 (based on Seb. Münster's rendering, *ad sublime aliquid*).

נִכְבָּד *glorious*: P.B.V. Ps. lxxxvii. 2.

נִשְׂגָּב *exalted*: P.B.V. Ps. cxxxix. 5 (A.V., R.V. high); P.B.V., A.V. Ps. cxlviii. 12 [A. V. 13] (R.V. exalted).

רֹאשׁ *head*, fig. *top, chiefness*: A.V. Ps. cxli. 5 (lit. oil of *chiefness*).

רֹב *abundance*: P.B.V., A.V., R.V. Ps. cl. 2 (lit. the *abundance* of his greatness).

נְגִידִים *princely things*: A.V., R.V. Prov. viii. 6.

יֶתֶר *superior*: A.V. Prov. xii. 26 (R.V. derives the word differently).

יֶתֶר *superiority*: A.V., R.V. Prov. xvii. 7 (lit. speech of *superiority*).

שָׁלִישִׁים *captain-like* (?), i.e. *noble* (?) things: A.V., R.V. Prov. xxii. 20.

---

[1] Used here in its weakened modern sense.

בחור *choice*: A.V., R.V. Cant. v. 15 ('excellent as the cedars').
גאון *majesty*: A.V., R.V. Is. iv. 2 (R.V. *marg.* majestic).
גאות *majesty*: A.V., R.V. Is. xii. 5.
הגדיל *to make great*: A.V., R.V. Is. xxviii. 29 ('is excellent [i.e. is surpassing] in wisdom,' lit. *maketh* wisdom *great*).
יתיר *surpassing*: A.V., R.V. Dan. ii. 31, iv. 36, v. 12, 14, vi. 3.

τὰ διαφέροντα *the things that excel* (or *are of value*, Mt. x. 31) R.V. Rom. ii. 18 (A.V. more excellent); A.V., R.V. Phil. i. 10.
μεγαλοπρεπής *magnificent, transcendent*, A.V., R.V. 2 Pet. i. 17.
In Ps. cxxxvi. 5 P.B.V. there is nothing in the Heb. corresponding to *excellent*, though it evidently means *surpassing*; and in Ez. xvi. 7 A.V., R.V., 'ornament of ornaments' (i.e. choicest ornament) is paraphrased by *excellent ornament(s)*.

More excellent is used in Eccl. vii. 11 R.V. for יותר *superior;* in Rom. ii. 18 A.V. for διαφέροντα; and in A.V., R.V. 1 Cor. xii. 31 in the rendering of τὴν καθ' ὑπερβολὴν ὁδόν; Heb. i. 4, viii. 6 for διαφορώτερος; Heb. xi. 4 for πλείων. *Most excellent* represents κράτιστος in A.V., R.V. Luke i. 3, Acts xxiii. 26, and in R.V. Acts xxiv. 3, xxvi. 25.

Cf. in the Collect for St Peter's Day, 'many *excellent* gifts,' in the Collect for Quinquagesima Sunday, 'that *most excellent* gift of charity' (with allusion to 1 Cor. xii. 31, just quoted), in the form of Solemnization of Matrimony, 'who hast consecrated the state of Matrimony to such an *excellent* mystery,' and in the Ordering of Priests, 'as your office is...of so great *excellency*,'—all in the sense of *pre-eminent, pre-eminency*.

In view of the weakened sense in which both these words are used in modern times, it is to be regretted that they have been retained in R.V. in passages in which the real meaning is something so very different. Let the reader mark on the margin of his Revised Version the true meaning of the Hebrew (and Greek) in the passages in which it is not already given; and he will find (in most cases) how greatly they gain in expressiveness and force.

CHAP. III. DANIEL'S THREE COMPANIONS RESCUED FROM THE FURNACE.

Nebuchadnezzar erects in the plain of Dura, near Babylon, a colossal golden image, and assembles for its dedication the high officials of his kingdom, all being commanded, under penalty of being cast into a burning fiery furnace, to fall down at a given signal and worship it (*vv.* 1—7). Daniel's three companions, Shadrach, Meshach, and Abed-nego, refusing to do this, are cast into the furnace; but, to the king's surprise, are wonderfully delivered from the power of the flame (*vv.* 8—27). Thereupon Nebuchadnezzar solemnly acknowledges the power of their God, issues a decree threatening death to any who presume to blaspheme Him, and bestows upon the three men various marks of favour (*vv.* 28—30).

v. 1.]   DANIEL, III.   35

Nebuchadnezzar the king made an image of gold, whose 3

The narrative has a didactic aim. It depicts a signal example of religious heroism; and at the same time presents a striking concrete illustration of the words of the second Isaiah (xliii. 2), 'When thou walkest through the fire, thou shalt not be burnt; neither shall the fire kindle upon thee.' Circumstances sometimes arise, under which it may be a point of duty for the faithful servant of God to prefer death to apostasy; and the three Jewish youths are represented as yielding themselves courageously to a martyr's death, without the least expectation that they would be delivered from it. In the time of the Maccabees (see 1 Macc. i. 62, 63; and the words of Mattathias, ii. 19—22), as also during the persecutions in the early centuries of Christianity, the alternative, martyrdom or apostasy, became a very real one; and constancy and faith won many splendid triumphs.

There was a popular Jewish legend respecting Abraham that for refusing to worship Nimrod's gods he was cast by him into a furnace of fire, and miraculously delivered[1].

1—7. Nebuchadnezzar's proclamation regarding the image.

1. *Nebuchadnezzar*] Sept., Theod., Pesh. prefix 'In the eighteenth year,' which would be the year before Jerusalem was finally taken by the Chaldaeans (2 Ki. xxv. 8). Sept. also has an addition stating the occasion on which the image was erected: it was while he was 'organizing (διοικῶν) cities and countries, and all the inhabitants of the earth, from India to Ethiopia.' The addition is probably nothing but a Midrashic embellishment: we at least know nothing from any other source of Nebuchadnezzar's empire as extending to the limits named, or of his conducting military expeditions except in the direction of Syria, Palestine, and Egypt (*ex*clusive of Ethiopia).

made an image of gold, &c.] The expression does not mean necessarily that it was of solid gold; it might be used of an image that was merely (in the ancient fashion) overlaid with gold: the 'altar of gold' of Ex. xxxix. 38 was in reality only overlaid with gold (Ex. xxx. 3). It is not expressly stated what the image represented; it is not however described as the image of a god, so in all probability it represented Nebuchadnezzar himself. It was a common practice of the Assyrian kings to erect images of themselves with laudatory inscriptions in conquered cities, or provinces, as symbols of their dominion, the usual expression in such cases being *ṣa-lam šarrû-ti-a* (*šur-ba-a*) *ipu-uš*, " a (great) image of my royalty I made "; see *KB*. i. 69, l. 98 f.; 73, l. 5; 99, l. 25; 133, l. 31; 135, l. 71; 141, l. 93; 143, l. 124; 147, l. 156; 155, l. 26, &c. (all from the reigns of Asshur-naṣir-abal, B.C. 885—860, and Shalmaneṣer II., B.C. 860—825). Jastrow (*Relig. of Bab. and Ass.*, 1898, p. 669) remarks that, inasmuch as in the inscriptions the victories of the armies were commonly ascribed to the help of the gods, a homage

---

[1] See Hastings' *Dict. of the Bible*, i. 17, Beer, *Leben Abraham's nach der Jüd. Sage*, p. 11 ff.; and cf. Ball, Pref. to the Song of the Three Children, in the *Speaker's Comm. on the Apocrypha*, ii. 305—7 (where also various Talmudic and Midrashic developments of the narrative of Dan. iii. are quoted).

height *was* threescore cubits, *and* the breadth thereof six cubits: he set it up in the plain of Dura, in the province of Babylon. Then Nebuchadnezzar the king sent to gather together the princes, the governors, and the captains, the

to some deity would be involved in the recital, though no instance is at present known of divine honours being paid to such statues.

threescore cubits, &c.] The image was thus some 90 feet high, and 9 broad. The disproportion of height and breadth—in the human figure the proportion is commonly 5—6 to 1—has not been satisfactorily explained. The dimensions themselves, also, are greater than are probable: but the 'India House Inscription,' by its descriptions of the decorations of temples, testifies to the amount of gold that was at Nebuchadnezzar's disposal: and Oriental monarchs have always prided themselves on the immense quantities of the precious metals in their possession.

set it up] "'to set up an image' (the same words in the Aram.) is the usual phrase in the heathen inscriptions of Palmyra and the Ḥaurān' (Bevan); see e.g. de Vogué, *Syrie Centrale* (1868), Nos. 4, 5, 7, 10, 11.

plain] properly a broad 'cleft,' or level (Is. xl. 4 *end*) plain, between mountains (see on Am. i. 5).

Dura] An inscription cited by Friedrich Delitzsch (*Paradies*, p. 216) mentions in Babylonia three places called *Dûru*. According to Oppert (*Expéd. en Mésopotamie*, i. 238 f.; cf. the chart of the environs of Babylon in Smith, *DB*., s.v. BABEL), there is a small river called the *Dura*, flowing into the Euphrates from the S., 6 or 7 miles below Babylon; and near this river, about 12 miles S.S.E. of Hillah, there are a number of mounds called the *Tolûl* (or *Mounds of*) *Dûra*. One of these, called *el-Mokhaṭṭaṭ*, consists of a huge rectangular brick structure, some 45 ft. square and 20 ft. high, which may, in Oppert's opinion, have formed once the pedestal of a colossal image.

2. *princes*] **satraps**, Aram. *'achashdarpan*,—both this and the Gk. ἐξατράπης, σατράπης, being corruptions of the Old Persian *kshatrapāwan*, lit. 'protector of the realm,' but denoting by usage (cf. on vi. 1) the chief ruler of a province. The term, as is well known, is a standing Persian one: in the O.T., it recurs *vv*. 3, 27, vi. 1, 2, 3, 4, 6, 7 (A.V. *princes*); and Ezr. viii. 36, Est. iii. 12, viii. 9, ix. 3 (A.V. *lieutenants*); R.V. always *satraps*. The use of the word here is an anachronism: both the name and the office were Persian, not Babylonian.

governors] **praefects**. The word (*s⁽gan*) explained on ii. 48.

captains] **governors** (R.V.), Aram. *pechah*, a term also (like *s⁽gan*) of Assyrian origin, often used in Assyrian of the governor of a conquered province. It found its way into Hebrew, and is used in the O.T. both of an Assyrian officer (Is. xxxvi. 9 = 2 Ki. xviii. 24: A.V., R.V. *captain*), of Babylonian officers (Jer. li. 57; Ez. xxiii. 6, 12, 23: A.V. *captains*, R.V. *governors*), and especially, in post-exilic writings, of the governor of a Persian province (Hag. i. 1, ii. 2; Mal. i. 8; Ezr. v. 3, 6; Neh. ii. 7, 9, and elsewhere); as well as once or twice more generally (1 Ki. xx. 24; Jer. li. 23, 28). In Dan. it recurs *vv*. 3, 27, vi. 7.

judges, the treasurers, the counsellors, the sheriffs, and all the rulers of the provinces, to come to the dedication of the image which Nebuchadnezzar the king had set up. Then 3 the princes, the governors and captains, the judges, the treasurers, the counsellors, the sheriffs, and all the rulers of the provinces, were gathered together unto the dedication of the image that Nebuchadnezzar the king had set up; and they stood before the image that Nebuchadnezzar had set

judges] So *v.* 3. Aram. *'adargāzar*, in all probability the old Pers. *andar-zaghar*, later Pers. *endarzgar*, 'counsel-giver,' a title which was still in use under the Sassanian kings (Nöldeke, *Tabari*, p. 462). R.V. *marg.* 'chief soothsayers' implies a very improbable etymology.

treasurers] So *v.* 3: Aram. *gᵉdābar*. An uncertain word. It *may* be a textual corruption, or a faulty pronunciation, of *gizbār*, 'treasurer' (Pehlevi *ganzavar*, Pers. *ganjvar*), which is found in Ezr. i. 8, vii. 21; it *may* have arisen by dittography from the following *dᵉthābar*[1]; it *may* be an error for *haddābar* (in the plur., גדבריא for הדבריא), the word which occurs in *vv.* 24, 27, iv. 36, vi. 7 (see on *v.* 24).

counsellers] **justices** (so *v.* 3): Aram. *dᵉthābar*, from the Old Pers. *dātabara*, Pehlevi *dātōbar*, Modern Pers. *dāwar*, properly 'law-bearer,' from *dāt*, 'law,' and *bar*, an affix meaning 'bearer.' Cf. the βασιλήϊοι δικασταί of Hdt. iii. 14, 31, v. 25, vii. 194. This word has been found by Hilprecht (frequently) in the commercial inscriptions belonging to the reigns of Artaxerxes I. and Darius II. (B.C. 465—425, 424—405), excavated recently at Nippur by the expedition organized by the American University of Pennsylvania.

sheriffs] Aram. *tiphtāyê*; only found besides in *v.* 3, and of very uncertain meaning. Bevan thinks it may be the mutilated form of some Persian title ending in *pat*, 'chief'; and so Behrmann compares the Sanskr. *adhipati*, which would correspond to an Old Pers. *adipati*, 'over-chief.' The word has been found recently as the name of an official in an Aramaic inscription from Egypt, dating B.C. 411[2]. *Lawyers* (R.V. *marg.*) depends upon an improbable connexion with the Arab. *'aftā*, to notify a decision of the law (whence *Mufti*, a jurisconsult).

and all the rulers of the provinces] conceived apparently as subordinate to the 'satraps,' and so as forming the class in which Shadrach, Meshach, and Abed-nego were included (ii. 49). It has often been asked, where was Daniel? Possibly he is to be regarded as not included in the classes of officials enumerated, on account of his exceptional position at the court (ii. 49): but in point of fact the narrative seems to be written without reference to Daniel; so that more probably the question is one which the author did not deem it necessary to answer.

3. The names of officials are the same as in *v.* 2.

---

[1] It is some support to this view that whereas the Aramaic text has in both *v.* 2 and *v.* 3 *eight* names of officials, the Sept. and Theod. have each only seven: see Lagarde's lucid exposition of the facts in *Agathangelus*, p. 157.

[2] *Répertoire d'épigraphie Sémitique*, i. No. 361.

4 up. Then a herald cried aloud, To you it is commanded,
5 O people, nations, and languages, *that* at what time ye hear
the sound of the cornet, flute, harp, sackbut, psaltery,

4. And the *herald cried aloud*] lit. *with might:* so iv. 14, v. 7; and
in Heb. (though the substantive is a different one) Jonah iii. 8.

peoples, nations, and languages] the same pleonastic combination,
vv. 7, 29, iv. 1, v. 19, vi. 25, vii. 14; cf. also Is. lxvi. 18. Similarly
Rev. v. 9, vii. 9, x. 11, xi. 9, xiii. 7, xiv. 6, xvii. 16. Here the
combination is no doubt used under the idea that strangers from
different countries ruled by Nebuchadnezzar, as well as from other
parts (such as were always to be found in Babylon: Is. xiii. 14*b*, xlvii.
15; Jer. l. 16), would be present on such an occasion.

peoples] i.e. nations, a sense not now expressed by the English
'people.' See the remarks on this word in the Preface to the Revised
Version of the O.T.

5. *cornet*] lit. *horn*: so *vv.* 7, 10, 15; elsewhere in this sense only
in the 'ram's horn,' Jos. vi. 5. The usual Hebrew name for this (or
some similar) instrument is *shōphār*. The word used here (*karnā*) is,
however, common in the same sense in Syriac.

flute] **pipe**, Aram. *mashrōḳītha* (from the root *shᵉraḳ*, to hiss, Heb.
שָׁרַק, Is. v. 26), not the word usually rendered 'flute,' and found besides
(in the O. T.) only in *vv.* 7, 10, 15. It occurs, though very rarely
(P. S. Col. 4339), in Syriac in the same sense.

harp] or *lyre*, Aram. *kitharos*, i.e. the Greek κίθαρις: so *vv.* 7, 10, 15.

sackbut] **trigon** (*vv.* 7, 10, 15), Aram. *sabbeka*, whence no doubt the
Gk. σαμβύκη was derived, which was a small triangular instrument, of
the nature of a harp, but possessing only four strings (see Athen. IV.
p. 175, *d, e*, where it is said to be a *Syrian* invention; XIV. p. 633 f.;
and the other passages cited by Gesenius in his *Thesaurus*, p. 935).
Sambucistriae and *psaltriae* (see the next word) are mentioned by Livy
(xxxix. 6) as a luxurious accompaniment at banquets, introduced into
Rome from the East in 187 B.C. (The mediaeval 'sackbut,'—Span.
sacabuche, a sackbut, and also a *tube* used as a pump: from *sacar*, to
draw out, and *bucha*, a box,—meaning properly a tube that can be
drawn out at will, was something quite different, viz. "a bass trumpet
with a slide like the modern trombone," Chappell, *Music of the most
Ancient Nations*, i. 35, as quoted in Wright's *Bible Word-Book*, s.v.)

psaltery] Aram. *psanṭērīn*, i.e. ψαλτήριον: so *vv.* 7, 10, 15. The
Greek ψαλτήριον, and the Latin *psalterium*, was a stringed instrument,
of triangular shape, like an inverted Δ: it differed from the *cithara* (as
Augustine repeatedly states) in having the sounding-board *above* the
strings, which were played with a plectrum and struck downwards[1].
The number of strings in the ancient psaltery appears to have varied.
The 'psaltery' is often mentioned in old English writers: in Chaucer it
appears in the form 'sawtrie,' or 'sauterie,' as *Manciple's Tale*, 17,200,

---

[1] Isid. *Etym.* iii. 22. 7; Cassiod. *Praef. in Psalm.* c. iv; Augustine on Ps. lvi.
(iv. 539 a—b, ed. Bened.), and elsewhere (see the Index); also Vergil, *Ciris* 177 'Non
arguta sonant tenui psalteria chorda.'

dulcimer, and all kinds of musick, ye fall down and worship the golden image that Nebuchadnezzar the king hath set up: and whoso falleth not down and worshippeth shall the same 6 hour be cast into the midst of a burning fiery furnace.

"Bothe harp and lute, gitern and *sauterie*"; and Shakespeare, for instance, speaks of "the trumpets, sackbuts, *psalteries*, and fifes" (*Coriol.* v. 4. 53). The name, in the form *sanṭīr*, passed also into Arabic; and the instrument, under this name, is mentioned in the *Arabian Nights*, and is in use also in modern Egypt[1].

dulcimer] bagpipe: Aram. *sūmpōnyāh*, i.e. the Greek συμφωνία. Συμφωνία, which in Plato and Aristotle has the sense of *harmony* or *concord*, came in later Greek to denote a *bagpipe*, an instrument consisting essentially of a combination of pipes, supplied with wind from a bladder blown by the mouth, and called 'symphonia,' on account of the combination of sounds produced by it, one pipe (called the 'chaunter') producing the melody, and three others the fixed accompaniments, or 'drones.' It is remarkable that Polybius employs the same word of the music used, on festive occasions, by Antiochus Epiphanes[2]. *Sūmpōnyāh* is found, in the same sense, in the Mishna[3]; and it passed likewise into Latin[4], and hence into several of the Romance languages, as Ital. *zampogna*; Old Fr. *Chyfonie, Chiffonie* (v. Ducange). In Syriac, it appears in the form צפוניא, which also denotes a kind of flute (Payne Smith, col. 3430). (The *dulcimer* was an entirely different kind of instrument, consisting of a trapèze-shaped frame, with a number of strings stretched across it, which was laid horizontally on a table, and played by a small hammer, held in the hand,—a rudimentary form of the modern pianoforte.)

worship] lit. *bow down to* (ii. 46). So regularly.

6. *the same hour*] Cf. *v.* 15, iv. 33, v. 5 (also 'hour' alone, iv. 16). The expression is common in Syriac, as in the Pesh. of Mt. viii. 3, xxvii. 48; Mk. i. 42; Acts xi. 11, 16; comp. (in the Greek) Mt. viii. 13, x. 19, xviii. 1, Luke ii. 38, vii. 21, x. 21, and elsewhere. 'Hour' (*shāʿāh*) does not occur in Biblical Hebrew; but it is common in

---

[1] Dozy, *Supplément aux Dict. Arabes*, i. 694; Lane, *Modern Egyptians*, ii. 70. The LXX used ψαλτήριον (sometimes) for the Heb. *nēbel* and *kinnōr*. Elsewhere in A.V. or R.V. where 'psaltery' occurs (as Ps. xxxiii. 2), it always represents *nēbel*.

[2] Polyb. xxvi. 10, as cited by Athen. v. 21, p. 193 d—e (and similarly x. 52, p. 439 a) Antiochus Epiphanes associated with very common boon companions—ὅτε δὲ τῶν νεωτέρων αἴσθοιτό τινας συνευωχουμένους, οὐδεμίαν ἔμφασιν ποιήσας παρῆν ἐπικωμάζων μετὰ κεραμίου (or κερατίου) καὶ συμφωνίας, ὥστε τοὺς πολλοὺς διὰ τὸ παράδοξον ἀνισταμένους φεύγειν; and xxxi. 4 (Athen. x. 53, p. 439 d) καὶ τῆς συμφωνίας προκαλουμένης ὁ βασιλεὺς ἀναπηδήσας ὠρχεῖτο καὶ προσέπαιζε τοῖς μίμοις ὥστε πάντας αἰσχύνεσθαι. (Κεράμιον is *a jar* [of wine?]; Diod. Sic. xxix. 32 has κερατιον, lit. *a little horn* [κέρας denoted the *Phrygian flute*]. Συμφωνία means very probably not a band, but—as in Dan., and in the passages cited in the next note but one—a musical instrument.)

[3] Levy, *NHWB.* iii. 492ᵃ (*Kelim* xi. 6, xvi. 8); cf. 513ᵃ.

[4] As Pliny, *H. N.* viii. 64 (=the αὐλὸς of Athen. xii. 19, p. 520 c), ix. 24; Prudentius, *Symm.* ii. 527 'signum symphonia belli Aegyptis dederat, clangebat buccina contra'; Fortunatus, *Vit. Martin.* iv. 48, 'Donec plena suo cecinit symphonia flatu.'

7 Therefore at that time, when all the people heard the sound of the cornet, flute, harp, sackbut, psaltery, and all kinds of musick, all the people, the nations, and the languages, fell down *and* worshipped the golden image that Nebuchadnezzar the king had set up.
8 Wherefore at that time certain Chaldeans came near, and
9 accused the Jews. They spake and said to the king Nebu-
10 chadnezzar, O king, live for ever. Thou, O king, hast made a decree, that every man that shall hear the sound of the cornet, flute, harp, sackbut, psaltery, and dulcimer, and all kinds of musick, shall fall down and worship the golden
11 image: and whoso falleth not down and worshippeth, *that* he should be cast into the midst of a burning fiery furnace.
12 There are certain Jews whom thou hast set over the affairs

Aramaic (Targums and Syriac) and later Hebrew. Originally it denoted any small interval of time, and was only gradually fixed definitely to what we call an 'hour.'

shall be cast, &c.] Cruel punishments were in vogue among both the Assyrians and the Babylonians. In Jer. xxix. 12 allusion is made to two Jews, Zedekiah and Ahab, whom (for some reason not stated) 'the king of Babylon roasted in the fire.' (The statement, sometimes made, that Asshurbanipal's rebel brother, Shamash-shum-ukin, was punished in this manner, appears to rest on a misconception: see *KB.* ii. 191 [Annals iv. 50 f.], and Maspero, *Passing of the Empires*, p. 422.)

7. *sackbut*] **trigon.**

8—18. The accusation brought against the three Jewish youths, and their answer to the king.

8. *certain Chaldeans*] probably, though not here necessarily, the learned class among the Babylonians (as i. 4, ii. 2 &c.). See p. 12 ff.

accused] The figure in the original is a peculiar one, lit. '*ate the (torn) pieces of* the Jews.' The expression has commonly in Aramaic the sense of *falsely accuse*, or *slander*, as Ps. xv. 3 in the Targ., and in Syriac (e.g. Luke xvi. 1 for διαβάλλειν; and '*ākhēl ḳarzā* for ὁ διάβολος, the false accuser, or 'devil,' Mt. iv. 1, and regularly): here and vi. 24 it is used at least in the sense of *accuse maliciously*.

9. *spake*] **answered** (R.V.): see on ii. 20.

the king Nebuchadnezzar] **Nebuchadnezzar the king**,—the regular order in Aramaic (*vv.* 1, 2, 5, 7 &c.), and often in late Hebrew (as Hag. i. 1, 15; Neh. ii. 1, v. 14). In early Hebrew the order is almost uniformly 'the king David,' 'the king Solomon,' &c.

O king, live for ever] Cf. on ii. 4.

10. *sackbut, psaltery, and dulcimer*] **trigon**, *psaltery*, and **bagpipe**.

12. *whom thou hast set*, &c.] See ii. 49. The 'Chaldeans' were, no doubt, jealous of the Jewish captives being promoted to high positions; and accordingly took advantage of their refusal to conform to Nebu-

of the province of Babylon, Shadrach, Meshach, and Abed-nego; these men, O king, have not regarded thee: they serve not thy gods, nor worship the golden image which thou hast set up.

Then Nebuchadnezzar in *his* rage and fury commanded 13 to bring Shadrach, Meshach, and Abed-nego. Then they brought these men before the king. Nebuchadnezzar spake 14 and said unto them, *Is it* true, O Shadrach, Meshach, and Abed-nego, do not ye serve my gods, nor worship the golden image which I have set up? Now if ye be ready that at 15 what time ye hear the sound of the cornet, flute, harp, sackbut, psaltery, and dulcimer, and all kinds of musick, ye fall down and worship the image which I have made; *well:* but if ye worship not, ye shall be cast the same hour into the midst of a burning fiery furnace; and who *is* that God that shall deliver you out of my hands? Shadrach, Meshach, 16 and Abed-nego, answered and said to the king, O Nebuchadnezzar, we *are* not careful to answer thee in this matter. If 17 it be *so*, our God whom we serve *is* able to deliver us from

chadnezzar's edict, in order to represent them as ungrateful and disloyal to their royal master.

regarded] The Aram. phrase, which is peculiar, recurs in vi. 13 (14).

14. Is it *true*] Probably this is right (cf. Theod. εἰ ἀληθῶς; Pesh. *in truth*), though it requires a slight change in the text (הַאִזְדָא [see ii. 5, 8] for הַצְדָא). R.V. (with Ges.) *of purpose* (Hitz., Keil, *of malicious purpose*): upon this view the word would be a Hebraism[1], from the rare root found in 1 Sam. xxiv. 11; Ex. xxi. 13; Num. xxxv. 20, 22[2]: this however rather means *to lie in wait* (see R.V. of the passages quoted), being used of one *aiming at* the life of another, and the word found here would not be derived correctly even from this verb.

15. *sackbut, psaltery, and dulcimer*] **trigon,** *psaltery, and* **bagpipe.**

well] an aposiopesis, as e.g. Gen. xxx. 27, Ex. xxxii. 32, Luke xiii. 9; *Il.* i. 135 f. (von Lengerke).

who is the *God*] The sense is not appreciably affected; but 'that' is not philologically correct (comp. on ii. 38). The question is a defiant challenge, like those of Sennacherib, and the Rab-shakeh, Is. xxxvi. 19 f., xxxvii. 11 f.

16. are *not careful*] **have no need** (R.V.).

17. *If it be* so, &c.] **If our God** *whom we serve is able to deliver us,* **he will deliver** *us from the burning fiery furnace,* **and out of** *thine*

---

[1] The Syr. verb *ẓᵉdā* with derivatives, cited by Ges. in his *Thes.*, is not recognized by Payne Smith (who has only *ẓᵉdad*, from which the word found here could not be derived).

[2] Levy, *NHWB.* iv. 170, quotes also three examples (in the sense of *lying in wait*, or *capturing*) from Talmud and Midrash (cf. *Chald. Wörterb.* ii. 316).

the burning fiery furnace, and he will deliver *us* out of thine
18 hand, O king. But if not, be it known unto thee, O king,
that we will not serve thy gods, nor worship the golden
image which thou hast set up.
19 Then was Nebuchadnezzar full *of* fury, and the form of
his visage was changed against Shadrach, Meshach, and
Abed-nego: *therefore* he spake, and commanded that *they*
should heat the furnace one seven *times* more than *it was*
20 wont to be heat. And he commanded the most mighty men
that *were* in his army to bind Shadrach, Meshach, and Abed-
21 nego, *and* to cast *them* into the burning fiery furnace. Then
these men were bound in their coats, their hosen, and their

hand, O king, i.e. we shall be harmed neither by the fire, nor by any
other punishment which the king may decree.

18. But even if He cannot, or will not, do this, still we can never
fall down and worship thy gods. The three men shew the same
courage, the same unflinching determination not to compromise their
faith, which were shewn by the loyal Jews in the age of the Maccabees
(1 Macc. i. 62, 63; 2 Macc. vi. 18 ff., vii. &c.).

19—27. The three youths delivered from the flames.

19. *full* of] **filled** (A.V. *marg.*) **with** would be both more accurate
and more forcible.

than it was *wont,* &c.] *than it was* **proper**—or, **the rule**[1]— *for it
to be heated.*

20. the *most*] **certain** (lit. *men*: cf. in Heb. Dt. xiii. 13 (14); Jud.
xix. 22; 1 Ki. xi. 17).

21. *coats*] The meaning of the Aram. *sarbāl* (only here and *v.* 27) is
uncertain (see the very full discussion in Ges. *Thesaurus*); but on the
whole **mantles** is the most probable. This is the sense which the word
has in the Talmud[2], in which it occurs frequently (Ges. p. 971; Levy,
NHWB, s.v.), so that it has ancient usage in its favour. On the other
hand, Aq. and Theod. (σαράβαρα), LXX. in *v.* 27 (94), Symm. (ἀναξυ-
ρίδες), Pesh., express the meaning *trousers* (though of a looser kind than
those worn by us),—an article of dress known independently (from
Herod., and other authorities) to have been worn at least by the ancient
Scythians and Persians, and to have been called by them σαράβαρα.
The word, in the same sense, passed into Arabic, in the form *sirwāl*
(e.g. in Saadyah's version of Lev. vi. 3), as well as into several of the
Romance languages. In both these senses the word may be originally
Persian: in that of *mantle,* meaning properly (according to Andreas) a
head-covering (* *sarabāra*), for which in Persia the peasants often use
their mantle; in that of *trousers,* corresponding to the Mod. Pers.

[1] See in Onkelos Lev. v. 10. ix. 16, Num. xxix. 6, 21 (for Heb. כמשפט); and
the Targ. of Jer. xxii. 13, xxxii. 11.
[2] And so also, as a loan-word from the Aram., the Arabic *sirbāl*: see Fränkel,
Aram. Fremdwörter im Arab. (1886), p. 47.

hats, and their *other* garments, and were cast into the midst of the burning fiery furnace. Therefore because the king's 22 commandment *was* urgent, and the furnace exceeding hot, the flame of the fire slew those men that took up Shadrach, Meshach, and Abed-nego. And these three men, Shadrach, 23 Meshach, and Abed-nego, fell down bound into the midst of the burning fiery furnace.

Then Nebuchadnezzar the king was astonied, and rose up 24 in haste, *and* spake, and said unto his counsellers, Did not we cast three men bound into the midst of the fire? They

shalwār, 'under-breeches.' The Syriac form of σαράβαρα has however a different sibilant from the one which is here used; and, as Mr Stanley A. Cook remarks[1], 'mantles, long flowing robes, and therefore extremely liable to catch the flames,' are more likely to be specially mentioned in the present connexion than trousers, or (R.V.) hosen.

their hosen] Another uncertain word (Aram. *paṭṭish*). Sept. and Theod. render τιάραι, 'turbans'; Pesh. uses the same word, which, however, seems otherwise to be known only to the Syriac lexicographers, who explain it sometimes as a 'tunic,' sometimes as 'trousers,' sometimes as a kind of 'gaiter' (Payne Smith, *Thes. Syr.* col. 3098). R.V. *tunics*; marg. 'Or, *turbans*.'

hats] The rendering *hats* (or *caps*) is supported by the fact that the same word *karbāl* (in the fem.) seems in post-Bibl. Hebrew (Levy, *s.v.*) to denote some kind of covering for the head, and means certainly, both in the Talmud and in Syriac (P.S. 1810), the *comb* of a cock. Others, comparing what is apparently the cognate verb in 1 Ch. xv. 27, render *mantle*; but the text of the passage quoted is uncertain.

22. *urgent*] rather, **sharp** (ii. 15).

24. *was astonied*] 'astonied' is the old, and more correct, form of *astonished* (Old Eng. *astony, astonie*, from Old Fr. *estonner*, Lat. **extonare*). Here, however, the meaning is rather, **was alarmed**, the Aram. *tĕwah* being used in the Targums for Heb. words signifying *to fear*, as Gen. xxvii. 33; 1 Ki. i. 49.

rose up] from the seat, from which he had been watching the preparations at the furnace.

spake] properly **answered**, as *v.* 9. So *vv.* 26, 28.

counsellers] **ministers** ('counseller' is used—rightly—for an entirely different word in Ezr. vii. 14, 15, 2 Sam. xv. 12, *al.*), a word (*haddābar*) peculiar to Dan. (*v.* 27, iv. 36, vi. 7), and of uncertain meaning. The termination *bar* shews that it is of Persian origin (cf. *dethābar*, 'lawbearer,' *gizbar*, 'treasurer'), but the sense of the first part of the word is not clear (Andreas). The explanation 'associate-judge' is questionable, as it implies a contracted, modern form of *dethābar*, 'judge,' viz. *dāwar*.

[1] 'On the articles of dress mentioned in Dan. iii. 21,' in the *Journ. of Philology*, XXVI. (1899), p. 306 ff.

25 answered and said unto the king, True, O king. He answered and said, Lo, I see four men loose, walking in the midst of the fire, and they have no hurt; and the form of
26 the fourth *is* like the Son of God. Then Nebuchadnezzar came near to the mouth of the burning fiery furnace, *and* spake, and said, Shadrach, Meshach, and Abed-nego, ye servants of the most high God, come forth, and come *hither*. Then Shadrach, Meshach, and Abed-nego, came forth of

25. *loose*] the fire had burnt away the fetters, but left the bodies of the three youths untouched.

form] **aspect, appearance**, as ii. 31.

is like the Son of God] *is like* a **son** *of* (the) **gods**, i.e. a heavenly being or angel: cf. the 'sons of God' (or, of the gods) in Gen. vi. 2; Job i. 6 (where see Davidson's note), xxxviii. 7. The rendering 'the Son of God' cannot stand: *'ĕlōhim* is, indeed, used with a singular force in Hebrew, but the Aram. *'ĕlāhīn* is always a true plural (ii. 11, 47, iii. 12, 18, iv. 8, 9, 18, v. 4, 11, 14, 23), 'God' being in the Aram. of Ezra and Dan. denoted regularly by the sing. *'ĕlāh*. The meaning is simply that Nebuchadnezzar saw an angelic figure (LXX, ὁμοίωμα ἀγγέλου Θεοῦ) beside the three youths (cf. *v.* 28, 'his angel').

Between *v.* 23 and *v.* 24 LXX, and Theodotion, and following them the Vulgate (but with notes prefixed and added to the effect that Jerome did not find the passage in the Heb. text, but translated it from Theodotion), have a long insertion (*vv.* 24—90), which, after describing how the three youths walked in the midst of the fire, praising God (*v.* 24), narrates the confession and prayer of Azarias (*vv.* 25—45), and then, after another short descriptive passage (*vv.* 46—50), represents the three as uttering a doxology (*vv.* 52—56), which leads on into the hymn known familiarly as the *Benedicite* (*vv.* 57—90). This insertion constitutes the Apocryphal book called the 'Song of the Three Children.'

26. *mouth*] Aram. *door*.

God Most High] so iv. 2, v. 18, 21: without 'God,' iv. 17, 24, 25, 32, 34, vii. 25 (first time); and with the adj. in a more Hebraistic form, vii. 18, 22, 25 (second time), 27. The title is found in Hebrew, Gen. xiv. 18, 19, 20, 22 (of the deity of Melchizedek, identified by the narrator with Jehovah); elsewhere only in poetry, especially in the Psalms, as lvii. 2, though usually without 'God,' as ix. 3, xviii. 13: as applied to Jehovah, it is a title of dignity and respect, denoting Him as one who is *supreme*, whether over the earth, as ruler and governor of the world (e.g. Ps. xlvii. 2), or over other gods (e.g. Ps. xcv. 3: cf. Cheyne on Ps. vii. 18). It occurs not unfrequently with the same force in the Apocrypha, being used sometimes by Israelites (cf. Luke i. 32, 35, 76), and sometimes (as here and iv. 2, 34, cf. Is. xiv. 14) placed in the mouth of heathen speakers (1 Esdr. ii. 3, vi. 31, viii. 19, 21, *al.*: cf. Mark v. 7, Acts. xvi. 17): it is also common (as a title, without 'God') in the Book of Enoch, and in Jubilees (see Charles on xxxvi. 16). See more fully the art. MOST HIGH in Hastings' *Dict. of the Bible.*

the midst of the fire. And the princes, governors, and 27 captains, and the king's counsellors, being gathered together, saw these men, upon whose bodies the fire had no power, nor was a hair of their head singed, neither were their coats changed, nor the smell of fire had passed on them. *Then* 28 Nebuchadnezzar spake, and said, Blessed *be* the God of Shadrach, Meshach, and Abed-nego, who hath sent his angel, and delivered his servants that trusted in him, and have changed the king's word, and yielded their bodies, that they might not serve nor worship any god, except their own God Therefore I make a decree, That every people, nation, 29 and language, which speak any thing amiss against the God of Shadrach, Meshach, and Abed-nego, shall be cut in pieces, and their houses shall be made a dunghill: because there is no other God that can deliver after this sort. Then 30 the king promoted Shadrach, Meshach, and Abed-nego, in the province of Babylon.

27. *princes, governors, and captains*] **satraps, praefects,** *and* **governors.** See on *v.* 2.

counsellors] **ministers** (*v.* 24).

upon whose bodies, &c.] **that** *the fire had no power* **upon their bodies,** *nor was* **the** *hair,* &c.

coats] either **mantles,** or **trousers** (*v.* 21).

changed] viz. for the worse, a sense which the word often has in Aramaic. Cf. v. 6.

28—29. Nebuchadnezzar's doxology, and edict of toleration.

28. *spake*] **answered.**

Blessed, &c.] cf. the confessions in 1 Ki. x. 9; 2 Ch. ii. 12.

sent his angel] cf. Gen. xxiv. 7, 40; Ex. xxxiii. 2; Numb. xx. 16.

changed] i.e. frustrated: cf. Ezr. vi. 11, 12 ('alter'); and Ps. lxxxix. 39 in the Targ., 'thou hast *altered* the covenant.'

29. *I make a decree*] the same phrase (lit. *a decree is made by me*), in iv. 6 (cf. vi. 26); Ezr. iv. 11 (at the end), 19, v. 17, vi. 8, 11, vii. 13, 21.

people, nation, and language] *vv.* 4, 7.

any thing amiss] lit. any *neglect* or *error*: cf. the same word in vi. 4; Ezr. iv. 22, vi. 9 ('fail'). In the Targums it stands for the Heb. *shegāgāh,* or *mishgeh,* oversight, inadvertence, Gen. xliii. 12; Lev. iv. 2, v. 18.

cut in pieces, and...made a dunghill] see on ii. 5. The terms of the edict, it will be noticed, are inexact: 'every people, nation, and language' must stand for 'every one belonging to any people, nation, and language.' ('Their houses' is in the Aram. *his house.*)

30. *promoted*] **made to prosper** (cf. vi. 28), i.e. supported them in different ways in the discharge of their office, and so ensured their success (ii. 49).

4 Nebuchadnezzar the king, unto all people, nations, and

CHAP. IV. NEBUCHADNEZZAR'S MADNESS.

Nebuchadnezzar makes a proclamation to all peoples of the earth, in which he extols the power and greatness of the God of Israel (*vv.* 1—3, 34—37). The occasion of the proclamation is explained in *vv.* 4—33. Nebuchadnezzar had a dream, which the 'Chaldeans' were unable to interpret, but which was explained to him by Daniel. It was a symbolical prediction that a great humiliation would overtake the king: for seven years his reason would leave him; he would be deposed from his high estate, and driven to consort with cattle in the open fields, until he should learn that the Most High was the disposer of the kingdoms of the earth (*vv.* 4—27). At the end of twelve months, as the king was contemplating from his palace the city which he had built, the prediction was suddenly verified, and Nebuchadnezzar was bereft of his reason for seven years (*vv.* 28—33). At the end of that time he recovered; and as an acknowledgement of God's power and goodness towards him he issued his present proclamation (*vv.* 34—37). The actual confession is confined to *vv.* 2, 3, 37: the rest of the proclamation consisting of a narration of Nebuchadnezzar's dream and its fulfilment, which in *vv.* 19 —33 lapses even into the third person.

The chapter, like the preceding ones, has a didactic purpose. The character of the Chaldaean king is idealized: he is represented as the typical despot, proud, self-sufficient, and godless; and an incident of his life, recorded (probably) by tradition, is made the basis of a narrative illustrating the truth, that 'Pride goeth before destruction, and a haughty spirit before a fall' (Prov. xvi. 18). In point of fact, Nebuchadnezzar is shewn by his inscriptions to have been an extremely reverent and religious king (Introd., p. xxv f.); and though, no doubt, in the 'India House Inscription' he narrates with pride his buildings in Babylon, he both begins and ends with a full acknowledgement of his dependence upon Marduk, and with prayers for the continuance of his blessing. That he did not know the God of Israel was, naturally, a result of the circumstances of his position.

1—3. The Prologue of Nebuchadnezzar's proclamation.

1. *all the peoples, nations, and languages*] iii. **4.**

that dwell in all the earth] The hyperbole seems to us extravagant; but it must be remembered that 'all the earth' in the O.T. has not the meaning which we attach to the expression, but denotes (substantially) Western Asia, from Elam and Media on the E., to Egypt and the 'isles of the sea' (i.e. the E. part of the Mediterranean Sea[1]) on the West, and that the greater part of this did fall within the real or nominal sovereignty of the Assyrian and Babylonian kings (cf. of Nebuchadnezzar himself, Jer. xxv. 26, "all the kingdoms which are upon the face of the earth," and the preceding enumeration, *vv.* 17—25; xxvii. 5—6). Standing titles of the Assyrian kings are 'king of multitudes' (=of the world), 'king of the four quarters of the earth'; and the same titles are adopted by Nabu-na'id, the last king of Babylon (*KB.* iii. 2, p. 97).

---

[1] Though of course a few places to the W. of this were known, e.g. Tarshish.

languages, that dwell in all the earth; Peace be multiplied unto you. I thought it good to shew the signs and wonders 2 that the high God hath wrought toward me. How great 3 *are* his signs! and how mighty *are* his wonders! his kingdom *is* an everlasting kingdom, and his dominion *is* from generation to generation.

I Nebuchadnezzar was at rest in mine house, and flourish- 4 ing in my palace: I saw a dream which made me afraid, 5 and the thoughts upon my bed and the visions of my head

The Persian kings call themselves similarly, 'the great king, the king of kings, the king of the lands, the king of this great earth' (*RP.*² ix. 73 ff.).

Peace be multiplied unto you] so vi. 25: cf. 1 Pet. i. 2; 2 Pet. i. 2.

2. *I thought it good*] better (R.V.) **It hath seemed good unto me.**

to shew] *to* **declare** (ii. 4). 'Shew' suggests here, at least to modern readers, a wrong sense.

signs and wonders] similarly in Darius's decree (vi. 27). Cf. 'signs and portents,' Deut. iv. 34, vi. 22, vii. 19 *al.* (where the Targ. of Pseudo-Jon. represents 'portents' by the same word 'wonders,' which is used here). The meaning is, significant and surprising evidences of power. The phraseology of the proclamation, both in *vv.* 2, 3, and also in *vv.* 34, 35, 37, betrays its Jewish author.

the high God] **God Most High** (iii. 26).

toward] lit. *with*, i.e. (in dealing) with: cf. Ps. lxxxvi. 17 Heb.

3. *an everlasting kingdom* (מלכות עלם)] cf. Ps. cxlv. 13 (מלכות כל עולמים).

is from, &c.] more exactly, (endureth) **with** *generation* **and** *generation* (i.e. successive generations): so *v.* 34 (Aram. 31). For 'with,' cf. also vii. 2, and Ps. lxxii. 5 Heb. The thought of this and the preceding clause, as *v.* 34 *b*, Ps. cxlv. 13: cf. also ii. 44, vii. 14 *b*, 18 *b*.

4—18. Nebuchadnezzar describes his dream, which, as the wise men of Babylon were unable to interpret it, he laid before Daniel.

4. *at rest*] or *at ease, prosperous.* The word suggests the idea of contentment and security,—in a good or a bad sense, according to the context (Job xvi. 12, Ps. cxxii. 6; Job xii. 6, Ps. lxxiii. 12).

flourishing] The word is applied properly to a tree, and means *spreading, luxuriant* (Deut. xii. 2; 1 K. xiv. 23, *al.*). A.V., R.V., 'green,' which is correct only in so far as a luxuriant tree is also commonly a 'green' one: it is used figuratively of persons, as here, in Ps. xcii. 14 (cf. lii. 8).

5. *the thoughts*] **imaginations** (without the art.); cf. R.V. *marg.* The word is a peculiar one, and is found only here in the O.T. The idea expressed by it is probably that of *fancyings, imaginings* (in Syr. it means a *mirage*); in the Targums it is used especially (like the cognate verb) of *sinful* imaginations, as Is. lvii. 17 (for the Heb. 'way'), Ez. xxxviii. 10.

visions of my head] ii. 28.

6 troubled me. Therefore made I a decree to bring in all the wise *men* of Babylon before me, that they might make
7 known unto me the interpretation of the dream. Then came in the magicians, the astrologers, the Chaldeans, and the soothsayers: and I told the dream before them; but they *did* not make known unto me the interpretation thereof.
8 But at the last Daniel came in before me, whose name *was* Belteshazzar, according to the name of my god, and in whom *is* the spirit of the holy gods: and before him I told
9 the dream, *saying*, O Belteshazzar, master of the magicians, because I know that the spirit of the holy gods *is* in thee, and no secret troubleth thee, tell *me* the visions of my dream
10 that I have seen, and the interpretation thereof. Thus *were*

troubled me] alarmed *me*. cf. *v.* 19, v. 6, 10, vii. 15, 28; also v. 9. The corresponding Hebrew word means to *perturb* or *dismay*.

6. The 'wise men' of Babylon (ii. 12) were summoned before the king, as on the occasion of his previous dream (ii. 2).

7. *the magicians, the* **enchanters**, *the Chaldeans, and the* **determiners** (of fates)] see on i. 21, ii. 2, and ii. 27.

8. *at the last*] It is difficult to understand how the Aram. can bear this meaning; though no doubt something substantially similar is what is intended. Behrmann renders, 'And (so it was) till another came in before me, (even) Daniel'; and Bevan (changing a point), 'And yet another came in before me, (even) Daniel.'

according to the name of my god] viz. Bel. The 'Bel' in Belteshazzar is not really the name of the god, but (as explained on i. 7) is part of the word *balâṭsu*, 'his life'; but it may be only an assonance, not an etymology, which the king is represented as expressing,—just as Hebrew writers say, for instance, that Cain or Moses was so called because of the verbs 'I have gotten,' 'I have drawn out,' although philologically Cain cannot possibly mean 'gotten,' or Moses 'drawn out.'

in whom is *the spirit*, &c.] imitated, it seems, from Gen. xli. 38 (of Joseph), 'a man in whom the spirit of God is.' On the sense of 'spirit' in the O.T., see on Joel ii. 28 (in the *Cambridge Bible*).

the holy gods] Nebuchadnezzar expresses himself as a polytheist: though in *vv.* 3, 34, 35 he uses language indistinguishable from that of pure monotheism. The same expression occurs in the Phœnician inscription of Eshmunazar, king of Sidon (3—4 cent. B.C.), lines 9 and 22[1]. On the sense attaching to the term 'holy' (which has here hardly any *ethical* connotation, and means rather what we should express by 'divine'), see Hastings' *Dict. of the Bible*, ii. 395–7; **and cf.** Sanday-Headlam, *Comm. on the Epistle to the Romans*, on i. 7.

9. *master of the magicians*] see ii. 48.

troubleth thee] **forceth, constraineth** *thee*, i.e. reduces thee to straits.

---

[1] Hogarth, *Authority and Archæology* (1899), p. 137 f.

the visions of mine head in my bed; I saw, and behold, a
tree in the midst of the earth, and the height thereof *was*
great. The tree grew, and was strong, and the height there- 11
of reached unto heaven, and the sight thereof to the end
of all the earth: the leaves thereof *were* fair, and the fruit 12
thereof much, and in it *was* meat for all: the beasts of the
field had shadow under it, and the fowls of the heaven dwelt
in the boughs thereof, and all flesh was fed of it. I saw in 13
the visions of my head upon my bed, and behold, a watcher

10—17. Nebuchadnezzar's dream was of a mighty tree, the head of which towered to heaven, while its branches sheltered, and afforded nutriment for, the beasts and fowl of the earth: as he watched it, he heard the command given that it should be hewn down to the earth, and only its stump left standing. For the imagery, cf. Ez. xxxi. 3—9, 10 ff. (where the Assyrian is compared to a magnificent cedar, towering up loftily in Lebanon, but suddenly and ignominiously cut down), esp. *v.* 6; and the dream of Xerxes, recorded in Herod. vii. *19*, in which the king saw himself crowned with the shoot of an olive-tree, the boughs of which covered the whole earth (τοὺς κλάδους γῆν πᾶσαν ἐπισχεῖν), until suddenly the crown about his head disappeared.

11, 12. The thoughts expressed by the symbolism of the dream are the central and commanding position taken in the world by Nebuchadnezzar's kingdom, its power, splendour, and prosperity, and the protection and support afforded by it, not only to those who strictly belonged to it, but also to all others who sought to enjoy the advantages supplied by it.

11. *grew*] **was grown.**

12. *meat*] in the old sense of the word (see on Am. v. 22; and cf. Gen. i. 29, 30), **food** in general, not what we now call 'meat.' So *v.* 21. The Aram. word occurs in Syr. and the Targums; and twice in the Heb. of the O.T., Gen. xlv. 23 (A.V. 'meat,' R.V. 'victual'), 2 Ch. xi. 23 (A.V., R.V. 'victual').

had shadow...dwelt...was fed of it] Better, **were sheltering..., dwelling..., was being fed from** *it*. The tenses of the original denote what was *habitual*, and therefore might be observed as taking place continuously at the time of the dream. Cf. for the thought Ez. xxxi. 6.

13. *a watcher*] i.e. not a *guardian*, but **a wakeful one** (Aq., Symm., ἐγρήγορος, Vulg. *vigil*); so *vv.* 17, 23. The term denotes an angel,—or, possibly, a particular class of angels,—so called, either as being ever ready to fulfil the Divine behests, or as being ever wakeful for some particular purpose (e.g. praise). It is of frequent occurrence in the Book of Enoch (in the Greek ἐγρήγοροι), where it is applied usually (i. 5, x. 9, 15, xii. 4, xiii. 10, xiv. 1, 3, xv. 2, xvi. 1, 2, xci. 15) to the fallen angels, but it is also (xii. 3, and perhaps xii. 2) used of the holy angels, though it is not perfectly clear (see the note in Dillmann's edition, p. 104 f.) whether it denotes them generally, or whether it is the name of a particular class (cf. Charles on i. 5, xxxix. 12): the use of

14 and a holy one came down from heaven; he cried aloud, and said thus, Hew down the tree, and cut off his branches, shake off his leaves, and scatter his fruit: let the beasts get 15 away from under it, and the fowls from his branches: nevertheless leave the stump of his roots in the earth, even with a band of iron and brass, in the tender grass of the field; and let it be wet with the dew of heaven, and *let* his portion *be* 16 with the beasts in the grass of the earth: let his heart be

the synonyms 'the holy angels who watch' in xx. 1 (in the Ethiopic, but not in the Greek text[1]) of six archangels, and 'those who sleep not' in xxxix. 12, 13, xl. 2, lxi. 12, lxxi. 7, of certain exalted angels who incessantly hymn the Almighty, and guard His throne, does not entirely remove the uncertainty. The same word which is used here is also often used of angels in Syriac; see Payne Smith, *Thes. Syr.* col. 2843-4.

and a holy one] another term denoting an angel: in the O.T., Job v. 1, xv. 15, Ps. lxxxix. 5, 7, Zech. xiv. 5, Dan. viii. 13 [A.V. 'saint' in these passages: see the note on viii. 13]; and repeatedly in the Book of Enoch, i. 9 (whence Jude 14), xii. 2, xiv. 23, xxxix. 5, &c. (see Charles' note on i. 9).

14. The strength and magnificence of the great tree are all to be stripped from it.

aloud] lit. *with might*, as iii. 4.

Hew down &c.] who are addressed, is not stated: as in other similar cases (Is. xiii. 2, xl. 3, lvii. 14, Jer. iv. 5, &c.), those whose duty it would naturally be to fulfil such a command are intended.

15. The destruction of the tree, however, is not to be total: a stump is to be left, which may ultimately grow again.

even in *a band of iron and brass*] Unless it might be supposed that it was customary, for any purpose, to place a metal band round the stump of a tree which had been cut down, the figure, it seems, must be here abandoned. Whether, however, that be the case or not, the reference, as the interpretation shews, is to something which Nebuchadnezzar would experience during his madness,—probably, either (Keil) the loss of mental freedom, or (Prince) the physical restraint and confinement to which he would naturally have then to submit.

in the tender grass of the field] There would be nothing remarkable in a tree being surrounded by grass; the tree, it is evident, must symbolize something for which such a position would be unnatural. What that is appears more distinctly in the sequel.

let his portion be, &c.] Let him share with them in the **herbage** of the earth.

herbage] the word used is a wider one than either 'grass' or 'tender (i.e. young) grass,' and includes vegetables and small shrubs (Gen. i. 11, 12).

16. *his heart*] i.e. his intelligence: let him receive the understanding

---

[1] See p. 356 in Charles' edition (Oxford, 1893).

changed from man's, and let a beast's heart be given unto him; and let seven times pass over him. *This* matter *is* by the decree of the watchers, and the demand *by* the word of the holy ones: to the intent that the living may know that the most High ruleth in the kingdom of men, and giveth it to whomsoever he will, and setteth up over it the basest of

of a beast (imagine himself an animal). The heart, in Hebrew psychology, is the seat not (as commonly with us) of tender feeling (a 'heartless' man), but of the *intellect:* cf. Hos. vii. 11, 'a silly dove, without *heart*,' i.e. without understanding, Jer. v. 21, 'a foolish people, without understanding,' lit. without heart.

seven times] i.e. seven *years:* cf. vii. 25, xii. 7 (Heb. *mô‘ēd*); Rev. xii. 14 (καιρός). With 'pass over,' comp. 1 Ch. xxix. 30.

17. This *matter*] either **The word** (i.e. *The sentence*, R.V., as Eccl. viii. 11 [cf. Est. i. 20, *the decree*, for the same word in Hebrew]), or (in a weakened sense), **The thing** (cf. iii. 16 'in this *matter*'), i.e. what has just been described.

by the decree &c.] implying that it is unalterably fixed.

of the watchers, &c.] in *v.* 24 the king's doom is said to be 'by the decree of the Most High.' God is represented in the O.T. as surrounded by an assembly of angels (1 Ki. xxii. 19), who form almost a kind of heavenly council, Job i. 6, ii. 1, xv. 8 (R.V. *marg.*), Jer. xxiii. 18, Ps. lxxxix. 7; and it seems that in Dan. the decree is regarded as possessing the joint authority of God and of His council. By the later Jews this assembly of angels was called God's 'court of judgement' (בית דין), or His 'family' (פמליא); and He was represented as taking counsel with it, or communicating to it His purposes (so Gen. i. 26 in the Targ. of Ps.-Jon.). In *Sanh.* 38*b* it is said, "The Holy One, blessed be He! does nothing without first consulting the family above, as it is said (Dan. iv. 17), 'By the decree of the watchers,' &c." See further Weber, *System der Altsynag. Theol.* p. 170 f.

the demand] probably **the matter** (R.V. *marg.*). The Aram. means either a *request* (1 K. ii. 16, Heb. and Targ., Luke xxiii. 24, Pesh. for αἴτημα), or a *question*, subject of discussion or dispute (Jer. xii. 1, Targ.); and is hence generally supposed to have here the weakened sense of *the matter*. ('Demand' must be understood in a sense analogous to that expressed by the verb in ii. 27 (see the note); there is no warrant for giving the Aram. word the sense of *authoritative* request.)

to the intent &c.] the humiliation of the mighty king is to teach all who witness it that God is supreme over the kingdoms of the world.

the basest] i.e. *the* **lowest** (R.V.),—viz. in rank and position, not in character. '*Base*' in Old English meant 'low, humble, not necessarily worthless or wicked,' (Wright, *Bible Word-Book, s.v.*). Polydore Vergil i. 70 (cited *ib.*), 'which *the baser sorte* [i.e. common people] doe som time superstitiouslye note as signs and wonders.' In 1 Cor. i. 28 the 'base things of the world' (τὰ ἀγενῆ τοῦ κόσμου) means merely 'things of no account'; and in 2 Cor. x. 1 St Paul in calling himself (A.V.) 'base

52 DANIEL, IV. [vv. 18—22.

18 men. This dream I king Nebuchadnezzar have seen. Now thou, O Belteshazzar, declare the interpretation thereof, forasmuch as all the wise *men* of my kingdom are not able to make known unto me the interpretation: but thou *art* able; for the spirit of the holy gods *is* in thee.
19 Then Daniel, whose name *was* Belteshazzar, was astonied for one hour, and his thoughts troubled him. The king spake, and said, Belteshazzar, let not the dream, or the interpretation thereof, trouble thee. Belteshazzar answered and said, My lord, the dream *be* to them that hate thee, and
20 the interpretation thereof to thine enemies. The tree that thou sawest, which grew, and was strong, whose height reached unto the heaven, and the sight thereof to all the
21 earth; whose leaves *were* fair, and the fruit thereof much, and in it *was* meat for all; under which the beasts of the field dwelt, and upon whose branches the fowls of the
22 heaven had their habitation: it *is* thou, O king, that art grown and become strong: for thy greatness is grown, and

among you,' of course really only means to say that he is 'lowly' (R.V.). Cf. Ez. xvii. 14, xxix. 14, 15. The same word which is used in the Aram. here is used also (in its Heb. form) in Job v. 11, 'to set up on high those that be *low*;' Ps. cxxxviii. 6, 'yet hath he respect unto the *lowly*,' and Is. lvii. 15 ('humble').

18. Nebuchadnezzar closes his description of his dream by appealing to Daniel to interpret it.

for the spirit &c.] See *v.* 8.

19—27. Daniel's interpretation of the dream.

19. *was astonied*] better, **was stupefied** or **appalled**, viz. as the meaning of the dream flashed across him. The root-idea of the word (שׁמם) seems to have been *to be motionless*,—sometimes (cf. on viii. 13) in the stillness of desolation, sometimes, as here, through amazement (so viii. 27). It is not the word used in iii. 24.

about *one hour*] In view of what was said on iii. 6, however, it is doubted by many whether *shāʻāh* is meant here to denote exactly what we call an 'hour'; and they render accordingly *for* **a moment.** Cf. Ex. xxxiii. 5, where nearly the same expression (שׁעה חדא) stands in the Targ. for the Heb. רגע אחד i.e. 'for a moment.'

his thoughts **alarmed** (*v.* 5) *him*] he dreaded, **viz., to foretell to the king his own disasters** The same phrase, v. 6, 10, vii. 28. The king, however, observing his confusion, and perceiving from it that he has found the interpretation of the dream, proceeds to reassure him.

20—21. The description repeated from *vv.* 11—12.

21. *meat*] food, as *v.* 12.

22. The tree represented Nebuchadnezzar himself, in the pride and greatness of his empire.

reacheth unto heaven, and thy dominion to the end of the earth. And whereas the king saw a watcher and a holy one 23 coming down from heaven, and saying, Hew the tree down, and destroy it; yet leave the stump of the roots thereof in the earth, even with a band of iron and brass, in the tender grass of the field; and let it be wet with the dew of heaven, and *let* his portion *be* with the beasts of the field, till seven times pass over him; this *is* the interpretation, O king, and 24 this *is* the decree of the most High, which is come upon my lord the king: that they *shall* drive thee from men, and 25 thy dwelling shall be with the beasts of the field, and they shall make thee to eat grass as oxen, and they *shall* wet thee with the dew of heaven, and seven times shall pass over thee, till thou know that the most High ruleth in the kingdom of men, and giveth it to whomsoever he will. And 26 whereas they commanded to leave the stump of the tree roots; thy kingdom *shall be* sure unto thee, after that thou shalt have known that the heavens do rule. Wherefore, O king, 27

to the end of the earth] Comp. what was said on *v*. 1.

23. Abbreviated from *vv*. 13—16.

24. *and* it is *the decree of the most High*, &c.] cf. *v*. 17 *a*.

25. The sense of *vv*. 15, 16, 17 *b* explained more distinctly: Nebuchadnezzar, imagining himself to be an animal, will act himself, and be treated by others, accordingly.

that they shall *drive thee...and they shall make thee to eat...and they shall* wet *thee*] R.V. *that* thou shalt be driven...*and* thou shalt be made *to eat...and* shalt be wet. In Aramaic, the 3rd pers. plur. with indef. subject is often used where we should employ the passive, even though the agent implicitly referred to is God, see e.g. ii. 30 (lit. 'that they should make known'), iii. 4 (lit. 'they command'), iv. 16 (lit. 'let them change...let them give'), 31 (lit. 'they speak'),—in all which passages A.V. itself paraphrases by the passive. The same usage occurs sometimes in Biblical Hebrew (see on i. 12); and it is frequent in the later language, as *Abhoth*, iv. 7 (cited on *v*. 26)[1]. Cf. Matth. v. 15; Luke vi. 38, 44, xii. 20 (ἀπαιτοῦσιν); Rev. xii. 6 τρέφωσιν (*v*. 14 τρέφεται).

26. *they commanded*] viz. the watchers (cf. *v*. 17). Or, in accordance with the principle just explained, *it was commanded.*

sure] i.e. *confirmed, secure:* cf. vi. 26 ('stedfast'). The object of the humiliation was (*v*. 25 *b*) to teach the king that his power was not his own, but delegated to him by God, the supreme ruler of the world; provision was therefore made that when he had learnt this lesson his kingdom should be restored to him (cf. *v*. 32 *b*).

that the heavens do rule] The use of 'heaven,' either as a metonym, or

---

[1] See further examples in Dalman, *Die Worte Jesu* (1898), p. 184.

let my counsel be acceptable unto thee, and break off thy sins by righteousness, and thine iniquities by shewing mercy to the poor; if it may be a lengthening of thy tranquillity.

as an expression of reverence, for God, does not occur elsewhere in the O.T.; but it is found in the Apocrypha, as 1 Macc. iii. 18, R.V. [contrast 1 Sam. xiv. 6], 19 (cf. *v.* 60), iv. 10, 24, 55, 2 Macc. ix. 20; and it is especially frequent in the Mishna, as *Abhoth*, i. 3, 'and let the fear of Heaven be upon you'; ii. 16, 'let all thy deeds be in the name of Heaven'; iv. 7, 'whoso profaneth the name of Heaven in secret, they punish him (i.e. he is punished) openly.' Cf. Luke xv. 18, 21[1].

In connexion with the phrase here employed, it may be remarked that the original Jewish sense of the expression, 'kingdom of heaven,' is the *rule*, or *government*, of heaven[2].

27. Daniel closes with a piece of practical advice addressed to the king.

break off] R.V. *marg.* 'Or, *redeem*'; LXX., Theod., λύτρωσαι. The word (*pᵉraḳ*), meaning properly to *tear away*, is common in Aram. (both Targums and Syriac) in the derived sense of *tearing away* from servitude, death, or danger, i.e. of *redeeming* (e.g. Lev. xxv. 25, 2 Sam. iv. 9); and occurs twice in that sense in Heb. (Lam. v. 8, Ps. cxxxvi. 24); but though sins might of course be 'atoned for,' or 'expiated,' it is doubtful whether they could be spoken of as 'redeemed': and hence no doubt the word is used here in its more original sense of *break off* (cf. in Heb. Gen. xxvii. 40 of a yoke, Ex. xxxii. 23, 24), i.e. *make a complete end of, cast absolutely away*.

by righteousness] i.e. by righteous conduct: cf. Prov. x. 2, 'righteousness delivereth from death'; xvi. 6, 'by kindness and truth iniquity is cancelled.' 'Righteousness' (צדקה) acquired, however, in late (post-Bibl.) Hebrew, as also in Aramaic (Targums, Talmud, Syriac), the special sense of *alms* or *almsgiving*: for instance *Abhoth*, v. 13 (Taylor 19), 'those who give *ṣedāḳāh* (i.e. alms)'; Jerus. *Taanith*, ii. 65 *b*, 'three things neutralize an evil fate, prayer, righteousness (almsgiving), and repentance.' Cf. Mt. vi. 1, where 'righteousness' (R.V.) is the true reading, and 'alms' (A.V.) the (correct) explanation, which has found its way into the *textus receptus*. In accordance with this usage, LXX. and Theod. (ἐλεημοσύναις), Pesh., Vulg., express the same sense here; but, in view of the context, the limitation of 'righteousness' to such a special virtue cannot be said to be probable[3]. On the contrary, 'righteousness' in its widest sense, especially towards subjects and dependents, is in the O.T. one of the primary virtues of a ruler (2 Sam. viii. 15; Jer. xxii. 15, &c.), which Nebuchadnezzar, as the ideal despot, is naturally pictured as deficient in.

by shewing mercy to the poor] cf. Prov. xiv. 21, where the same two words occur in their Hebrew form.

if **haply there** *may be a lengthening* (vii. 12 Aram.) *of thy* **prosperity**]

---

[1] See further examples in Dalman, *l.c.*, pp. 178—180; and cf. Schürer[2], ii. 454.
[2] Dalman, pp. 75—77.
[3] LXX also render *ṣedāḳāh* by 'alms' in Deut. vi. 25, xxiv. 13; Ps. xxiv. 5, xxxiii. 5, ciii. 6; Is. i. 27, xxviii. 17, lix. 16; Dan. ix. 16; and 'alms delivereth from death' in Tob. iv. 10, xii. 9, seems based upon Prov. x. 2, similarly interpreted.

All this came upon the king Nebuchadnezzar. At the 28, 29
end of twelve months he walked in the palace of the kingdom
of Babylon. The king spake, and said, *Is* not this great 30
Babylon, that I have built for the house of the kingdom by
the might of my power, and for the honour of my majesty?
While the word *was* in the king's mouth, there fell a voice 31
from heaven, *saying*, O king Nebuchadnezzar, to thee it is
spoken; The kingdom is departed from thee. And they 32
shall drive thee from men, and thy dwelling *shall be* with
the beasts of the field: they shall make thee to eat grass as
oxen, and seven times shall pass over thee, until thou know

the last word being the subst. corresponding to the adj. rendered *at
ease* or *prosperous* in *v.* 4. A.V. *marg.*, and R.V. *marg.*, 'an healing of
thy error' (so Ewald), implies changes of punctuation in the two substantives: *'arūkhāh*, 'healing,' Is. lviii. 8 *al.* (lit. *fresh flesh* over a
wound), for *'arkhāh*, and *shālūthākh*, 'thy error' (iii. 29, vi. 4) for
shᵉlēwᵉthākh. Theod. (ἴσως ἔσται μακρόθυμος τοῖς παραπτώμασίν σου ὁ
θεός), Vulg., Pesh., also, presuppose the same reading of the last word
(though their renderings of the first word are inadmissible).

28—33. The fulfilment of the dream.

29. *he* **was walking upon** *the* **royal palace** *of Babylon*] 'upon'
means *on the roof of*: cf. 2 Sam. xi. 2.

30. *spake*] **answered** (ii. 20).

great Babylon] Rev. xvi. 19 (in a figurative sense); cf. Jer. li. 58.

I] The pronoun is emphatic.

for the house of the kingdom] *for* **a royal dwelling-place (or
residence)**.

honour] glory (as ii. 37).

The 'India House Inscription' of Nebuchadnezzar is a fine commentary on the words here put into the mouth of the great king: see
the abstract of it given in the Introduction, p. xxiv f.

31. The divine rebuke alights immediately upon the king.

there fell a voice from heaven] such as was called by the later Jews a
Bath Ḳôl, lit. 'the daughter of a voice' (the accompanying verb being
usually 'came forth'), the term applied by them to a divine voice unaccompanied by any visible manifestation. Cf. *Apoc. of Baruch*, xiii. 1,
'a voice came from heaven,' xxii. 1; and see further Weber, *System
der Altsynag. Theol.* p. 187 f., Dalman, *Die Worte Jesu*, p. 167 f.,
Edersheim, *Life and Times of Jesus*, i. 286, and the particulars given
in Hamburger's *Real-Encyclop. für Bibel u. Talmud*, vol. ii., s. v.
BATHKOL. The voices from heaven in the N.T. (as Matth. iii. 17,
xvii. 5; John xii. 28; Acts xi. 7, 9; Rev. x. 4) would all, in Jewish
phraseology, be so described.

32. *And* **thou shalt be driven...shalt be made** *to eat grass as
oxen*] The passives, as *v.* 25,—with which, indeed, except that one
clause is omitted, the present verse agrees almost verbally.

that the most High ruleth in the kingdom of men, and
33 giveth it to whomsoever he will. The same hour was the
thing fulfilled upon Nebuchadnezzar: and he *was* driven
from men, and did eat grass as oxen, and his body was wet
with the dew of heaven, till his hairs were grown like eagles'
34 *feathers*, and his nails like birds' *claws*. And at the
end of the days I Nebuchadnezzar lift up mine eyes unto heaven,
and mine understanding returned unto me, and I blessed
the most High, and I praised and honoured him that liveth
for ever, whose dominion *is* an everlasting dominion, and
35 his kingdom *is* from generation to generation: and all the
inhabitants of the earth *are* reputed as nothing: and he
doeth according to his will in the army of heaven, and
among the inhabitants of the earth: and none can stay his

33. *The same hour*] iii. 6.
the thing] or, *the* word, i.e. the announcement of *vv*. 31, 32.
did eat...was wet] The tenses express what was habitual (cf. *v.* 12).
till his hairs were grown, &c.] The delusion under which he was suffering leading him naturally to neglect his person.
34—37. At the end of the appointed time, Nebuchadnezzar's reason returned to him: he owned the sovereignty of the Most High, and was restored to his kingdom; and now, in thankful acknowledgement of His power, he issues his present proclamation.
34. *the days*] i.e. the seven 'times' of *vv*. 16, 23, 25, 32.
lift up mine eyes unto heaven] The mute, half-unconscious acknowledgement of the God who rules in heaven, was followed by the return of the king's human consciousness.
and I blessed, &c.] The king gave open and conscious expression to his gratitude, acknowledging and glorifying the power of the Most High.
him that liveth for ever] So xii. 7; cf. vi. 26, also Rev. iv. 9, 10, x. 6.
and his kingdom (endureth) **with** *generation* **and** *generation*] *v.* 3.
35. are *reputed as nothing*] better, *are as* **persons of no account** (Bevan). The expression is in part, no doubt, suggested by Is. xl. 17 (where the verb rendered 'counted' is the same as that which in the partic. is here rendered 'reputed').
and he doeth &c.] He rules alike in heaven and earth.
the army of heaven] The Aram. equivalent (representing it also in the Targums) for the Heb. 'host of heaven'—an expression which denotes sometimes the angels (1 Ki. xxii. 19; Neh. ix. 6 *b*), sometimes the stars (Deut. iv. 19, Jer. xxxiii. 22, *al.*; cf. Neh. ix. 6 *a*)[1]. Here angelic beings, as opposed to the 'inhabitants of the earth,' are doubtless meant: cf., for the general thought, Ps. ciii. 20.
stay his hand] strike *his hand*, viz. for the purpose of arresting it.

---

[1] See the art. HOST OF HEAVEN in Hastings' *Dictionary of the Bible.*

hand, or say unto him, What doest thou? At the same 36
time my reason returned unto me; and for the glory of my
kingdom, mine honour and brightness returned unto me;
and my counsellors and my lords sought unto me; and I
was established in my kingdom, and excellent majesty was
added unto me. Now I Nebuchadnezzar praise and extol 37
and honour the King of heaven, all whose works *are* truth,
and his ways judgement: and those that walk in pride he *is*
able to abase.

The same idiom occurs in the Targ. of Eccl. viii. 4 *b* (perhaps borrowed from here); it occurs also in the Talm. more than once, in the sense of *to forbid*, and (with another word for *strike*) in Arabic as well. See Ges. *Thes.* p. 782; Levy, *NHWB.* iii. 72.

or say unto him, What **hast** *thou* done?] Cf. Is. xlv. 9; Job ix. 12; Eccl. viii. 4 *b*.

36. *reason*] The word is the same as that which in *v.* 34 is rendered *understanding*.

mine honour] **my majesty** (R.V.), as the word is rendered in A.V. in *v.* 30. In Heb. the word is regularly used of the majesty of a king (or of God), as Ps. xxi. 5, xxix. 4, xlv. 3, 4.

and **my splendour**] i.e. my royal state (cf. Ps. xxi. 6 Pesh. [for Heb. הדר], 1 Chr. xxix. 25 Pesh. and Targ. [for Heb. הוד]); though others, comparing v. 6, 9, 10, vii. 28, think the recovered **brightness** of the countenance to be meant. The 'glory' of Nebuchadnezzar's 'kingdom' had been impaired by his absence: it was restored when he reappeared in his usual place and resumed his former royal state.

my **ministers** (iii. 24, 27) *and my lords sought unto me*] They welcomed him back, and again consulted him on affairs of state.

excellent majesty] **surpassing greatness.** See on ii. 31; and, for 'greatness,' cf. *v.* 22, vii. 27 (A.V. *greatness*), v. 18, 19 (R.V. *greatness*).

37. Nebuchadnezzar's final doxology.

extol] or *exalt*: Ps. xxx. 1, cxviii. 28, cxlv. 1, &c.

the King of heaven] Cf. 3 Macc. ii. 2, Tob. xiii. 7, 11; Dalman, p. 143.

truth.. judgement] cf. Ps. cxi. 7.

and those that walk in pride, &c.] Cf. Ez. xvii. 24; **Ps. xviii. 27,** lxxv. 7; also Prov. xvi. 18. Nebuchadnezzar recognizes that the humiliation which he has experienced is a punishment for his pride.

"The Bible always represents to us that pride and arrogant self-confidence are an offence against God. The doom fell on Nebuchadnezzar while the haughty boast was still in the king's mouth. The suddenness of the nemesis of pride is closely paralleled by the scene in the Acts of the Apostles in which Herod Agrippa I. is represented as entering the theatre to receive the deputies of Tyre and Sidon"; and, in spite of the ominous warning, which according to the story in Josephus he had received just before, as accepting the blasphemous adulation of the multitude, and as being stricken immediately by a mortal illness (Acts xx. 20—23; Jos. *Ant.* XIV. viii. 2). "And something like this we see again and again in what the late Bishop Thirlwall called the 'irony of history'—the cases in which men seem to have been elevated to the very summit of power only to heighten the dreadful precipice over which they immediately fell. He mentions the cases of Persia, which was on the verge of ruin when with lordly arrogance she dictated the peace of Antalcidas; of Boniface VIII., in the Jubilee of 1300, immediately preceding his deadly overthrow; and of Spain, under Philip II., struck down by the ruin of the Armada at the zenith of her wealth and pride. He might have added the instances of Ahab, Sennacherib [cf. Is. x. 12—19, 33—34], Nebuchadnezzar, and Herod Antipas, of Alexander the Great, and of Napoleon" (Farrar, p. 198 f.).

Additional Note on Nebuchadnezzar's madness.

The malady from which Nebuchadnezzar is represented as suffering agrees, as Dr Pusey has pointed out (p. 425 ff.), "with the description of a rare sort of disease, called Lycanthropy, from one form of it, of which our earliest notice is in a Greek medical writer of the 4th cent. A.D., in which the sufferer retains his consciousness in other respects, but imagines himself to be changed into some animal, and acts, up to a certain point, in conformity with that persuasion." Persons thus afflicted imagine themselves for instance to be dogs, wolves, lions, cats, cocks, or other animals, and cry or otherwise behave themselves in the manner of these animals. Marcellus (4 cent. A.D.) says, "They who are seized by the kynanthropic or lykanthropic disease, in the month of February go forth by night, imitating in all things wolves or dogs, and until day especially live near tombs." Galen mentions the case of one who crowed, and flapped his arms, imagining himself to be a cock; and many similar cases are on record in modern times. Dr Pusey states that he found no notice of the exact form of the disease with which Nebuchadnezzar was afflicted (which would be *Boanthropy*); but there seems to be no intrinsic reason why an ox should not be the animal whose nature was thus assumed. A man who imagined himself to be an ox might naturally enough eat grass like an ox; but a perverted appetite, including, in particular, a desire to devour grass, leaves, twigs, &c., is also an independent characteristic of many forms of insanity. At the same time, persons suffering in these ways are often not entirely, or continuously, bereft of their reason; they are at times aware that they are not what they imagine themselves to be; and frequently (as visitors to lunatic asylums sometimes notice) make on many subjects acute and sensible remarks; so that there is no difficulty in supposing that Nebuchadnezzar could, as seems to be represented in *v*. 34, have recognized God in prayer even before his reason had wholly returned to him. Dr Pusey refers at some length to the case of Père Surin, who, in exorcising others, fell for many years into a strange malady, in which he believed himself to be possessed, and acted outwardly in the manner of a maniac, and yet remained fully conscious of religious verities, and was inwardly in perfect peace and communion with God.

If therefore it were clear that the narrative in Daniel was the work of a contemporary hand, there does not seem to be any sufficient reason why the account of Nebuchadnezzar's insanity should not be accepted as historical: it is supported by physiological analogies; and the objections that it is not mentioned by other ancient writers, and that his empire would not have been preserved to him during such a long illness, are hardly of a nature to be conclusive; our records of his reign are imperfect[1], and an arrangement may have been made by which the chief courtiers continued to rule in the king's name,—as in the similar cases of Charles VI. of France, Christian VII. of Denmark, George III. of England, and Otho of Bavaria, referred to by Dr Farrar (p. 201).

The question assumes, however, a different complexion, if it be true that the book is a work of the Maccabæan age. We then have no contemporary evidence for the fact; and it becomes an open question, whether it is more than a popular tradition which the writer has followed, and which he has adopted for the purpose of teaching one of the great lessons of his book. Some support is given to this opinion by the curious, though imperfect, parallel quoted by Eusebius (*Praep. Evang.* ix. 41) from the Assyrian history of Abydenus (prob. 2 cent. A.D.):—

"Megasthenes says that Nebuchadnezzar became stronger than Herakles, and made wars upon Libya and Iberia, and having conquered these countries settled a part of their inhabitants on the right of Pontus. After this, it is said by the Chaldæans, he ascended the roof of his palace, and being possessed by some god or other, cried aloud: 'O Babylonians, I, Nebuchadnezzar, announce to you beforehand the coming misfortune, which Bel my ancestor and the Queen Beltis are alike powerless to persuade the Fates to avert. A Persian mule [i.e. Cyrus] will come, having your own deities as his allies[2], and will bring slavery. He who will help him in this undertaking will be Mēdēs[3], the boast of Assyria[4]. Would that, before my citizens were betrayed, some Charybdis or sea might receive him, and utterly extinguish him! or else that, betaking himself elsewhere, he might be driven through the desert, where is no city nor track of man, where wild beasts have their pasture, and birds do roam, and that among rocks and ravines he might wander alone! and that I, before he imagined this, might meet with some happier end!' Having uttered this prophecy, he forthwith disappeared; and Evilmaluruchus [Evil-merodach], his son, succeeded him on the throne."

Megasthenes was a contemporary of Seleucus Nicator (B.C. 312—280); but the statements about Nebuchadnezzar's prophecy are made on the authority of the 'Chaldaeans.' Prof. Bevan, following Prof. Schrader[5],

---

[1] The statement of Berosus (ap. Jos. *c. Ap.* i. 20) that 'falling into a sickness (ἐμπεσὼν εἰς ἀρρωστίαν), he ended his life,' is too vague to be regarded as confirmatory of the narrative in Daniel: Berosus uses almost the same expression (ἀρρωστήσας) in speaking (*ib.* i. 19) of the death of Nabopolassar; besides, it is implied that from this sickness Nebuchadnezzar did not recover.

[2] Cyrus, in his 'Cylinder-Inscription,' represents himself as led into Babylon by Merodach, the supreme god of Babylon (cf. the Introd. p. xxxi, *bottom*).

[3] Schrader, following a conjecture of von Gutschmid's, reads 'the son of a Median woman,' i.e. Nabu-na'id, who certainly made himself unpopular by his neglect of the gods of Babylon, and may well have been regarded as in great measure responsible for its capture by Cyrus.

[4] Used in the sense of *Babylonia*.

[5] In his Essay on 'Nebuchadnezzar's Madness' in the *Jahrbücher für Protest. Theol.*, 1881, p. 618 ff.

points out well the historical significance of the passage, and its bearing on the Biblical narrative. "Obscure as the passage is in some of its details, one part may be regarded as certain, viz. that we have here a popular legend of Babylonian origin, coloured of course by the Greek medium through which it has passed. The prophecy put into the mouth of Nebuchadnezzar evidently refers to the overthrow of the Babylonian empire by Cyrus, the 'mule.'...The resemblances between the narrative in Daniel and the Babylonian legend can hardly be accidental": in both the king is on the roof of the palace; in the one case a prophetic voice declares to him that he will be driven from men, and have his abode with the beasts of the field, in the other he invokes a similar fate upon his nation's foe. "But to suppose that either narrative has been directly borrowed from the other is impossible. It would appear that of the two, that in Abydenus is on the whole the more primitive. Its local character,"—notice, for instance, the interest evinced by it in the history of Babylon,—"is strongly marked; and it shews no signs of having been deliberately altered to serve a didactic purpose. In Daniel, on the other hand, we find a narrative which contains scarcely anything specifically Babylonian, but which is obviously intended to teach a moral lesson. It is therefore probable that some Babylonian legend on the subject of Nebuchadnezzar had, perhaps in a very distorted form, reached the ears of the author of Daniel, who adapted the story in order to make it a vehicle of religious instruction."

Chap. V. Belshazzar's Feast.

While Belshazzar and his lords are at a feast, impiously drinking their wine from cups which had belonged once to the Temple at Jerusalem, the fingers of a man's hand appear writing upon the wall. The king, in alarm, summons his wise men to interpret what was written; but they are unable to do so (*vv.* 1—9). At the suggestion of the queen Daniel is called, who interprets the words to signify that the days of Belshazzar's kingdom are numbered, and that it is about to be given to the Medes and Persians (*vv.* 10—28). Daniel is invested with purple and a chain of gold, and made one of the three chief ministers of the kingdom (*v.* 29). The same night Belshazzar is slain, and "Darius the Mede" receives the kingdom (*vv.* 30—31).

Nearly 70 years have elapsed since the events narrated in ch. i.; so that Daniel must now be pictured as an aged man, at least 80 years old.

On Belshazzar, see the Introduction. Nebuchadnezzar reigned from B.C. 604 to 561; and Babylon fell into the hands of Cyrus 23 years after his death, B.C. 538. The inscriptions have made it clear that Belshazzar was not king of Babylon, as he is here represented as being: Nabu-na'id (who reigned for 17 years, from 555 to 538) was the last king of Babylon; Belshazzar is called regularly "the king's son," and he bore this title to the day of his death. For a series of years, during his father's reign, he is mentioned as being with the army in the country of Akkad (N. Babylonia). *After* Gubaru and Cyrus had entered Babylon, and governors had been established by them in the city, he is said (according to the most probable read-

Belshazzar the king made a great feast to a thousand of **5**
his lords, and drank wine before the thousand. Belshazzar, **2**

ing[1]) to have been slain by Gubaru 'during the night,' i.e. (apparently) in some assault made by night upon the fortress or palace to which he had withdrawn. Nabu-na'id was a quiet, unwarlike king; and Belshazzar, as general, may have distinguished himself, at the time when Cyrus took possession of Babylon, in such a manner as to eclipse his father,—with the result that in the imagination of later ages he was himself regarded as 'king' of Babylon.

Nebuchadnezzar in ch. iv. was the personification of pride: Belshazzar is the personification of profanity as well; and his fall is all the more tragic and complete: in a single night the brilliant revel is changed, first into terror and bewilderment, and then into disaster and death. Herodotus (i. 191), and Xenophon (*Cyrop.* VII. v. 15—31), testify to the existence of a tradition that Babylon was taken by Cyrus during the night, while the inhabitants were all feasting. This tradition is shewn now by the inscriptions (p. xxxi) to be unhistorical, at least in the form in which these writers report it; but it is, of course, not impossible that Belshazzar was holding a feast in the night on which he was slain by Gubaru. Even, however, though this may have been the case, there are features in the representation of the present chapter which so conflict with history as to make it evident that we are not dealing with an account written by a contemporary hand, but with a narrative, constructed doubtless upon a basis supplied by tradition, but written, as a whole, for the purpose of impressing a moral lesson. Those who regard the Book as dating from the reign of Antiochus Epiphanes often think that the chapter may be intended indirectly to allude to him: his audacity and impiety are mentioned pointedly in viii. 10, 11, xi. 36—38; in 1 Macc. i. 21—24 we read that he 'entered proudly into the sanctuary' and robbed it of the golden altar, and most of the other sacred vessels; and so it is thought that the fate which is elsewhere (viii. 25, xi. 45) distinctly predicted for the impious Syrian prince, is here indirectly hinted at by the nemesis which overtakes the profanity of Belshazzar.

1. *Belshazzar*] Babyl. *Bêl-shar-uṣur*, 'Bel, protect the king!' LXX. Theod. and Vulg. confuse this name with Belteshazzar (i. 7), representing both by Βαλτασαρ, 'Baltassar.'

to a thousand of his lords] in accordance with the magnificence of Eastern monarchs.

and drank, &c.] *and before the thousand* **was drinking** *wine*. By 'before' is no doubt meant, facing the guests, at a separate table, on a raised dais at the end of the banqueting-hall. We have little or no information respecting the custom of the king at state-banquets in Babylon: but something similar is reported, or may be inferred, of royal banquets among the Persians (Athen. iv. 26, p. 145 c, ll. 1—3; cf. Rawl. *Anc. Mon.*[4] iii. 215), and Parthians (Athen. iv. 38, p. 153 a—b).

---

[1] See above, p. xxx, ll. 22, 23.

62   DANIEL, V.   [vv. 2—4.

whiles *he* tasted the wine, commanded to bring the golden and silver vessels which his father Nebuchadnezzar had taken out of the temple which *was* in Jerusalem; that the king, and his princes, his wives, and his concubines, might 3 drink therein. Then they brought the golden vessels that were taken out of the temple of the house of God which *was* at Jerusalem; and the king, and his princes, his wives, 4 and his concubines, drank in them. They drank wine, and praised the gods of gold, and of silver, of brass, of iron, of wood, and of stone.

2. *whiles*] tne genitive sing. of the subst. *while* (as in ' for a *while* '), used adverbially (cf. ' need*s*,' ' upward*s* '). It occurs in A.V. ix. 20, 21; Ez. xxi. 29 (twice), xliv. 17; Hos. vii. 6; Matt. v. 25; Acts v. 4; 2 Cor. ix. 13; and several times in Shakespeare, as *Much Ado*, iv. 1, 221, ' What we have we prize not to the worth, *Whiles* we enjoy it,' *Meas. for Meas.* iv. 3, 84; *Jul. Caes.* i. 2. 209.

whiles he *tasted the wine*] in the taste—i.e. enjoyment—of *the wine*, when he began to feel the influence of the wine.

commanded, &c.] an act, under the circumstances, of wanton and defiant impiety.

the golden and silver vessels, &c.] see i. 2.

his father] Belshazzar is not known to have been related to Nebuchadnezzar: his father was Nabu-na'id, a usurper, the son of one Nabo-balâtsu-ikbi, and expressly said (see Introd. pp. xxvii, li) to have been unconnected with Nebuchadnezzar's family.

'Father' may, however, by Hebrew usage, be understood to mean grandfather (Gen. xxviii. 13, xxxii. 10; cf. 1 Kings xv. 13 for great-grandfather); and there remains the *possibility* that Nabu-na'id may have sought to strengthen his position by marrying a daughter of Nebuchadnezzar, in which case, of course, Nebuchadnezzar would be Belshazzar's grandfather on his mother's side (see however, p. li, *n.*).

2. *princes*] lords, as *v.* 1. So *v.* 3.

his wives] *his* consorts: so *vv.* 3, 23. The word is a rare one, being found otherwise in the O.T. only in Neh. ii. 6 (of the queen of Artaxerxes), and Ps. xlv. 9[1].

concubines] so *vv.* 3, 23. Not the usual Hebrew word, but one found also in the Aramaic of the Targums. Cf. Cant. vi. 8, where ' queens ' and ' concubines ' are mentioned side by side.

The presence of women at feasts was not usual in antiquity (cf., of Persia, Est. i. 10—12); but there is some evidence, though slight, that it was allowed in Babylon (Xen. *Cyrop.* v. ii. 28; and, in the age of Alexander, Curtius v. i. 38). The LXX. translator, feeling probably some difficulty in the statement, omits the clause relating to the ' wives and concubines ' both here and *vv.* 3, 23.

---

[1] It is read by some scholars conjecturally in Jud. v. 30 ('for the neck of the consort,'—שֵׁגַל for שָׁלָל). The cognate verb means *to ravish* (Is. xiii. 16 *al.*).

In the same hour came forth fingers of a man's hand, 5
and wrote over against the candlestick upon the plaister
of the wall of the king's palace: and the king saw the part
of the hand that wrote. Then the king's countenance was 6
changed, and his thoughts troubled him, so that the joints
of his loins were loosed, and his knees smote one against
another. The king cried aloud to bring in the astrologers, 7
the Chaldeans, and the soothsayers. *And* the king spake,

5. *In the same hour*] in the midst of their godless revelry (*v.* 4). Cf. for the expression iii. 6, 15, iv. 33.

over against] **in front of**, or **opposite to**, *the candlestick;* and hence a part of the wall where the light was particularly bright.

the plaister] lit. *the chalk.* The place was consequently white : and any dark object moving upon it would be immediately visible. In the great halls of Babylonian palaces the brick walls were probably, as in the palaces of Assyria, lined to a height of 10—12 ft. above the ground with slabs of a kind of alabaster, ornamented with elaborate basreliefs, and often brilliantly coloured (cf. Ez. xxiii. 4): in their upper part, also, the walls seem to have been usually painted, but the plaster may sometimes have been left white. Comp. Layard, *Nineveh and its Remains*[5], i. 254—7, 262 f., *Nineveh and Babylon*, p. 651, Rawl., *Anc. Mon.*[4] ii. 283.

the part] *the* **palm** *or* **hollow** ; the word (in the fem.) is used in the Targums and in Syriac in this sense (e.g. 1 Kings xviii. 44). "We must suppose the hand to have appeared above the place where the king was reclining" (Bevan).

6. *countenance*] lit. **brightness** (i.e. healthy freshness and colour): cf. iv. 36. So *vv.* 9, 10, vii. 28. Cf. the Targum (Onk.) of Deut. xxxiv. 7, 'And the glorious *brightness* of his face was not *changed*.'

was changed] i.e. grew pale through fear. If the text be correct, the word used can be rendered only ' was changed *for him* ' (hence R.V. *in him*) ; but the construction which this rendering presupposes, though found occasionally in Hebrew[1], is doubtful in Aramaic. Probably *was changed* is right, though two letters in the Aram. should be omitted.

his thoughts alarmed *him*] Cf. iv. 19. 'Troubled' is altogether too weak.

the joints of his loins were loosed, &c.] He trembled violently, and could not stand firm. Cf. Od. xviii. 341 λύθεν δ' ὑπὸ γυῖα ἑκάστης Ταρβοσύνῃ.

7. *aloud*] lit. *with might*, as iii. 4, iv. 14. Not simply 'commanded,' but 'cried aloud': the king's alarm was reflected in the tones of his voice.

the enchanters, *the Chaldeans, and the* **determiners** (of fates)] Cf. iv. 7 ; and see on i. 21, ii. 2, 27.

spake] **answered** (ii. 20). So *v.* 10.

---

[1] Ges.-Kautzsch, § 117. 4, Rem. 3.

64 DANIEL, V. [vv. 8—10.

and said to the wise *men* of Babylon, Whosoever shall read this writing, and shew me the interpretation thereof, shall be clothed with scarlet, and *have* a chain of gold about his neck, and shall be the third ruler in the kingdom. 8 Then came in all the king's wise *men*: but they could not read the writing, nor make known to the king the interpretation thereof. 9 Then *was* king Belshazzar greatly troubled, and his countenance *was* changed in him, and his lords *were* astonied.

10 Now the queen, by reason of the words of the king and

the wise men *of Babylon*] ii. 12, 14, &c.
shew me] declare to me (ii. 4, 6, &c.).
scarlet] purple (R.V.), as Ex. xxv. 4; Jud. viii. 26, &c. So *vv*. 16, 29. Purple was a royal, or princely, colour among the Persians (Est. viii. 15; Xen. *Anab*. I. v. 8), the Medes (*Cyrop*. 1. iii. 2, II. iv. 6), and also (it may be inferred) among the Seleucidae (1 Macc. x. 20, 62, 64, xiv. 43 f.; cf. viii. 14).

a chain of gold about his neck] Cf. Gen. xli. 42, where Pharaoh decorates Joseph similarly. A golden necklace was worn also by Persians of rank (cf. Xen. *Anab*. I. v. 8, viii. 29); and was given sometimes by the Persian kings as a compliment or mark of distinction: in Hdt. iii. 20 Cambyses sends 'a purple garment, a golden necklace, bracelets,' with other presents, to the Ethiopians; and in Xen. *Anab*. I. ii. 27 the younger Cyrus gives one to Syennesis. (The word, *hamnuk* or *hamnīk*, occurs in the O.T. only here and *vv*. 16, 29. It is probably of Persian origin [*hamyānak*], a diminutive from *hāmyān* 'girdle.' It is found in the Targums, in the form *mĕnīk*, and in Syriac as *hamnīk* and *hemnīk* (see Gen. xli. 42, Onk. and Pesh.); and it made its way into Greek as μανιάκης, LXX. Theod. here, Polyb., &c.).

and shall rule as one of three in the kingdom] So R.V. *marg*. The expression (which recurs *vv*. 16, 29) is difficult. The rendering of A.V. is however certainly not tenable. The word rendered 'third' in A.V. is not that which is used anywhere else (either in the Targums or in Daniel) to denote the ordinal; but resembles most closely the word (*tiltā* or *tūltā*) which both in the Targums and in Syriac means *a third part* (e.g. 2 Kings xi. 5, 6, 'a *third part* of you'). Hence the literal rendering appears to be, 'shall rule *as a third part* in the kingdom,' i.e. have a third part of the supreme authority in the country, be one of the three chief ministers, 'rule as one of three.' Cf. LXX. δοθήσεται αὐτῷ ἐξουσία τοῦ τρίτου μέρους τῆς βασιλείας.

8. The wise men, however, failed either to read or to explain the writing.

9. *greatly troubled*] greatly alarmed,—a climax upon *v*. 6.
and his brightness *was changed* upon *him*] 'upon' in accordance with the principle explained on ii. 1.
were astonied] were confused or (R.V.) perplexed.

10. *the queen*] probably, as most commentators assume,—partly

his lords, came into the banquet house: *and* the queen spake and said, O king, live for ever: let not thy thoughts trouble thee, nor let thy countenance be changed. There 11 is a man in thy kingdom, in whom *is* the spirit of the holy gods; and in the days of thy father light and understanding and wisdom, like the wisdom of the gods, was found in him; whom the king Nebuchadnezzar thy father, the king, *I say*, thy father, made master of the magicians, astrologers, Chaldeans, *and* soothsayers; forasmuch as an excellent spirit, 12 and knowledge, and understanding, interpreting of dreams, and shewing of hard sentences, and dissolving of doubts,

because she is distinguished from the 'wives' or 'consorts' mentioned in *v.* 2, partly on account of the manner in which she speaks in *v.* 11 of what had happened in the days of Nebuchadnezzar,—the queen-mother, i.e. (in the view of the writer) Nebuchadnezzar's widow[1]. In both Israel and Judah the mother of the reigning king is mentioned as an influential person, 1 Ki. xv. 13; 2 Ki. x. 13, xxiv. 12, 15; Jer. xiii. 18, xxix. 2.

O king, live for ever] Cf. on ii. 4.
trouble] **alarm**, as *v.* 6.
11. *in whom* is *the spirit*, &c.] As iv. 8, where see the note.
thy father] see on *v.* 2.
like the wisdom of (the) gods] Cf. 2 Sam. xiv. 20. The queen, however, speaks as a polytheist.
made master of the magicians, &c.] See ii. 48 and iv. 9.
enchanters, *Chaldeans, and* **determiners** (of fates)] As *v.* 7.

12. *an excellent spirit*] *a* **surpassing** *spirit*, i.e. pre-eminent ability. Cf. *v.* 14, vi. 3; and see on ii. 31. The Aramaic word used stands often in the Syriac version of the N.T. for πλεῖον and περισσότερον, as Matth. vi. 25, xi. 9, xii. 42.

interpreting...dissolving] These two English words are, of course, substantives. The meaning of the passage is, no doubt, given correctly, but it involves a change of punctuation: in the original, the two words, as actually pointed, are participles and out of construction with the context.

shewing of hard sentences] **declaring** *of* **riddles**. As Prof. Bevan remarks, the two Aramaic words here used correspond exactly to the two Hebrew words found in Judg. xiv. 14, 15, 19, and there rendered 'declare the riddle.' 'Hard' or (R.V.) 'dark sentences,' or 'sayings' (Ps. xlix. 4, lxxviii. 2; Prov. i. 6) is an obscure expression, the retention of which in the R.V. is to be regretted. The Hebrew word is the same as that which is used in 1 Ki. x. 1 of the 'hard questions' with which the Queen of Sheba plied Solomon. It is also used of an allegory Ez. xvii. 2, of an 'enigma' of life, Ps. xlix. 4, of a truth taught

[1] Nabu-na'id's actual mother died eight years previously, in his ninth year, as is expressly stated in the 'Annalistic Tablet,' ii. 13 (*KB*. iii. 2, p. 131; *RP*.[2] v. 160).

were found in the same Daniel, whom the king named Belteshazzar: now let Daniel be called, and he will shew 13 the interpretation. Then was Daniel brought in before the king. *And* the king spake and said unto Daniel, *Art* thou that Daniel, which *art* of the children of the captivity of Judah, whom the king my father brought out of Jewry? 14 I have even heard of thee, that the spirit of the gods *is* in thee, and *that* light and understanding and excellent 15 wisdom is found in thee. And now the wise *men*, the astrologers, have been brought in before me, that they should read this writing, and make known unto me the interpretation thereof: but they could not shew the inter-16 pretation of the thing: and I have heard of thee, that thou canst make interpretations, and dissolve doubts: now if thou canst read the writing, and make known to me the

indirectly Ps. lxxviii. 2, and of a satirical poem, containing indirect, taunting allusions, Hab. ii. 6. Orientals love both actual riddles and also indirect, figurative modes of speech; and the power of explaining either the one or the other is highly esteemed by them.

dissolving of doubts] **loosing of knots**: i.e. either *solving of difficulties* (cf. the same word in the Talm., *Jebamoth* 61ᵃ ('I see a *knot* [difficulty] here,' 107ᵇ 'they made two *knots* [raised two difficulties] against him'; it has also the same sense of *perplexity* in Syriac, P. S. col. 3591); or (Bevan) *untying of magic knots* or *spells* (cf. this sense of the word in Syriac, 'tiers of *knots*,' of a species of enchanters, 'incantations and *knots*,' P. S. *l. c.*), to accomplish which demanded special skill.

whom the king named Belteshazzar] See i. 7.
and he will shew] declare (*v.* 7).
13. *spake*] **answered**.
Art *thou that Daniel*] *Art* **thou** *Daniel*. The pron. *thou* is emphatic; but 'that' implies a false view of the syntax of the sentence (cf. on ii. 38 and iii. 15).
who is *of the children of the* **exile** *of Judah*, &c.] See ii. 25.
Jewry] Judah. 'Jewry,' i.e., the country of the Jews, is an old English expression for Judah (or Judæa): in A.V. it occurs besides in Luke xxiii. 5 and John vii. 1, as well as frequently in the Apocrypha. It is a standing expression in Coverdale's version of the Bible (1535); and from him it passed into Ps. lxxvi. 1 in the P.B.V. Shakespeare uses it seven times; e.g. 'Herod of Jewry,' *A. and Cl.* i. 2, 28, iii. 3, 3.
14. *I* **have heard** (R.V.), &c.] *v.* 11.
excellent wisdom] surpassing (*v.* 12) *wisdom* (*v.* 11).
15. *the astrologers*] *the* **enchanters** (i. 20).
shew] **declare**.
16. *make*] better *give* (R.V.); lit. *interpret*.
dissolve doubts] **loose knots**. See on *v.* 12.

interpretation thereof, thou shalt be clothed with scarlet, and *have* a chain of gold about thy neck, and shalt be the third ruler in the kingdom. Then Daniel answered and said before the king, Let thy gifts be to thyself, and give thy rewards to another; yet I will read the writing unto the king, and make known to him the interpretation.

O thou king, the most high God gave Nebuchadnezzar thy father a kingdom, and majesty, and glory, and honour: and for the majesty that he gave him, all people, nations, and languages, trembled and feared before him: whom he would he slew; and whom he would he kept alive; and whom he would he set up; and whom he would he put down. But when his heart was lifted up, and his mind hardened in pride, he was deposed from his kingly throne,

thou shalt be clothed with **purple**, &c.] As *v.* 7.
and **rule as one of three** *in the kingdom*] See on *v.* 7.
17. Daniel rejects the proffered honours: he will read the writing; but he will do so quite irrespectively of any promises made to him by the heathen king.
before the king] cf. on ii. 8.
rewards] See the note on ii. 6.
yet] **nevertheless** (R.V.) brings out the force of the adverb used more distinctly (cf. iv. 15, 23 [R. V.]).
18—24. Before interpreting the writing Daniel reads the king a lesson. Nebuchadnezzar's pride, combined with his refusal to recognize the sovereignty of the true God, had brought upon him a bitter humiliation: Belshazzar has exhibited the same faults yet more conspicuously: and the present sign has been sent in order to warn him of the impending punishment.
18. the *kingdom*, **and greatness**, *and glory*, *and* **majesty**] Cf. iv. 22, 36.
19. *and* **because of** *the* **greatness** *that he gave him, all peoples, nations, and languages*, &c.] Cf. iii. 4.
trembled and feared before him] dreading what he might do next.
whom he would he slew, &c.] he acted as though he possessed the attributes of Deity, and was accountable to no superior. Similar expressions are used elsewhere of the action of God: e.g. Deut. xxxii. 39; 1 Sam. ii. 6, 7; Ps. lxxv. 7.
set up] *lifted up* (or *exalted*): the word used in Ps. lxxv. 7, lxxxix. 19, cxiii. 7, &c.
20. *was lifted up*] Cf. Deut. viii. 14, xvii. 20; Ez. xxxi. 10, &c.
and his **spirit was hardened that he dealt proudly** (R.V.)] 'was hardened' is literally *was strong* (i.e. stiff, unyielding): the same word (*t^ekaph*) is used in the Targums for the Hebrew *ḥāzaḳ*, *ḥizzēḳ* 'to be *or* make strong (hard)' in Ex. vii. 13, 22, ix. 12, 35, &c. (of Pharaoh's heart). Cf. Deut. ii. 30.

21 and they took *his* glory from him: and he *was* driven from the sons of men; and his heart was made like the beasts, and his dwelling *was* with the wild asses: they fed him with grass like oxen, and his body was wet with the dew of heaven; till he knew that the most high God ruled in the kingdom of men, and *that* he appointeth over it whom-
22 soever he will. And thou his son, O Belshazzar, hast not
23 humbled thine heart, though thou knewest all this; but hast lifted up thyself against the Lord of heaven; and they have brought the vessels of his house before thee, and thou, and thy lords, thy wives, and thy concubines, *have* drunk wine in them; and thou hast praised the gods of silver, and gold, of brass, iron, wood, and stone, which see not, nor hear, nor know: and the God in whose hand thy breath *is*, and whose *are* all thy ways, hast thou not glori-
24 fied: then *was* the part of the hand sent from him; and
25 this writing *was* written. And this *is* the writing that *was*
26 written, MENE, MENE, TEKEL, UPHARSIN. This *is*

they took his *glory*] or, *his glory was taken*, according to the principle explained on iv. 25.
21. See iv. 25, 32, 33.
the wild asses] An untamable animal, which roamed in the open plains (see Job xxxix. 5—8; and cf. Gen. xvi. 12): to dwell with the wild asses would thus be a special mark of wildness and savagery.
they fed him] or he was fed (R.V.): iv. 25, 32 ('make to eat').
till he knew, &c.] iv. 25, 32.
appointeth] setteth up (R.V.), as iv. 17 (A.V.) for the same word. 'Appointeth' is not strong enough.
22—23. But Belshazzar, in spite of the warning afforded by Nebuchadnezzar's fate, has sinned still more deeply, and by wanton sacrilege has deliberately defied the God of heaven.
23. *and they have brought*, &c.] See *vv.* 2—4.
which see not, nor hear, nor know] Cf. Deut. iv. 28; Ps. cxv. 5—6, cxxxv. 16—17.
in whose hand thy breath is] who is the author of thy life and being. Cf. Gen. ii. 7; Job xii. 10.
thy ways] i.e. thy destinies. Cf. Jer. x. 23.
24. *Then* was *the* palm (*v.* 5) *of the hand* sent forth from before him; *and this writing* was inscribed] *v.* 5. *Then* is here equivalent, virtually, to *hence, therefore*.
25—28. The reading and interpretation of the writing.
25. *written*] inscribed (R.V.). The word is not the one that ordinarily means *to write*, but one that means rather *to print* or *stamp*.
MENE (pron. *měnê*, to rhyme with *bewray*), MENE, TEKEL (pron. *těkêl*, to rhyme with *bewail*), UPHARSIN] in the explanation (*v.* 28),

the interpretation of the thing: MENE; God hath numbered thy kingdom, and finished it. TEKEL; Thou art 27 weighed in the balances, and art found wanting. PERES; 28 Thy kingdom is divided, and given to the Medes and Persians.

Then commanded Belshazzar, and they clothed Daniel 29 with scarlet, and *put* a chain of gold about his neck, and

we have, for *upharsīn*, *pĕrēs* (to rhyme with *deface*), which is just the singular of *parsīn* (or, where a vowel, as here u, precedes, *pharsīn*), *u* being 'and.' *Mĕnê*, as the pass. part. of *mĕnâ*, to number, might mean 'numbered'; but if the present vocalization is correct, *tĕḳêl* cannot mean 'weighed,' nor *pĕrēs* 'divided.' These two words, as they stand, must be substantives. The true explanation of the four words is probably that which was first suggested by Clermont-Ganneau[1], and which has since been adopted by Nöldeke and others. They are really the names of three *weights*, *mĕnê* being the correct Aramaic form of the Hebrew *māneh*, the *m'na* (μνᾶ), *tĕḳêl* being the Aramaic form of the Hebrew *sheḳel*, and *pĕrēs* (or more correctly *pĕrās*), properly *division*, being a late Jewish word for a half-m'na. Thus the four words are really A M'NA, A M'NA, A SHEKEL, AND HALF-M'NAS. The puzzle consisted partly in the character or manner in which they were supposed to have been written —an unfamiliar form of the Aramaic character, for instance, or, as the mediæval Jews suggested, a vertical instead of a horizontal arrangement of the letters; partly in the difficulty of attaching any meaning to them, even when they were read: what could the names of three weights signify?[2] Here Daniel's skill in the 'declaring of riddles' (*v.* 12) comes in. *Mĕnê* itself means 'numbered,' as well as 'a m'na': it is accordingly interpreted at once as signifying that the days of Belshazzar's kingdom are 'numbered,' and approaching their end. *Tĕḳêl*, '*sheḳel*,' suggests *tĕḳîl*, 'weighed': 'Thou art *weighed* in the balances, and art found wanting.' *Parsin*, 'half-m'nas,' or *pĕrēs* (*pĕrās*), 'a half-m'na,' points allusively to a double interpretation: 'Thy kingdom is *divided* (*pĕrīs*)[3], and given to the Medes and *Persians*' (Aramaic *pāras*).

26. *finished it*] **completed** *it*, given it its full and complete measure of time. Cp. the cognate adj. in Gen. xv. 16 ('full,' 'complete').

28. *the Medes and Persians*] See on *v.* 31.

29. Belshazzar fulfils the promise given in *v.* 16. The unconcern exhibited by the king at Daniel's interpretation, especially in presence of what (as *v.* 30 shews) could hardly have been a distant or unsuspected danger, is scarcely consistent with historical probability.

scarlet] **purple**, as *vv.* 7, 16.

---

[1] *Journal Asiatique*, Juillet-Août, 1886, p. 36 ff. Reprinted in *Recueil d'Archéol. Orientale*, i. (1888), p. 136 ff.
[2] For the names of common objects interpreted significantly, see Jer. i. 11, 12 xix. 1, 7 (Heb.), Am. viii. 1.
[3] The word occurs in Heb. in this sense, *e.g.* Lev. xi. 3, 4, 5; and of dividing bread, Is. lviii. 7 ('deal'), Jer. xvi. 7 (R.V. 'break').

made a proclamation concerning him, that *he* should be
30 the third ruler in the kingdom. In that night *was* Bel-
31 shazzar the king of the Chaldeans slain. And Darius the
Median took the kingdom, *being* about threescore and two
years old.

that he *should be ruler* as one of three *in the kingdom*] See on *v.* 7.
31. *And Darius the Median* (or *the* **Mede**, as xi. 1) **received** *the
kingdom*] The idea of the writer appears to be that the Medes and
Persians were acting in concert at the time of the capture of
Babylon (*v.* 28); but that when the city was taken, 'Darius the Mede,'
by a joint arrangement between the two peoples (or their rulers),
'received' the kingdom, or (ix. 1) 'was made king,' and (ch. vi) took
up his residence in Babylon as his capital. Darius, though bound by
the laws of the two allied peoples, the 'Medes and Persians' (vi. 8,
12, 15), clearly, in ch. vi, acts not as viceroy for another but as an
independent king, organising his kingdom into satrapies (vi. 1), otherwise both acting as king and receiving the title of 'king' (vi. 3, 7, 8,
&c., 25): his reign, moreover, precedes, and is distinct from, that of
Cyrus (vi. 28: see also ix. 1, 2, xi. 1, as compared with x. 1; and cp.
on viii. 3). It is true, this representation does not agree with what is
known from history, for though the Medes (see on ii. 39) joined Cyrus
in B.C. 549, and formed afterwards an important and influential element
in the Persian empire[1], there is no trace of their exercising afterwards
any independent rule; in the Inscriptions, Cyrus begins his reign in
Babylon immediately after the close of that of Nabu-na'id. Contemporary monuments allow no room for a king, 'Darius the Mede,'
between the entry of Babylon by Cyrus and the reign of Cyrus himself.
The figure, it seems, must be the result of some historical confusion,—
perhaps (see the Introd. p. liv) a combination of Gubaru, the 'governor'
(*peḥāh*), who first entered Babylon, and took command in it, at the
time of Cyrus' conquest, with (cf. Sayce, *Monuments*, pp. 528—30)
Darius Hystaspis, father (not *son*) of 'Ăhashwērōsh=Xerxes (ix. 1).

about threescore and two years old] We do not know upon what tradition, or chronological calculation, the age assigned to 'Darius the
Mede' depends.

CHAP. VI. DANIEL IN THE LIONS' DEN.

Darius the Mede appoints over his kingdom 120 satraps with three
presidents over them, one of the latter being Daniel (*vv.* 1—2). On
account of the regard shewn to him by the king, the satraps and
presidents, being moved with envy, seek an opportunity to ruin him
(*vv.* 3—4). They accordingly persuade Darius to issue a decree,
forbidding any one to ask a petition of God or man, except the king,
for thirty days (*vv.* 5—9). Daniel, however, continues as before to

---

[1] Under the Persian kings, Medes are repeatedly mentioned as holding high and
responsible positions (Rawl., *Herod.* App. to Bk. i, Essay iii, § 2). On the large
amount contributed by Media to the Persian revenue see Rawl., *Anc. Mon.*[4] ii. 428.

It pleased Darius to set over the kingdom an hundred **6**
and twenty princes, which should be over the whole kingdom; and over these three presidents; of whom Daniel **2**

pray three times a day at his open window towards Jerusalem. The king, upon information being brought to him, reluctantly yielding obedience to the law, orders Daniel to be cast into a den of lions (*vv.* 10—17). Next morning, to his astonishment and joy, he finds him uninjured; and publishes a decree enjoining men, in all parts of his dominion, to stand in awe of the God of Daniel, who had given such wonderful evidence of His power (*vv.* 18—28).

Daniel has hitherto been uniformly prosperous: success and honours have attended him under each monarch with whom he has had to do (i. 19, 20; ii. 26 ff., 48, 49; iv. 19—27; v. 17 ff., 29), even including Darius (vi. 2, 3). But, in his old age, his trial also comes. His loyalty to his God, his determination not to disown the public profession of his faith, is put severely to the test. It is not, as with his three companions in ch. iii., a question of a positive sin which he will not commit, but of a positive duty which he will not omit. He finds himself placed in a position in which, if he worships the God of his fathers in his accustomed manner, he will become guilty of a capital offence. The situation is, in all essential features, the same as that of the faithful Jews under the persecution of Antiochus Epiphanes (see 1 Macc. i. 41—64). The story of Daniel's deliverance, notwithstanding certain improbabilities which (quite apart from the details which are avowedly miraculous) it seems, to some minds, to present, is a vivid exemplification of the value, in God's sight, of courageous loyalty to Himself. Of course, in the ordinary operation of Providence, God's servants are not delivered from bodily peril by a direct miraculous intervention of the character here described: but the narrative, like that in ch. iii., must be judged by the principle laid down in the Introduction (p. lxxii): the lesson, not the story in which it is embodied, is the point which the narrator desires to impress, and on which the reader's attention ought to be fixed.

1. *an hundred and twenty* **satraps**] see on iii. 2. No other notice of this organization has come down to us. The Persian empire was first organised into provinces under 'satraps' by Darius Hystaspis (522—485 B.C.); and then the satrapies were only 20 in number (Herod. III. 89[1]). The statement, upon independent grounds, is not probable; and if it is true that there was no king 'Darius the Mede,' some error or confusion must manifestly underlie it. It may have been suggested by the 127 provinces, into which, according to Est. i. 1, viii. 9, the Persian empire was divided under Xerxes.

over] in, i.e. (R.V.) **throughout.**

2. *three presidents*] Aram. *sārak*, prob. a form derived from the

---

[1] The Behistun Inscription of Darius (col. I. par. 6) enumerates 23 provinces; the later (sepulchral) inscription of Naksh-i-Rustam (l. 7—19), 29: see *RP.*[1] i. 111, v. 151 f. Darius, in the first of these inscriptions, mentions the 'satrap' of Bactria, and the 'satrap' of Arachotia (col. iii. par. 3 and 9). See further details in Rawl., *Anc. Mon.*[4] iii. 417 ff.

72 DANIEL, VI. [vv. 3—6.

was first: that the princes might give accounts unto them,
3 and the king should have no damage. Then this Daniel
was preferred above the presidents and princes, because
an excellent spirit *was* in him; and the king thought to
set him over the whole realm.

4 Then the presidents and princes sought to find occasion
against Daniel concerning the kingdom; but they could
find none occasion nor fault; forasmuch as he *was* faithful,
5 neither was there any error or fault found in him. Then
said these men, We shall not find any occasion against
this Daniel, except we find *it* against him concerning the
6 law of his God. Then these presidents and princes

Pers. *săr*, 'head,' 'chief,' 'prince.' In the O.T. it is found only in this chap. (*vv.* 2, 3, 4, 6, 7): in the Targums it stands often for the Heb. *shōtēr*, 'officer,' as Ex. v. 6, 10; Deut. i. 15, xx. 5; Josh. i. 10; Prov. vi. 7 ('overseer').

was first] was one: so R.V. rightly.

that these satraps *might give* account *unto them*] strictly, *might be giving account*, i.e. might be permanently answerable to them, that the interests and revenues of the king were properly guarded. No such officials are mentioned elsewhere,—except in so far as they may be regarded as the successors of the three Babylonian ministers, presupposed in v. 7, 16, 29. Darius Hystaspis, as a check upon his satraps, appointed in each satrapy an independent military commandant, and a royal 'scribe,' or secretary, whose business it was to report to the king the doings of the satrap (Hdt. iii. 128; Rawl., *Anc. Mon.*⁴ iii. 424).

3. *was preferred*] distinguished himself, or (R.V.) was distinguished. The root idea of the word is *to shine*, hence *to be illustrious*. It is common in Syriac in the sense of *praeclare se gessit*, representing for instance the Greek διαλάμπειν, εὐδοκιμεῖν, εὐδοξεῖν (Payne Smith, col. 2438). 'Was preferred' means here *was advanced* or *promoted*, in accordance with the old sense of 'prefer,' preserved now only in 'preferment'; see Est. ii. 9; John i. 15, 27; and the *Bible Word-Book*.

princes] satraps. So *vv.* 4, 6, 7.

an excellent spirit] *a* surpassing *spirit*, as v. 12.

4. *sought to find occasion*, &c.] They were evidently jealous that a man of alien race and creed should be exalted above themselves.

concerning] as touching (R.V.): lit. *from the side of*. The meaning of course is, any charge of disloyalty, or any remissness or neglect in the discharge of his public office.

error] or *negligence*: iii. 29.

5. *law*] *dāth*, the same Persian word, which is found in ii. 9, 13, 15, and also in vi. 8, 12, 15, and constantly in Esther. Here, as in Ezr. vii. 12, 14, 21, 25, 26, it denotes the Jewish law (Heb. *tôrāh*).

assembled *together* to the king, and said thus unto him, King Darius, live for ever. All the presidents of the kingdom, 7 the governors, and the princes, the counsellors and the captains, have consulted together to establish a royal statute, and to make a firm decree, that whosoever shall ask a petition of any God or man for thirty days, save of thee, O king, he shall be cast into the den of lions.

6. *assembled* together] **came thronging** (A.V. *marg.*; R.V. *marg.* **came tumultuously**). The word occurs several times in the Aramaic of the Targums, where it corresponds to Heb. words signifying *to be in commotion* or *tumult*, as Ps. xlvi. 6, 'nations *were in tumult*,' Ruth i. 9, 'and all the inhabitants of the city *were in commotion* on account of them'; and it occurs once in Heb., Ps. ii. 1, 'Why do the nations *throng tumultuously?*[1]' The expression is thus a more vivid and graphic one than would be inferred from the rend. of A.V.: the courtiers, in their animosity against Daniel, are represented as flocking tumultuously to the king, for the purpose of gaining his co-operation in their plan.

live for ever] see on ii. 4.

7. *All the presidents*] of course, with the exception of Daniel, who was one of them (*v.* 2). But the misrepresentation may be meant to be intentional, as though to lead the king to suppose that the proposal had Daniel's approval.

the governors, and the princes, the counsellers and the captains] the **praefects** (ii. 48), *and the* **satraps**, *the* **ministers** (iii. 24), *and the* **governors** (iii. 2). Cf. the enumeration of officials in iii. 2, 3, 27.

to establish a royal statute] Of course, indirectly,—by prevailing upon the king to take action. A.V. *marg.* 'that the king should establish a statute, and make' &c., expresses the meaning more distinctly; but it is a less natural rendering of the Aramaic.

and to make a firm decree] *and to* **make a stringent interdict.** 'Interdict' (so A. V. *marg.*, and R.V.) is lit. a *binding*, or *restraining;* and almost the same word is used in Num. xxx. 2, 3, 4, &c. of a restraining vow (A.V., R.V., 'bond'). The passive partic. of the cognate verb is common in the Mishna in the sense of 'prohibited.'

a petition] The meaning probably is, not any petition absolutely, but any petition of the nature of a prayer, or request addressed formally to a superior. The interdict has been deemed an incredible one; but some allowance must be made for what an oriental despot might prescribe in a freak of humour. Nevertheless, it is remarkable that the king should accede so readily to the proposal made to him, without either consulting the minister whose judgement he specially trusted (*v.* 3), or reflecting upon the difficulties in which it might involve him.

the den of lions] the reference is "to the custom which existed already among the Assyrians, and from them was passed on to the

---

[1] Cf. the cogn. subst. *throng*, Ps. lv. 14 (so R.V.), lxiv. 2 (R.V. 'tumult,' marg. 'throng').

8 Now, O king, establish the decree, and sign the writing,
9 that *it* be not changed, according to the law of the Medes and Persians, which altereth not. Wherefore king Darius signed the writing and the decree.
10 Now when Daniel knew that the writing *was* signed, he went into his house; and his windows being open in his chamber toward Jerusalem, he kneeled upon his knees

Persians, of keeping lions for the chase" (Bevan): cf. Ez. xix. 9. The word rendered 'den' means properly a *pit* or *dungeon:* see the Targ. of Gen. xxxvii. 22; Jer. xxxviii. 6, 7; and cf. *v.* 23 ('taken up'), and *v.* 24, *end.*

8. *decree*] **interdict.**
altereth not] lit. *passeth not away.* On the unalterableness of the edicts of a Persian king, cf. Est. i. 19 ('let it be written among the laws of the Persians and Medes, that it *pass not away*'), viii. 8 (a royal edict, properly signed and sealed, 'may no man reverse').

9. *decree*] **interdict.**

10. *and his windows,* &c.] more exactly, and also more clearly, **now he had** *in his* **roof-chamber open windows fronting** *Jerusalem.* The clause is parenthetical, and describes the constant and habitual arrangement of Daniel's windows.

roof-chamber] usually rendered *upper chamber,* which however does not at all suggest to an English reader what is intended. The 'roof-chamber' was (and still is) an apartment 'raised above the flat roof of a house at one corner, or upon a tower-like annex to the building, with latticed windows giving free circulation to the air' (Moore on Judg. iii. 20). It was thus cool in summer (Judg. *l. c.*), and a part of the house to which anyone would naturally retire if he wished to be undisturbed (cf. 1 Ki. xvii. 19; 2 Ki. i. 2, iv. 10, 11). In the N.T. the roof-chamber is mentioned as a place of meeting for prayer (Acts i. 13, xx. 8; cf. x. 9: see also ix. 37, 39). Comp. Thomson's *The Land and the Book,* ed. 2, II. 634, 636 (with an illustration).

open] i.e., either without lattices at all, or without fixed lattices (cf. 2 Ki. i. 2, xiii. 17) opp. to 'closed windows' (Ez. xl. 16, xli. 16, 26), or 'windows with closed wood-work' (1 Ki. vi. 4), the lattices of which did not admit of being opened.

toward Jerusalem] To pray, turning towards Jerusalem—or, if in Jerusalem, towards the Temple—became in later times a standing Jewish custom: we do not know how early it began; but it was based doubtless upon 1 Ki. viii. 35, 38, 44, 48 (in this verse with reference to exiles in a foreign land), cf. Ps. v. 7, xxviii. 2. The custom is alluded to in the Mishna (*Běrāchōth,* iv. 5, 6); and in *Sifrê* 71[b] it is said that those in foreign lands turn in prayer towards the land of Israel, those in the land of Israel towards Jerusalem, and those in Jerusalem towards the Temple. Mohammed at first commanded his disciples to pray towards Jerusalem; but afterwards he altered the *ḳibla* ('facing-point') to Mecca.

and he continued kneeling.... **and praying, and giving** *thanks* three times a day, and prayed, and gave thanks before his God, as he did aforetime. Then these men assembled, ¹¹ and found Daniel praying and making supplication before his God. Then they came near, and spake before the ¹² king concerning the king's decree; Hast thou not signed a decree, that every man that shall ask *a petition* of any God or man within thirty days, save of thee, O king, shall be cast into the den of lions? The king answered and said, The thing *is* true, according to the law of the Medes and Persians, which altereth not. Then answered they ¹³ and said before the king, *That* Daniel, which *is* of the children of the captivity of Judah, regardeth not thee, O king, nor the decree that thou hast signed, but maketh his petition three times a day. Then the king, when he ¹⁴ heard *these* words, was sore displeased with himself, and

before his God, **forasmuch as he had been wont to do** (it) *aforetime*] inasmuch as it had been his regular custom, he still adhered to it.

three times a day] Cf. Ps. lv. 17 ('at evening, and at morning, and at noonday will I complain and moan'). In later times, the three hours of prayer were—not as is often supposed, the third, sixth and ninth hours, but—the time when the morning burnt-offering was offered (תפלת שחר), in the afternoon at the ninth hour (our three o'clock; cf. Acts iii. 1, x. 30), when the evening meal-offering was offered (תפלת מנחה), and sunset (תפלת הערב): see Schürer, ii. 237. The custom may well have arisen before the 2nd cent. B.C. On the prayers which, at least in later days, were used at the three times, see Hamburger, *Real-Encyclop.* vol. ii., arts. MORGEN-, MINCHA-, and ABENDGEBET.

before his God] a usage of the later Jews (as in the Targum constantly), who, from a feeling of greater reverence, said 'to speak, pray, confess, &c. *before* God,' rather than '*to* Him.' Cf. *v.* 22, *end*; also ii. 9, with the note. The later Jews even extended the same usage to cases in which God was really the agent: cf. Matt. xi. 26 (οὕτως ἐγένετο εὐδοκία ἔμπροσθέν σου), xviii. 14 (see R.V. *marg.*); Luke xii. 6 (ἐπιλελησμένον ἐνώπιον τοῦ Θεοῦ); Num. xiv. 8 Onk. ('if there is good pleasure in us *before Jehovah*'); and see Dalman, *Die Worte Jesu*, pp. 172—174.

11. *assembled*] **came thronging** (*v.* 6),—flocking tumultuously about Daniel's house.

12. *before the king*] cf. *v.* 10; and see on ii. 9.
decree (twice)] interdict. So *v.* 13.
altereth not] lit. *passeth not away* (*v.* 8).
13. *children of the* **exile** *of Judah*] ii. 25, v. 13.
14. *was sore displeased with himself*] **was sore displeased** (R.V.):

set *his* heart on Daniel to deliver him: and he laboured
15 till the going down of the sun to deliver him. Then these
men assembled unto the king, and said unto the king,
Know, O king, that the law of the Medes and Persians
is, That no decree nor statute which the king establisheth
16 may be changed. Then the king commanded, and they
brought Daniel, and cast *him* into the den of lions. *Now
the king spake and said unto Daniel, Thy God whom
17 thou servest continually, he will deliver thee.* And a stone
was brought, and laid upon the mouth of the den; and
the king sealed it with his own signet, and with the signet
of his lords; that the purpose might not be changed concerning Daniel.

'with himself' is incorrect. The expression is the Aram. equivalent of the Heb. phrase found in Jonah iv. 1; Neh. ii. 10, xiii. 8.

laboured] rather, **continued striving**; Theod. ἠγωνίσατο, Pesh. מתכתש הוא. The idea expressed by the word is that of *struggling*.

to deliver him (second time)] *to* **rescue him** (R.V.: so *v.* 27 A.V.); a different word from the one rendered 'deliver' just before.

15. *assembled*] **came thronging** or **tumultuously**, as *v.* 6.

Know, O king, &c.] The courtiers, in their violence against Daniel, address Darius, as in *v.* 12, abruptly and peremptorily, without any respectful words of introduction (*v.* 6).

decree] **interdict.**

16. Now *the king spake*, &c.] **The king answered**, &c. The asyndetic construction is characteristic of the Aramaic portion of the book: iii. 19, 24, 26, v. 7, 13, vi. 20 (notice italics in A.V.), *al.*

he will deliver thee] Rather, **may he** (emph.) *deliver thee!* The king hopes, even against hope, that Daniel may by some means or other be spared his fate. Throughout the narrative Darius shews solicitude for Daniel (cf. *vv.* 14, 18—20). He does not willingly consign him to death: he has been entrapped by his courtiers; and in acting as he has done, he has merely, like Herod (Matth. xiv. 9), yielded to what he supposes to be the necessities of his position.

17. *sealed it with his own signet*] seals were in common use alike among the Assyrians, Babylonians (cf. Hdt. I. 195, 'every one has a seal'), and Persians; and numbers, especially from Babylonia and Assyria, have been brought to European museums during the past half century. The signet cylinder of Darius Hystaspis represented the king as engaged in a lion hunt (Rawlinson, *Anc. Mon.* III. 226, 227). Cf. (in Israel) 1 Ki. xxi. 8; and (in Persia) Est. iii. 12, viii. 8, 10.

that **nothing** *might be changed concerning Daniel* (R.V.)] i.e. that nothing might be done, either by the king, or by anyone else, to rescue Daniel. The word, meaning properly *will, purpose*, is here used in the weakened sense of *thing*, which it has in the Aramaic

Then the king went to his palace, and passed the night 18 fasting: neither were instruments of musick brought before him: and his sleep went from him. Then the king arose 19 very early in the morning, and went in haste unto the den of lions. And when he came to the den, he cried with 20 a lamentable voice unto Daniel: *and* the king spake and said to Daniel, O Daniel, servant of the living God, is thy God, whom thou servest continually, able to deliver thee from the lions? Then said Daniel unto the king, 21

of Palmyra (Lidzbarski, *Handbuch der Nordsemitischen Epigraphik* (1898), p. 464, l. 6, 'about these *things*'), as well as constantly in Syriac, as Ecclus. xxxii. 19 (Pesh.) ' Do not *anything* without counsel.'

18. *instruments of musick*] The meaning of the word thus rendered is unknown. The root in Aram. and Heb. means *to thrust, overthrow* (Ps. xxxvi. 12, cxviii. 13). In Arab. it means further *to spread, spread out*, and is also used specially in the sense *compressit feminam*. The ancient translators and commentators conjectured a meaning suited to the context. Theod. (ἐδέσματα), Pesh., Jerome (*cibi*), render *food*; Rashi (12 cent.), *a table* (cf. A.V. *marg.*); Ibn Ezra, *stringed instruments* (supposing, improbably, *to thrust* to be used in the sense of *to strike*); Saad. (10 cent.), *dancing-girls*; many moderns (from the Arab. meaning of the root, mentioned above), *concubines*. But it is very doubtful whether it is legitimate to explain an Aram. word from a sense peculiar to Arabic, and there, moreover, only secondary and derived. By assuming a very small corruption in the text (דחון for לחנן), we should, however, obtain the ordinary Aram. word for *concubines* (v. 2, 3, 23): so Marti, Prince. But whatever the true meaning, or reading, of the word may be, the general sense of the verse remains the same: the king did not indulge in his usual diversions.

fled (R.V.) *from him*] lit. *fled* upon *him*: in accordance with the idiom explained on ii. 1. For 'fled' cf. Gen. xxxi. 40; Est. vi. 1.

19. *Then the king arose* at dawn, as soon as it was light] lit. *at dawn, in the brightness*. The words used imply that day had fully broken. The first word ('dawn') stands in the Targ. for 'morning' in Is. lviii. 8; and the second ('brightness'), in its Heb. form, in Is. lxii. 1.

in haste (iii. 24)] So anxious was he to learn how Daniel had fared.

20. *when he came*] as he drew near.

with a lamentable voice] or, *with a* pained *voice*. The same expression (with an inappreciable difference of form) occurs in the Targ. (Ps.-Jon.) of Ex. xii. 31, and in that of Est. iv. 1.

and the king, &c.] the king answered *and said*.

the living God] The same emphatic and significant title, found in Deut. v. 26; Josh. iii. 10; 1 Sam. xvii. 26, 36; 2 Ki. xix. 4, 16; Jer. x. 10, xxiii. 36; Hos. i. 10; Ps. xlii. 2, lxxxiv. 2.

22 O king, live for ever. My God hath sent his angel, and hath shut the lions' mouths, that they have not hurt me: forasmuch as before him innocency was found in me; and
23 also before thee, O king, have I done no hurt. Then was the king exceeding glad for him, and commanded that *they* should take Daniel up out of the den. So Daniel was taken up out of the den, and no manner of hurt was found
24 upon him, because he believed in his God. And the king commanded, and they brought those men which had accused Daniel, and they cast *them* into the den of lions, them, their children, and their wives; and the lions had the mastery of them, and brake all their bones in pieces or ever they came at the bottom of the den.

21. *O king, live for ever*] cf. *v.* 6.
22. *sent his angel*] cf. iii. 28.
shut &c.] cf. Heb. xi. 33 (ἔφραξαν; Theod. here ἐνέφραξεν).
before thee] see on *v.* 10 end, and ii. 9; and cf. Luke xv. 18, 21.
23. *for him*] to be omitted (like 'with himself' in *v.* 14).
because he believed—or (R.V.) **trusted**—*in his God*] cf. Heb. xi. 33.
24. The king's vengeance on the men who had maliciously accused Daniel.
accused] see on iii. 8.
their children, and their wives] according to the rough justice—or, to our minds, injustice—of antiquity: cf. Josh. vii. 24—25; 2 Sam. xxi. 5—9; Est. ix. 13, 14; Hdt. iii. 119. Cf. Mozley's *Ruling Ideas in Early Ages*, p. 87 ff., in explanation of the principle involved.
had the mastery of them] or *fell upon them*—a sense which the Aram. phrase, properly meaning *to rule over*, has in the Targums (*e.g.* Judg. xv. 12; 2 Sam. i. 15).
in pieces] These words should be followed by a comma (as in R.V.), the words *or ever* &c., having reference to both the preceding clauses (the order in the Aram. is 'and they reached not the bottom of the pit, ere the lions' &c.).
or ever] i.e. *before;* the expression being a pleonastic, reduplicated form of *ere* (A.S. *ær*, Germ. *eher*), frequent in Old English. So Prov. viii. 23 (A.V., R.V.), Ps. liii. 8 (P.B.V.), xc. 2 (P.B.V., A.V., R.V.), Cant. vi. 12 (A.V., R.V.), Acts xxiii. 15 (A.V., R.V.); Is. lxv. 24, in Coverdale's version, '*Or ever* they call, I shal answere them'; and several times in Shakespeare. Mr Wright (*Bible Word-Book*, s.v.) quotes from Latimer's *Sermons*, 'The great man was gone forth about such affairs as behoved him, *or* [=*ere*] I came.'
25—27. The edict of Darius, enjoining all his subjects to dread and fear the God of Daniel. Cf. the decree of Nebuchadnezzar in iii. 29, forbidding men anywhere to speak against Him; and his proclamation in iv. 1—3, 37, declaring to mankind His doings. The thought and phraseology of the edict are strongly Jewish.

Then king Darius wrote unto all people, nations, and 25
languages, that dwell in all the earth; Peace be multiplied
unto you. I make a decree, That in every dominion of 26
my kingdom *men* tremble and fear before the God of
Daniel: for he *is* the living God, and stedfast for ever, and
his kingdom *that* which shall not be destroyed, and his
dominion *shall be even* unto the end. He delivereth and 27
rescueth, and he worketh signs and wonders in heaven
and in earth, who hath delivered Daniel from the power
of the lions. So this Daniel prospered in the reign of 28
Darius, and in the reign of Cyrus the Persian.

25. *unto all the peoples,...unto you*] verbally identical with iv. **1**.
26. *I make a decree*] almost exactly as iii. 29.
in every dominion] *in* **all the** *dominion* &c.
tremble and fear before] Cf. v. 19 (of the dread felt towards Nebuchadnezzar).
stedfast] or *subsistent, enduring*,—a common epithet of God in the Targums, and often representing the Heb. 'living,' as in the passages quoted on *v.* 20[1]. The combination, 'living and enduring' (קָיָם וְחַי), is also frequent in post-Biblical Jewish literature.
and his kingdom &c.] Cf. ii. 44, iv. 3, 34 *b*; also vii. 14, 27.
27. *He delivereth and rescueth*] And not Darius (*v.* 14): cf. iii. 28, 29.
signs and wonders] iv. 2, 3.
from the power] Aram. *from the hand*, as in Heb., Ps. xxii. 20 (21), xlix. 15 (16), &c.
28. After this signal deliverance Daniel's gainsayers were silenced; and prosperity attended him through the rest of the reign of Darius, as well as in that of his successor Cyrus.

CHAPTERS VII.—XII.

The *second* part of the book, describing the four visions seen by Daniel in the reigns of Belshazzar (ch. vii., viii.), Darius the Mede (ch. ix.), and Cyrus (ch. x.—xii.).

CHAP. VII. THE VISION OF THE FOUR BEASTS.

A vision, seen by Daniel in a dream, in the first year of Belshazzar. The vision was of four beasts emerging from the agitated sea, a lion with eagle's wings, a bear, a leopard with four wings and four heads, and a fourth beast, with powerful iron teeth, destroying all things, and with ten horns, among which another 'little horn' sprang up, 'speaking proud things,' before which three of the other horns were rooted up (*vv.* 1—8). Hereupon a celestial assize is held: the Almighty appears, seated on a throne of flame, and surrounded by myriads of attendants;

---

[1] Also regularly in the phrases, '(As) I *live*,' '(As) Jehovah *liveth*,' 1 Sam. xiv. 39; Ez. v. 11, &c.

80 DANIEL, VII. [vv. 1, 2.

7 In the first year of Belshazzar king of Babylon Daniel had a dream and visions of his head upon his bed: then he wrote the dream, *and* told the sum of the matters.
2 Daniel spake and said, I saw in my vision by night, and behold, the four winds of the heaven strove upon the great

the beast whose horn spake proud things is slain; and a figure in human form comes with the clouds of heaven into the presence of the Divine Judge, and receives from Him a universal and never-ending dominion (*vv.* 9—14). After this, the vision is interpreted to Daniel: the four beasts are explained to signify four kingdoms; and after the destruction of the fourth, the 'people of the saints of the Most High' will receive the dominion of the entire earth (*vv.* 15—28).

The vision is parallel to the dream of Nebuchadnezzar in ch. ii.; and the kingdoms symbolized by the four beasts are generally allowed to be the same as those symbolized by the four parts of the image which Nebuchadnezzar saw in his dream. The animal symbolism of the vision is an extension of that found in some of the later prophets, as Ezek. xvii. 3, xix. 1—9, xxix. 3—5, xxxii. 2—6; Is. xxvii. 1.

1. *In the first year of Belshazzar*] The visions (c. 7—12) are not a continuation of the narratives (c. 1—6), but form a series by themselves: the author accordingly no longer adheres to the chronological order which he has hitherto followed, but goes back to a date anterior to that of ch. v. (see v. 30). In view of what was said at the beginning of ch. v. it is, of course, impossible to estimate the 'first year' of Belshazzar in years B.C.

had] lit. saw.

visions of his head upon his bed] The same phrase in ii. 28.

then he wrote the dream] With reference to the sequel (*v.* 2 ff.), in which Daniel speaks in the first person, and which in these words is represented as having been committed to writing by Daniel himself. The first person (with the exception of x. 1) continues from *v.* 2 to the end of the book.

the sum of **words** (or **things**)] contained in the revelation, i.e. its essential import.

2. *Daniel* **answered** *and said, I saw*] properly, *I was seeing* (or *beholding*), as iv. 10, 13: so *vv.* 4, 6, 7, 9, 11 (twice), 13, 21. LXX. and Theod. rightly render by ἐθεώρουν.

the four winds of the heaven] The same expression, viii. 8, xi. 4; Zech. ii. 6, vi. 5; 2 Esdr. xiii. 5.

strove upon] **were breaking forth** (see Jud. xx. 33 Heb.) **on to**, creating a great disturbance of the waters. A.V. *strove* is to be explained from the sense which the word has in the Targums. The root means *to break* or *burst forth*, of water (as Job xxxviii. 8); but in the Targums it is common, in the conjug. here used, in the sense of *to wage war*, lit. *to cause war to break forth*, as Deut. xx. 4, and even with 'war' omitted, Josh. xxiii. 3 *al.*; hence *strove*. However, the prep. which here follows does not mean *upon*, but *to*.

the great sea] a name of the Mediterranean Sea, Josh. i. 4, ix. 1 *al.*

sea. And four great beasts came up from the sea, diverse 3
one from another. The first *was* like a lion, and had 4
eagle's wings: I beheld till the wings thereof were pluckt,
and it was lifted up from the earth, and made stand upon
the feet as a man, and a man's heart was given to it.

However, that sense is not to be pressed here; the 'great sea,'
tossed up by the four winds of heaven, symbolizes the agitated world
of nations (cf. *v.* 3 with *v.* 17; and comp. Rev. xvii. 15: also Is. xvii.
12).

3. *came up from the sea*] Cf. Rev. xiii. 1; 2 Esdr. xi. 1, xiii. 3
(R.V.).

4. The first beast.

eagle's wings] The 'eagle' (*nesher*) of the O.T., as Tristram has shewn
(*Nat. Hist. of the Bible*, p. 172 ff.), is properly a **vulture**,—though not
the ordinary carrion vulture, but the **Griffon-Vulture**, or **Great Vulture**,
a "majestic bird, most abundant, and never out of sight, whether on the
mountains or the plains of Palestine. Everywhere it is a feature in the
sky, as it circles higher and higher, till lost to all but the keenest sight,
and then rapidly swoops down again" (Smith's *Dict. of the Bible*, ed. 2,
i. 815).

were pluckt] were plucked off.

lifted up from the earth] on which, as an animal, it had been
lying.

upon the feet] *upon* **two** *feet*.

a man's heart] i.e. a man's intelligence: cf. on iv. 16.

The first beast was like a lion, with the wings of the Griffon-Vulture:
it combined consequently the characteristics of the noblest of quadrupeds and of one of the most majestic of birds—the indomitable strength
of the lion, and the power of the vulture to soar securely on high, to
descry its prey from afar, and to alight unerringly upon it. It corresponds to the head of gold in Nebuchadnezzar's dream (ii. 32, 38), and
denotes, analogously to that, the Babylonian empire (comp. the simile
of the lion applied to Nebuchadnezzar in Jer. xlix. 19, and that of the
Griffon-Vulture to either Nebuchadnezzar, or his armies, in Jer. xlix. 22;
Hab. i. 8; Ez. xvii. 3 (see *v.* 12); Lam. iv. 19). After a time however a
change passes over the figure. Its wings are taken away, i.e. it is
deprived of the power of flight; its rapidity of conquest is stopped;
nevertheless it is lifted up into an erect position, and receives both the
form and intelligence of a man. It seems that Ewald, Keil, Pusey
(p. 69 f.) and others are right in seeing here an allusion to what is
narrated in ch. iv.: the empire is regarded as personified in its head;
in Nebuchadnezzar's loss of reason its powers were crippled: during
this time he is described (iv. 16) as having *a beast's heart;* afterwards,
when his reason returned, and he glorified God (iv. 34, 37), he gave
proof that he possessed *the heart* (intelligence) *of a man;* the animal
(i.e. heathen) character of the empire disappeared, and it was, so to say,
humanized in the person of its representative.

5 And behold, another beast, a second, like to a bear, and
it raised up itself on one side, and *it had* three ribs in the
mouth of it between the teeth of it: and they said thus
6 unto it, Arise, devour much flesh. After this I beheld,
and lo another, like a leopard, which had upon the back

5. The second beast.

like to a bear] The bear is a voracious[1] animal, living indeed principally upon roots, bulbs, fruits, and other vegetable products, but, especially when pressed by hunger, ready to attack both the smaller wild and domestic animals, and even man[2]. In the O.T. it is spoken of as being, next to the lion, the most formidable beast of prey known in Palestine (1 Sam. xvii. 34; Am. v. 19; cf. 2 Ki. ii. 24; Hos. xiii. 8); at the same time it is inferior to the lion in strength and appearance, and is heavy and ungainly in its movements. The kingdom denoted by it corresponds to the 'silver' kingdom of ii. 32, which was 'inferior' (ii. 39) to that of Nebuchadnezzar, i.e. the empire of the Medes; as was pointed out on ii. 39, the book of Daniel represents the Chaldæan empire as succeeded not immediately by Cyrus, but by a *Median* ruler, Darius.

it **had raised up** *one side*] This is the Massoretic reading; R.V. *it* **was raised up on** *one side*, follows a reading (implying a change of only one point) found in some MSS. and editions, but possessing less authority. The two readings do not however differ materially in meaning; though what either is intended to denote cannot be said to be altogether clear. Perhaps, on the whole, the most probable view is that the trait is intended to indicate the animal's aggressiveness: it is pictured as raising one of its shoulders, so as to be ready to use its paw on that side. (The rendering of A.V. and R.V. *marg.*, 'raised up one dominion,' implies sh^{e}tar for s^{e}tar; and is not probable.)

and it had *three ribs*, &c.] as the prey which it had seized. Those who regard the bear as symbolizing the Medo-Persian empire generally suppose the three ribs to denote Lydia, Babylonia, and Egypt, three prominent countries conquered, the first two by Cyrus, and the third by Cambyses; but it is quite possible that the ribs in the creature's mouth are meant simply as an indication of its voracity, and are not intended as an allusion to three particular countries absorbed by the empire which it represents.

and they said] or, *and* **it was said**: see on iv. 25.

Arise, devour much flesh] as its nature would prompt it to do. The Medes are the people whom the Heb. prophets of the exile represent as summoned to destroy Babylon (Is. xiii. 17, xxi. 2; Jer. li. 11, 28); and Is. xiii. 17, 18 gives a graphic picture of the insolence and cruelty of their attack.

6. The third beast. A leopard.

upon the back of it] The Aram. word means both *back* and *side*;

---

[1] Arist. *H. N.* VIII. 5 παμφάγον (with reference, as the explanation following shews, to its eating fruits, roots, &c., as well as flesh).
[2] See many illustrations from different authorities collected by Bochart, *Hieroz.* III. ix. (ii. 138 ff., ed. Leipz. 1794).

of it four wings of a fowl; the beast had also four heads; and dominion *was* given to it. After this I saw in the night visions, and behold, a fourth beast, dreadful and terrible, and strong exceedingly; and it had great iron teeth: it devoured and brake in pieces, and stamped the residue with the feet of it: and it *was* diverse from all the

and, as the Heb. text (*K'tîb*) has the mark of the plural, perhaps we ought to render **on its sides** (so Bevan, Behrmann).

of a fowl] i.e., as we should now say, *of a bird*.

The leopard is a fierce, carnivorous animal, remarkable for the swiftness and agility of its attack (cf. Hab. i. 8, where the horses of the Chaldæans are said to be 'swifter than leopards'). It is particularly dangerous to cattle; and "specially noted for the patience with which it waits, extended on the branch of a tree, or a rock near a watering-place, expecting its prey, on which it springs with a deadly precision. Hence Hos. xiii. 7, 'as a leopard by the way will I observe them'; Jer. v. 6" (G. E. Post, in Hastings' *Dict. of the Bible*, s. v.).

Here the four wings upon the leopard's back indicate that it is invested with more than ordinary agility of movement; while the four heads, looking, it may be presumed, towards the four quarters of the earth, are meant apparently to indicate that the empire which it symbolised was to extend in every direction[1]. It was thus a fit emblem of the Persian empire, the founder of which, Cyrus, astonished the world by the extent and rapidity of his conquests.

and dominion was *given to it*] emphasizing the vastness of its rule: cf. ii. 39, where the corresponding empire is described as 'ruling over all the earth.'

7, 8. The fourth beast.

7. *dreadful and terrible*] The same two words occur in combination in the Targ. of Hab. i. 7, 'terrible and dreadful are they.' The rendering of the second word in R.V., *powerful*, follows a slightly different reading (*'emtānī* for *'ĕmtānī*), found in some editions, but less well attested and less probable (it would be a ἅπαξ εἰρημένον in Aram., and explicable only from the Arabic).

and stamped the residue with the feet of it] in wanton destructiveness and ferocity.

and it was *diverse,* &c.] Each of the beasts was 'diverse' from the others (*v.* 3); but the terrible appearance of this differentiated it materially from the other three, and placed it in a class by itself. The fourth beast has, moreover, no name; for no one creature, or even combination of creatures (as the lion with vulture's wings in *v.* 4), could adequately represent it; only words expressive of terribleness, ferocity, and might are accumulated for the purpose of characterizing it. The empire meant (if the two preceding ones are explained correctly)

---

[1] So at least Keil, Meinhold, Behrmann. Others, however, as von Lengerke, Ew., Hitz., Delitzsch, Kuenen, Bevan, Prince, think that the four heads denote the four kings of Persia referred to in xi. 2.

8 beasts that *were* before it; and it had ten horns. I considered the horns, and behold, there came up among them another little horn, before whom there were three of the first horns pluckt up by the roots: and behold, in this horn *were* eyes like the eyes of man, and a mouth speaking great *things*.

will be that of Alexander the Great: comp. viii. 5, 21, xi. 3. Cf. the description of the fourth kingdom in ii. 40, as 'strong as iron,' and 'breaking in pieces and bruising.'

and it had ten horns] A horn is commonly in the O.T. the figure of strength to attack and repel (e.g. Deut. xxxiii. 17; Mic. iv. 13); but in the imagery of Daniel's visions it represents either a king (see *v.* 24; and cp. viii. 5, 8 *a*, 9, 21), or a dynasty of kings (viii. 3, 6, 7, 8 *b*, 20, 22), rising up in, or out of, the empire symbolized by the creature to which the horn belongs. Here the reference is apparently to the ten successors of Alexander on the throne of Antioch (see more fully the Additional Note, p. 101). Cf. the 'ten toes of the feet' in the corresponding part of ch. ii. (*vv.* 41, 42).

8. *I considered the horns, and*] *I* was contemplating *the horns,* when, &c. The force of the verb is apparent from its use in the Targ. of Onk., as Ex. iii. 6, 'he feared to *gaze upon* the glory of Jehovah,' and Num. xxi. 9, 'when he *looked attentively at* (or *contemplated*) the serpent of brass.'

another little horn, &c.] R.V. (avoiding a possible ambiguity in the English) another horn, a little one, *before* which, &c. With 'little' cf. viii. 9. No doubt the meaning is, little in its beginning, but soon increasing in power, till 'three of the first horns were rooted up from before it.' If the fourth beast symbolizes the empire of Alexander, the 'little horn' will be Antiochus Epiphanes, whose persecution of the Jews (B.C. 168—165) forms certainly the subject of viii. 10—14, 24, 25, and xi. 31—33, and who, in viii. 9 (see viii. 23), is also represented by a 'little horn.' The descriptions at the end of the present verse, and in *vv.* 21, 25, also suit Antiochus Epiphanes. For further particulars respecting the events of his reign, see the notes on xi. 21 ff., 30—35, 36 ff., and p. 194 f.

and behold, in this horn, &c.] Another marvel: the horn had the eyes and mouth of a man. *The eyes like the eyes of a man* imply the faculty of keen observation and insight, and so indirectly the possession of intellectual shrewdness.

and a mouth speaking great things] i.e. proud, presumptuous things, especially against God, or His people. Cf. Ps. xii. 3, 'the tongue that speaketh *great things*,' Obad. 12, lit. 'neither *make thy mouth great*,' Rev. xiii. 5, where the beast with ten horns is given '*a mouth speaking great things* and blasphemies.' Comp. xi. 36, where it is said of Antiochus Epiphanes that he will 'speak marvellous things against the God of gods'; and 1 Macc. i. 24, where it is stated that, after despoiling the Temple (B.C. 170), he went away, and 'spake great presumptuousness' ($\dot{\epsilon}\lambda\dot{\alpha}\lambda\eta\sigma\epsilon\nu$ $\dot{\upsilon}\pi\epsilon\rho\eta\phi\alpha\nu\dot{\iota}\alpha\nu$ $\mu\epsilon\gamma\dot{\alpha}\lambda\eta\nu$).

I beheld till the thrones were cast *down*, and the 9
Ancient of days did sit, whose garment *was* white as snow,
and the hair of his head like the pure wool: his throne
was like the fiery flame, *and* his wheels *as* burning fire.

9—14. The judgement on the Gentile powers. The scene is majestically conceived. Thrones are set for the heavenly powers, the assessors of the Judge: the Almighty Himself appears in the likeness of an aged man, seated on a throne of flame: angels in countless myriads stand in attendance around Him: and the books recording the deeds of the Gentile rulers are opened. The four beasts are given over to destruction: while a figure in human form is brought before the Almighty in the clouds of heaven, and receives from Him an everlasting dominion.

9. *till* **thrones were placed** (R.V.)] for the angelic assessors of the Judge, who are not further mentioned, but who are naturally to be distinguished from the hosts which 'stand,' ministering before Him, in *v.* 10. A.V. means, 'till the thrones of the Gentile powers were *overthrown*'; but the rendering of R.V. is much preferable. Exactly the same expression occurs in the Targ. of Jer. i. 15, 'and they shall *cast down* (i.e. set down, place) each his throne in front of the gates of Jerusalem.' Cf. Rev. iv. 2 (ἔκειτο).

the Ancient of days] The expression does not mean what the English words seem to imply, one who had existed from the days of eternity; it means simply an *aged man*; and the R.V., one that was *ancient of days*, is meant to indicate this. Exactly the same expression occurs in the Syriac version of Wisd. ii. 10 for an 'old man,' and in Ecclus. xxv. 4 (in the plural) for 'elders.' 'What Daniel sees is not the eternal God Himself, but an aged man, in whose dignified and impressive form God reveals Himself: cf. Ez. i. 26' (Keil).

his raiment was *white as snow*] symbolizing purity (Is. i. 18; Ps. li. 7). The white hair would have the same symbolism, though this would be natural independently in an aged man. The imagery of Rev. i. 14 is derived from the present passage.

like pure *wool*] The imagery of the visions in the Book of Enoch is based largely upon that of the present passage of Daniel. With the words quoted, cf. Enoch xlvi. 1 (cited below, p. 106), and lxxi. 10.

his throne **was fiery flames, and the wheels thereof** *burning fire*] in accordance with the usual representation of God as surrounded by, or manifested in, fire, the most immaterial of elements, and at the same time the agency best suited to represent symbolically His power to destroy all that is sinful or unholy: cf.—in different connexions—Gen. xv. 17; Ex. iii. 2; Numb. xvi. 35; Deut. iv. 24; Ps. xviii. 12, 13, l. 3, xcvii. 3; Is. xxx. 27; Ez. i. 4, 13, x. 2, 6, 7 (fire between the cherubim supporting the Divine throne), i. 27, viii. 2 (fire representing the Divine form). With the description itself, comp. also Enoch xiv. 18—22 (in the Greek text, p. 347 of Charles' edition): 'And I beheld, and saw a lofty throne...And underneath the throne there came forth rivers of flaming fire; and I could not look thereon. And the Great

10 A fiery stream issued and came forth from before him: thousand thousands ministered unto him, and ten thousand times ten thousand stood before him: the judgement was
11 set, and the books were opened. I beheld then because

Glory sat thereon, and His raiment was brighter than the sun, and whiter than any snow...Fire burnt round about, and a great fire stood beside Him, and no one approacheth Him round about: thousand thousands stand before Him, and every word of His is deed.'

the wheels **thereof**] The throne is pictured implicitly as a chariot, as in Ez. i. 15—28. The representation of the throne and wheels as *being* fire is, however, more than is found even in the visions of Ezekiel.

10. *a* **stream of fire**...*from before him*] For 'from before,' cf. v. 24; and on vi. 10. Comp. also Rev. i. 14, 'his eyes were as a flame of fire.'

thousand thousands] Cf. Deut. xxxiii. 2, R.V. (if the existing Heb. text of line 4 is correct); also 1 Ki. xxii. 19; Zech. xiv. 5 *end*, R.V.; Enoch i. 9 (cited, with slight verbal differences [see Charles' ed. p. 327], in Jude 14, 15 [for 'saints' in *v.* 14, A.V., see the note on Dan. viii. 13]). The present passage is doubtless the source of Enoch xiv. 22 (cited on *v.* 9), xl. 1 (cited below, p. 106); cf. lx. 1, lxxi. 8, 13; and of **Rev. v. 11.**

ministered...stood] Better, **were ministering...were standing**, the tenses being as in iv. 12.

stood before him] viz. in attendance: cf. for the idiom 1 Ki. x. 8.

the judgement was set] i.e. (in accordance with the old English sense of the expression) **was seated**: the Aram. is lit. *sat*, 'judgement' being used here in a concrete sense for *the judges*; cf. LXX., Theod., τὸ κριτήριον ἐκάθισεν, Vulg. *judicium sedit*; and see *v.* 26, 'shall *sit*'. The Almighty is represented as holding a court of judgement. For *was set* in this sense see in A.V., Matth. v. 1 ('when he *was set*,' i.e. was seated), xxvii. 19; Heb. viii. 1 (R.V. *sat down*); Ps. ix. 4 (P.B.V), 'thou *art set* (i.e. hast seated thyself) in the throne that judgest right.' W. A. Wright quotes, from an old writer, 'When they were *sette*' (viz. at table).

and the books were opened] the books in which the deeds of men are recorded—in particular the deeds of the four 'beasts,' representing the four empires. Cf. Rev. xx. 12, 'And I saw the dead, great and small, standing before the throne; and books were opened;...and the dead were judged out of the things which were written in the books, according to their works:' also 2 Esdras vi. 20; Apoc. of Baruch xxiv. 1; Ascension of Isaiah (ed. Dillmann, 1877), ix. 22; Enoch xlvii. 3 (cited on p. 106), lxxxix. 70, 71, 76, 77, xc. 20, xcviii. 7, 8, civ. 7,—all passages speaking of the deeds of men being recorded in books, which are afterwards opened in heaven. See further Charles's note on Enoch xlvii. 3; and comp. *Abhoth* ii. 1, 'Know what is above thee, a seeing eye, and a hearing ear, and all thy deeds written in a book.' The germ of the representation is to be found most probably in the figurative

of the voice of the great words which the horn spake: I beheld *even* till the beast *was* slain, and his body destroyed, and given to the burning flame. As concerning the rest 12 of the beasts, they had their dominion taken away: yet

expressions in Is. lxv. 6 ('Behold, it is *written before me*': cf. Jer. xvii. 1); Mal. iii. 16 (cf. Est. vi. 1); Ps. lvi. 8.

11. The beast representing the fourth empire is slain, and utterly destroyed, on account of the blasphemies of Antiochus Epiphanes (*v.* 8), the idea being that the guilt of the empire culminated in him. The writer thinks of *empires* only, not of individuals; and it is impossible to say what he pictured to himself as being the fate of the individuals of whom the fourth empire consisted.

I beheld, &c.] The second 'I beheld' is resumptive of the first, after the intervening clause introduced by *because*—a construction of which there are many examples in Hebrew (e.g. Lev. xvii. 5; Jud. xi. 31; Zech. viii. 23). *I beheld till*, as *v.* 9. The clause *because*, &c., though apparently giving the reason for 'I beheld,' gives in reality the reason for 'the beast was slain,' &c.

and his body destroyed] The empire being represented by an animal, its 'body' will correspond to the fabric, or political organization, of the State. This is to be utterly brought to an end.

and he was given to be burned with fire (R.V.)] lit. *to the burning of fire* (cf. Is. lxiv. 11, lit. 'has become *for the burning of fire*), i.e. to complete destruction. It is hardly likely that there is any allusion here to the torments of the wicked after death, for though in parts of Enoch, written probably within 50 years of Daniel (x. 13, xxi. 7—10, xc. 24—27), mention is made of a fiery place of punishment for wicked angels and men, had that been intended here it is probable that it would have been indicated more distinctly,—to say nothing of the fact that, as remarked just above, it is the fate of *empires*, not of individuals, that the writer has in view. Rev. xix. 20, xx. 10 are not sufficient proof that the author of Daniel had the idea here in his mind.

12. *the rest of the beasts*] Commentators are divided as to whether the three beasts of *vv.* 4—6, or the seven horns left after the three had been rooted up (*v.* 8), are intended: but the expression used ('beasts') strongly favours the former interpretation. In the abstract, it is true, the latter interpretation might be deemed the more probable; for, as the 'beasts' represent successive kings, or kingdoms (*vv.* 17, 23), the dominion of the first three would naturally be at an end long before the period of the judgement on the fourth, whereas the seven 'horns' might well be conceived as subsisting still. In point of fact, however, the kingdoms, though in reality successive, are in the vision represented as contemporaneous: nothing is said in *vv.* 3—7 about the disappearance of one beast when a second appears; all continue visible, side by side. So in ch. ii. the four kingdoms represented by the image are destroyed simultaneously: the entire image remains intact until the stone falls upon the feet (representing the fourth and last kingdom), when the whole of it breaks up together.

13 their lives were prolonged for a season and time. I saw in the night visions, and behold, *one* like the Son of man came with the clouds of heaven, and came to the Ancient
14 of days, and they brought him near before him. And there *was* given him dominion, and glory, and a kingdom, that all people, nations, and languages, should serve him: his dominion *is* an everlasting dominion, which shall not pass away, and his kingdom *that* which shall not be destroyed.

they (indef.) **took away** *their dominion*] i.e. (see on iv. 25) *their dominion* was taken away (R.V.).

but a prolonging in life was given them (A.V. *marg.*)] The three first beasts are humbled, but not, like the fourth beast, destroyed; their dominion was taken away from them, but they were permitted to remain alive: i.e. the Gentile powers, represented by the beasts, were to survive for a while as *nations*, though deprived of empire.

until *a* **time** *and a* **season** (ii. 21)] i.e. until the unspecified time, determined for each in the counsel of the Most High (Keil).

13, 14. The kingdom of the saints.

13. *and behold* **there appeared coming** *with the clouds of heaven* **one like unto a son** *of man*] lit. *there was coming*, &c., the graphic partic. with the finite verb, which is so frequent in Daniel (Theod. LXX. καὶ ἰδοὺ μετὰ [LXX. ἐπὶ] τῶν νεφελῶν τοῦ οὐρανοῦ ὡς υἱὸς ἀνθρώπου ἐρχόμενος [LXX. ἤρχετο]): though in English '*was coming*' is too weak to express its force adequately. The rendering of A.V., 'the Son of man,' is quite untenable: the expression of the original is indefinite, and denotes simply, in poetical language (cf. Num. xxiii. 19; Ps. lxxx. 17; Is. li. 12, lvi. 2), a figure in human form (comp. Rev. i. 13, xiv. 14, R.V.). What the figure is intended to represent can be properly determined only after the explanation in *v.* 16 ff. has been considered (see p. 102 ff.). If the terms of *vv.* 18, 22 *b*, 27 are to be taken as deciding the question, it would seem that it must describe the ideal and glorified people of Israel.

with the clouds of heaven] in superhuman majesty and state. The passage is the source of the expression in Mk. xiv. 62 (Mt. xxvi. 64 'on'); Rev. i. 7, 'behold, he cometh with the clouds:' cf. Mt. xxiv. 30 ('on')=Mk. xiii. 26 ('in')=Lk. xxi. 27 ('in'); and Rev. xiv. 14 ('one sitting on a cloud, like unto a son of man'), 15, 16.

and he came even to the ancient of days] see on *v.* 9.

and they brought him near] The subject might be angelic beings; or, which is probably better, it may be indefinite, like the 'they' of *vv.* 5, 12, i.e. *and* he was *brought near* (see on iv. 25).

14. A universal and never-ending dominion is given to him. The expressions in the first half of the verse resemble in part those used in v. 18, 19 of Nebuchadnezzar. *Serve* does not necessarily mean *worship*: like the word which has the same meaning in Heb. (עֲבַד), it may be used of obedience to either God (iii. 12, 14 *al.*) or a human ruler (vii. 27; and the Targ. of Jer. xxvii. 6, 7, 8, &c.). With the

I Daniel was grieved in my spirit in the midst of *my* 15
body, and the visions of my head troubled me. I came 16
near unto one of them that stood *by*, and asked him the
truth of all this. So he told me, and made me know the
interpretation of the things.

These great beasts, which *are* four, *are* four kings, *which* 17

second half of the verse comp. ii. 44, and especially iv. 3 *b*, 34 *b* (of the
kingdom of God). *All peoples, nations*, &c., as iii. 4.

15—28. The explanation of the vision.

15. **As for me** *Daniel*, **my spirit was pained]** or **distressed**: in
modern English we should not say 'grieved' in such a connexion.

in the midst of **the sheath]** or, with a change of punctuation, **its
sheath**, fig. for the body, as the soul's *sheath*, or receptacle. The word
is of Persian origin (*nidâna*, 'vessel,' 'receptacle'): it occurs once
again in late Heb., 1 Ch. xxi. 27, of the sheath of a sword; and (in the
form *lidneh* for *nidneh*) several times in the Targums (e.g. Ez. xxi. 8)
in the same sense. Levy quotes two passages from the later Jewish
literature where it is used in the same application as here: *Sanh.* 108ᵃ
'that their soul should not return to *its* sheath,' and *B'rêshith Rabbā*
§ 26 (p. 118 in Wünsche's transl.) 'in the hour (viz. of resurrection)
when I bring back the spirit to its sheath, I do not bring back their
spirits to their sheaths.' The usage is nevertheless a singular one; and
these two passages may be simply based upon this one of Daniel.
The emendation *on this account* (בגין דנה for בגו נדנה) has been
proposed (Weiss, Buhl, Marti); and LXX. (ἐν τούτοις) may partly
support it: it is, however, some objection to it that בגין, though
found in the Palest. Targums, does not otherwise occur in Biblical
Aramaic[1].

troubled] alarmed (iv. 5). *Visions of my head*, as *v*. 1 and iv. 5.

16. *one of them that* **were standing** (there)] One of the angels
that 'stood' before the Almighty (*v*. 10), who happened to be nearer
than the others to Daniel himself. For the part of interpreter taken by
an angel in a vision, cf. Zech. i. 7—vi. 8 *passim*; and the Apocalypses
of Enoch and 2 Esdras. It is characteristic of the later prophecies:
in the visions of the earlier prophets (as Am. vii. viii., Is. vi., Jer. i.,
Ez. ii.—v., viii. ix., &c.), Jehovah speaks Himself to the prophet. We
have the transition in Ez. xl.—xlviii., where an angel conducts the
prophet, and usually explains things to him (Ez. xl. 3, 4, &c.), though
sometimes Jehovah also speaks Himself (xliii. 7—9, xliv. 2, 5, &c.).

of all this] better, **concerning** *all this* (R.V.).

17. The four beasts represent four kings, or (*v*. 23) four kingdoms,
the 'king' in each case being not an individual king, but a typical
king, embodying the characteristics of the empire ruled by him. The
angel does not however dwell more fully on the 'beasts,' or interpret
their symbolism; but hastens (*v*. 18) to explain the nature of the
kingdom which is to succeed theirs.

---

[1] Nestle would read simply 'in my body' (בגוייתי, or בגוישמי).

18 shall arise out of the earth. But the saints of the most High shall take the kingdom, and possess the kingdom
19 for ever, even for ever and ever. Then I would know the truth of the fourth beast, which was diverse from all the others, exceeding dreadful, whose teeth *were of* iron, and his nails *of* brass; *which* devoured, brake in pieces, and

18. The four kingdoms of the Gentiles will pass away; and be succeeded by the kingdom of the saints of the Most High, which will endure for ever. The saints of the Most High seem here, as also in *vv.* 22, 27, to take the place of the 'one like unto a son of man' in *v.* 13, and to receive the same never-ending dominion.

the saints] lit. *the holy ones*; so *vv.* 21, 22, 25, 27, viii. 24 (cp. xii. 7). Cf. Ps. xvi. 3, xxxiv. 9. (The word is entirely different from the one (*ḥasid*) rendered 'saints' everywhere else in the Psalms, as Ps. xxx. 4, xxxi. 23, xxxvii. 28, &c., and in 1 Sam. ii. 9 [A.V.]; 2 Chron. vi. 41, Prov. ii. 8.) The term, in this application, is an extension of the use of the word 'holy' to denote Israel in its ideal character (Ex. xix. 6; Lev. xi. 44, 45, xix. 2, xx. 7, 26; Deut. vii. 6, xiv. 2, 21, xxxiii. 3 and elsewhere).

the Most High] See on iii. 26. The Hebraizing (and plural) form found here (עֶלְיוֹנִין) recurs *vv.* 22, 25 (second time), 27. The plural is probably the so-called 'plural of majesty,' which we have, for instance, in the Heb. of 'holy' in Josh. xxiv. 19, and Prov. ix. 10.

shall receive (v. 31) *the kingdom*] They will not establish it by their own power (cf. *v.* 27 'shall be given, &c.).

and possess the kingdom for ever, &c.] Cf. *v.* 14 *b*.

19—22. Daniel asks for further information respecting the fourth beast, and the means by which its power was broken.

19. *Then I desired to know the truth concerning*, &c. (R.V.)] 'Would' in Old English has often the sense of 'willed,' 'desired'; but in modern English it is not strong enough in a passage like the present. Cf. *will* in W. A. Wright's *Bible Word-Book*, who points out that in the A.V. it is sometimes more than a mere auxiliary verb: e.g. Matt. xi. 27 '.and he to whomsoever the Son *will* [R.V. *willeth to*] reveal him,' Luke xiii. 31 'for Herod *will* [R.V. *would fain*] kill thee;' John vii. 17 (R.V. *willeth to*), 1 Tim. v. 11 (R.V. *desire to*). The case is similar with *would*, as Col. i. 27, 'To whom God *would* make known,' &c. (R.V. '*was pleased to* make known,'—ἠθέλησεν γνωρίσαι), John i. 43 (also for ἠθέλησεν, R.V. *was minded to*[1]).

The description of the fourth beast is in the main repeated from *vv.* 7, 8; but some traits are noticed here which were not mentioned before.

and his nails of **bronze** (ii. 32)] Not in *v.* 7.

---

[1] See a useful little volume, Clapperton's *Pitfalls in Bible English* (1899), p. 89.

stamped the residue with his feet; and of the ten horns 20
that *were* in his head, and *of* the other which came up,
and before whom three fell; even *of* that horn that had
eyes, and a mouth that spake very great *things*, whose
look *was* more stout than his fellows. I beheld, and the 21
same horn made war with the saints, and prevailed against
them; until the Ancient of days came, and judgement *was* 22
given to the saints of the most High; and the time came
that the saints possessed the kingdom. Thus he said, 23
The fourth beast shall be the fourth kingdom upon earth,
which shall be diverse from all kingdoms, and shall devour

20. *And* concerning *the ten horns that were* on *his head,* and the *other which came up, and before* which, &c.] See *v.* 8.
even of *that horn,* &c.] and as regards *that horn,* it had eyes, &c.
very great things] great things: the expression is exactly the same as in *v.* 8.
whose look, &c.] whose appearance *was* greater *than* (that of) its *fellows.* The adj. is the usual one for 'great' in Aramaic. The horn, though called a 'little' one (*v.* 8), must be supposed to have grown rapidly to a portentous size: cf. esp. viii. 9.

21—22. A recapitulation of the substance of *vv.* 9—12, and of *vv.* 13—14,—the latter in the phraseology of *v.* 18,—with a mention of the fact not noticed before, that a war with the 'little horn' had preceded the triumph of the saints.

21. *made war with the saints*] Alluding to the violent efforts made by Antiochus Epiphanes to denationalize the Jews and to suppress their religion: cf. *v.* 25, viii. 10—14, 24, 25.
and prevailed against them] The war was a desperate one; and the 'little horn' would have conquered, had it not been for the intervention of the Most High (*v.* 22).

22. *the Ancient of days*] *vv.* 9, 13.
judgement was *given* for, &c. (R.V. *marg.*)] i.e. was pronounced in their favour. Bevan and Kamph. agree, however, that Ewald was perhaps right in conjecturing that the words יתב ושלטנא have dropped out by *homœoteleuton* before יהב: the verse would then run, 'and the judgement [sat, and dominion] was given to the saints,' &c. (cf. *vv.* 10 *b*, 14; 26, 27). The rendering *to* (with the existing text) means that judgement was committed into their hands (1 Cor. vi. 2), an idea alien to the present context: God Himself is here the judge, and by His judgement secures justice for His saints.
and the time came, and, &c.] The time appointed by God for the purpose. Cf. *v.* 18.

23—27. The answer of the angel.
23. *shall be* a *fourth kingdom,* &c.] The fourth beast represents a kingdom different in character from all the kingdoms, i.e. from any of the previous kingdoms, and far more terrible in its operation.

the whole earth, and shall tread it down, and break it in pieces. And the ten horns out of this kingdom *are* ten kings *that* shall arise: and another shall rise after them; and he shall be diverse from the first, and he shall subdue three kings. And he shall speak *great* words against the most High, and shall wear out the saints of the most High, and think to change times and laws: and they shall be

the whole earth] To be understood with the same limitations as when it is said (ii. 39; cf. also on iv. 1) that the Persian empire should include 'the whole earth.'

tread it down] The word is used in Hebrew, and at least sometimes in Aramaic, of *threshing* (which was performed in ancient times by the feet of oxen, Deut. xxv. 4): hence R.V. *marg.* 'Or, *thresh it.*' Cf. for the figure Mic. iv. 13; Is. xli. 15.

24. The ten horns are ten kings.

and he (emph.) *shall be diverse from the* **former ones**] The king represented by the 'little horn' will differ from the others, viz. by being aggressive and presumptuous.

and he shall subdue three kings] put down (R.V.), as the same word is rendered in the A.V. of v. 19 and Ps. lxxv. 7. *Abase, bring down, lay low*, is the idea of the word (Is. ii. 12, xxv. 11, 12, xxvi. 5). Cf. *v.* 8. On the interpretation, see the Additional Note at the end of the Chapter.

25. Expansion of the 'great things' of *v.* 8 *end*. He will blaspheme the Most High (cf. xi. 36 'will speak marvellous things against the God of gods'), and seek to ruin His saints.

wear **away**] LXX, κατατρίψει. An expressive figure for continuous persecution and vexation. The idea of the word is *to wear* or *rub away*, applied often to clothes (Deut. viii. 4; Josh. ix. 13; Is. l. 9, *al.*), though in the usual rendering of A.V., R.V., 'wax old,' this is unfortunately obliterated. Cf. Job xiii. 28 'and he, like a rotten thing, *weareth* (or *falleth*) *away*'; 1 Ch. xvii. 9 'neither shall the children of unrighteousness any more *wear* them *away*' (altered from the 'afflict' of 2 Sam. vii. 10); Is. iii. 15, Targ. 'and the faces of the poor ye *wear* away' (for Heb. *grind*).

think to change **times and law**] The phrase is worded generally; and it is true that Antiochus, according to 1 Macc. i. 41, 42, sought to interfere arbitrarily even with heathen cults: but the allusion is more particularly to the attempts made by him to suppress the Jewish religion by prohibiting the observance of religious festivals and other ordinances of the Law (see 1 Macc. i. 44—49). 'Think' means *plan* or even *hope*, a sense which the word used has often in the Targums and in Syriac (Luke xxiv. 21, Pesh.). For 'times' in the sense of *fixed times* (here, the times fixed for religious observances, the Hebrew *mō'ădîm*, Lev. xxiii. 2, 4 [R.V. *set feasts*], Is. i. 14 [A.V., R.V., *appointed feasts*], xxxiii. 20 [A.V., R.V., *solemnities*]), see in the Targ. Gen. i. 14; Ex. xiii. 10, xxiii. 15; Numb. xxviii. 2; Is. xxxiii. 20 (for 'solemnities'); Jer. viii. 7. By 'law' is meant the Mosaic law, as vi. 5.

given into his hand until a time and times and the dividing
of time. But the judgement shall sit, and they shall take 26
away his dominion, to consume and to destroy *it* unto the
end. And the kingdom and dominion, and the greatness 27
of the kingdom under the whole heaven, *shall be* given
to the people of the saints of the most High, whose kingdom
is an everlasting kingdom, and all dominions shall serve

until a time and times and half a time (R.V.)] The saints will be
given into the hand of this godless king for three years and a half.
'Time' (a different word from that in the preceding clause, and in the
note on *v.* 12 rendered *season*) has the same sense of *year*, which it had
in iv. 16: the same expression (in its Hebrew form) recurs in xii. 7 (also
of the duration of Antiochus' persecution) ; comp. also Rev. xii. 14.
For the particulars of Antiochus' persecution, see the notes on xi. 31.
It began with the mission of Apollonius against Jerusalem, probably
about June 168, and with the edict of Antiochus which was immediately
afterwards put in force (1 Macc. i. 20—53); and it ended (substantially)
with the re-dedication of the Temple, after its three years' desecration,
on the 25th of Chisleu [Dec.], 165 (1 Macc. iv. 52 f.). This, in all
probability, is the period of $3\frac{1}{2}$ years which is here intended. The
$3\frac{1}{2}$ years might also, however, be reckoned from the erection of the
heathen altar in the court of the Temple, on the 15th of Chisleu, B.C.
168, to the death of Antiochus, which took place probably about the
middle of 164 (see on viii. 14): the *terminus a quo* would then agree
with that of the 1290 days in xii. 11, and the two periods would be
(approximately) the same; but the six months before December 168
are more likely to have been included in the period of persecution,
than the six months after December 165, when the victories of Judas
had stemmed the tide of the persecution, and public worship had been
resumed in the Temple.

26—27. At the end of $3\frac{1}{2}$ years his power will be taken away from
him ; and the persecuted saints will receive the kingdom of the entire
world.

26. *the judgement shall sit*, &c.] *vv.* 10^b, 11^b.

they shall take away his dominion] or, *his dominion* shall be taken
away (cf. *v.* 12).

to destroy *and* cause it to perish even unto *the end*] i.e. finally, for
ever. 'Even unto the end,' as vi. 26.

27. *of the kingdom*s *under the whole heaven*] not merely the kingdom ruled by the 'little horn,' but all the kingdoms of the earth, will
be given then to the saints of the Most High. 'Under the whole
heaven,' as Deut. ii. 25, iv. 19 ; cf. Job xxviii. 24, xxxvii. 3, xli. 11.

its *kingdom is*, &c.,...*shall serve and obey* it] The pronouns, as
the context shews, must refer to 'people,' not to 'the Most High.'
In this verse, even more distinctly than in *vv.* 18, 22, the universal and
never-ending dominion, which in *v.* 14 is given to the 'one like unto a
son of man,' seems to be conferred upon the people of the saints. For

28 and obey him. Hitherto *is* the end of the matter. *As for* me Daniel, my cogitations much troubled me, and my countenance changed in me: but I kept the matter in my heart.

the same idea, adapted to a N.T. standpoint, cf. Rev. v. 10 *b*, xi. 15, xii. 10, xxii. 5; also xx. 4, 6.

28. Concluding remark on the vision.

Hitherto] *To this point* : we should say **Here** (R.V.). Cf. xii. 6, lit. '*Until when* shall be the end of the wonders?'

the end of the matter] i.e. of the entire revelation, including both the vision and the interpretation.

my **thoughts** *much* **alarmed** *me*] The expression, exactly as iv. 19, v. 6, 10.

and my **brightness** *was changed* **upon** *me*] As v. 9; cf. v. 6, 10.

but I kept, &c.] Cf. Luke ii. 19, and especially ii. 51.

Additional Note on the Four Empires of Daniel II., VII.

It is generally agreed that the four empires represented by the composite image in ch. ii. are the same as those represented by the four beasts in ch. vii.: there is also no doubt that the first empire in ch. vii. is the same as the first empire in ch. ii., which is expressly stated in ii. 38 to be that of Nebuchadnezzar, and that the kingdom which is to succeed the fourth is in both chapters the kingdom of God: but the identification of the second, third, and fourth empires in the two chapters has been the subject of much controversy. It is also further a question, to which different answers have been given, whether the same three kingdoms in these two chapters are or are not identical with those denoted by the two horns of the ram, and by the he-goat in viii. 3—5, i.e. (as is expressly explained in viii. 20, 21), with the kingdoms of Media, Persia, and Greece. The following tabular synopsis (based upon that of Zündel) of the two principal interpretations that have been adopted, will probably assist the reader in judging between them.

A.

Ch. ii.	Ch. vii.	Ch. viii.	
Golden head	= Lion with eagle's wings	=	= Babyl. empire
Silver breast and arms	= Bear with three ribs in mouth	= Ram with two unequal horns	= Medo-Persian
Bronze belly and thighs	= Leopard with four wings	= Goat with one horn, followed by four horns, out of one of which came a little horn	= Grecian (Alexander and his successors)
Iron legs, feet and toes partly iron partly clay	= Beast with iron teeth, and ten horns, among which came up one little horn		= Roman

B.

Ch. ii.	Ch. vii.	Ch. viii.	
Golden head	= Lion with eagle's wings		= Babyl. empire
Silver breast and arms	= Bear with three ribs in mouth	= First and shorter horn of ram	= Median
Bronze belly and thighs	= Leopard with four wings	= Second and longer horn of ram	= Persian
Iron legs, feet and toes partly iron partly clay	= Beast with iron teeth, and ten horns, among which came up one little horn	= Goat with one horn, followed by four horns out of one of which came a little horn	= Grecian (Alexander and his successors)

The difference between the two interpretations comes out most markedly in the explanation given of the fourth empire: A, for convenience, may, therefore, be termed the *Roman* theory, and B the *Grecian* theory.

A. This interpretation is first found[1] in the apocryphal book of 2 Esdras (written probably under Domitian, A.D. 81—96), xii. 11 f., where the eagle, which Ezra is supposed to see in his vision and which unquestionably represents the imperial power of Rome, is expressly identified with the fourth kingdom which appeared to Daniel: though (it is added) the meaning of that kingdom was not expounded to Daniel as it is expounded to Ezra now. The same view of the fourth kingdom is implied in Ep. Barnab. iv. 4—5 (*c.* 100—120 A.D.), where the writer, in proof that the time of trial, preceding the advent of the Son of God, is at hand, quotes the words from Dan. vii. 7, 8, 24, respecting the little horn abasing three of the ten horns[2]. Hippolytus (*c.* 220 A.D.) expounds Dan. ii. and vii. at length in the same sense (ed. Lagarde, 1858, pp. 151 ff., 171 ff., 177 ff.). The same interpretation was also general among the Fathers; and it is met with likewise among Jewish authorities. Among modern writers, it has been advocated by Auberlen, Hengstenberg, Hofmann (*Weissagung und Erfüllung*, 1841, p. 276 ff.), Keil, Dr Pusey, and others.

Upon this view, the fourth empire being the Roman, the ten toes, partly of iron and partly of clay, of the image in ch. ii., and the ten horns of the fourth beast in ch. vii., represent ten kingdoms, into which the Roman empire is supposed to have broken up, each retaining to a certain extent the strength of the Roman, but with its stability greatly impaired by internal weakness and disunion[3]: the 'mouth speaking great things,' which is to arise after the ten kingdoms and to destroy three of them, being Antichrist, who is identified by some with the Papacy, and by others is supposed to be a figure still future.

---

[1] It is implied also (apparently) in Joseph. *Ant.* x. xi. 7.
[2] The writer seems to have understood by the 'horns' the Roman emperors: but there is great difficulty in determining precisely which are meant; see in Gebhardt and Harnack's edition (1878), p. lxix f.
[3] Cf. Hippolytus, p. 172, 'The legs of iron are the Romans, being as strong as iron; then come the toes, partly of iron, partly of clay, in order to represent the democracies which are to arise afterwards' (similarly, p. 152); p. 153, 'the little horn growing up among the others is Antichrist.'

Thus Dr Rule[1] writes: 'This little horn is too like the Papacy to be mistaken for anything else; and taking this for granted, as I believe we may venture to do, ten kingdoms must be found *that came into existence previously to the establishment of the Pope's temporal power in Italy*.' Accordingly the ten kingdoms enumerated by him are—

1. The kingdom of the *Vandals* in Africa, established A.D. 439.
2. *Venice*, which became an independent state in A.D. 452, and long maintained an extremely important position in the affairs of Christendom.
3. *England*, which, properly so called, was founded in A.D. 455, and in spite of the Norman Conquest still retains her independence.
4. *Spain*, first Gothic, A.D. 476, then Saracenic, and *still Spain*.
5. *France*. Gaul, conquered by the Romans, lost to Rome under the Visigoths, and transferred to the Franks under Clovis, A.D. 483.
6. *Lombardy*, conquered by the Lombards, A.D. 568.
7. The exarchate of *Ravenna*, which became independent of Constantinople in 584, and flourished for long as an independent state.
8. *Naples*, subdued by the Normans about 1060.
9. *Sicily*, taken by the Normans under Count Roger about 1080.
10. *Rome*, which assumed independence under a Senate of its own in 1143, and maintained itself so till 1198. 'The tumultuary revolution headed in Rome by Arnold of Brescia, tore away the ancient city from its imperial relations and brought the prophetic period of the ten kingdoms to its close.'

The 'little horn diverse from the ten, having eyes and a mouth speaking very great things,' is Pope Innocent III. (A.D. 1198—1216), who immediately after his consecration restored, as it was called, the patrimony of the Church, by assuming absolute sovereignty over the city and territory of Rome, and exacting of the Prefect of the city, in lieu of the oath of allegiance which he had hitherto sworn to the Emperor of Germany, an oath of fealty to himself, by which he bound himself to exercise in future the civil and military powers entrusted to him, solely in the interests of the Pope. 'Here is the haughty speech, and here are the watchful eyes to survey the newly usurped dominion, and to spy out far beyond.' Of the three 'horns' which fell before Innocent III. and his successors, the first was thus the Roman Senate and people, with the so-called patrimony of St Peter, in the year 1198; the other two were the two kingdoms of Naples and Sicily, which having in 1060 and 1080 fallen under the rule of the Dukes of Normandy, were afterwards offered by Urban IV. to the Duke of Anjou, to be held by him in subjection to the Church, with the result that ultimately, in 1266, 'the two Sicilies,' as they were afterwards called, fell under the subordinate rule of a branch of the house of Bourbon, and so remained until recent times. The war on the saints is referred to the Inquisition, organized by Innocent III. and carried on by his successors, and abetted 'by every device of oppressive legislation, and artful diplomacy.' 'Concerning the change of times and laws, a few words will suffice. "He shall think to change times" by the substitution of an ecclesiastical calendar for the civil. He shall ordain festivals, appoint jubilees, and so enforce observance of such times and years as to set aside civil obligations, and even supersede the sanctification of the Lord's days by the multiplication of saints' days. With regard to laws he will enforce Canon Law in contempt of Statute Law, and sometimes in contradiction to the Law of God.'

Auberlen, on the other hand[2], points more generally to the many different ways in which the influence of Rome has perpetuated itself even in modern Europe. The various barbarian nations out of which have developed gradually the states of modern Europe, have, he observes, fallen largely under the spell of Roman civilization. 'Roman culture, the Roman church, the Roman language, and Roman law have been the essential civilizing principles of the Germanic world. The Romance nations are a monument of the extent to which the influence of Rome has penetrated even into the blood of the new humanity: they are the products of the admixture "by the seed of men." But they do not cohere together: the Roman element is ever re-acting against the Germanic. The struggles between Romans and Germans have been the determining factor of modern history: we need mention only the contests between the Emperor and the Pope, which stirred the Middle Ages, and the Reformation, with the consequences following from it, which have continued until the present day. The fourth empire has thus a genuine Roman tenacity and

---

[1] *An Historical Exposition of Daniel the Prophet*, 1869, p. 195 ff.
[2] *Der Prophet Daniel* (1857), pp. 252—4.

force; at the same time, since the Germans have appeared on the scene of history, and the iron has been mixed with the clay, it has been much divided and broken up, and its different constituent parts have shewn themselves to be unstable and fragile (Dan. ii. 41, 42). The Roman element strives ever after universal empire, the German element represents the principles of individualism and division.' Hence the ever fresh attempts, whether on the part of the Pope, or of a secular prince, as Charlemagne, Charles V., Napoleon, and even the Czar, to realize anew the ideal of Roman unity. Against these attempts, however, the independent nationalities never cease to assert as persistently their individual rights. Politically and religiously, the Roman, the German, and the Slavonic nationalities stand opposed to one another: in the end, however, after many conflicts, they will resolve themselves into ten distinct kingdoms, out of one of which Antichrist—a kind of exaggerated, almost superhuman, Napoleon—will arise, and realise, on an unprecedented scale, until Providence strikes him down, the 'dæmonic unity' of an empire of the world.

So far as the mere symbolism of the vision goes, there is no objection to this interpretation. The kingdom which is to 'tread down and break in pieces,' with the strength of iron, 'the whole earth' (vii. 23; cf. vii. 7, ii. 40) might well be the empire of the Romans, who by their military conquests subdued, one after another, practically all the nations of the then known world; and it has been contended, not without some show of plausibility, that the imagery of the second kingdom agrees better with the Medo-Persian than with the Persian empire: the bear, it is urged, with its slow and heavy gait would be the most suitable symbol of the Medo-Persian empire, of which 'heaviness,' as exemplified by the vast and unwieldy armies which its kings brought into the field[1], was the leading national characteristic, while the three ribs in its mouth are more naturally explained of three provinces absorbed by the empire of the Persians[2], than of any conquests made by the Medes. These explanations of the imagery, however, though they *fall in* with the interpretation in question, cannot be said to be so certain, upon independent grounds, as to *require* it: Alexander's military successes were also such that he might be spoken of as subduing the whole earth; and we do not *know* that the suggested interpretation of the symbolism of the bear is really that which was in the mind of the writer of the chapter.

The great, and indeed fatal, objection to this interpretation is, however, that it *does not agree with the history*. The Roman empire, the empire which conquered and ruled so many nations of the ancient world[3],—whether it be regarded as coming to its close when in A.D. 476 Romulus Augustulus, at the bidding of Odoacer, resigned his power to the Emperor of the East, or whether that act be regarded merely as a transference of power from the West to the East, and its real close be placed, with Gibbon, at the capture of Constantinople by the Turks in 1453, or whether, lastly, it be held, with Bryce, to have prolonged a legal existence till in 1806 the Emperor Francis II resigned the imperial crown,—has passed from the stage of history; nor, whichever date be

---

[1] Darius Hystaspis was said to have led 700,000 men into Scythia: Xerxes' expedition against Greece numbered 2,500,000 fighting men; Darius Codomannus, at the fatal battle of Issus, commanded 600,000 men (Pusey, p. 71).
[2] Media, Assyria, and Babylonia (Hippolytus); Persia, Media, and Babylonia (Jerome, Ephr. Syr.); Lydia, Babylonia, and Egypt (Hofmann, Keil, Pusey, p. 70).
[3] 'Empire' is of course used here generally in the sense of 'power': at the time when many of these conquests were made, the Romans, as is well known, were under the rule of neither 'emperors' nor 'kings.'

assigned for its close,—and, in the natural sense of the word, the 'Roman empire' ceased to exist at the first of these dates,—can any 'ten' kingdoms be pointed to, as in any sense arising out of it? The non-natural character of the 'praeterist' explanation of Dr Rule must be patent to the reader. 'Futurist' expositors suppose that the kingdoms represented by the ten horns are yet to appear[1]. But these kingdoms are to 'arise out of' the fourth empire (Dan. ii. 24): clearly therefore the fourth empire must still exist when they appear; but the Roman empire is beyond controversy an empire of the past. Auberlen's explanation, ingenious as it is, cannot be deemed satisfactory[2].

The interpretation under discussion is in fact one which, in view of the circumstances of the age, might readily have suggested itself to Christian expositors of Daniel, while the Roman empire was still the dominant power in the world; but it is one which the progress of history has shewn to be untenable. The early Christians believed that they were living in an age in which the end of the world was imminent; and it was in this belief, as Mr (now Bishop) Westcott has pointed out, that the interpretation in question originated. 'It originated at a time when the triumphant advent of Messiah was the object of immediate expectation, and the Roman empire appeared to be the last in the series of earthly kingdoms. The long interval of conflict which has followed the first Advent formed no place in the anticipation of the first Christendom; and in succeeding ages the Roman period has been unnaturally prolonged to meet the requirements of a theory which took its rise in a state of thought which experience has proved false[3].'

B. This interpretation appears first[4] in Ephrem Syrus (*c.* 300—350

---

[1] Auberlen, as cited above; Keil, p. 224; Dr Pusey, p. 78 f.

[2] It is remarkable, if Daniel's vision really extends so far as to embrace the history of Europe, that the first coming of Christ, and the influences wrought by Christianity, should be ignored in it. The explanation that Daniel, "being a statesman and an Israelite, saw nothing of the Church" (Aub. p. 252) is artificial and improbable.

[3] Smith's *Dict. of the Bible*, s.v. DANIEL. The view is, in fact, just a re-interpretation, and re-application, of the unfulfilled prophecy of Daniel: see Charles, *Eschatology* (1899), p. 171 f.; Cooke, *Expositor*, March, 1909, p. 206.

[4] Or, at least, for the first time distinctly; for a passage in the so-called 'Sibylline Oracles' (see the Introduction, p. lxxxiii) makes it probable that the 'ten horns' were understood of the Seleucidae as early as *c.* 140 B.C. After describing (iii. 381—7) how Macedonia will bring great woe upon Asia, and overcome Babylon (alluding manifestly to Alexander the Great), the 'Sibyl' continues (388 ff.):—

ἥξει καί ποτ' ἄπυστ [εἰς] Ἀσσίδος ὄλβιον οὖδας
ἀνὴρ πορφυρέην λώπην ἐπιειμένος ὤμοις,
390 ἄγριος, ἀλλοδίκης, φλογόεις· ἤγειρε γὰρ αὐτὸν
πρόσθε κεραυνός φῶτα· κακὸν δ' Ἀσίῃ ζυγὸν ἕξει
πᾶσα, πολὺν δὲ χθὼν πίεται φόνον ὀμβρηθεῖσα.
ἀλλὰ καὶ ὡς πανάϊστον ἄπαντ' Ἀΐδης θεραπεύσει·
ὧν δὴ περ γενεὴν αὐτὸς θέλει ἐξαπολέσσαι,
395 ἐκ τῶν δὴ γενεῆς κείνου γένος ἐξαπολεῖται·
ῥίζαν ἴαν γε διδούς, ἣν καὶ κόψει Βροτολοιγὸς
ἐκ δέκα δὴ κεράτων, παρὰ δὲ φυτὸν ἄλλο φυτεύσει.
κόψει πορφυρέης γενεῆς γενετῆρα μαχητήν,
καὐτὸς ἀφ' υἱῶν, ὧν ἐς ὁμόφρονα αἴσιον ἄρρης
400 φθεῖται· καὶ τοτὲ δὴ παραφυόμενον κέρας ἄρξει.

The 'man clad with purple, fierce, unjust, fiery, lightning-born,' who is to enslave Asia is, it seems, Antiochus Epiphanes (whose invasion of Egypt is certainly

A.D.)¹; it was adopted afterwards by several later and mediæval scholars; more recently it has been advocated in England by Mr (now Bishop) Westcott, and Prof. Bevan; and on the Continent by Ewald, Bleek, Delitzsch², Kuenen, Meinhold, and others³. The strongest arguments in its favour are derived (1) from the positive objections stated above, to the 'Roman' interpretation,—for an intermediate view, which has been suggested, viz. that the four empires are the Babylonian, the Medo-Persian, the Macedonian, and the Syrian, has little to recommend it: and (2) from the description of the 'little horn' in Dan. vii., viewed in connexion with what is said in other parts of the book. In ch. viii. there is a 'little horn,' which is admitted on all hands to represent Antiochus Epiphanes, and whose impious character and doings (viii. 10—12, 25) are in all essentials identical with those attributed to the 'little horn' in ch. vii. (vii. 8 *end*, 20, 21, 25): as Delitzsch remarks, it is extremely difficult to think that where the description is so similar, two entirely different persons, living in widely different periods of the world's history, should be intended. It is true, there are *details* in which the two descriptions differ,—ch. viii. dwells for instance a good deal more fully on the *particulars* of Antiochus' assaults upon the faith: but entire identity would be tautology; the differences affect no material feature in the representation; and there is consequently no better reason for supposing that they point here to two different personalities than for supposing that similar differences in the representations of ch. ii. and ch. vii. point there to two different series of

referred to in ll. 611—615). The race which he wishes to destroy, but by which his own race will be destroyed, is that of his brother Seleucus IV. (B.C. 187—175), whose son, Demetrius I., caused the 'one root' which Antiochus left, viz. his son and successor, Antiochus V. Eupator (164—162), to be put to death (1 Macc. vii. 1—4): this the writer expresses by saying, 'the destroyer (Ares, the god of war) will cut him off out of ten horns', i.e. as the last of ten kings. The (illegitimate) 'plant' planted beside him is Alexander Balas, who defeated and slew Demetrius I., the 'warrior father of a royal race' in 150 (1 Macc. x. 49 f.), and usurped the throne of Syria from 150 to 146. In 146, however, Alexander Balas (l. 399) was attacked and defeated by Demetrius II., son of Demetrius I., and his father in-law, Ptolemy Philometor, and soon afterwards murdered (1 Macc. xi. 8—19; Jos. *Ant.* XIII. iv. 8). The 'horn' growing alongside, that was then to rule, is the *parvenu* Trypho, guardian of the youthful Antiochus VI., who having procured the death of his ward, held the throne of Syria from 142 to 137 (1 Macc. xii. 39, xiii. 31 f., xv. 37). If this highly probable interpretation is correct (and it is accepted by Schürer), the 'ten horns,' though not entirely, are nevertheless largely (see p. 101 f.) the same Seleucid princes as in Dan.; and it is reasonable to regard the passage as indicating the sense in which the 'horns' of Dan. were understood at the time when it was written (see further Schürer, ii. p. 798 f.).

2 Esdr. xii. 11 (cited p. 95), where the interpretation of Dan. vii. 7, 8 given in *vv.* 23—26 seems to be corrected, may also perhaps justify the inference that this interpretation had previously been the prevalent one: it would be but natural that, when the empire of the Greeks had passed away, without the prophecy being fulfilled, it should be re-interpreted of the Romans (cf. Charles, *Eschatology, Hebrew, Jewish and Christian*, p. 173).

¹ See the Commentary on Daniel in vol. ii. of his Syriac works (ed. 1740).
² In his art. DANIEL, in the 2nd edition of Herzog's *Real-Encyklopädie* (1878). It is also adopted by Buhl in the corresponding article in the 3rd edition (1898) of the same work.
³ It is adopted also in the art. DANIEL in Hastings' *Dict. of the Bible*, by Prof. E. L. Curtis, of Yale, and in that in Black's *Encyclopaedia Biblica* (col. 1007), by Prof. Kamphausen, of Bonn.

empires. Again, the period during which the persecution in ch. vii. is to continue is 'a time, times, and half-a-time' (i.e. 3½ years)—exactly the period during which (xii. 7: cf. *v.* 11; and on ix. 27) the persecution of Antiochus is to continue: is it likely that entirely different events should be measured by precisely the same interval of time? And thirdly, if the overthrow of Antiochus Epiphanes is in xii. 1—3 (see the notes) followed immediately by the Messianic age, is it probable that in chs. ii. and vii. this should be represented as beginning at an indefinite date in the distant future? The age of Antiochus Epiphanes is in fact the *limiting horizon of the book*. Not only does the revelation of chs. x.—xii. culminate in the description of that age, which is followed, without any interval, by the period of final bliss, but the age of Antiochus himself is in viii. 19 (as the sequel shews) described as the 'time of the end': can there then, asks Delitzsch, have been for Daniel a 'time of the end' *after* that which he himself expressly describes as the 'end'? 'There might have been, if the visions which *ex hyp.* represent the Roman age as following that of Alexander and his successors, were *later* in date than those which do not look beyond the period of the Seleucidae. In point of fact, however, the dream of ch. ii., and the vision of ch. vii., are both of earlier date than the visions of ch. viii. and ch. ix.[1]'

For these reasons it is impossible to think either that the 'little horn' of ch. vii. represents any other ruler but Antiochus Epiphanes, or that the fourth empire of ch. ii. and ch. vii. is any other than the Greek empire of Alexander's successors. That the symbolism of the two visions leaves 'nothing to be desired' upon this interpretation, has been shewn by Delitzsch. "By the material of the feet being heterogeneous is signified the division of the kingdom, in consequence of which these offshoots ('Ausläufer') of it arose (cf. xi. 5); by its consisting of iron and clay is signified the superior strength of the one kingdom as compared with the other (xi. 5); by the iron and clay being mingled, without being organically united, is signified the union of the two kingdoms by matrimonial alliances (xi. 6, 17), without any real unity between them being attained. And how naturally are the silver breast and arms referred to the Median empire, and the brazen belly and loins to the Persian! 'After thee,' says Daniel to Nebuchadnezzar (ii. 39), 'will arise another kingdom, inferior to thine.' Was then the Persian empire inferior to the Chaldaean? It may be answered that it was so in its Median beginnings. But what justification is there for referring the word 'inferior' to the beginnings of the second empire, rather than to the period when it displayed most fully its distinctive character? The reference is to the Median Empire which, because it was in general of less importance than the others, is passed by in the interpretation (ii. 39) in few words. Of the third empire, on the contrary, it is said (*ibid.*) that it will 'bear rule over all the earth.' That is the Persian empire. Only this is again a universal empire, in the fullest sense of the term, as the Chaldaean was. The inter-

---

[1] The arguments in the preceding paragraph are substantially those of Delitzsch, in his article just referred to, p. 474.

DANIEL, VII.

mediate Median empire, weaker than both, merely forms the transition from the one to the other[1]."

What, however, upon this interpretation of the fourth empire, is denoted by the 'ten horns'? The most probable view is that they represent the successors of Alexander upon the throne of Antioch, the line out of which Antiochus Epiphanes, the 'little horn,' ultimately arose. 'That all ten appear simultaneously is a consequence of the vision [comp. in ch. ii. how the four successive empires appear as parts of the same image], and does not authorize the conclusion that all were contemporary, though of course the three uprooted by Antiochus must have been contemporary with him' (Delitzsch). The first seven of these successors are: (1) Seleucus (I.) Nicator (B.C. 312—280); (2) Antiochus (I.) Soter (279—261); (3) Antiochus (II.) Theos (260—246); (4) Seleucus (II.) Callinicus (245—226); (5) Seleucus (III.) Ceraunus (225—223); (6) Antiochus (III.) the Great (222—187); (7) Seleucus (IV.) Philopator (186—176). The last three are reckoned differently. According to some[2], they are (8) Heliodorus, the chief minister of Seleucus Philopator, who, having poisoned his master, aimed at the throne for himself, and would, no doubt, have secured it, had not Antiochus Epiphanes returned from Rome in time, with the help of Attalus and Eumenes of Pergamum, to prevent it (see further on xi. 20)[3]; (9) Demetrius, son of Seleucus Philopator and nephew of Antiochus Epiphanes, who after his father's murder was the legitimate heir to the throne, but who was detained as hostage at Rome in lieu of Antiochus Epiphanes, and only actually succeeded to the throne after Antiochus Epiphanes' death; (10) Ptolemy (VII.) Philometor, king of Egypt, also nephew of Antiochus Epiphanes (being son of his sister Cleopatra), whom, according to Jerome, a party in Syria desired to place on the throne, but whom Antiochus 'by simulating clemency' displaced[4]: Philometor afterwards laid claim to the Syrian provinces of Coele-Syria and Palestine, but being attacked by Antiochus, he fell into his uncle's hands, and had it not been for the interference of the Romans, would, in all probability, have permanently lost the crown of Egypt (see more fully on xi. 21). These three men, as Ewald points out, were all politically prominent at the time; they all stood in Antiochus's way, and had in one way or another to be put aside before he could secure his crown: they might thus, in the

---

[1] Delitzsch had already shewn, substantially as is done above, in the note on ii. 39, that according to the representation of the Book of Daniel, there was a Median empire, following the Chaldaean, and at the same time distinct from the Persian.

[2] Bertholdt, von Lengerke, Ewald, Meinhold; cf. Delitzsch, p. 476.

[3] Cf. Appian, *Syr.* 45: τὸν δὲ Ἡλιόδωρον...εἰς τὴν ἀρχὴν βιαζόμενον ἐκβάλλουσιν; and (of Antiochus) τῆς ἀρχῆς ἁρπαζομένης ὑπὸ ἀλλοτρίων βασιλεὺς οἰκεῖος ὤφθη.

[4] The statement, sometimes made, that Cleopatra herself claimed the throne of Syria for her son, is only matter of inference (cf. Pusey, p. 150). It is, however, true that the claim was afterwards (148—147 B.C.) raised, and even acted on by the Roman senate (Polyb. xxxiii. 16), on behalf of Philometor's son-in-law, Alexander Balas; and that Philometor, having marched into Syria to assist Alexander in enforcing his claim, was actually for a short time king of Syria (1 Macc. xi. 13; Polyb. xl. 12; Jos. *Ant.* xiii. 4: see Mahaffy, *The Empire of the Ptolemies*, p. 366, and the coin figured on p. 376).

imagery of the vision, be well described as 'plucked up' (vii. 8), 'falling down' (vii. 20), or 'abased' (vii. 24), before him. Others[1], arguing that the fourth beast represents the Greek supremacy as a whole, consider that Alexander, the first king, should not be excluded from the enumeration: they accordingly begin the list with him, obtaining then (8) Seleucus Philopator; (9) Heliodorus; (10) Demetrius: upon this view it is supposed that the murder of Seleucus Philopator, though in fact the work of Heliodorus, was attributed popularly at the time to the suggestion, or instigation, of Antiochus (who, indeed, almost immediately succeeded his brother, and consequently was the one who, to all appearance, benefited most materially by his removal). The exclusion of Ptolemy Philometor from this enumeration, is thought to be a point in its favour; for before the accession of Antiochus, he was not, it is pointed out, king of Syria, and it is doubtful (p. 101, *note*) whether even any claim to the throne was then made on his behalf. Others[2], again, doubt whether Demetrius is rightly included among the ten kings (for though he was the lawful heir after his father's death, he was not actually king at the time here referred to), and prefer, therefore, (8) Seleucus Philopator; (9) Heliodorus; (10) an unnamed brother of Demetrius, who, according to a fragment of John of Antioch, was put to death by Antiochus[3]. One or other of these alternatives may be reasonably adopted, as sufficiently satisfying the requirements of the case; our knowledge of the times does not, unfortunately, enable us to decide with confidence which deserves the preference.

Bleek supposed that the ten horns represented the parts of Alexander's empire which, after his death, became independent kingdoms, the number ten being chosen in view of the generals who, in the partition of B.C. 323, obtained the chief provinces, viz. 1 Craterus (Macedonia), 2 Antipater (Greece), 3 Lysimachus (Thrace), 4 Leonatus (Little Phrygia on the Hellespont), 5 Antigonus (Great Phrygia, Lycia, and Pamphylia), 6 Kassander (Caria), 7 Eumenes (Cappadocia and Paphlagonia), 8 Laomedon (Syria and Palestine), 9 Pithon (Media), 10 Ptolemy Lagi (Egypt). However, according to Justin (xiii. 4) the entire number of provinces was not 10, but 28, and the principle upon which 10 are selected out of them appears to be arbitrary; moreover, these provinces were not independent kingdoms, but satrapies of an empire still regarded as one and undivided (see Pusey, p. 153 ff).

Additional Note on the expression 'one like unto a son of man' in Dan. vii. 13[4].

The question what this expression in Dan. vii. 13 denotes has been much disputed. On the one hand, the current interpretation has, no doubt, been that it denotes the *Messiah*; on the other hand, there are strong reasons, derived from the text of Daniel itself, for holding that it denotes the glorified and ideal *people of Israel*.

---

[1] Hitzig, Cornill, Behrmann, Prince,—though Behrmann is disposed to treat the number symbolically, and to doubt whether particular individuals are referred to: the 'ten horns' he regards as symbolizing generally the divided rule of the Diadochi (p. 46). We cannot feel *sure* what the author means, so that this view must at least be admitted as a possible one.
[2] Von Gutschmid, Kuenen, Bevan.
[3] Müller, *Fragm. hist. Graec.* iv. 558.
[4] See further, esp. on the N.T. usage, the writer's art. in *DB.* iv. 579 ff.

1. *The meaning of the expression*[1]. In *Hebrew*, 'sons of man' (or 'of men'—אדם being a collective term) is a common expression for mankind in general (Ps. xi. 4, xii. 1, 8, xiv. 2 &c.): the sing. 'son of man' also occurs (*a*) in the address to Ezekiel (בן אדם), Ez. ii. 1, 3, iii. 1, 3 and more than 90 times besides (so also Dan. viii. 17); (*b*) poetically, here and there, usually in parallelism with איש or אנוש, as Num. xxiii. 19; Is. li. 12, lvi. 2; Jer. xlix. 18 (=*v*. 33=l. 40=(nearly) li. 43); Ps. viii. 4, lxxx. 17, cxlvi. 3 (∥ נדיבים 'nobles'); Job xvi. 21 (∥ גבר)[2], xxv. 6, xxxv. 8; cf. Ps. cxliv. 3 בן־אנוש (∥ אדם).

In *Aramaic*, *bar 'ĕnāsh* (or, contracted, *bar-nāsh*) is common in some dialects (but not in others) in prose (and not merely in poetry) in the ordinary sense of *man*. It does not occur in this sense elsewhere in Bibl. Aramaic, or in the Targum of Onkelos, or in the Targum on the Prophets (except in Is. lvi. 12; Jer. xlix. 18, 33, l. 40, li. 43; Mic. v. 6 [Heb. בני אדם], where it is suggested directly by the Hebrew): but it is frequent in the somewhat different dialects of the Targums on the Hagiographa (about 7 cent. A.D.)[3], the Palestinian Targums on the Pent.[4], the Palestinian Talmud (3—4 cent. A.D.), the Palestinian Evangeliarium (about 5 cent. A.D.)[5], and Syriac[6].

On the strength of the poetical usage in Heb., and the usage which prevailed, at least in later times, in Aramaic, it may be said that 'son of man' in Dan. vii. 13 does not substantially denote more than a 'man,' though it is[7] a choice, semi-poetical expression for the idea. It is, however, a *man*, as opposed to a brute, humane as well as human— perhaps, also, as Dalman urges (pp. 198 f., 217 f.), *only* a man, in himself frail and helpless, powerless by his own might to conquer the world, and destined, if he is to become ruler of the world, to 'receive' his kingdom at the hands of God.

2. *The interpretation of the expression.* In the Book of Daniel itself there is nothing which lends support to the Messianic interpretation. In the explanation of the vision which follows (vii. 15 ff.) the place occupied by the 'one like unto a son of man' is taken, not by the Messiah, but by the ideal people of God: in *v*. 14 the 'one like unto a son of man' appears when the dominion of the four beasts, and the persecution of the 'little horn,' are both over, and receives a universal kingdom which shall never pass away; and in *vv*. 18, 22, 27, when the dominion of the four kingdoms corresponding to the four beasts is at an end, and the persecution of the king corresponding to the 'little horn' has ceased, the 'saints of the Most High,' or (*v*. 27) the 'people of the saints of the Most High,' receive similarly a universal kingdom (*v*. 27),

---

[1] Cf. Dalman, *Die Worte Jesu*, p. 191.

[2] But read here probably וּבֵן אָדָם ('and *between* a man,' &c.).

[3] *E.g.* Ps. viii. 5 (twice), lvi. 12, lx. 13, cxv. 4, cxviii. 6, 8, cxix. 134.

[4] *E.g.* Lev. iv. 2, v. 1, 2, 4, 21, vii. 21, xvii. 4, 9, xix. 8 in the Targ. of 'Pseudo-Jonathan.'

[5] In both, for instance, often in the expression חַד בַּרְנָשׁ 'a certain *man*' (did so and so). Numerous examples are quoted by Lietzmann, *Der Menschensohn* (1896), pp. 32 ff.

[6] *E.g.* Ex. xiii. 13, 15; Lev. xviii. 5; Matth. iv. 4, xii. 12, 43, &c.

[7] At least, this is an inference suggested by the fact that the expression does not occur elsewhere in Dan. for 'man.'

and possess it for ever and ever (*v.* 18). The parallelism between the vision and the interpretation is complete: the time is the same, the promise of perpetual and universal dominion is the same: and hence a strong presumption arises that the subject is also the same, and that the 'one like unto a son of man' in *v.* 13 corresponds to, and represents, the 'saints of the Most High' of *v.* 18, and the 'people of the saints of the Most High' of *v.* 27, i.e. the ideal Israel, for whom in the counsels of God the empire of the world is designed. If the writer by 'the one like unto a son of man' meant the Messiah, the head of the future ideal nation, his silence in the interpretation of the vision is inexplicable: how comes it that he there passes over the Messiah altogether, and applies the terms which (*ex hyp.*) are used of him in *vv.* 13, 14 to the people of Israel in *vv.* 18, 22, 27?

The explanation of the vision *given in the chapter itself* is thus the primary and fundamental argument of those who hold the ideal people of Israel to be intended in vii. 13. If, however, this interpretation be considered further, it will be seen to be both supported by the symbolism of the vision, and to harmonize with the representations of the ideal future given elsewhere in the book. In the first place, the realities of history are represented in the vision not as they actually are, but in a *figurative* form: the four beasts are not four actual beasts, but represent four kingdoms; the horns are not actual horns, but represent kings: by analogy, therefore, the figure in human form would not represent an actual man, but would stand for something else, the nature of which is explained, exactly as in the case of the four 'beasts' and of the 'horns,' in the interpretation. It is not difficult to suggest a reason why in the vision the last figure should appear in human form. Humanity is contrasted with animality; and the human form, as opposed to the bestial, teaches that the last kingdom will be, not like the Gentile kingdoms, a supremacy of brute force, but a supremacy essentially humane and spiritual. It is another figurative element in the vision, that the Gentile empires rise out of the sea (*v.* 3), by which is meant (see *v.* 17) that they are of this world: by analogy, the statement that the last empire comes with the clouds of heaven, will be a figurative indication of the fact that it will be ushered in by the power of God (cf. Bevan, p. 119). And, secondly, this explanation agrees with the representations given in other parts of the book. Both in ii. 44 and xii. 3, where the establishment of the future kingdom of God is spoken of, the author is as silent respecting a personal Messiah as its head, as he is in vii. 22, 27: the inference is that the Messiah was not a prominent figure in the prophet's thoughts, and the conclusion supports the opinion, derived in the first instance from ch. vii. itself, that he is not intended in vii. 13.

Various considerations have been advanced for the purpose of meeting these arguments. It has been said, for instance, that 'the kingdom is not to be thought of without its king,' and 'that the prophets habitually picture the future happiness of their nation as bestowed upon it by the Messiah.' But the author of Daniel expressly says that in this case the kingdom was to be possessed by the people of the saints; and that the dominion was to belong, not to the Messiah, but either to the people, or to the Almighty Himself (according to the interpretation adopted of the pronoun 'his' in vii. 27). Nor is it true to say that the figure of the Messiah is a constant feature in prophecy: there is no Messiah in Amos (ix. 11 ff.), Zephaniah (iii. 9 ff.), Joel (ii. 23—iii. 21), or in the remarkable eschatological prophecy preserved in Isaiah xxiv.—xxvii., or even in the brilliant visions of the future drawn by the second Isaiah (liv. 11—17, lx.—lxii., lxv. 17—25 &c.)[1]; in Hosea, also, the figure of the Messiah is a shadowy one, hardly more than a resuscitated David (iii. 5), and it is absent altogether from the picture of Israel's future ideal felicity drawn in ch. xiv. Thus while some prophets speak of a Messiah, others do not; there is no uniform practice on the subject; and whether or not the Messiah is referred to in a particular passage is a question which, antecedently, is perfectly open, and can be settled only by exegetical considerations. It has further been argued that coming with the clouds of heaven denotes 'omnipotent judicial power.' This, however, is far from being self-evident. It denotes certainly exaltation and majesty; but the judgement is *completed* (*vv.* 10—12) before the 'one like unto a son of man' appears (*v.* 13), and the purpose for which he is brought to the Almighty is not to exercise judicial functions, but to receive a dominion which should never pass away (*v.* 14). The two verses which refer to him describe, not a judgement, but the solemn inauguration of a divine kingdom upon earth[2].

Though the title, however, it thus seems, does not in Daniel directly denote the Messiah, it was at an early date interpreted personally, and applied to him. The earliest example of this application is found in the 'Similitudes' of the apocryphal Book of Enoch (cc. 37—71), a part of this (composite) book, which is generally considered to date from the first century B.C.[3] The 'Similitudes' consist of a series of visions supposed to be seen by Enoch, in which is represented in particular the judgement to be finally passed upon the world. The imagery of the writer is in several instances suggested evidently by Dan. vii. Enoch is carried in his vision into heaven, where he sees the 'Lord of Spirits' (the Almighty), the 'Elect One' (the Messiah: Is. xlii. 1), in His immediate presence, and the angels, who, like the seraphim in Is. vi., eternally hymn the Creator (c. 39).

---

[1] The passages (Is. xlii. 1—4, &c.) speaking of Jehovah's ideal Servant are in no contradiction with this statement: the 'Messiah,' or 'Anointed One,' is the ideal *King* of Israel (just as the actual king is called 'Jehovah's anointed,' 1 Sam. xxiv. 6, &c.); and the figure of the ideal *Servant* in Is. xl.—lxvi. (though equally fulfilled in the person of our Lord Jesus Christ) is something quite different from this. See the present writer's *Isaiah, his life and times*, pp. 175—180.

[2] For a discussion of some other arguments on the same side, see Drummond, *The Jewish Messiah* (1877), pp. 226—241.

It has been disputed whether the figure like a son of man which appeared in the clouds of heaven came originally from heaven, or was lifted up from the earth. The dispute implies a misconception of the nature and limits of the symbolism. The four beasts appeared emerging from the sea, and yet it is certain that the kingdoms which they represented did not rise out of the sea likewise.

[3] According to Dillmann, from before B.C. 64; according to Mr Charles from either B.C. 94—79 or B.C. 70—64; according to Schürer, at the earliest from the time of Herod (B.C. 37—B.C. 4).

The general picture of the future, as exhibited in these visions, is as follows[1]: In the latter days sin will flourish in the world; and the kings and the mighty will oppress the people of God (lxii. 11). But suddenly the Head of Days (another title of the Almighty in this book, based on the "aged of days" of Dan. vii. 13) will appear, and with Him the Son of Man (xlvi. 1—4), to execute universal judgement. All Israel will be raised from the dead (li. 1: cf. Dan. xii. 2), and judgement on men and angels alike will be committed to the Son of Man (lxix. 27). The fallen angels will be cast into a fiery furnace (liv. 6); the kings and the mighty will be tortured in Gehenna by the angels of punishment (liii. 3—5, liv. 1, 2); and the remaining sinners and godless will be destroyed from the face of the earth (liii. 2, lxix. 27). Heaven and earth will be transformed (xlv. 4, 5; cf. Is. lxv. 17); and the righteous will become angels in heaven (li. 4), and dwell for ever in presence of the Elect One (xxxix. 6, xlv. 4).

This outline will be sufficient to indicate what details of the picture are derived from Daniel, and what details are new. Some passages in the description are however of sufficient interest to be quoted in full[2]:—

xl. 1. 'And after that I saw thousands of thousands, and ten thousand times ten thousand, a multitude beyond number and reckoning, who stood before the Lord of Spirits' (cf. Dan. vii. 10; Rev. v. 11).

xlvi. 1. 'And there I saw One who had a head of days, and His head was white like wool [Dan. vii. 9], and with him was another being whose countenance had the appearance of a man, and his face was full of graciousness, like one of the holy angels. 2. And I asked the angel who went with me and shewed me all the hidden things, concerning that Son of Man, who he was, and whence he was, and why he went with the Head of Days. 3. And he answered and said unto me, "This is the Son of Man who hath righteousness, with whom dwelleth righteousness, and who reveals all the treasures of that which is hidden, because the Lord of Spirits hath chosen him, and his lot before the Lord of Spirits hath surpassed everything in uprightness for ever. 4. And this Son of Man whom thou hast seen will arouse the kings and the mighty ones from their couches and the strong from their thrones, and will loosen the reins of the strong and grind to powder the teeth of the sinners...6. And he will put down the countenance of the strong, and shame will cover them."'

xlvii. 3. 'And in those days I saw the Head of Days when He had seated Himself on the throne of His glory, and the books of the living were opened before him, and His whole host which is in heaven above and around Him stood before Him.'

li. 1. 'And in those days will the earth also give back those who are treasured up within it, and Sheol also will give back that which it has received, and hell will give back that which it owes. 2. And he will choose the righteous and holy from among them; for the day of their redemption hath drawn nigh.'

The judgement is described most fully in ch. lxii.

---

[1] Cf. R. H. Charles, in Hastings' *Dict. of the Bible*, i. 744.
[2] From Mr Charles' translation (Oxford, 1893).

lxii. 2. 'And the Lord of Spirits seated him (*viz.* the Messiah) on the throne of His glory, and the spirit of righteousness was poured out upon him, and the word of his mouth slew all the sinners, and all the unrighteous were destroyed before his face. 3. And there will stand up in that day all the kings and the mighty, and the exalted, and those who hold the earth.... 5. And their countenance will fall, and pain will seize them when they see that Son of Man sitting on the throne of His glory.' Then, when it is too late, they will be ready to acknowledge and worship the Son of Man; but 'the angels of punishment' will take them in charge and make them 'a spectacle for the righteous and for His elect.' The righteous and elect, however, 'will be saved on that day and will never again from thenceforth see the face of the sinners and unrighteous. 14. And the Lord of Spirits will abide over them, and with that Son of Man will they eat and lie down and rise up for ever and ever.'

lxiii. The kings and the mighty make a further appeal for mercy to the angels of punishment; but it is without avail, and they are banished for ever from the presence of the Son of Man.

lxix. 29. 'And from henceforth there will be nothing that is corruptible; for the Son of Man has appeared and sits on the throne of His glory, and all evil will pass away before his face and depart; but the word of the Son of Man will be strong before the Lord of Spirits[1].'

Another development of Dan. vii. 13 is found in the Second (Fourth) Book of Esdras, an apocalypse written most probably under Domitian (A.D. 81—96), though c. 13, by some critics, is assigned to a rather earlier date, before A.D. 70. In c. 13 of this book a dream is described, in which 'a wind arose from the sea, that it moved all the waves thereof [cf. Dan. vii. 2]. And I beheld, and lo, this wind caused to come up from the midst of the sea as it were the likeness of a man, and I beheld, and lo, that man flew with the clouds of heaven; and when he turned his countenance to look, all things trembled that were seen under him.' Afterwards, an innumerable multitude of men 'from the four winds of heaven,' were gathered together, 'to make war against the man that came out of the sea. And I beheld, and lo, he graved himself a great mountain, and flew up upon it.' The multitudes then advance against him; he lifts up against them neither sword nor spear, but destroys them by a 'flood of fire' and 'flaming breath' proceeding out of his mouth, which in a moment reduces them to cinders. After this, he summons to himself another, peaceable multitude; but before what he is going to do with this has transpired the seer awakes (xiii. 1—13). The interpretation of the vision follows (*v.* 21 ff.). The man coming up out of the sea is he whom the Most High has reserved to be a deliverer and a judge (i.e. though the word itself is not used, the Messiah):

---

[1] The expressions used in Enoch are 'that Son of Man' (referring back to xlvi. 1), xlvi. 2, 4 ('this'), xlviii. 2, lxii. 5, 9, 14, lxiii. 11, lxix. 26, 29, lxx. 1, lxxi. 17, and 'the Son of Man' xlvi. 3, lxii. 7, lxix. 27. In the other parts of the book this title is not found; the Messiah is alluded to (figuratively) in the section c. 83—90, at least in passing (xc. 37, 38), but as hardly more than an ordinary man, and without any supernatural powers or attributes: in cv. 2, also, he is spoken of by God as 'My Son.'

in those days cities and peoples will all be fighting against one another, but in the midst of these tumults 'my Son will be revealed, whom thou sawest (as) a man ascending'; when the nations hear his voice, they will leave their own wars, and proceed to fight against him; but he will stand upon the top of Mount Sion, and rebuke and destroy them. The peaceable multitude is then explained to be the Ten tribes, who after their exile by the king of Assyria, had migrated into a still more distant region of the earth that they might keep the law of their God, but are now brought back to their own land (*vv.* 35—47).

The Messianic interpretation of Dan. vii. 13 is also implied in the often quoted saying of R. Joshua ben Levi (c. 250 A.D.), the intention of which is to reconcile the apparently discrepant descriptions here and in Zech. ix. 9: If Israel are worthy, he will come 'with the clouds of heaven;' if Israel are not worthy, he will come 'afflicted and riding upon an ass[1].' On the strength of the same interpretation, the Jews even identify the 'Anānī (a name formed from '*ānān*, cloud, and signifying in appearance the 'cloud-one'), who forms the close of the Davidic genealogy in 1 Chron. iii. 24, with the Messiah[2]. Another Rabbinical title of the Messiah, which perhaps presupposes the same explanation, is *bar niphlê*, if this is rightly explained as 'filius νεφελῶν[3].'

It is a question, however, how far the fact that the passage was thus interpreted, even in early times, by the Jews, is evidence as to its original meaning, and sufficient to neutralize the arguments in support of the other interpretation supplied by the book of Daniel itself. The passage is one which, *taken alone*, might readily give rise to the impression that the Messiah was intended; while early Jewish writers might easily neglect to make the comparison of other passages necessary to correct the impression. The ultimate decision of the question must depend upon the relative weight, which, in the reader's opinion, ought to be attached to the *primâ facie* impression made by *vv.* 13, 14, and to what (to use Schürer's words) "is said by the author distinctly and expressly in his interpretation of the vision, in *vv.* 18, 22, 27[4]."

[1] (*Sanh.* 98ᵃ, זכו ישראל עם ענני שמיא לא זכו עני ורוכב על חמור) and elsewhere: see references in Dalman, *Der Leidende und der Sterbende Messias der Synagoge*, 1888, p. 38 *n.*).

[2] See, *e.g.*, the (late) Targum on this passage: '...and Delaiah and Anani, that is, the Anointed King, who is to be revealed (הוא מלכא משיחא דעתיד לאתגלאה).' Comp. Pearson, *On the Creed*, art. vii. fol. 292—3; and Dalman, *l.c.*

[3] Levy, *NHWB.* iii. 422; Dalman, *l.c.* p. 37 f.; *Die Worte Jesu*, p. 201.

[4] The opinion that the 'one like unto a son of man' denotes the Messiah has been maintained in modern times not only by Häv., Hengst., Keil, Pusey, Zöckler, &c., but also by Von Lengerke, Ewald, Bleek (*Jahrb. für Deutsche Theol.* 1860, p. 58 *n.*), Hilgenfeld (*Jüd. Apok.* p. 45 f.), Riehm, *Messianic Prophecy* (Edinb. 1891), p. 193 ff., Behrmann; Schultz, *O. T. Theol.* ii. 439, also inclines to it: the view that it represents the people of Israel is in antiquity that of Ephrem Syrus, in modern times it has been defended by Hitzig, Hofmann (*Weissagung u. Erfüllung*, i. 290 f.), Bevan, Meinhold, Drummond, Stanton (*Jewish and Christian Messiah*, p. 109), Schürer (*Gesch. des Jüd. Volkes*², ii. 426 [E. T. II. ii. 137]), Dalman (*Die Worte Jesu*, p. 197), Sanday (in Hastings' *Dict. of the Bible*, ii. 622); cf. Farrar, pp. 249—51.

A consideration of the use and meaning of the term, 'the son of man,' in the N. T. does not belong properly to a Commentary on Daniel; nevertheless the subject is sufficiently germane to the present passage of Daniel for a few words on it not to be out of place here. The expression ὁ υἱὸς τοῦ ἀνθρώπου is used frequently, both in the Synoptic Gospels and in St John, as a designation of Christ, but exclusively—for John xii. 34 is hardly an exception—in the mouth of Christ Himself: elsewhere in the N.T.[1] it occurs only in the words of Stephen, Acts vii. 56. There is no evidence that it was a current Jewish title of the Messiah[2]. It is commonly supposed to have been directly derived from Daniel vii. 13. But, as Prof. (now Bishop) Westcott pointed out long ago[3], this is not quite correct. 'In reality the passage (Dan. vii. 13) in which the title is supposed to be found has only a secondary relation to it. The vision of Daniel brings before him not 'the Son of man,' but one 'like a son of man.' The phrase is general, and is introduced by a particle of comparison. The thought on which the seer dwells is simply that of the human appearance of the being presented to him' (cf. above, *ad loc.*). '*The* son of man' differs evidently from '*one like a* son of man.' The former, it cannot reasonably be doubted, was chosen purposely by Jesus to express His own view of His office. It may be doubted, however, whether in its origin it was connected by Him with Dan. vii. 13. It seems clearly to represent Him as the true child of man, the ideal son of the human race, the representative of humanity. It is used most frequently in passages which refer to the earthly work of the Lord in the time of His humility[4], especially where the thought is prominent of His lowliness, or physical weakness, or true humanity. These however are not the associations that would be naturally suggested by Dan. vii. 13. But the title is used also on other occasions where the reference is to His future coming in glory (as Matt. xiii. 41, xvi. 27 f., xix. 28, xxiv. 27, 30, 37, 39, 44, xxv. 31, xxvi. 64). It is, however, only in passages belonging quite to the close of our Lord's ministry, viz. Matt. xxiv. 30, 'coming on the clouds of heaven' (|| Mk. xiii. 26; Luke xxi. 27), and xxvi. 64 (|| Mk. xiv. 62), that it is brought distinctly into connexion with Dan. vii. 13. The passages in which the title is used of our Lord as Judge are strikingly similar to some of those quoted above from the Book of Enoch. But the more primary use and sense of the expression seem to lie in the first group of passages; and it is in these, it would seem, that its original meaning must be sought. The employment of the title in the second group of passages may have been suggested by its use in the Book of Enoch, or (in Matt. xxiv. 30, xxvi. 64 and || ||) by Dan. vii. 13. And the reference in Matt. xxiv. 30 may be not unreasonably held to imply that, as the ideal representative of Israel, our Lord claimed to fulfil the promise of dominion made to Israel (if the view adopted in this note is correct) in Dan. vii. 14. But our Lord was not only '*like a* son of man,' He was '*the* Son of man'; so that, even in so far as He bases His use of the term upon Dan. vii.

---

[1] In Rev. i. 13, xiv. 14, there is no article in the Greek (see R. V.).
[2] Dalman, p. 197 ff., 204.   [3] *Speaker's Comm.* on St John, p. 33 f.
[4] Westcott, *l.c.* p. 34 (§ 9), quotes and classifies the passages.

8 In the third year of the reign of king Belshazzar a vision appeared unto me, *even unto* me Daniel, after that which
2 appeared unto me at the first. And I saw in a vision;

13, He certainly reads into it a larger and fuller meaning than it there possesses. And it is a question whether the sense which He appears to attach to the title is not more naturally deducible from Ps. viii. 4—a Psalm of which the theme is the contrast between the actual lowliness and the ideal dignity of man—than from Dan. vii. 13.

CHAP. VIII. ANTIOCHUS EPIPHANES AND THE DESECRATION OF THE SANCTUARY.

A vision of Daniel in the third year of Belshazzar. A ram with two horns appeared, pushing towards the west, north, and south, until a he-goat, with a 'notable horn' between its eyes, emerged from the west, and, drawing nigh, attacked the ram, and broke its two horns (*vv.* 1—7). After this, the he-goat increased in strength; but ere long its horn was broken; and in place of it there rose up four other horns, looking towards the four quarters of the earth (*v.* 8). Out of one of these there came forth a little horn, which, waxing great towards the land of Judah, exalted itself against the host of heaven and against its Prince (God), desecrating His sanctuary, and interrupting the daily sacrifice for 2300 half-days (*vv.* 9—14). The meaning of this vision was explained to Daniel by the angel Gabriel. The ram with two horns was the Medo-Persian empire; the he-goat was the empire of the Greeks, the 'notable horn' being its first king, Alexander the Great: and the four horns which followed were the four kingdoms into which, after his death, his empire was ultimately resolved (*vv.* 15—22). The little horn, which arose out of one of these, represented a king who, though not named, is shewn, by the description of his doings (*vv.* 23—25), to be Antiochus Epiphanes.

Although the vision is dated in the third year of Belshazzar, its main subject is thus the empire of the Greeks, especially the reign of Antiochus Epiphanes, whose character and policy are clearly depicted in it. The vision differs from the one in ch. vii. in that it dwells more exclusively upon the *human* side of the history, and describes with greater particularity Antiochus' dealings with the Jews.

1. *In the third year* &c.] See the note on vii. 1.

at the first] properly, **at the beginning** (Gen. xiii. 3, xli. 21, xliii. 18, 20). The reference is to ch. vii. where the first of Daniel's visions is recorded.

2. *And I saw in* the *vision; and it came to pass, when I saw, that I* was **in Shushan, the citadel,** *which* is **in Elam, the province;** *and I saw in* the *vision, and I was by* **the stream Ulai**] The verse is awkwardly worded, and in part tautologous; its object is to describe where Daniel seemed to find himself in the vision. 'Elam' is the Heb. form of the Sumerian (or 'Accadian') *Êlam-ma*, 'highland,' which in Ass. assumed the fem. term. and became *Êlamtu*: it de-

and it came to pass, when I saw, that I *was* at Shushan *in* the palace, which *is* in the province of Elam; and I

noted originally (Delitzsch, *Paradies*, p. 320 f.) 'the mountainous region beginning N. and E. of Susa, and corresponding roughly to the modern Khusistan.' Persia proper was S. E. of it. It is mentioned frequently both in the O.T. (Gen. x. 22; Is. xi. 11; Jer. xlix. 34, &c.), and also in the Assyrian Inscriptions: Anshan, or Anzan, the home of Cyrus, was the district in the S.-W. of Elam, bordering on what is now the lower course of the Tigris, but what in ancient times was the upper part of the Persian Gulf (called by the Assyrians the *Nâr Marratum*, or *Bitter* (salt) *River*[1]). Shushan (Susa) was the capital of Elam. Asshurbanipal (B.C. 668—626) invaded Elam more than once, and has left a full and vivid account of the occasion on which he stormed and sacked Shushan (*KB.*, ii. 203 ff.). Darius Hystaspis appears to have been the first Persian king who erected palaces at Shushan, or held his court there[2]; and from his time onwards, as the principal residence of the Persian kings (cf. Neh. i. 1; Est. i. 2, and *passim*), it held for nearly two centuries a commanding position in the ancient world. 'From Susa, during this period, the peoples of W. Asia and E. Europe awaited their destiny; in the Apadâna tributary princes, ambassadors, and satraps, including the noblest of the Greeks, as Antalkidas (387 and 372), Pelopidas and Ismenias (367), did homage at the feet of the Great King. In the palaces of the citadel were enacted bloody harem-tragedies, in which eunuchs and women were the actors (Esther, Amytis, Amestris, Parysatis, Statira). Here Xerxes fell under the daggers of Artabanus and Aspamithras, and here Bagoas poisoned two kings' (Billerbeck, *Susa*, p. 154). Susa was thus a suitable spot at which the seer should find himself in a vision that portrayed with some prominence both the rise and the fall of the Persian power (*vv.* 3—7). See further, on Susa, p. 125 f.

For other instances of visionary transference to a distant locality, see Ez. viii. 3—xi. 24, xl. 2 ff.

Shushan, *the* citadel] the standing title of Shushan in the O. T. (Neh. i. 1; Est. i. 2, 5, ii. 3, 5, 8, iii. 15, viii. 14, ix. 6, 11, 12). The word rendered 'citadel' (*birah*) is peculiar to the later Hebrew, being found otherwise only in 1 Chr. xxix. 1, 19; Ezra vi. 2; Neh. ii. 8 (see Ryle's note), vii. 2. It is probably the Ass. *birtu*, 'castle' (Delitzsch, *Ass. Handwörterbuch*, p. 185), and denotes a castellated building or enclosure, a castle, citadel, or acropolis.

Elam, the province] Cf. Ezr. vi. 2, 'Media, the province.' It is, however, extremely doubtful whether Elam, especially after the rise and successes of Cyrus, was a 'province' (iii. 2, 3) of the Babylonian empire: the word seems rather a reminiscence of the time when the district in which Susa lay was a principal 'province' of the Persian empire.

---

[1] Maspero, *Struggle of the Nations* (with Map), p. 30 f.
[2] Billerbeck, *Susa* (1893), pp. 128, 129, 133 ff.

112   DANIEL, VIII.   [vv. 3, 4.

3 saw in a vision, and I was by the river of Ulai. Then I lifted up mine eyes, and saw, and behold, there stood before the river a ram which had two horns: and the two horns *were* high; but one *was* higher than the other, and the
4 higher came up last. I saw the ram pushing westward, and northward, and southward; so that no beasts might stand before him, neither *was there any* that could deliver out of his hand; but he did according to his will, and became

the stream *Ulai*] The word rendered *stream* occurs only here and *vv.* 3, 6; but it appears to differ only phonetically from the one found in Jer. xvii. 8, and (in a slightly different form) in Is. xxx. 25, xliv. 4. The Ulai is the Ass. *U-la-a-a*—the waters of which Asshurbanipal, on his first invasion of Elam, states that he 'coloured with blood like wool' (*KB.* ii. 183)—the Eulaeus of the classical writers, which Pliny (*H. N.* vi. 27) says flowed close by Susa. The difficulties which were formerly felt in identifying the Eulaeus have been cleared up by the surveys of Loftus and Dieulafoy. There are at present three rivers flowing near Susa, from the mountains on the north, into the Persian Gulf. On the S.-W. of Susa, some four or five miles from the site of the ancient acropolis, flows the Kerkha (the ancient Choaspes): on the east is the Abdizful (the Coprates), which runs into the Karun (the Pasitigris); and the Eulaeus was a large artificial canal some 900 feet broad, of which traces remain, though it is now dry, which left the Choaspes at Pai Pul, about 20 miles N.-W. of Susa, passed close by the town of Susa on the N. or N.-E., and afterwards joined the Coprates.

3. And *I lifted up my eyes*] in the vision: cf. x. 5; Gen. xxxi. 10; Zech. i. 18, ii. 1, v. 1, 9, vi. 1.

a **ram standing** *before the* **stream, and it** *had* **two** *horns; and the* **two** *horns* were *high*, &c.] The ram is an emblem of power and dominion: cf. Ez. xxxix. 18. The symbolism of the figure is explained in *v.* 20: the ram, as a whole, represents the combined power of the Medes and Persians; but the strength of the animal lying in its horns, these are taken as representing more particularly the two powers separately, that of Persia, as being the stronger, and arising after that of Media, being represented by the higher horn, which came up last. On the distinction between the two empires, see the notes or ii. 39 and v. 31.

4. *pushing*] i.e. *butting:* cf. Ex. xxi. 28 ('gore'); and applied figuratively to peoples, Deut. xxxiii. 17; Ps. xliv. 5 ('push down,' properly 'butt').

stand before him] so *v.* 7. For the expression cf. 2 Ki. x. 4.

did according to his will] did exactly what he pleased; cf. xi. 3, 16, 36, Neh. ix. 24, Est. i. 8, ix. 5 (the Heb. in all being the same).

and became great] *and* **did greatly,** or (R.V.) **magnified himself.** The verb (in the conjug. here used) means *to shew greatness, to do greatly,* usually in a bad sense; e.g. Ps. lv. 12; Jer. xlviii. 26, 42;

great. And as I was considering, behold, a he goat came 5 from the west on the face of the whole earth, and touched not the ground: and the goat *had* a notable horn between

Lam. i. 9. So *vv.* 8, 11, 25. The verse describes the irresistible advances of the Persian arms, especially in the direction of Palestine, Asia Minor, and Egypt, with particular allusion to the conquests of Cyrus and Cambyses.

5—7. A he-goat, with a conspicuous horn between its eyes, appearing from the west, attacked the ram, and beat it down to the ground. The empire of the Greeks; the horn (cf. *v.* 21) being Alexander the Great.

5. *considering*] *paying attention, reflecting* (מֵבִין): not, as in vii. 8 (where the word is a different one), *contemplating.*

a he goat] For the he-goat (though the Heb. word is different), the leader of the flock, as a symbol of a prince or ruler, cf. Is. xiv. 9, xxxiv. 6; Ezek. xxxix. 18; Zech. x. 3.

on] **over**; its course carried it over the whole earth (the hyperbole, as in iv. 1,—though it is true that Alexander penetrated further to the east than any Assyrian or Babylonian king of whom we know). Cf. 1 Macc. i. 3, where it is said of him that he 'went through to the ends of the earth' (διῆλθεν ἕως ἄκρων τῆς γῆς).

and touched not the ground] as though flying,—such was the incredible rapidity of its course. The Heb. is properly, 'and there was *none* touching the earth,'—a more graphic and forcible expression than simply, 'and *it* touched not the earth.' One is reminded involuntarily of Homer's description of the horses of Erichthonius (*Il.* XX. 226—9), and of Vergil's of the huntress Camilla (*Aen.* VII. 807—811, 'Illa vel intactae segetis,' &c.).

a notable horn] **a conspicuous** *horn*; lit. *a horn of sight.* Explained in *v.* 21 to signify Alexander.

Alexander the Great crossed the Hellespont in the spring of B.C. 334. Having routed the Persian forces, which had assembled to oppose his advance, at the Granicus, he marched through Asia Minor, receiving the submission of many cities and peoples; and in Nov. B.C. 333, defeated Darius Codomannus, with great loss, at Issus, on the E. border of Cilicia. Having reduced Tyre (July 332), he marched through Palestine and conquered Egypt, founding in memory of the event the afterwards celebrated city of Alexandria. In 331 he crossed the Euphrates, and gave the final blow to the power of Persia at Arbēla, a little E. of Nineveh. Having made a triumphal entry into Babylon, he took possession of Persepolis and Susa, the two official capitals of the Persian kings. Darius meanwhile had fled into Bactria, where he was slain by conspirators; and Alexander, pursuing after him (330), secured only his corpse. Alexander then started for the further East. First, he invaded Hyrcania (on the S. of the Caspian Sea), then he passed on to Bactria and Sogdiana, after which, retracing his steps, he crossed (327) the Indus, and found himself in the country now called the Punjaub. Defeating Porus, a powerful Indian king, he

6 his eyes. And he came to the ram that had two horns, which I had seen standing before the river, and ran unto
7 him in the fury of his power. And I saw him come close unto the ram, and he was moved with choler against him, and smote the ram, and brake his two horns: and there was no power in the ram to stand before him, but he cast him down to the ground, and stamped upon him: and there was none that could deliver the ram out of his hand.
8 Therefore the he goat waxed very great: and when he was strong, the great horn was broken; and for it came up four notable ones toward the four winds of heaven.

subjugated the country; and then, with a large fleet, sailed down the Indus to its mouth. Thence (326) he returned through Gedrosia and Carmania (N. of the Persian Gulf) to Persepolis; and afterwards (325) to Susa. In 324 he was again in Babylon. There ambassadors from Greece and other parts were waiting to salute him, and greet him as the conqueror of Asia. He was planning further conquests,—in particular, an expedition into Arabia,—when he was seized with a fever, which after 11 days carried him off (June 28, B.C. 323), at the early age of 32.

6. Alexander's attack upon Persia.
that had two horns] *that had* **the two** *horns* (v. 3).
the river] *the* **stream** (v. 2).
ran unto him] **at** or (R.V.) **upon** him (Job xv. 26).

7. The collapse of the Persian power before Alexander, especially in the two great defeats of Issus and Arbela.
was moved with choler] an effective rendering; so xi. 11. The Heb. is lit. *embitter himself*, or *be embittered*, i.e. be maddened, enraged: cf. in Syriac, Euseb. v. 1, 50 for ἠγριώθη, and elsewhere for μαινόμενος (Payne Smith, col. 2200).
stamped] **trampled** (R.V.), viz. in contempt: so v. 10. Cf. Is. xxvi. 6, lxiii. 3. Not the word used in vii. 7, 19.
and there was none, &c.] The 'ram' was now as defenceless before the 'he-goat,' as others had once (v. 4) been before it.

8. *Therefore*, &c.] **And** *the he goat* **did very greatly** (v. 4) i.e. performed great exploits.
and when he was strong, the great horn—the '**conspicuous** horn' of v. 5—*was broken*] Alexander was struck down by his fatal malady, just when he had risen to the summit of his power.
and **instead of it** *came up four notable ones*] lit. *a sight of four*, which is explained to mean 'four conspicuous ones' (cf. v. 5, though the expression there is not quite the same). But the explanation is forced: and from v. 22, *end*, it would seem also that these four horns were by no means so 'conspicuous,' or 'notable,' as the original horn; so that very probably LXX and Theod. are right in reading, with a slight change (אחרות for חזות), *four* **other** *ones*.
toward the four winds of heaven] cf. Jer. xlix. 36; Ez. xlii. 20; 1 Chr. ix. 24; and esp. (in the same connexion) ch. xi. 4. See also vii. 2.

vv. 9, 10.]   DANIEL, VIII.   115

And out of one of them came forth a little horn, which 9
waxed exceeding great, toward the south, and toward the
east, and toward the pleasant *land*. And it waxed great, 10

Alexander left no legitimate heir (though his widow, Roxana, gave
birth to a son shortly after his death); and hence his empire became
the prey of rivalries and disputes between his generals. A division
of the provinces was agreed upon at a military council held the day
after his death; but the only permanent elements in this were the
allotment of Egypt to Ptolemy Lagi, and Thrace to Lysimachus. After
the death of Perdikkas (who had acted as regent) in 321, a fresh distribution took place at a meeting of generals held at Triparadisus
in Syria; and another one, after a four years' war, undertaken for the
purpose of checking the ambitious designs of Alexander's veteran general
Antigonus, in 311. The final settlement was brought about by the
battle of Ipsus (in Phrygia), in 301, in which Antigonus was defeated and slain by Ptolemy, Seleucus, and Lysimachus, who had
coalesced against him. The result of this victory was that Cassander
obtained Macedonia and Greece, Lysimachus Thrace and Bithynia,
Seleucus Syria, Babylonia, and other Eastern countries as far as the
Indus, while Ptolemy remained in possession of Egypt. These are
the four kingdoms (cf. *v.* 22) denoted here by the four 'horns.'

9—14. Antiochus Epiphanes (B.C. 175—164), and his assaults upon
the religion of the Jews (cf. *vv.* 23—25).

9. *out of one of them*] The history of Seleucus himself and his
immediate successors is passed over: and the prophecy proceeds at
once to Antiochus Epiphanes (B.C. 175—164), whose reign was fraught
with such momentous consequences for the Jews.

a little horn] cf. vii. 8. The general sense is, no doubt, given
correctly; but the exact meaning of the Heb. (which is very peculiar)
is far from clear. The explanation which is least forced is 'a horn
(arising) *out of* (being) a small one.' It is quite possible, however,
that the text is slightly in error: by omitting one letter, we should
obtain the ordinary Hebrew for 'a little horn'; and by altering two
letters, we should get 'another horn, a little one' (cf. vii. 8). Probably
one of these is the true reading: LXX. Theod. support the former.

toward the south] i.e. Egypt, as in ch. xi. (*v.* 5, &c.). On the wars
of Antiochus against Egypt, see more fully on ch. xi. 21 ff.

toward the east] Antiochus led an expedition into Elymais (on the
E. of Babylonia) in the last year of his life (see on xi. 40).

and toward the **beauteous** (land)] lit. *the beauty*; but the full expression 'land of beauty,' or 'beauteous land,' occurs in xi. 16, 41.
It is a title of honour for the land of Israel, based upon Jer. iii. 19,
where Canaan is called 'the heritage of *beauty* (i.e. the most beauteous
heritage) of the hosts of the nations,' and Ez. xx. 6, 9, 'the land flowing
with milk and honey, which is the *beauty* of all lands' (or, as we
might say, the crown of all lands).

10. The horn 'waxed great,' in the vision, not only over the surface
of the earth (*v.* 9); it even towered up to heaven, struck and hurled

even to the host of heaven; and it cast down *some* of the host and of the stars to the ground, and stamped
11 upon them. Yea, he magnified *himself even* to the prince of the host, and by him the daily *sacrifice* was taken
12 away, and the place of his sanctuary was cast down. And

down to the earth some of the stars, and then trampled contumeliously upon them.

even to] **as far as**, so as even to reach. Cf. Is. xiv. 13—14; Job xx. 6; and 2 Macc. ix. 10, 'the man (Ant. Ep.) that a little afore *supposed himself to touch the stars of heaven.*' The 'host of heaven' are the stars (as Deut. iv. 19, Jer. viii. 2, xxxiii. 22, and elsewhere[1]). Antiochus did not merely (cf. the passages quoted) *touch* heaven in his pride: he is represented further, with allusion to his insolent assaults upon the religion of the Jews, and to the martyrs who fell in consequence (*v.* 24; cf. 1 Macc. i. 24, 30, 57, 63, &c.), as audaciously attacking it, and hurling down some of the stars to the earth.

and it cast, &c.] better, R.V. **and some of** *the host and of the stars it cast down to the ground, and* **trampled** (*v.* 7) *upon them*. The stars are intended to symbolize the faithful Israelites: cf. Enoch xlvi. 7.

11. And even unto *the prince of the host* **it magnified itself**] it not only mounted to the stars, but in impious defiance it *shewed greatness* (*vv.* 4, 25), i.e. continued its acts of pride and presumption, *even to* the throne of *the prince of the host*, i.e. of God himself.

and it took away from him (i.e. from the prince of the host) *the* **continual** (burnt-offering)] So the Heb. text (*K'tîb*): the Heb. marg. (*Qrê*) has, *and* **by it** *the* **continual** (burnt-offering) **was taken away.** The allusion is to Antiochus' suspension of the temple-services for three years (1 Macc. i. 45, 59, iv. 52 f.); see further on xi. 31.

The daily burnt-offering is called in Ex. xxix. 42 and elsewhere the 'continual (i.e. daily recurring) burnt-offering,' lit. 'the burnt-offering of continuance (Heb. *tāmîd*)': from this expression, the daily burnt-offering came in later Heb. to be spoken of simply as 'the *tāmîd*'; and this usage is found here, and in *vv.* 12, 13, xi. 31, xii. 11. It does not occur elsewhere in the O.T., but it is common in the Mishna, &c., where the word is even used in the plural, 'the *tāmîds*' (תמידין).

and the place of his sanctuary was cast down] or, by a change of points, which has the effect of improving the sentence, *and cast down the place*, &c. The Temple does not seem to have been literally 'cast down' by Antiochus: but it suffered severely at his hands: its sacred vessels were carried away (1 Macc. i. 21—23); the sanctuary is described as being 'laid waste like a wilderness' (*v.* 39), and 'trampled down (καταπατούμενον)' (iii. 45); and in 1 Macc. iv. 38 we read that when Judas and his brethren went up to mount Zion for the purpose of re-dedicating it, they 'saw the sanctuary laid desolate, and the altar profaned, and the gates burned up, and shrubs growing

---

[1] See HOST OF HEAVEN in Hastings' *Dict. of the Bible*. It denotes them as a *disciplined army*, obedient to the commands of its leader (Is. xl. 26).

a host was given him against the daily *sacrifice* by reason of transgression, and it cast down the truth to the ground; and it practised and prospered. Then I heard one saint 13 in the court as in a forest or in one of the mountains, and the priests' chambers pulled down' (cf. *v*. 48, 'and they *built* the holy place (τὰ ἅγια), and the inner parts of the house ').

place] not the usual word, but a rarer word, chiefly poetical, and meaning properly *fixed* or *established* place, used mostly of God's abode, whether on earth, Ex. xv. 17, 1 Ki. viii. 13, or in heaven, Is. xviii. 4, 1 Ki. viii. 39, 43, 49, Ps. xxxiii. 14, *al.*

12. *And a host*, &c.] The first part of this verse is difficult and uncertain; but the most natural rendering is, '*And a host* **was appointed** [or, **a warfare** (Is. xl. 2) **was undertaken**] **against**[1] **the continual** (burnt-offering), **with** *transgression* (i.e. wickedly).' The allusion, with this rendering, will be to the violent measures adopted by Antiochus for the purpose of suppressing the sacred rites of the Jews—in particular, perhaps, to the armed garrison established by him in the 'city of David' with the object of overawing the worshippers, which remained there for many years (1 Macc. i. 33—38; cf. *v*. 51, ii. 15, 31 f., iv. 41). R.V. has '*And the host* [better, with Meinhold, Keil, &c. **an** *host*]—i.e. an army of Israelites, the figure of *vv*. 10, 11 being kept up—**was given over** to it (i.e. into the power of the horn) **together with** *the continual* (burnt-offering) **through** *transgression* (i.e. on account of the apostasy of the Hellenizing Jews): this has the advantage of taking 'host,' 'give' (i.e. *give up*, *abandon*[2]), and 'transgression,' in the same senses as in *v*. 13; but the rendering *together with* is not here very natural.

and it cast down **truth** *to the ground*] i.e. overthrew the true religion. 'Truth' is commonly used in Heb. subjectively of a moral quality; but here it denotes that which is true objectively, a body of true principles, i.e. true religion. So ix. 13, Ps. xxv. 5.

As pointed, the verb 'and it cast down' ought strictly to be construed as a future; but the rest of the description is in the past time; and probably the punctuation should be altered accordingly. The other two verbs in the verse may denote either future or past time; they must be rendered, therefore, so as to agree with the tense of 'cast down.'

and it **did**, *and prospered*] cf. *v*. 24. 'Did' is used in a pregnant sense, *acted* (viz. with effect), *carried through his purpose;* hence R.V. '*did* (its pleasure)'. Cf. 2 Chr. xxxi. 21 'And in every work that he

---

[1] A.V. and the first marg. of R.V. do not differ in general sense; but 'was appointed' (absolutely) is better than 'was given (to it).' The 2nd marg. of R.V. renders (nearly as Ewald) 'was set over the continual (burnt-offering)'—viz. to lay compulsion upon it, or to suppress it—also with no difference in the general sense. For the rendering *appoint* (or *set*) see 2 Ch. xx. 22, Neh. ix. 17; and with *over*, 2 Ch. xxxii. 6, Neh. ix. 37.

[2] In Heb. *to give* may mean, according to the context, either to *set*, *place* (as Gen. i. 17, and frequently), or to *give over*, *deliver* (Deut. i. 27, &c.), and abs. (though this usage is rare) *to give up*, *abandon*, Numb. xxi. 3; 1 Ki. xiv. 16; Mic. v. 3; Dan. xi. 6.

speaking, and another saint said unto that certain *saint* which spake, How long *shall be* the vision *concerning* the

began..., he *did* (i.e. *acted*) with all his heart, *and prospered*;' also the absolute use of 'do' of God, Ps. xxii. 31 and lii. 9 (there is no 'it' in the Heb.), xxxvii. 5 (lit. 'and he will *do*'). Comp. ch. xi. 28, 30, 32.

13, 14. A dialogue between two angels, which is overheard by Daniel, and the object of which is evidently to inform Daniel how long the suspension of the daily sacrifices and the desecration of the Temple are to continue.

13. *one saint*] **a holy one**, i.e. an angel, as iv. 13 (where see the note). So in the next line, *and another* **holy one.** In A. V. 'saint' is used, in an application which is now obsolete, of the *angels*: see Deut. xxxiii. 2, Job v. 1, xv. 15, Ps. lxxxix. 5, 7, Zech. xiv. 5, Jude 14, and probably 1 Thess. iii. 13. But the term, as limited by modern usage, yields an incorrect sense; and hence, in all the passages quoted, except the last, 'holy one(s)' has been substituted in R.V.

speaking] What was said is not stated: but the question which follows shews that it had some reference to the vision which Daniel had just seen.

unto that certain **one** *which spake*] The indef. expression is used (cf. 1 Sam. xxi. 3; Ruth iv. 1), as the speaker could not be specified more closely.

How long (shall be) *the vision? the* **continual** (burnt-offering), *and the transgression* **causing appalment, the giving** *both the sanctuary and the host* (to be) **trampled** *under foot?*] The sentence (if the text is correct) is harshly constructed; but the words following 'vision' must be understood to be in apposition with that word, and to indicate the contents of the vision. The rendering of LXX. might suggest that 'taken away' had dropped out after 'continual (burnt-offering)'; at any rate, whether actually read by the translators or not, this is a correct interpretation of the sense. 'The transgression causing appalment' is the heathen worship established by Antiochus in the Temple, with special reference, perhaps (cf. xi. 31, xii. 11), to the heathen altar erected by him on the altar of burnt-offering in the Temple court, which was naturally an object of extreme abhorrence to the pious Jews (see 1 Macc. i. 47, 51, 54, 59).

causing appalment] Except in Daniel, the word used means either *laid waste, desolated*[1] (Is. xlix. 8; Lam. i. 4, 13, 16, iii. 11), or *appalled*[1] (2 Sam. xiii. 20): but the passive sense is unsuitable both here, and in ix. 27 (last word), xii. 11; and the active, whether *causing appalment*, or *causing desolation*, being defensible (see Ges.-Kautzsch, §§ 55 *c, f*; 52 *s*; König, *Lehrgebäude*, ii. p. 106), must be adopted. Comp. ix. 27, xi. 31 (where a probable explanation of the expression is mentioned in the note), xii. 11: and the note on p. 151.

---

[1] On the connexion between these two senses, see the note on iv. 19. In the corresponding verb, the sense *to be appalled, horror-struck*, is common, as Jer. ii. 12, xviii. 16, Ez. xxvi. 16, xxvii. 35 (A.V., R.V., *be astonished*).

daily *sacrifice*, and the transgression of desolation, to give both the sanctuary and the host to be trodden under foot? And he said unto me, Unto two thousand and three hundred days; then shall the sanctuary be cleansed. 14

the giving both] The meaning *both* is uncommon, though instances occur: perhaps, with a redivision of the words (תתו קדש for תת וקדש), we should read '**his giving** *the sanctuary*,' &c., or (Bevan, Marti) מתתו '*since he hath given*,' &c.

the host] i.e. *the army*, fig. of the Israelites, as in *v*. 10.

(to be) **trampled** *under foot*] lit. (to be) *a trampling* (or *treading down*), exactly as Is. x. 6 (cf. R.V. *marg.*). See *vv*. 10 *end* (where the figure is the same), 11 *end*.

14. *unto me*] Sept. Theod. Pesh. *unto* **him**, which is adopted by most moderns, and is probably right.

unto two thousand and three hundred **evenings, mornings**] i.e. successive evenings and mornings: cf. *v*. 26 'the vision of the evenings and the mornings.' The expression is peculiar; but it seems to have been suggested by the fact that the burnt-offering (*vv*. 11, 13) was offered morning and evening daily (Ex. xxix. 38—42); the meaning consequently is that this offering would cease for 2300 times, i.e. during 1150 days (so most commentators). In vii. 25 (where see the note), xii. 7, the period of persecution is to last 3½ years, i.e. (if the year be reckoned at 360 days) 1260 days, or, if account be taken of the varying possibilities of the Calendar in use in the 2nd century B.C.[1], 1274 or 1309 days; and, according to 1 Macc. i. 54, iv. 52, 53, the interval which actually elapsed between the erection of the heathen altar upon the altar of burnt-offering, on the 15th of Chisleu, B.C. 168, and the dedication of the new altar on the 25th of Chisleu, B.C. 165, was 3 years and 10 days (i.e. 1090, 1102—3, or 1132—3 days). The period assigned here is some months less than 3½ years; it is not however identified with the entire period of the persecution, but only with that part of it during which the daily sacrifice was interrupted and the Temple desecrated. It seems therefore (cf. xii. 11) that 15 Chisleu B.C. 168 must be the *terminus a quo*, the end of the period assigned not agreeing precisely with the event. Cornill's supposition (pp. 22—26) that the edict of Antiochus (1 Macc. i. 44—6) is the *terminus a quo*, in spite of the very ingenious argument by which he seeks to shew that this edict might have been issued just 1150 days before 25 Chisleu, B.C. 165, hardly does justice to the terms of *v*. 13 (which lay stress on the *cessation of the daily sacrifice* as the beginning of the period referred to); cf. Bevan, p. 128 f.

By some commentators the expression 'evening, morning' has been understood as equivalent to *day* (cf. Gen. i. 5 *b*, 8 *b*, &c.); and the 2300 days have been reckoned either from the time when Menelaus, in 171, purchased for himself the high-priesthood from Antiochus (see on ix. 26) to the dedication of the Temple in Dec. 165, or from the profanation

---

[1] Cornill, *Die Siebzig Jahrwochen Daniels* (1889), p. 22.

15 And it came to pass, when I, *even* I Daniel, had seen the vision, and sought for the meaning, then behold, there **16** stood before me as the appearance of a man. And I heard a man's voice between *the banks of* Ulai, which called, and said, Gabriel, make this *man* to understand the vision.

of the Temple in Dec. 168 to the great victory of Judas over Nicanor at Adasa, near Beth-horon (1 Macc. vii. 43—50) on Adar 13, B.C. 162 (cf. Hävernick, Pusey, p. 219). But either of these periods seems to embrace much which is not legitimately included in the terms of the question in *v.* 13. And as against the second period suggested, the reference to an event some two years after the death of Antiochus is not probable.

then shall the sanctuary be justified] i.e. have justice done to it, be shewn not to have deserved desecration. "The justification of the sanctuary is the vindication of its cause, for as long as it is polluted it lies under condemnation" (Bevan).

15—27. Daniel seeks to know the meaning of the vision, which is imparted to him, as in vii. 16 ff., by an angel.

15. that I *sought* to understand (it), and, *behold*, &c.] cf. vii. 19.

there was standing in front of me] appearing suddenly, some little way off (see *v.* 17, 'came near').

as the appearance of a man] The expression 'as the appearance of' is borrowed from Ez. (i. 13, 14, 26, 27, 28, viii. 2, x. 1, xl. 3, xlii. 11), and recurs below, x. 6, 18. The word for man (*geber*)—different from that in x. 18—is evidently chosen with allusion to the name 'Gabriel,' 'man of God' [not the word used in the common phrase, 'man of God,' for a prophet].

16. *between Ulai*] This singular expression can, it seems, mean only '*between* (the banks of) *Ulai*' (*v.* 2): the voice seemed to come to Daniel from above the waters of the river (cf. xii. 6, 7).

Gabriel] mentioned also in ix. 21 as explaining to Daniel Jeremiah's prophecy of the 70 years, and in Luke i. 19, 26, as foretelling the birth of John the Baptist to Zacharias, and acting as the angel of the Annunciation to Mary. Gabriel is also often mentioned in non-canonical Jewish writings. In Enoch ix. 1 and xx. 7, he is one of the four (or seven) principal angels or 'archangels' (see their names on x. 13); in xl. 3—7, 9, he is one of the four 'presences' (Michael, Raphael, Gabriel, and Phanuel; so liv. 6, lxxi. 8, 9, 13), who bless, or make intercession, or ward off the accusing 'Satans,' before God (comp. Luke i. 19, 'I am Gabriel, that *stand in the presence of God*'); in x. 9 he is commissioned to destroy the wicked giants. Gabriel is also mentioned not unfrequently in the later (post-Christian) Jewish literature (Weber, *System der altsynag. Theologie*, pp. 162, 163—4, 167—8, 366): so, for instance, in the Targ. of Pseudo-Jon. on Gen. xxxvii. 15, he is the 'man' who shews Joseph the way to his brethren, and in the Targ. on Job xxv. 2 he is said to stand on God's left hand, while Michael is at His right. See, further, on x. 13.

So he came near where I stood: and when he came, I 17
was afraid, and fell upon my face: but he said unto me,
Understand, O son of man: for at the time of the end
shall be the vision. Now as he was speaking with me, I 18
was in a deep sleep on my face toward the ground: but
he touched me, and set me upright. And he said, Behold, 19
I *will* make thee know what shall be in the last end of

17. *afraid*] **affrighted** (R.V.), as Is. xxi. 4, A.V. (Job vii. 14 *al.*
'terrify'): 'afraid' is not strong enough. At the approach of the celestial being Daniel is terrified.

fell upon my face] a mark of awe or respect (Gen. xvii. 3; Jud. xiii. 20; Ruth ii. 10, *al.*); cf. in the visions of Ezekiel, Ez. i. 28, iii. 23, ix. 8, xi. 13, xliii. 3, xliv. 4.

son of man] Borrowed, no doubt, from the book of Ezekiel, where it is the standing title by which the prophet is addressed (ii. 1, 3, 6, 8, iii. 1, 3, 4, 10, 17, 25, &c.—more than a hundred times altogether).

for the vision belongeth to the time of the end] and therefore deserves attention. The 'time of the end' is a standing expression in Daniel (xi. 35, 40, xii. 4, 9; cf. 'the appointed-time [מוֹעֵד] of the end' viii. 19, and 'the end' ix. 26 *b*), and means (spoken from Daniel's standpoint) the period of Antiochus's persecution, together with the short interval, consisting of a few months, which followed before his death (xi. 35, 40), that being, in the view of the author, the 'end' of the present condition of things, and the divine kingdom (vii. 14, 18, 22, 27, xii. 2, 3) being established immediately afterwards. This sense of 'end' is based probably upon the use of the word in Am. viii. 2, Ez. vii. 2, 'an end is come, the end is come upon the four corners of the land,' 3, 6: cf. also 'in the time of the iniquity of the end,' Ez. xxi. 25, 29, xxxv. 5; and Hab. ii. 3, 'For the vision is yet for the appointed-time [has reference to the time of its destined fulfilment], and it hasteth toward the end.'

18. *I fell into a dead sleep*] Daniel was alarmed when the angel approached (*v.* 17): when he spoke to him, he fell paralysed and motionless—or, as we might say (in a figurative sense), *stunned*—upon his face (cf. the similar passage, x. 9). The word is used of a deep sleep, Jud. iv. 21; Ps. lxxvi. 6 (here of the sleep of death): cf. the corresponding subst., Gen. ii. 21, xv. 12; Sam. xxvi. 12; Is. xxix. 10 (here fig. of insensibility).

set me upright] lit. *made me stand upon my standing* (cf. *v.* 17 Heb.), a late Heb. idiom for *in my place, where I had stood* (R.V. *marg.*), 2 Ch. xxx. 16, xxxiv. 31, Neh. xiii. 11, *al.*: in the same application as here, Dan. x. 11. For the fear occasioned by a vision, and the restoration by an angelic touch, cf. x. 8, 10, 16, 18; Enoch lx. 3, 4; 2 Esdr. v. 14, 15; also Rev. i. 17.

19. *in the latter time* (R.V.) *of the indignation*] The 'indignation' is the Divine wrath implied in Israel's subjection to the nations: the persecution by Antiochus is the last stage of this indignation: when

the indignation: for at the time appointed the end *shall*
20 *be*. The ram which thou sawest having two horns *are* the
21 kings of Media and Persia. And the rough goat *is* the
22 king of Grecia: and the great horn that *is* between his
eyes *is* the first king. Now that being broken, whereas
four stood up for it, four kingdoms shall stand up out of
23 the nation, but not in his power. And in the latter time

that is over, the kingdom of the saints will be set up. Cf. xi. 36,
'and he (Antiochus) shall prosper till the *indignation* be accomplished;' and 1 Macc. i. 64, 'and there came exceeding great wrath upon Israel.' The word may be suggested by Is. x. 25, xxvi. 20.

for it (i.e. the vision, *v.* 17) **belongeth to the appointed-time of the end**] The sentence seems suggested by Hab. ii. 3 (quoted on *v.* 17), though the word 'end' has not there the special sense which it has acquired in Daniel.

20—26. The explanation of the vision.

20. *having* **the two** *horns*] see on *v.* 3.

21. *the rough* **he-***goat*] *v.* 5. The word rendering 'rough' (*sā'īr*), treated as a subst., is the usual old Hebrew word for a he-goat (Gen. xxxvii. 31, &c.): the word here rendered 'he-goat' (*sāphīr*) being properly the Aramaic word for the same animal (Ezra vi. 17, and in the Targums), and being found in Heb. only in late passages (*vv.* 5, 8; 2 Ch. xxix. 21; Ezra viii. 35). Perhaps, therefore, *sā'īr* is not intended here to be an adj., but is simply the old Heb. synonym of *sāphīr*, added by way of explanation; and the whole expression should be rendered simply **the he-goat**.

Grecia] or, as we should now say, **Greece**. So x. 20, xi. 2 (but Zech. x. 13 'Greece'); and similarly *Grecians* for *Greeks*, Joel iii. 6, Acts vi. 1 *al*. The Heb. (both here and elsewhere) is *Yavan*, Gen. x. 2, 4 = 1 Ch. i. 5, 7; Is. lxvi. 19; Ez. xxvii. 13, 19 (?), i.e. Ἰάϝων, Ἰάϝον-ες, the name by which the 'Greeks' were known also to the Assyrians and Egyptians. The reason is to be found in the fact that the 'Ionians' on the west coast of Asia Minor were that branch of the Greeks which was the earliest to develope civilization, and to engage extensively in commerce; it was thus the first to become generally known in the Eastern world.

the first king] i.e. Alexander the Great.

22. **And as for that which was broken, in the place whereof** *four stood up* (R.V.), *four kingdoms shall stand up*, &c.] see on *v.* 8.

stand up] i.e. *arise*. Late Hebrew uses '*āmad*, 'to stand,' or 'stand up,' where early Hebrew would say *ḳûm*, 'to arise' (e.g. Ex. i. 8): similarly *v.* 23, and several times in ch. xi.

out of the nation] There is no art. in Heb.; and the passage, as it stands, reads baldly. Read probably, with LXX, Theod., Vulg., '*his* nation' (*gōyō* for *gōy*), i.e. Alexander's.

but not with his power] None of the four kingdoms which ultimately (see on *v.* 8) took the place of the Macedonian empire possessed the power which Alexander enjoyed. Cf. xi. 4 *b*.

of their kingdom, when the transgressors are come to the full, a king of fierce countenance, and understanding dark sentences, shall stand up. And his power shall be mighty, 24 but not by his own power: and he shall destroy wonderfully, and shall prosper, and practise, and shall destroy the

23—25. A fuller description of the character and policy of Antiochus Epiphanes.

23. *in the latter time of their kingdom*] in the closing period of the rule of the Diadochi (which the author pictures as brought altogether to an end at the death of Antiochus).

when the transgressors **have completed** (their guilt)] i.e. filled up the measure of their transgressions (cf., though the Heb. word is not the same, Gen. xv. 16). Or, with 'transgressions' for 'transgressors' (Sept., Theod., Pesh., Ew., Meinh.: the difference affects only the vocalization), *when they* (or *men*) *have completed transgressions*. It is disputed whether the reference is to the Israelites (Keil, Behrm.) or their heathen oppressors (Hitz., Meinh., Bevan). In the former case, the meaning will be that when the measure of Israel's guilt is full, this final and severest of persecutions will fall upon them: in the latter case, Antiochus will be viewed as the climax of heathen impiety.

a king of **hard** *countenance*] i.e. *unyielding, unmoved*, **defiant**: lit. '*strong* of countenance,' i.e. hard, firm (in a bad sense). The expression is borrowed from Deut. xxviii. 50: cf., with the corresponding verb, Prov. vii. 13 (of the harlot), 'she made her face *strong*,' i.e. hard, impudent, xxi. 29; 'a wicked man *hardeneth* his face,' Eccl. viii. 1.

and understanding **riddles** (v. 12)] a master of dissimulation, able to conceal his meaning under ambiguous words, and so disguising his real purposes. Cf. *v.* 25, 'deceit,' xi. 27, 'obtain the kingdom by smooth sayings.' Examples are afforded by his treatment of his nephew, Ptolemy Philometor, and the manner in which he completely misled the legates who were sent by the Romans for the purpose of ascertaining his feelings towards them (see on xi. 27, 40). Antiochus was habitually successful in concealing his real motives and intentions when his interests required it.

24. *his power shall be mighty, but not by his own power*] but rather, so it is implied in this rendering, by the permission of God (Häv., Hitz.). The rendering **not by his power** (but rather **by** intrigues) is, however, preferable: the first two clauses of the verse will thus contain an oxymoron. R.V. *marg.* '*Or, with his power.* See ver. 22' seems to refer the pron. (with Ewald) to Alexander; but such a reference is here far-fetched.

destroy wonderfully] work destruction in an extraordinary degree;— the idea of 'wonder,' 'wonderful' in Heb. is properly that of something *distinctive, exceptional, extraordinary.* Cf. xi. 36, xii. 6.

prosper, and **do**] cf. *v.* 12.

25 mighty and the holy people. And through his policy also he shall cause craft to prosper in his hand; and he shall magnify *himself* in his heart, and by peace shall destroy many: he shall also stand up against the Prince of princes;
26 but he shall be broken without hand. And the vision of

the mighty] them that are *mighty* (indef.), alluding to Antiochus' political foes.

and the people of the holy ones (or saints)] i.e. Israel: cf. vii. 25 ('and shall wear away the holy ones (*or* saints) of the Most High').

25. *And through*—properly, *on* (the basis of)—*his* understanding] or *insight, cleverness*,—usually in a good sense (1 Sam. xxv. 3, Job xvii. 4, *al.*), here in a bad sense = *astuteness*.

he (without 'also'[1]) *will cause* deceit *to prosper in his hand*] his intrigues will prove successful (cf. xi. 23, also of Antiochus). For 'in his hand,' cf. Gen. xxxix. 3, Is. liii. 10.

and in his heart he will shew greatness] i.e. here (cf. on *v*. 4), devise proud, presumptuous schemes. Comp. the expression '*greatness* of heart' Is. ix. 9, x. 12 (A.V. 'stoutness,' 'stout').

and in (time of) security he will *destroy many*] i.e. he will come upon them unawares, and destroy them while off their guard. Many modern scholars render indeed by unawares, supposing that the Heb. expression (בְּשַׁלְוָה 'in tranquillity') is used with the force of a similar Aramaic idiom מִן שְׁלִי *suddenly, unawares*, (lit. *out of quiet*): see e.g. Jer. iv. 20, Pesh. The same expression recurs in ch. xi. 21, 24 (LXX. both times ἐξάπινα), also of Antiochus. Comp. 1 Macc. i. 29, 30, where it is related how Antiochus's chief collector of tribute, Apollonius, came to Jerusalem, and 'spake words of peace unto them in subtilty, and they gave him credence; and he fell upon the city suddenly (ἐξάπινα: Pesh. מִן שְׁלִי),' and killed many of its inhabitants (cf. 2 Macc. v. 23—26).

the Prince of princes] i.e. God, the 'prince of the host' of *v*. 11. Cf. ii. 47; and the 'Lord of lords' of Deut. x. 17, Ps. cxxxvi. 3.

broken without hand] i.e. not by human means, but by a Divine intervention; cf. ii. 34, with the note. Antiochus died suddenly, in B.C. 164, a few months after the re-dedication of the Temple (25 Chisleu [Dec.], 165), apparently from some mental disorder, such as might well suggest the idea of a Divine stroke, at Tabae in Persia (see p. 196 f.).

26. *the vision of the evening*s *and morning*s (*v*. 14) *which* hath been *told*, is *true*] a solemn asseveration of the truth of what has been told (cf. x. 1, xi. 2, xii. 7; also Rev. xix. 9, xxi. 5, xxii. 6), intended here as an encouragement to the persecuted Israelites, who may rest assured that their sufferings will ere long reach the appointed limit.

[1] See on the construction Ges.-Kautzsch, § 112. 5, or the writer's *Hebrew Tenses*, § 123 γ. It is against the reading of LXX (followed by Grätz and Bevan), that שֵׂכֶל does not signify διανόημα, or 'mind.'

the evening and the morning which was told *is* true: wherefore shut thou up the vision; for *it shall be* for many days. And I Daniel fainted, and was sick *certain* days; afterward 27 I rose up, and did the king's business; and I was astonished at the vision, but none understood *it*.

but thou (emph.), *shut thou up the vision*] keep it secret (cf. xii. 4). The vision is supposed to have been seen in the third year of Belshazzar (*v.* 1), but it relates to the age of Antiochus; it is consequently to remain hidden till then, partly because it would not be intelligible before, partly in order to explain why no one had ever heard of it till the days of Antiochus himself. For the idea of a revelation given in the interests of a distant future, cf. Enoch i. 2, civ. 13.

for it **belongeth to** *many days* (to come)] i.e. it relates to a distant future. The expression is exactly the same (in the Heb.) as in Ez. xii. 27.

27. *fainted*] The expression is peculiar: if correct, it must mean *I was done with, exhausted*, the verb being the same that is used in ii. 1 in the passage 'his sleep was *done with* upon him.' It does not occur in this sense elsewhere in the O.T.

for (some) *days*] so Gen. xl. 4 (A.V., R.V., 'a season'); Neh. i. 4.

rose up] from his bed of sickness, as Ps. xli. 8.

the king's business] what business is not stated; nor can we be sure (cf. v. 13) that the writer pictured him as still holding the office to which Nebuchadnezzar had appointed him some 60 years previously (ii. 48). For the expression, cf. Est. ix. 3.

was astonished] cf. on iv. 19.

but none understood it] The expression is strange, and difficult to reconcile with what has preceded: if the vision was to be 'shut up,' the remark that no one understood it would seem to be superfluous. Perhaps 'none' may be used as in *v.* 5; and Daniel himself may be really meant (cf. xii. 8): the meaning will then be that, though the vision had been partly explained to him, he did not understand it fully: *vv.* 23—25 are, for instance, expressed enigmatically, and without any name being given (Hitz., Bevan). Other renderings are, *but no one perceived* it (cf. 1 Sam. iii. 8 Heb.), i.e. no one perceived that Daniel had had a vision, or of what nature it was (Meinh.); or *but no one gave heed* (cf. Is. lvii. 1 Heb.; A.V. 'considering'), viz. to Daniel's astonishment (Behrm.).

Additional Note on the Ruins of Susa.

The site of Susa was visited, and partly excavated, by Mr Loftus in 1852: it was excavated much more completely, and with more important results, by M. Dieulafoy, a French architect and engineer, in 1884—6. The site of the city, which was distinct from the 'castle' (cf. Est. iii. 15), and in fact separated from it by the stream, is marked only by hardly perceptible undulations of the plain; but three huge mounds, forming a rhomboidal mass, 4500 feet long from N. to S., and 3000 feet broad from E. to W., are a standing witness to the size and magnificence of the buildings which formed the ancient citadel or acropolis. The plan of the citadel, and many remains of the buildings of which it consisted, have been recovered by M. Dieulafoy. Artaxerxes, in an inscription found on one of the columns, says, "My ancestor Darius built this *Apadâna* in ancient times. In the reign of Artaxerxes, my grandfather, it was consumed by fire. By the grace of Ahuramazda, Anaïtis, and Mithras, I have restored this *Apadâna*." An *Apadâna* (see on Dan. xi. 45) was a large hall or throne-room. The *Apadâna* of Susa stood on the N. of the acropolis: it formed a square of about 250 feet each way. The roof (which consisted of rafters and beams of cedar, brought from Lebanon) was supported by 36 columns in rows of six; the sides and back were composed of walls of brick, each pierced by four doors; the front of the hall was open. The columns were slender shafts of limestone, delicately fluted, and topped by magnificently carved capitals. In front of the hall, on each side, was a pylon or colonnade, with a frieze at the top 12 feet high, formed of beautifully enamelled bricks, the one decorated by a procession of lions, the other by a procession of 'Immortals,' the armed life-guards of the Persian kings[1]. A garden surrounded the *Apadâna*, and in front of it, on the south, was a large square for military manœuvres, &c. Adjoining it, on the east, was a large block of buildings forming the royal harem (the 'house of the women' of Est. ii. 3, &c.): south of this was the royal palace, with a court in the centre (Est. iv. 11, v. 1). The entire acropolis covered an area of 300 acres.

It was this entire complex of buildings that was called the *Birah*, or 'citadel[2].'

CHAP. IX. THE PROPHECY OF THE SEVENTY WEEKS.

In the first year of 'Darius the Mede,' Daniel, considering that the 70 years of desolation prophesied by Jeremiah (xxv. 11; cf. *v.* 12, xxix. 10) were drawing to their close, implores God to forgive His people's sin, and to look favourably upon His ruined city and sanctuary (*vv.* 1—19). The angel Gabriel explains to Daniel that it would be, not 70 years, but 70 weeks of years (i.e. 490 years), before the iniquity of the people would be pardoned, and the promised deliverance be finally effected (*vv.* 20—24). The period of 70 weeks is then divided into three smaller ones, 7+62+1; and it is said: (*a*) that 7 weeks (=49 years) will elapse from the going forth of the 'word' for the rebuilding of Jerusalem to 'an anointed one, a prince;' (*b*) that for 62 weeks (=434 years) the city will be rebuilt, though

---

[1] In one of the galleries at the Louvre several rooms are devoted to sculptures, &c., brought from Susa, and to a restoration of parts of the *apadâna*.

[2] See further Evetts, *Fresh Light on the Bible*, p. 229 ff.; Vigouroux, *La Bible et les découvertes modernes*, ed. 6, 1896, iv. 621 ff.; and esp. Dieulafoy, *L'Acropole de Suse* (Paris, 1890—92), *passim*: also Mme. Dieulafoy, *À Suse, Journal des Fouilles, 1884—6* (1888), and *La Perse, la Chaldée, et la Susiane* (1887), Chap. xxxix.—all with numerous illustrations and Maps; also, more briefly, Billerbeck's excellent monograph, *Susa* (1893).

In the first year of Darius the son of Ahasuerus, of 9
the seed of the Medes, which was made king over the
realm of the Chaldeans; in the first year of his reign I
Daniel understood by books the number of the years, 2
where*of* the word of the LORD came to Jeremiah the
prophet, that *he* would accomplish seventy years in the

in straitened times; (*c*) that at the end of these 62 weeks 'an anointed one' will be cut off, and the people of a prince that shall come will 'destroy' the city and the sanctuary: he will make a covenant with many for 1 week (=7 years), and during (the second) half of this week he will cause sacrifice and meal-offering to cease, until his end come, and the destined doom overtake him (*vv.* 25—27). The general sense of these verses is to postpone the fulfilment of the promises given by Jeremiah to the end of 490 years; and to describe in outline the troubles which must be gone through, in the closing years of this period, before the fulfilment can take place.

1. *Darius*] i.e. 'Darius the Mede,' v. 31 : cf. vi. 1 ff. The date is fixed suitably: the first year after the conquest of Babylon would be a time when, in view of the promises of Jeremiah and the second Isaiah (e.g. Is. xliv. 28, xlv. 13), thoughts of restoration would naturally be stirring in the minds of the Jewish exiles.

the son of Ahasuerus] Ahasuerus,—properly *'Ăchashwērōsh*, also in Ezr. iv. 6, and Esther, *passim*—is the Hebrew form of the Persian *Khshayārshā*, the Greek Xerxes, called in contemporary Aramaic *Chshiarsh* (חשיארש)[1]. Cf. p. liv, and on v. 31.

of the seed of the Medes] See v. 31. For the expression cf. Est. vi. 13.

was made king] See on v. 31, 'received the kingdom.'

2. *by the books*] i.e. the sacred books, the Scriptures. The neglect of the Heb. article in the A.V. obscures here an important point; for '*the* books' can only be naturally understood as implying that, at the time when the passage was written, some definite collection of sacred writings already existed (comp. Ryle, *Canon of the Old Test.*, p. 112). We do not however learn more respecting its contents except that it included the prophecies of Jeremiah. The phrase might also be rendered (Hitz., Keil, Behrm.) *observed* in *the books*.

which *the word of* **Jehovah** *came to Jeremiah the prophet that he would accomplish* **for** *the desolations of Jerusalem*, (even) **seventy years**] See Jer. xxv. 12, and especially xxix. 10, which, being followed by promises of restoration, addressed to Israel, seems to have been particularly in the writer's mind. Cf. 2 Ch. xxxvi. 21.

3—19. Daniel's prayer, consisting (1) of a confession of national transgression, and of the justice of God's punishment (*vv.* 4—14), and (2) of a supplication for mercy and restoration (*vv.* 15—19). The prayer evinces great depth and fervour of religious feeling. In style it is Deuteronomic; in fact, it is composed largely of reminiscences of

---

[1] See the writer's *Introduction*, p. 512 (ed. 6, p. 546), *note*.

₃ desolations of Jerusalem. And I set my face unto the Lord God, to seek *by* prayer and supplications, with fasting,
₄ and sackcloth, and ashes: and I prayed unto the LORD my God, and made my confession, and said,

O Lord, the great and dreadful God, keeping the covenant and mercy to them that love him, and to them
₅ that keep his commandments; we have sinned, and have committed iniquity, and have done wickedly, and have rebelled, even by departing from thy precepts and from thy

---

Deut., the prayer of Solomon in 1 Ki. viii., and (especially) of Jeremiah (in particular, of Jer. xxvi., xxxii., xliv.): there are also some noticeable parallels with the prayers in Neh. i., ix., and Ezra ix. (see on *vv.* 4, 6, 7, 9, 14, 15, 18). The most striking resemblances are, however, with parts of the confession and supplication in Baruch i. 15—iii. 18; on which see further the Introd. p. lxxiv f.

3. *set my face*] i.e. directed myself: cf. 2 Ch. xx. 3 (lit. '*set his face* to seek unto Jehovah').

to **seek prayer**, &c.] i.e. to apply myself to prayer, &c.

with fasting, and sackcloth, and ashes] marks of mourning, and the usual accompaniments of supplication, penitence, and confession. Cf. Is. lviii. 5; Ezr. viii. 23; Neh. ix. 1; Jonah iii. 5, 6; Est. iv. 1, 3, 16.

4. *and* **made confession**] Lev. v. 5, xvi. 21, xxvi. 40, Num. v. 7, 2 Ch. xxx. 22; and in a context similar to the present one, Ezr. x. 1, Neh. i. 6, ix. 2, 3, as well as below, *v.* 20.

O Lord] Ah, **now!** *Lord*, beginning with a strong particle of entreaty. So Neh. i. 5, where the same particle is equally obliterated in A.V., R.V. In Neh. i. 11, Is. xxxviii. 3, Ps. cxvi. 4 (but not in *v.* 16), cxviii. 25, it is rendered *I* (or *we*) *beseech thee*.

the great...commandments] A quotation from Deut. vii. 9, with the substitution of *great and* **terrible** (as Deut. vii. 21) for *faithful*. The whole verse, from *and said*, is also almost identical with Neh. i. 5 (cf. Neh. ix. 32 a).

5. *We have sinned, and have* **dealt perversely**, *and have done wickedly*] from 1 Ki. viii. 47, with extremely slight differences, indicated in R.V. by the substitution of *done* for *dealt*, and of *dealt* for *done*. Ps. cvi. 6 is based similarly on 1 Ki. viii. 47.

and have turned aside *from thy* **commandments**] Cf. Deut. xvii. 20; Ps. cxix. 102. 'Even' with the infin. is quite false; the construction of the Heb. is one with which every tyro is familiar (Gen. xli. 43, Ex. viii. 11, &c.).

judgements] i.e. *ordinances*, as the word is sometimes rendered (Josh. xxiv. 25; 2 Ki. xvii. 34, 37; Is. lviii. 2). Properly a *judicial decision*, which being made legally binding, becomes a standing *ordinance*; the word being then generalized, it is applied to moral and religious ordinances, as well as to statutes of the civil and criminal law, Ex. xxi. 1). See e.g. Lev. xviii. 4, 5, 26; Deut. iv. 1, 5, 8, 14, &c.

vv. 6—9.] DANIEL, IX. 129

judgements: neither have we hearkened unto thy servants the 6
prophets, which spake in thy name to our kings, our princes,
and our fathers, and to all the people of the land. O Lord, 7
righteousness *belongeth* unto thee, but unto us confusion
of faces, as *at* this day; to the men of Judah, and to the
inhabitants of Jerusalem, and unto all Israel, *that are* near,
and *that are* far off, through all the countries whither thou
hast driven them, because of their trespass that they have
trespassed against thee. O Lord, to us *belongeth* confusion 8
of face, to our kings, to our princes, and to our fathers,
because we have sinned against thee. To the Lord our 9
God *belong* mercies and forgivenesses, though we have

6. The guilt is the greater, because Israel had been warned, but had not listened to the warning.
neither have we hearkened unto thy servants the prophets] A reminiscence of Jer. xxvi. 5; cf. vii. 25, xxv. 4, xxix. 19, xxxv. 15, xliv. 4 (all containing the expression 'my servants the prophets,' followed by 'and ye (or they) hearkened not').
to our kings, our princes, and our fathers, and to all the people of the land] The same combination in Jer. xliv. 21; cf. 'our fathers, our kings, and our princes,' Jer. xliv. 17: comp. Neh. ix. 32, 34.
7. Thus righteousness belongs only to God: to the sinful people only confusion and shame. With *vv.* 7, 8 *b*, cf. Baruch i. 15—17.
confusion of faces, &c.] Cf. Ezr. ix. 7, 'and for our iniquities have we, our kings, and our priests, been delivered...to confusion of face, as (it is) this day.' Lit. 'shame of face,' as the same expression is rendered in 2 Ch. xxxii. 21; cf. Ps. xliv. 15, 'shame of my face;' Jer. vii. 19, 'the shame of their own faces'; also Ps. lxix. 7. The meaning is the shame (i.e. disappointment) which is visible upon the face after a repulse, disaster, &c.
as (it is) *this day*] as experience shews is now the case.
the men (lit. *man*,—collectively) *of Judah, and to the inhabitants of Jerusalem*] A combination found otherwise only in Jer. (8 times),— e.g. iv. 4, xxxii. 32,—and 2 Ki. xxiii. 2 (= 2 Ch. xxxiv. 30). An evident reminiscence of the language of Jer.: cf. 'all the countries whither thou hast driven them' from Jer. xvi. 15, xxiii. 3, 8, xxxii. 37.
that are near and that are *far off*] Jer. xxv. 26; cf. Is. lvii. 19.
their **unfaithfulness wherein** *they have* **dealt unfaithfully** *against thee*] The idea of *māʻal* is disloyalty rather than 'trespass.' The same phrase Lev. xxvi. 40; Ez. xvii. 20, xviii. 24, xxxix. 26; 1 Ch. x. 13. Both the subst. and the cognate verb are almost confined to the priestly sections of the Hexateuch, to Ezek., and the Chronicles: cf., however, the subst. in Ezr. ix. 2, 4, x. 6, and the verb in Ezr. x. 2, 10; Neh. i. 8, xiii. 27.
8. *to our kings*, &c.] Cf. Jer. xliv. 17 (quoted on *v.* 6).
9. *mercies*] The word often rendered 'tender mercies' (Ps. xxv. 6,

DANIEL 9

10 rebelled against him; neither have we obeyed the voice of the LORD our God, to walk in his laws, which he set
11 before us by his servants the prophets. Yea, all Israel have transgressed thy law, even by departing, that *they* might not obey thy voice; therefore the curse is poured upon us, and the oath that *is* written in the law of Moses the servant of God, because we have sinned against him.
12 And he hath confirmed his words, which he spake against us, and against our judges that judged us, by bringing upon us a great evil: for under the whole heaven hath not
13 been done as hath been done upon Jerusalem. As *it is* written in the law of Moses, all this evil is come upon us: yet made we not our prayer before the LORD our God, that

xl. 11, &c.). The cognate verb and adj. are often rendered by *have compassion on* (e.g. Is. xlix. 15), and *full of compassion* (e.g. Ps. lxxviii. 38). **Compassion** would be the best word to adopt uniformly for this word and its cognates.

forgivenesses] Ps. cxxx. 4, 'With thee is forgiveness'; and Neh. ix. 17, 'a God of forgivenesses.'

though] **because** or **for.** The clause explains how it is that there is need for the exercise of forgiveness by God.

10. *obeyed* (lit. *hearkened to*) *the voice*, &c.] So Ex. xv. 26, xix. 5; and especially in Deut. (as iv. 30, ix. 23, xxviii. 1, 2, 15), and Jer. (as iii. 13, ix. 13, xliv. 23). Cf. with this verse Bar. i. 18, ii. 10.

to walk in his laws] Cf. Jer. xxvi. 4, xxxii. 23, xliv. 10, 23.

which he set before us] See Deut. iv. 8, xi. 32; Jer. ix. 13, xliv. 10, and esp. xxvi. 4 (cf. the last clause).

11. *even by departing*] **and have turned aside,** as *v.* 5.

so as not to obey (*hearken to*) *thy voice*] as Jer. xviii. 10, xlii. 13 (Heb.).

and so there hath been poured out upon us **the curse and the oath,** *that is written*, &c.] 'Poured out,' as Jer. xlii. 18, xliv. 6 (of anger): 'the curse that is written in,' as Deut. xxix. 20, the reference being here to Deut. xxviii. 15 ff.; 'curse' strengthened by 'oath,' as Num. v. 21, Neh. x. 29.

Moses, the servant of God] Neh. x. 29: and (with *Jehovah* for *God*) Deut. xxxiv. 5, and often in Josh. (as i. 1, 13, 15, viii. 31, 33).

12. *confirmed his words*] The phrase as Neh. ix. 8; cf. Deut. ix. 5, 1 Ki. viii. 20, *al.* with this verse, cf. Bar. ii. 1, 2.

judges] apparently a general term for rulers, as Ps. ii. 10.

by bringing, &c.] to 'bring evil upon' is a phrase common **in Jer.,** as xxxv. 17, xxxvi. 31 (where 'pronounced' is lit. *spake*, as here).

for] better, **so that, such that,** 1 Ki. iii. 12.

under the whole heaven] cf. on vii. 27.

13. *As* it is *written*, &c.] Cf. Deut. xxviii. 15 *b*, xxx. 1.

yet **have** *we* **not intreated the favour of** (R.V.)] lit. *made the face sweet* (i.e. gracious), the idiom used with reference to a human object

we might turn from our iniquities, and understand thy truth. Therefore hath the LORD watched upon the evil, 14 and brought it upon us: for the LORD our God *is* righteous in all his works which he doeth: for we obeyed not his voice. And now, O Lord our God, that hast brought thy 15 people forth out of the land of Egypt with a mighty hand, and hast gotten thee renown, as *at* this day; we have sinned, we have done wickedly. O Lord, according to all 16 thy righteousness, I beseech thee, let thine anger and thy

in Job xi. 19; Ps. xlv. 12; Pr. xix. 6, and frequently with reference to God, as Ex. xxxii. 11; 1 Sam. xiii. 12; Jer. xxvi. 19, *al.* Cf. Bar. ii. 8.

understand thy truth] better (R.V.), **have discernment in** *thy truth,* 'truth' being used in the objective sense which it has in viii. 12, and the meaning being (Keil, Prince) to acquire insight into God's revealed will, and to think and act in accordance with it. The words might, however, also be rendered (R.V. *marg.*) **deal wisely** (viz. in amending our ways) **through**[1] *thy truth* (v. Lengerke, Behrm.), i.e. through Thy revealed word. The verb has the former meaning (*understand, discern*) in *v.* 25; and the latter in xi. 33, 35, xii. 3, 10..

14. And (so) Jehovah hath watched over] The same expression in Jer. i. 12, xxxi. 28, xliv. 27 ('I watch over them for evil and not for good'), the meaning being that Jehovah is *wakeful* or *vigilant* over the evil, that it may duly be brought when the right moment arrives. Cf. Bar. ii. 9.

is *righteous*] cf. Jer. xii. 1, Lam. i. 18, Ezr. ix. 15, Neh. ix. 8 *end*, 33.

in the matter of *all his works which he* **hath done**] cf. (with the same peculiar use of the prep. *'al*) Neh. ix. 33, 'and thou art righteous *in the matter of* all that is come upon us.'

and we have not *obeyed* (lit. *hearkened to*) *his voice*] cf. *v.* 10.

15—19. The confession passes now gradually into a supplication for help. Cf. Bar. ii. 11, 12 *a*, 13 *a*, 14 *a*, 16 *b*, 17 *a*, 19.

15. *that hast brought,* &c.] Deut. vi. 21, ix. 26, xxvi. 8; cf. Jer. xxxii. 21.

and hast **made thee a name,** *as at* **this day**] verbatim (in the Heb.), though not quite *literatim*, as Jer. xxxii. 20 and Neh. ix. 10; *to make oneself a name* (i.e. to gain renown), also, Gen. xi. 4, and (of God) Is. lxiii. 12, 14, and (with a syn. in the Heb. for *make*) 2 Sam. vii. 23.

we have sinned, we have done wickedly] 1 Ki. viii. 47.

16. *according to all thy righteousness***es**] The plural, of righteousness exhibited in deeds, or, in other words, of **acts of righteousness**: so Jud. v. 11; 1 Sam. xii. 7; Mic. vi. 5; Ps. ciii. 6. **God's deliverance** of His people, according to His covenant-promise, when and in so far as it deserves it, is regarded as a manifestation of His righteousness. As in the last verse, God's acts of mercy towards His people and His interpositions on its behalf, in the past, are appealed to as a ground why He should interpose similarly now.

[1] There is a similar ambiguity in the verb and accompanying prep. in Ps. ci. 2.

fury be turned away from thy city Jerusalem, thy holy mountain: because for our sins, and for the iniquities of our fathers, Jerusalem and thy people *are become* a reproach
17 to all *that are* about us. Now therefore, O our God, hear the prayer of thy servant, and his supplications, and cause thy face to shine upon thy sanctuary that is desolate, for
18 the Lord's sake. O my God, incline thine ear, and hear; open thine eyes, and behold our desolations, and the city which is called by thy name: for we do not present our

let thine anger, &c.] for the expression, cf. Num. xxv. 4, Jer. xxiii. 20, xxx. 24, Is. xii. 1.

thy city] *v.* 19: cf. 'my city,' Is. xlv. 13.

thy holy mountain] Ps. xv. 1, xliii. 3, and elsewhere. So *v.* 24.

the iniquities of our fathers] Cf. Lev. xxvi. 39, Jer. xi. 10, Is. lxv. 7, Neh. ix. 2; also Ps. lxxix. 8.

a reproach to all that are *round about us*] Cf. Ps. xliv. 13, lxxix. 4; also Ez. xxv. 3, 6, 8; xxxv. 10, 12, 13. The words may, however, also glance at "the position of the faithful Jews under Antiochus, since in addition to the tyranny of the king they had to endure the taunts of their heathen neighbours, the Edomites, the Ammonites, etc." (Bevan).

17—19. The supplication becomes more urgent, especially in *vv.* 18, 19.

17. hearken unto *the prayer*, &c.] A reminiscence of 1 Ki. viii. 28 (= 2 Ch. vi. 19). Similarly Neh. i. 6, 11 (from 1 Ki. viii. 29).

cause thy face to shine upon] i.e. be favourable to: Num. vi. 25; Ps. lxvii. 1, lxxx. 3, 7, 19 (in a prayer for help, as here), cxix. 135.

desolate] The word (*shāmēm*) used in Lam. v. 18, 'mount Zion, which is *desolate*' (cf. 1 Macc. iv. 38), chosen perhaps at the same time with allusion to the transgression, or abomination, 'causing appalment' (*shōmēm*, *měshōmēm*), of viii. 13, ix. 27, xi. 31, xii. 11.

for the Lord's sake] The words in themselves occasion no difficulty (cf. *v.* 19; Is. xlviii. 11, 'for mine own sake'), though *for thy name's sake* would be more usual (Jer. xiv. 7, 21; Ps. lxxix. 9): Jehovah's honour, or reputation, it is implied, would be impaired, if His sanctuary remained longer in abasement; out of regard to Himself, therefore, He is entreated to interfere. But the *third person* in the midst of a series of petitions in the second person, is very strange: it is probable, therefore, that either a letter or a word has dropped out in the Heb., and that we should read, either with Theod., Prince, *for thine own sake, O Lord* (cf. *v.* 19), or with LXX, Bevan, Marti, *for thy servants' sake, O Lord* (as in the very similar appeal of Is. lxiii. 17).

18. *incline...and behold* (lit. *see*)] Almost exactly the words in Hezekiah's prayer, 2 Ki. xix. 16 (= Is. xxxvii. 17).

desolations] *v.* 26: cf. Is. xlix. 19, lxi. 4 (twice).

over which *thy name* **hath been called**] i.e. of which Thou art the Owner. The sense of the expression appears from 2 Sam. xii. 28, 'lest

supplications before thee for our righteousnesses, but for thy great mercies. O Lord, hear; O Lord, forgive; O Lord, hearken and do; defer not, for thine own sake, O my God: for thy city and thy people are called by thy name.

And whiles I *was* speaking, and praying, and confessing my sin and the sin of my people Israel, and presenting my supplication before the LORD my God for the holy mountain of my God; yea, whiles I *was* speaking in prayer, even the man Gabriel, whom I had seen in the vision at the

I take the city, and *my name be called over it*,' in token, viz. of my having conquered it. The expression is often used, especially in Deuteronomic writers, of the people of Israel, Jerusalem, or the Temple, as *v.* 19; Deut. xxviii. 10; Jer. vii. 10, 11, 14, 30, xiv. 9, xxv. 29; 1 Ki. viii. 43; Is. lxiii. 19. The paraphrase of A.V., R.V., 'which is called by my name,' weakens and obscures the real force of the expression. Cf. further on Am. ix. 12.

present] lit. *cause to fall*: so *v.* 20, Jer. xxxviii. 26, xlii. 2, 9; cf. xxxvi. 7 (lit. '*their supplication will fall* before Jehovah'), xxxvii. 20 (here in the sense of being accepted). The expression does not occur elsewhere in the O.T.: Prof. Kirkpatrick compares, however, Baruch ii. 19 (οὐ...καταβάλλομεν τὸν ἔλεον we do not *cast down* our supplication).

for...for] properly *on* (the ground of).

thy great compassions] *v.* 9. The same expression in Neh. ix. 19, 27, 31 (A.V., R.V., 'manifold mercies'): cf. 2 Sam. xxiv. 14 ('for his compassions are great'), Ps. cxix. 156.

19. *hear...forgive*] The combination is, no doubt, suggested by 1 Ki. viii. 30 *b*, 34, 36, 39.

hearken] attend, as the word is often rendered in the Psalms, xvii. 1, lv. 2, lxi. 1, lxxxvi. 6, cxlii. 6.

and do] cf. Jer. xiv. 7, 'though our iniquities testify against us, O Jehovah *do* for thy name's sake': see also on viii. 12.

defer not: for thine own sake, O my God, because, &c. (R.V.). The Hebrew accentuation places the main break in the verse at *defer not*.

defer not] as Ps. xl. 17 (=lxx. 5: in A.V., R.V., *make no long tarrying*).

for thine own sake] see on *v.* 17, *end*.

because *thy name* hath been called over *thy city and thy people*] see on *v.* 18.

20—23. Daniel's prayer heard; and the angel Gabriel sent with the answer.

20. *whiles*] So *v.* 21. See on *v.* 2.

confessing] *v.* 4.

for the holy mountain of my God] cf. *v.* 16.

21. *even the man*] 'even' arises from an incorrect apprehension of the syntax, and should be omitted (as is done in R.V.).

in the vision at the beginning] viii. 16.

beginning, being caused to fly swiftly, touched me about the
22 time of the evening oblation. And he informed *me*, and
talked with me, and said, O Daniel, I am now come forth to
23 give thee skill and understanding. At the beginning of thy
supplications the commandment came forth, and I am
come to shew *thee;* for thou *art* greatly beloved: therefore

being caused to fly swiftly] The Hebrew is peculiar, and has been
variously understood. The first word may be derived equally from
two different verbs, meaning respectively *to fly* and *to be weary;* the
second word, as it stands, could only be derived naturally from the latter
verb: thus we get the two renderings, **being made to fly in weariness**
(i.e. being exhausted by his flight), and (Ges., Keil, Meinh.) **being
made weary in weariness** (cf. R.V. *marg.* 'being sore wearied'), the
words in the latter case being referred either (Ges.) to Gabriel, or
(Keil, Meinh.) to Daniel ('whom I had seen..., when exhausted,'
&c.), in accordance with what is said in viii. 17 f. Neither explanation is satisfactory, but the present text admits of nothing better.
'Swiftly' (A.V.), though found in the ancient versions (LXX, τάχει
φερόμενος, Vulg. *cito volans*), is a very questionable paraphrase. The
second word might have arisen by an erroneous and incorrect repetition
of the first. Of the first word, **being made to fly** is the more natural
rendering. Angels are elsewhere in the O.T. represented as possessing
human form, but not as winged (only seraphim, Is. vi. 2, and cherubim,
Ez. i. 6, have wings): winged angels (unless one is presupposed here,
or in xii. 6, 1 Chr. xxi. 16?) appear first in Enoch lxi. 1, 'And I saw in
those days how cords were given to those angels, and they took to
themselves wings and flew, and they went towards the north'; cf.
Rev. xiv. 6.

touched me] **was approaching close to me.**

the evening meal offering] 2 Ki. xvi. 15; Ezr. ix. 4, 5; Ps. cxli. 2:
cf. 1 Ki. xviii. 29, 36.

22. *and he informed* me] better, **made** (me) **to understand,** as in
viii. 16. But the pron. is (in the Heb.) much desiderated; and very
probably we should read, with LXX, Pesh., **And he came** (ויבא) for
(ויבן): so Bevan, Behrm., Marti.

to give thee skill and understanding] R.V. (from A.V. *marg.*) *to*
make thee skilful (cf. i. 4, 17) **of** *understanding.* The verb might also
be rendered *to give thee discernment* or *make thee wise* (cf. *v.* 13 *end*).

23. *the commandment came forth*] **a word went forth** (cf. Est.
vii. 8; Is. lv. 11). The reference is not to the commandment given to
Gabriel to go to Daniel, but to the Divine declaration contained in
vv. 24—27.

to shew thee] *to* **declare** (it): cf. on ii. 2.

greatly beloved] **greatly desired,** or (R.V. *marg.*) **very precious:**
lit. *desirable things* or *desirablenesses;* cf. x. 11, 19, ' a man of desirablenesses,' the plural being intensive[1].

---

[1] For the Heb. idiom here employed cf. Ps. cix. 4, cx. 3: and see Ges.-Kautzsch,
§ 141 c.

understand the matter, and consider the vision. Seventy **24** weeks are determined upon thy people and upon thy holy city, to finish the transgression, and to make an end of

The cognate verb means *to desire* (Ps. xix. 10; Ex. xx. 17, 'covet'); and when applied to men has usually reference to their personal attractiveness (Is. liii. 2; Ps. xxxix. 11, 'his desirableness,' A.V., R.V., 'his beauty'). The word here used, properly *desired*, is elsewhere rendered *precious* (2 Ch. xx. 25; Ezr. viii. 27; Dan. xi. 43), or *pleasant* (Dan. x. 3, xi. 38) : hence R.V. *marg.* 'very precious.'

understand...consider] R.V. *consider...understand*. The two words in the Heb. are different forms of one and the same verb: R.V. transposes the renderings, probably on the ground that 'understanding' implies more than 'consideration,' and would naturally follow it.

the matter] *the* **word** (x. 1), i.e. the prophetic word following (*vv.* 24—27).

the vision] viii. 16, 27, x. 1. Also a term descriptive of the revelation following, and implying that the appearance of Gabriel to Daniel took place in a vision. The word (מראה) is not the one found in Is. i. 1 (חזון), which does sometimes mean no more than 'prophecy'.

24. The 70 years foretold by Jeremiah are to be understood as 70 weeks of years (i.e. 490 years); at the end of that period sin will be done away with, and the redemption of Israel will be complete. Jeremiah's promises, which, while the city and nation are being made the prey of Antiochus, seem a dead letter, will, with this new explanation of their meaning, receive their fulfilment; and (as *vv.* 26, 27 shew) the time when this will take place is not now far distant. Perhaps, as Prof. Bevan observes, this explanation may have been suggested to the writer by the terms of Lev. xxvi. 18, 21, 24, 28, where it is emphatically declared that the Israelites are to be punished *seven times* for their sins : "the 70 years of Jeremiah were to be repeated seven times, and at the end of the 490th year the long-promised deliverance might be confidently expected." The Chronicler had already brought the idea of the 70 years of Judah's desolation into connexion with heptads, or 'weeks,' of years, by his remark (2 Ch. xxxvi. 20 f.) that they were the penalty exacted by God for the 'sabbatical' years, which Israel had neglected to observe whilst in possession of its land (cf. Lev. xxvi. 34 f.).

weeks] i.e. (as the sequel shews) *weeks of years*, a sense not occurring elsewhere in Biblical Hebrew, but found in the Mishna.

determined] **decreed** (R.V.). The word is a different one from that rendered 'determined' in *vv.* 26, 27, and occurs only here in Biblical Hebrew. In the Talm. it means *to determine in judgement, decide.*

to finish the transgression] to bring it to an end. The verb rendered *finish* is anomalous in form, and might also be rendered *to confine* (as in a prison, Jer. xxxii. 2), or *restrain* (Num. xi. 28), viz. so that it could no longer spread or continue active (so R.V. *marg.*). But the former rendering is preferable; and is that adopted both by the ancient versions and by the great majority of modern commentators.

and to make an end of sins] parallel with *to finish transgression* : cf.

sins, and to make reconciliation for iniquity, and to bring in everlasting righteousness, and to seal up the vision and

for the meaning of the verb, Ez. xxii. 15 ('consume'). So the Heb. marg. (*Qrê*), Aq., Pesh., Vulg. The Heb. text (K'tib) and Theod. have *to seal up* (חתם for התם), which is explained (in agreement with *restrain* in the last clause), as meaning partly to preclude from activity, partly to preclude from forgiveness (cf. Job xiv. 17): but this explanation is forced; and the *Qrê* yields here a meaning in better harmony with the context.

and to **cancel** *iniquity*] The verb *kipper* means originally, as seems to be shewn by Arabic, *to cover*; in Hebrew, however, it is never used of literal covering, but always in a *moral* application, viz. either of *covering* the face of (i.e. appeasing[1]) an offended person, or of *screening* an offence or an offender. When, as here, the reference is to sin or iniquity, the meaning differs, according as the subject is the priest, or God: in the former case the meaning is to *cover* or *screen* the sinner by means (usually) of a propitiatory sacrifice[2], and it is then generally rendered *make atonement* or *reconciliation* for (as Lev. iv. 20, 26, 31); in the latter case it means *to treat as covered, to pardon* or *cancel*, without any reference to a propitiatory rite, as Jer. xviii. 23; Ps. lxv. 3, lxxviii. 38, lxxix. 9 (A.V. *to purge away* or *forgive*)[3]. Here no subject is mentioned: it would most naturally (as in the case of the other infinitives) be God; moreover, when, in the ritual laws, the subject is the priest, the object of the verb is never, as here, the *guilt*. The rendering of R.V. *marg.* ('to purge away'), though somewhat of a paraphrase, is thus preferable to that of A.V.

everlasting righteousness] The expression does not occur elsewhere. In thought, however, Is. xlv. 17, 'Israel is saved through Jehovah with an everlasting salvation: ye shall not be put to shame, and ye shall not be confounded, for ever and ever,' lx. 21, 'Thy people shall be all of them righteous, for ever shall they inherit the land,' are similar. The general sense of the four clauses, of which this is the last, is that the Messianic age is to be marked by the abolition and forgiveness of sin, and by perpetual righteousness. It thus expresses in a compendious form the teaching of such passages as Is. iv. 3 f. (the survivors of the judgement to be all *holy*), xxxii. 16, 17 (righteousness the mark of the ideal future), xxxiii. 24 ('the people that dwell therein shall be forgiven their iniquity'), Ez. xxxvi. 25—27; Is. xlv. 17, lx. 21.

and to **seal vision** *and* **prophet**] i.e. to set the seal to them, to ratify and confirm the prophets' predictions, the figure (cf. John iii. 33, vi. 27) being derived from the custom of affixing a seal to a document, in order to guarantee its genuineness (Jer. xxxii. 10, 11, 44). The close of the 70 weeks will bring with it the confirmation of the prophetic utterances (such as those just quoted) respecting a blissful future.

A.V., R.V., 'seal *up*,' means to close up, preclude from activity, the

---

[1] See Gen. xxxii. 20 [Heb. 21]; and cf. Prov. xvi. 14 ('pacify').
[2] Occasionally without one, as Ex. xxx. 15, 16, Num. xvi. 46 f., xxv. 13.
[3] See more fully the note in the writer's *Deuteronomy*, p. 425 f.; or the art. PROPITIATION in Hastings' *Dict. of the Bible*.

prophecy, and to anoint the most Holy. Know there- 25
fore and understand, *that* from the going forth of the

sense of the expression, upon this view, being supposed to be that, prophecies being fulfilled, prophet and vision will be needed no more.

and to anoint **a most holy**] 'most holy' or 'holy of holies' (lit. *holiness of holinesses*) is an expression belonging to the priestly terminology and is variously applied. It is used of the altar of burnt-offering (Ex. xxix. 37, 'and the altar shall be *most holy*,' xl. 10), of the altar of incense (Ex. xxx. 10), of the Tent of meeting, with the vessels belonging to it (*ib. vv.* 26—29; cf. Num. iv. 4, 19, Ez. xliv. 13); of the sacred incense (*ib. v.* 36), of the shew-bread (Lev. xxiv. 9), of the meal-offering (Lev. ii. 3, 10, vi. 17, x. 12), of the flesh of the sin- and guilt-offering (Lev. vi. 17, 25, vii. 1, 6, x. 17, xiv. 13, Num. xviii. 9; cf. Lev. xxi. 22, Ez. xlii. 13, Ezr. ii. 63, 2 Ch. xxxi. 14); of things 'devoted' to Jehovah (Lev. xxvii. 28); of the entire Temple, with the territory belonging to it, in Ezekiel's vision (Ez. xliii. 12, xlv. 3, xlviii. 12); and once (perhaps) of the priests (1 Ch. xxiii. 13), 'And Aaron was separated, to sanctify him as (a thing) most holy[1], him and his sons for ever, to burn incense, &c.': '*the* holy of holies,' or '*the* most holy (place),' is also the name, in particular, of the inmost part of the Tent of meeting, and of the Temple, in which the ark was (Ex. xxvi. 33, and frequently). As no object is called in particular 'a most holy (thing),' general considerations, viewed in the light of the context, can alone determine what is here intended. A material object, rather than a person, is certainly most naturally denoted by the expression, and most probably either the altar of burnt-offering (which was in particular desecrated by Antiochus Epiphanes), or the Temple generally, is what is meant. The term *anoint* is used both of the altar of burnt-offering in particular, and of the Tent of meeting and vessels belonging to it in general, in Ex. xxix. 36, and xxx. 26—28 (cf. xl. 9—11; Lev. viii. 10, 11; Num. vii. 1, 10, 84, 88),—each time immediately preceding the passages quoted above for the use in the same connexion of the term 'most holy.' The consecration of a temple in the Messianic age (cf. Is. lx. 7; Ez. xl. ff.) is, no doubt, what is intended by the words.

25—27. The 70 weeks are now broken up into three periods of 7, 62, and 1 week, respectively; and the events by which each of these periods is to be marked are signalized.

25. The 7 weeks and the following 62 weeks.

understand] R.V. **discern**,—the Hebrew word being the same as that rendered *have discernment* in *v.* 13 (R.V.), and different from the one rendered *understand* in *vv.* 2, 23.

the going forth of the **word**] cf. (for the expression) *v.* 23, Is. lv. 11. The reference is to the Divine word spoken by Jeremiah (Jer.

---

[1] The words ought however, perhaps, to be rendered (cf. A.V., R.V.) 'that he should sanctify that which was most holy, he and his sons for ever,'—the reference being to the sanctuary and sacred vessels (cf. Ex. xxx. 29), and to the various sacrifices mentioned above.

commandment to restore and to build Jerusalem unto the Messiah the Prince *shall be* seven weeks, and threescore and two weeks: the street shall be built again, and the wall,

xxx. 18, xxxi. 38 f.), the meaning of whose predictions is here interpreted (cf. *v.* 2).

to restore] lit. *to cause to return* or *bring back*, often used of exiles (as Jer. xii. 15), but not used elsewhere of *restoring* (i.e. rebuilding) a city. To *repeople* (הָשֵׁיב for הָשִׁיב),—lit. *to cause to sit*, figuratively of a city, *to cause to be inhabited*,—is a plausible emendation (Bevan): cf. the same word in Is. xliv. 26 ('she shall be *made to be inhabited*,' lit. *be made to sit*), Jer. xxx. 18 (see R.V. marg.: lit. *shall sit*), Ez. xxxvi. 33 (lit. *cause the cities to sit*, followed by 'and the waste places shall be builded').

unto an anointed one, a prince] The term 'anointed' is used most frequently in the O.T. of the theocratic ruler of Israel ('Jehovah's anointed,' 'his, my, anointed,' &c., 1 Sam. xii. 3, Ps. xviii. 50, &c., but never '*the* anointed'); of the high-priest, Lev. iv. 3, 5, 16, vi. 22 ('the high-priest, the anointed one'), 2 Macc. i. 10; in a figurative sense also of Cyrus, as the agent commissioned by Jehovah for the restoration of His people, Is. xlv. 1, and of the patriarchs, Ps. cv. 15 ('Touch not mine anointed ones'). On the rend. of A.V., see further p. 144.

prince (נָגִיד),—properly *one in front, leader*,—is used (*a*) of the chief ruler of Israel, 1 Sam. ix. 16, x. 1, xiii. 14 and frequently; (*b*) of a foreign ruler, Ez. xxviii. 2; (*c*) of some high official connected with the Temple, Jer. xx. 1 ('who was *prince*-overseer in the house of Jehovah'), 1 Ch. ix. 11, 2 Ch. xxxi. 18, xxxv. 8, Neh. xi. 11; (*d*) in the Chronicles, more generally, of a leader (1 Ch. ix. 20, xiii. 1, xxvii. 16), commander (2 Ch. xi. 11), or superintendent (1 Ch. xxvi. 24, 2 Ch. xxxi. 12). The 'anointed one, the prince,' who is here meant, is apparently (see more fully below) Cyrus (Is. xlv. 1), who is called in Is. xlv. 1 Jehovah's 'anointed,' and who, it is said in Is. xliv. 26, 28, xlv. 13, will give command for the rebuilding of Jerusalem, which is here, it will be observed, just the subject of the following clause. Grätz and Bevan, however, suppose that Jeshua, son of Jozadak, the first high-priest after the restoration (Ezr. iii. 2; Hag. i. 1; Zech. iii. 1), is intended. The date would suit in either case: the prophecies contained in Jer. xxx.—xxxi. were delivered probably shortly before the fall of Jerusalem, about B.C. 587, and 49 years from 587 would be 538, which was just the date of the capture of Babylon by Cyrus. Jeshua is mentioned among those who returned to Jerusalem with Zerubbabel (Ezr. ii. 2).

shall be **seven weeks: and for** *threescore and two weeks* **it** *shall be built again*, (with) **broad place and moat (?); and that, in strait of** *times*] so, according to the Heb. interpunction, in manifest agreement with what the sense requires. Seven weeks are to elapse from the 'word' commanding the rebuilding of Jerusalem to the 'anointed one, the prince'; then it will be built again, as a complete city, with 'broad place' and moat (?), but in strait of times,—with allusion, viz. to the subject, and sometimes oppressed, condition of Jerusalem from B.C. 538

even in troublous times. And after threescore and two 26
weeks shall Messiah be cut off, but not for himself: and

to 171 (comp. for the earlier part of the period Ezr. iv., Neh. vi., ix. 37): Jerusalem would, indeed, be rebuilt, after the restoration in 538, with material completeness, but would not until long afterwards enjoy the splendour and independence which the prophets had promised (e.g. Is. lx.). A 'broad place,' or as we might say 'a square,' was a standing feature in an Eastern city: see in A.V. Jer. v. 1, and in R.V. 2 Ch. xxix. 4, xxxii. 6, Ezr. x. 9 (one before the Temple), Neh. viii. 1, 3, 16, —unhappily, in A.V. nearly always[1], and even in R.V. often, misrendered *street*, and so confused with something entirely different. The word rendered 'moat' does not occur elsewhere in the O.T.: the root signifies *to cut, make incisions*, and in the Mishna almost the same word is used of a *trench* in a field or vineyard. Whether these facts justify the definite sense of *moat* is, perhaps, questionable, especially as 'walls' and 'towers' are more commonly mentioned in connexion with the defences of Jerusalem. Prof. Bevan, following the Pesh., suggests the plausible emendation, 'broad place and *street*' (חרוץ for חריץ), two words often found in parallelism: see in A.V. Jer. v. 1; in R.V. Prov. i. 20, vii. 12, Is. xv. 3; also Cant. iii. 2, Am. v. 16, Nah. ii. 4 (here, badly, *broad ways*). Whether, however, the text be altered or not, the general sense remains the same: Jerusalem will be rebuilt with the usual material completeness of an Eastern city; but will not enjoy political ease and freedom.

in strait of *times*] For the expression cf. Is. xxxiii. 6, 'stability (i.e. security) of thy *times*': for 'times,' also, 1 Ch. xxix. 30.

26, 27. The 70th week (B.C. 171 to 164).

26. *And after* the *threescore and two weeks shall* **an anointed one** *be cut off*, **and shall have no**......] The 'anointed one' cannot be the same as the 'anointed one' of *v.* 25; for he lives 62 'weeks' (i.e. 434 years) after him. The language is intentionally allusive and ambiguous. The term 'anointed' (see on *v.* 25) is used sometimes of the high-priest; and the reference, it seems, is here to Onias III. Onias III. was highpriest till B.C. 175, when he was superseded by his brother Jason, who by the offer of 440 talents of silver purchased the office from Antiochus for himself (2 Macc. iv. 7—9). Jason held office for three years, at the end of which time a certain Menelaus, whom he had employed as his agent to carry the 440 talents to the king, took advantage of the occasion to secure the high-priesthood for himself by offering Antiochus 300 talents more. The money promised by Menelaus not being paid, he was summoned before the king. When he arrived he found Antiochus absent in Cilicia and a courtier named Andronicus representing him at Antioch. Menelaus, anxious to secure Andronicus's favour, presented him with some golden vessels which he had stolen from the Temple. Onias, who was in the neighbourhood, hearing of what he had done, rebuked him sharply for his sacrilege; and Menelaus, resenting

---

[1] As Gen. xix. 2; Deut. xiii. 16; 2 Sam. xxi. 12 (see R.V. *marg.*); Jer. ix. 21; Lam. ii. 11, 12; Zech. viii. 4, 5.

the people of the prince that *shall* come shall destroy the

the rebuke, prevailed upon Andronicus to assassinate Onias. Antiochus, upon his return home, was vexed with what had occurred, and (according to 2 Macc.) had Andronicus put to death at the very spot at which he had murdered Onias (2 Macc. iv. 7—9, 23—38). The assassination of one who was the lawful high-priest was an occurrence which might well be singled out for mention in the prophecy; and how the godly character of Onias, and his unjust end, impressed the Jews, appears from what is said of him in 2 Macc. iii. 1, 2, iv. 2, 35—37, xv. 12[1]. On the chronological difficulty involved in the verse, see below, p. 146 f.

and shall have no.....] The clause is difficult; though the same text (ואין לו) was perhaps already read (but rendered incorrectly) by the LXX. (καὶ οὐκ ἔσται), and is distinctly implied by Aq., Symm., and the Pesh. The rendering 'and shall have **nothing**' may be defended by Ex. xxii. 3 [Heb. 2], though, it is true, the 'thing' lacking is there more easily supplied from the context than is the case here; but the sense obtained is not very satisfactory, and the sentence (in the Heb.) reads also incompletely; we should have expected, 'and shall have no [helper],'—as Grätz would actually read, comparing xi. 45,— or '[successor],' or '[seed],' or something of the kind. Still, if the text be sound, this, it seems, must be the meaning: the 'anointed one,' when he is 'cut off,' *will have nought*, i.e. he will be left with *nothing*, —no name, no house, no legitimate successor. (LXX. *and be no more*, would be the correct rendering of ואיננו; but this reading is suspiciously easy.) The rendering of A.V., 'but not for himself,' is an impossible one: אין is not a synonym of לא, but always includes the substantive verb, 'there is not,' 'was not,' 'shall not be' (the tense being supplied according to the context).

the people of a prince that shall come] viz. against the land, the verb being used in the same hostile sense which it has in i. 1, xi. 13, 16, 21, 40, 41. The allusion is to the soldiery of Antiochus Epiphanes, who set Jerusalem on fire, and pulled down many of the houses and fortifications, so that the inhabitants took flight, and the city could be described as being 'without inhabitant, like a wilderness' (1 Macc. i. 31, 32, 38,

---

[1] This account of the end of Onias III. is accepted generally by historians (e.g. Ewald, v. 295; Schürer[2], i. 152; Grätz ii. 2, 303): but 2 Macc. (which alone records it) is known to contain much that is not historical; and Josephus not only does not mention the assassination of Onias, but, while he sometimes (*Ant.* XII. ix. 7, XIII. iii. 1—3, XX. x.) speaks of Onias' *son* as fleeing to Egypt, and founding there the temple at Leontopolis, elsewhere (*B. J.* I. i. 1, VII. x. 2—3) says that Onias himself, after Antiochus' attack upon Jerusalem in 170 (Introduction, p. xliii.), fled to Egypt, and founded the temple at Leontopolis (cf. Bäthgen, *ZATW*, 1886, pp. 278—282). On these and some other grounds, Wellhausen (*Gött. Gel. Anz.* 1895, pp. 950—6; *Isr. u. Jüd. Gesch.*[2], 1897, pp. 244—7), partly following Willrich (*Juden u. Griechen vor der Makkab. Erhebung*, 1895, pp. 77—90), regards the account of Onias' murder in 2 Macc. as apocryphal: see, however, on the other side, Büchler, *Die Tobiaden u. die Oniaden* (1899), pp. 106—124, 240 f., 275 f., 353—6, whose conclusion on this subject has the weighty support of the historian Niese, *Kritik der beiden Makk.-bücher*, 1900, p. 96 f. *If* Wellhausen's view is correct, the reference in this verse of Dan. will be to the cessation of the legitimate high-priesthood, when Jason was superseded by the Benjaminite (2 Macc. iv. 23, cf. iii. 4; Büchler, p. 14) Menelaus.

city and the sanctuary; and the end thereof *shall be* with a flood, and unto the end of the war desolations *are* determined. And he shall confirm the covenant with many *for* one week: and *in* the midst of the week he shall cause

iii. 45)—'people' being used as in 2 Sam. x. 13, Ez. xxx. 11, &c., of a body of troops. On the treatment which the Temple received at the same time, see above on viii. 11.

but his *end* (shall be) *with a flood*] he will be swept away in the flood of a Divine judgement. The word (cf. xi. 22) may be suggested by Nah. i. 8; cf. the cognate verb (also of an overwhelming Divine judgement) in Is. x. 22 ('*overflowing* with righteousness,' i.e. judicial righteousness, judgement), xxviii. 2, 15, 17, 18, xxx. 28.

and **until** *the end* (shall be) *war*, (even) **that which is determined of** *desolations*] until the end (i.e. until the close of the seventieth week,—the period pictured by the writer (see on viii. 17) as the 'end' of the present dispensation), the war waged by Antiochus against the saints (vii. 21) will continue, together with the accompanying 'desolations,' determined upon in the Divine counsels. The word rendered 'that which is determined,' which recurs in *v.* 27, and xi. 36, is a rare one; and is manifestly a reminiscence of Is. x. 23, xxviii. 22. For 'desolations,' comp. 1 Macc. i. 39, iii. 45, iv. 38 (quoted in the notes on viii. 11).

27. *And he shall* **make a firm** *covenant with many for one week*] Lit. *make mighty* a covenant. The expression is a peculiar one; but apparently (the Heb. being late) *make mighty* is used in the weakened sense of *make strong* or *confirm*; cf. Ps. ciii. 11, cxvii. 2 (where 'is great' ought rather to be *is mighty*: the word is also sometimes rendered *prevail*, as Gen. xlix. 26, Ps. lxv. 3). The subject is naturally the 'prince' just named (*v.* 26). If the text be sound, the allusion will be to the manner in which Antiochus found apostate Jews ready to cooperate with him in his efforts to extirpate their religion: see on xi. 30; and cf. 1 Macc. i. 11—15, where, conversely, the Hellenizing Jews say, 'Let us go and make a covenant with the nations that are round about us.'

and **for half** *of the week he shall cause* **sacrifice** *and* **meal-offering** *to cease*] alluding to the suspension of the Temple services by Antiochus from the 15th of Chisleu, B.C. 168, to the 25th of Chisleu, B.C. 165 (1 Macc. i. 54, iv. 52 f.: see the note on ch. viii. 14). The 'half-week' does not seem to coincide exactly with the three and a half years of vii. 25 and xii. 7; for xii. 11 appears to shew that the suspension of the legitimate services did not precede the erection of the heathen altar on the 15th of Chisleu, B.C. 168; as the reckoning here is by weeks, the half-week is in all probability meant merely as a round fraction for what was strictly a little more than three-sevenths of a 'week,' three years and ten days. 'Sacrifice' and 'meal-offering' are mentioned as representing sacrifices generally: cf. 1 Sam. ii. 29, iii. 14, Am. v. 25, Is. xix. 21. The 'meal-offering' (*minḥāh*) was properly the accompaniment of the burnt-offering, and, as such, offered daily: see Ex. xxix. 40,

the sacrifice and the oblation to cease, and for the overspreading of abominations he *shall* make *it* desolate, even until the consummation, and that determined shall be poured upon the desolate.

41. The word *might*, however, be used in its more general sense, and signify 'offering' or 'oblation' generally (1 Sam. ii. 17, xxvi. 19).

and **upon the wing** *of abominations* (shall be) **a desolator**] or better (cf. on viii. 13 and xi. 31) **one that causeth appalment**: in contrast to Jehovah, who rides upon the cherub (Ps. xviii. 10), the heathen foe will come against the sanctuary, riding upon a winged creature, which is the personification of the forces and practices of heathenism[1]. 'Abomination' (*shikkūẓ*) is often used as a contemptuous designation of a heathen god or idol, or an object connected with idolatrous rites: see e.g. Deut. xxix. 17; 1 Ki. xi. 5, 7; Jer. vii. 30. It would be better rendered—for the sake of distinction from *tō'ēbāh*, also 'abomination'— **detestation** or **detestable thing** (as it is actually rendered in A.V. when it occurs by the side of *tō'ēbāh*, Ez. v. 11, vii. 20, xi. 18, 21); but 'abomination' is, through the N.T. (Matt. xxiv. 15; Mark xiii. 14), so inseparably connected with the Book of Daniel, that the time-honoured rendering may be left undisturbed.

Whether, however, the rendering given above expresses the real meaning of the passage may be doubted. The figure of the 'wing' is not in harmony with the context; and in xi. 31 the same two words 'abomination' and 'desolator (*or* appaller),' differently construed, recur, with clear reference to Antiochus's persecution, 'And they shall profane the sanctuary, (even) the stronghold, and take away the continual (burnt-offering), and set up *the abomination that maketh desolate* (or *appalleth*)' (cf. xii. 11 'from the time when the continual burnt-offering was taken away, and *the abomination that maketh desolate* (or *appalleth*) set up'; and above, viii. 13); and it is highly probable that, slightly changing the text, we should read here, similarly, 'and **in its place** (כנו for כנף: so Van Lennep, Kuenen, Bevan, Kamphausen, Prince; cf. xi. 38) shall be **the abomination that maketh desolate** (*or* **appalleth**)' (שקוץ משומם), as xi. 31, for שקוצים משומם,—a מ erroneously repeated, and then שׁמם written *plene* שׁמים), i.e. instead of the legitimate 'sacrifice' and 'meal-offering' on the altar of burnt-offering, there will be the detestable heathen altar (see on xi. 31), built upon it by Antiochus.

and that, *until the consummation,* **and that which is** *determined* (i.e. the determined doom), *be poured upon the* **desolator** (or **appaller**)] the heathen abomination will remain upon the altar until the destined judgement come down upon its author (Antiochus). The phrase, *the*

---

[1] R.V. *marg.* 'upon the *pinnacle* of abominations'; but though πτερύγιον (Matth. iv. 5) means a *pinnacle*, there is no evidence that the Heb. or Aram. כנף acquired this sense. A.V. 'for (i.e. on account of) the *overspreading*,' &c., follows David Kimchi, who takes 'wing' as a figure for *spreading abroad, diffusion*,—'on account of the diffusion of abominations, men will be appalled.' But such a metaphorical sense of the word is very improbable.

consummation, &c., from Is. x. 23, xxviii. 22. *Be poured* is often used of *anger* or *fury* (Jer. xlii. 18, xliv. 6 *al.*).

Additional Note on the Prophecy of the Seventy Weeks.

Probably no passage of the Old Testament has been the subject of so much discussion, or has given rise to so many and such varied interpretations, as this. Already Jerome wrote[1], 'Scio de hac quaestione ab eruditissimis viris varie disputatum et unumquemque pro captu ingenii sui dixisse quod senserat'; after which he proceeds to give, in some cases quoting the explanations in full, nine different interpretations: though, deeming it 'dangerous' to decide between the opinions of *magistri Ecclesiae* and to prefer one above another, he leaves it to his reader to determine which he will adopt. Since the time of Jerome the number of divergent interpretations has greatly increased. They differ primarily in the *terminus ad quem* which it is desired, or which it is thought possible, to reach; this necessitates differences in the *terminus a quo* adopted, and also in the manner of calculating the 'weeks,' which have been treated sometimes as consisting of solar years, sometimes of lunar years, sometimes as jubile-periods of 7×7 years, sometimes as mystic or symbolic periods, not necessarily equal in length; the order $7 + 62 + 1$, implied apparently by the text, has been inverted, and altered into $62 + 7 + 1$, or $62 + 1 + 7$; the 62 weeks, instead of following the 7, have been made to begin concurrently with them; intervals, not taken account of in the prophecy, have been assumed in the period covered by it; the author, it has been supposed, has followed an erroneous chronology. The reason why commentators have had recourse to these varied and often singular expedients is that, understood in the plain and obvious meaning of the words,—the 'week' being naturally allowed to signify a week of years,—the prophecy *admits of no explanation, consistent with history, whatever;* and hence, if it is to be explained at all, an assumption, or assumptions, of some kind or other, *must* be made; and the only question that can arise is, What assumption is the least violent one, or most adequately meets the requirements of the case? It will be unnecessary to review at length the bewildering mass of explanations that have been offered[2]: the majority are so artificial, or extravagant, that they cannot be regarded as having a serious claim on the reader's attention. The two principal explanations will however be noticed in some detail; and specimens of others will be placed before the reader.

Two exegetical conditions may be premised, which it seems reasonable that any sound interpretation ought to satisfy: (1) the 'weeks' must have the same value throughout; (2) they must be distributed in the order in which they appear in the prophecy, i.e. 7, 62, and 1. It

---

[1] *Comm. on Dan., ad loc.* (ed. Vallarsi, v. 681; ed. Migne, v. 542). They may be seen summarized in Zöckler, p. 187. None of the interpretations which he mentions has found a sponsor in modern times.

[2] A synopsis will be found in Zöckler's *Comm.* (1870), p. 185 ff.; and in Van Lennep's *De Zeventig Jaarweken van Daniel*, 1888, p. 99 ff.

is the plain intention of the prophecy to answer Daniel's questionings and supplication (*vv.* 2, 18, 19, 22), by assigning certain dates, marking stages in the future history of Jerusalem and ending with the consummation of the Divine purpose towards it; and if these dates were to be fixed by variable standards, or if the stages were to be taken as following one another in an inverted order, not indicated in the terms of the text, no definite information would be conveyed by the vision, and the intention of the prophecy would be frustrated.

(i) The traditional explanation of the passage makes it a prediction of the Advent (*v.* 25) and Death (*v.* 26) of Christ, of the abolition of Levitical sacrifices by His sacrifice, once for all, upon the Cross (*v.* 27), and of the destruction of Jerusalem by the Romans under Titus (*v.* 26). There are, no doubt, expressions in the version of Theodotion and the Vulgate, and still more in the Authorized Version, which directly suggest this interpretation,—for instance, 'to anoint the most Holy' (τοῦ χρῖσαι ἅγιον ἁγίων, ut...ungatur sanctus sanctorum), 'unto the Messiah the Prince' (ἕως χριστοῦ ἡγουμένου, usque ad Christum ducem), 'shall Messiah be cut off, but not for himself' (occidetur Christus; et non erit eius populus, qui eum negaturus est; Theod. here ἐξολοθρευθήσεται χρῖσμα¹, καὶ κρῖμα οὐκ ἔστιν ἐν αὐτῷ), 'and he shall confirm the covenant with many for one week; and in the midst of the week he shall cause the sacrifice and the oblation to cease' (Theod. and Vulg. here, somewhat less pointedly, καὶ δυναμώσει διαθήκην πολλοῖς ἑβδομὰς μία· καὶ ἐν τῷ ἡμίσυ τῆς ἑβδομάδος ἀρθήσεταί μου θυσία καὶ σπονδή, confirmabit autem pactum multis hebdomada una; et in dimidio hebdomadis deficiet hostia et sacrificium); but these renderings are interpretations, of which one ('but not for himself') is impossible, while the others are, to say the least, exegetically doubtful, and certainly in no case necessary (see the notes *ad locc.*). Thus, to take here but one expression, the crucial term 'Messiah' depends upon a wholly uncertain exegesis: nowhere else in the O.T. does *māshīaḥ*, used absolutely, denote the ideal, or even the actual, ruler of Israel: the expression used is always either 'Jehovah's anointed,' or 'my, thy, his anointed'; and though the later Jews unquestionably used the term *mᵉshīḥā* 'the anointed one' (the Μεσσίας of the N.T.) to denote Israel's expected ideal king, it is just the question when this usage began, and whether it was current as early as when the book of Daniel was written: certainly, if the book was written by Daniel himself, its appearance in it would be extremely unlikely. Even, indeed, if more than this were conceded, and it were granted that the word *might* have this sense in Daniel, there would be no proof that it *must* have it, and the rendering would still remain exegetically a matter of uncertainty.

When, moreover, the passage is examined in detail, positive objections of a serious, not to say fatal kind, reveal themselves.

(1) If the Crucifixion (A.D. 29) is to fall (*v.* 27 A.V.) in the middle of the last week, the 490 years must begin *c.* 458 B.C., a date which coincides with the decree of Artaxerxes, and the mission of Ezra (Ezr. vii.), and which is accordingly assumed as the *terminus a quo* by Auberlen, Pusey, and

---

¹ i.e. מָשֻׁח for מָשִׁיחַ: so LXX. (ἀποσταθήσεται χρῖσμα καὶ οὐκ ἔσται).

others. Unfortunately, however, this decree is silent as to any command to 'restore and build Jerusalem'; nor was this one of the objects of Ezra's mission to Judah. Others, therefore, adopting the same general view of the meaning of the prophecy, assume as the *terminus a quo* the permission given by Artaxerxes to Nehemiah, in his 20th year, to visit Jerusalem for the purpose of rebuilding the walls (Neh. i.—iii.). To urge the objection that at this time Jerusalem itself was already rebuilt (cf. Hag. i. 4), and that the work of Nehemiah was only to rebuild the walls of the city, might be deemed hypercritical: it is a more substantial objection that Artaxerxes' 20th year was B.C. 445, which brings the *terminus ad quem* 13 years too late,—a serious discrepancy, when the prediction is a minute one, and given (*ex hyp.*) by a special supernatural revelation. In so far also as this interpretation is usually adopted by those who believe the book to have been written by Daniel himself, it can hardly be considered probable that the *terminus a quo* should be a point some 80 years or more subsequent to the date (B.C. 538) at which the prophecy itself is stated to have been given (ch. ix. 1).

(2) The interpretation depends upon the unnatural interpunction of *v*. 25 adopted in A.V., viz. 'unto an anointed one, a prince, shall be seven weeks, and threescore and two weeks; it shall be built again, with broad place and moat, and that in strait of times': the division of the 69 weeks into 7 weeks and 62 weeks, without the mention of anything to mark the close of the 7 weeks, is improbable, while at the same time some mention of the time at which or during which the city is to be 'built again' is desiderated. Those who adopt this interpretation generally suppose the 49 years (which would end *c.* 409 B.C.) to mark the close of the rebuilding of Jerusalem which was begun by Nehemiah: but there is really no ground for the supposition that this work continued till then. Nehemiah rebuilt, not the city, but the walls, and that, not after the destruction by Nebuchadnezzar, but after some more recent catastrophe[1]; the work was accomplished rapidly (Neh. vi. 15), and even on the occasion of his second visit to Jerusalem in 432 (Neh. xiii. 6 ff.), there is no indication that any rebuilding, whether of the city or the walls, was still going on. With the interpretation and rendering of *v*. 25 adopted in R.V., the possibility ceases of identifying the 'anointed one, the prince' of *v*. 25 with the 'anointed one' of *v*. 26, and also of referring either—except upon such strained interpretations as those quoted below, pp. 148, 149—to Christ. (3) Christ did not 'confirm a covenant with many for one week' (= 7 years); His ministry lasted at most somewhat over 3 years; and if, in the years following, He is regarded as carrying on His work through the agency of His apostles, the limit, 'seven years,' seems an arbitrary one; for the apostles continued to gain converts from Judaism for many years subsequently. The preaching of the Gospel to the Samaritans (Acts viii.), which may have happened 3—4 years after the Crucifixion, and which has been suggested as the limit intended in the prophecy, did not mark such an epoch in the establishment of Christianity as could be naturally regarded as closing the period during which the Messiah would 'make a firm covenant with many.'

[1] See Ryle on Neh. i. 3. On Neh. ii. 5 *end*, and vii. 4, see also Ryle's notes.

(4) The destruction of Jerusalem by Titus (A.D. 70), which is supposed upon this view to be predicted in *v.* 26*b*, follows the date of the Crucifixion by 40—41 years. It not only, therefore, is out of place before *v.* 27, but does not even come within the limits of the 490 years at all. Were the prophecy perfectly general in its terms, it would, no doubt, be unreasonable to press an objection of this kind; but where periods of 7 and 3½ years, in the distant future, are (*ex hyp.*) exactly discriminated, *à fortiori* a period of 40 years should be so discriminated. Auberlen, it is true, argues that the final destruction of Jerusalem is rightly excluded from the 70 weeks, because after Israel rejected the Messiah it was no longer an object of sacred but only of profane history; but if such an argument be a sound one, it surely ought to apply to the prophecy, not less than to the history, and the event in question ought not to be referred to in the prophecy at all. It is, however (*ex hyp.*), referred to in it; and is there, to all appearance, placed before the commencement of the 70th week.

(5) If the R.V. of *v.* 27 be correct,—and it is certainly the natural meaning of the Heb.,—a reference to the death of Christ is excluded altogether; for the verse does not then describe the final *abolition* of material sacrifices, but their temporary *suspension* for 'half of the week.'

(ii) The principal alternative interpretation is the one adopted in this Commentary in the notes on ix. 24—27. According to this view the *terminus a quo* is B.C. 587—6, the probable date of the promises that Jerusalem should be rebuilt contained in Jer. xxx. 18, xxxi. 38—40; the 7 weeks of *v.* 25 end with B.C. 538, the date of the edict of Cyrus (the 'anointed one, the prince' of this verse); the 62 weeks, reckoned from 538, end with B.C. 171 (the date of the murder of Onias III., the 'anointed one' of *v.* 26); the last week extends from B.C. 171 to B.C. 164, the reference in *vv.* 26 *b*, 27, being to Antiochus Epiphanes, and to his acts of violence and persecution against the Jews. This interpretation does entire justice to the terms of the text: but it labours under one serious difficulty. The number of years from 538 to 171 is not 434 (=62 'weeks'), but 367; the number assigned in the prophecy is thus too large by 67. The difficulty is usually met, on the part of those who adopt this explanation, by the supposition that the author of Daniel followed an incorrect computation. There is no intrinsic improbability, it is urged, in such a supposition: for (1) the difficulty of calculating dates in the ancient world was much greater than is often supposed. Until the establishment of the Seleucid era, in B.C. 312, the Jews had no fixed era whatever; and a writer living in Jerusalem (*ex hyp.*) under Antiochus Epiphanes would have very imperfect materials for estimating correctly the chronology of the period here in question; the continuous chronology of the O.T. ceases with the destruction of Jerusalem B.C. 586,—or at least (2 K. xxv. 27) with the 37th year of the captivity of Jehoiachin (= B.C. 562): and though mention is made in the O.T. of the 70 years of the Chaldaean supremacy, or (cf. on ch. ix. 2) of the desolation of Judah, the length of the period between Cyrus and Alexander the Great could be ascertained exactly only by means of a knowledge of secular history which a Jew, living in such an age, was

DANIEL, IX. 147

not likely to possess. There would thus be nothing unreasonable in the assumption of a mis-computation for the interval between 538 and 171.

Cornill makes the clever suggestion that, in the absence of any fixed era for the period before B.C. 312, the 490 years were arrived at by a calculation based on the generations of high-priests. From the destruction of Jerusalem to Onias III. there were just 12 generations in the high-priestly family: 1. Jehozadak (1 Ch. vi. 15); 2. Jeshua (Ezr. iii. 2); 3. Joiakim; 4. Eliashib; 5. Joiada; 6. Jonathan; 7. Jaddua (Neh. xii. 10, 11); 8. Onias I. (Jos. *Ant.* XI. viii. 7); 9. Simon I. the 'Just' (*ib.* XII. ii. 4); 10. Onias[1] II. (*ib.* XII. iv. 1); 11. Simon II.; and 12. his son Onias III. (*ib.* XII. iv. 10): and a generation being reckoned at 40 years, 12 generations (=480 years) might readily suggest 69 weeks (=483 years) for the period from the destruction of Jerusalem to the date of the death of Onias, and 70 weeks (=490 years) for the entire interval contemplated by the author.

(2) It is remarkable that, as has been pointed out by Schürer[2], precisely similar chronological mistakes are made by other Jewish writers. Thus Josephus (*B. J.* VI. iv. 8) says that there were 639 years between the second year of Cyrus (B.C. 537 or 536) and the destruction of Jerusalem by Titus (A.D. 70): the real interval was thus reckoned by him as longer by some 30 years than it should be. Further, the same writer reckons (*Ant.* XX. x.) 434 years from the Return from the Captivity (B.C. 538) to the reign of Antiochus Eupator (B.C. 164—162), i.e. 374 years, and (*Ant.* XIII. xi. 1) 481 years from the same date to the time of Aristobulus (B.C. 105—4) i.e. 433 years,—the former calculation being 60 years, and the latter nearly 50 years, in excess of the true amount. The Hellenistic Jew, Demetrius (Clem. Al. *Strom.* i. 21, § 141), reckons 573 years from the Captivity of the Ten Tribes (B.C. 722) to the time of Ptolemy IV. (B.C. 222), i.e. 500 years; he thus over-estimates the true period by 73 years[3]. There seems in fact, as Schürer has remarked, to have been a traditional error in the ancient chronology of the period here in question: it was over-estimated,—by Demetrius to approximately the same extent as by the author of Daniel. There is thus nothing astonishing in the fact 'that an apocalyptic writer of the date of Epiphanes, basing his calculations on uncertain data to give an allegoric interpretation to an ancient prophecy, should have lacked the records which would alone have enabled him to calculate with exact precision' (Farrar, *Daniel*, p. 291).

What may be termed a modification of this interpretation has been adopted by Hilgenfeld[4], also by Behrmann, the most recent commentator on Daniel. According to this view, the *terminus a quo* is B.C. 606 or

---

[1] Son of Simon I., though not his immediate successor in the high-priestly office: being an infant at the time of his father's death, he was preceded in the office first by his own uncle Eleazar, and then by Eleazar's uncle, Manasseh (*Ant.* XII. ii. 4, iv. 10).

[2] *Gesch. des Jüd. Volkes im Zeitalter Jesu Christi*, ii. 616 (Engl. tr. II. iii. p. 54).

[3] As Behrmann, however, has pointed out, this mistake is not quite certain; for in the figures of Demetrius, as quoted by Clement, there is some confusion: he reckons, viz., from the Captivity of Israel to that of Judah 128 years, 8 months, and from that of Judah to Ptol. IV. 338 years, 3 months,—both together thus equalling 466 years, 11 months; and yet for the whole period from the Captivity of Israel to Ptol. IV. he assigns 573 years, 9 months!—König (*Expos. Times*, 1899, p. 256 f.) explains a curious (early mediæval) example of the opposite error (327 years from Uzziah to Alexander, and the Persian period contracted to 52 years).

[4] *Die Jüdische Apokalyptik* (1857), p. 29 f.

605, the date of Jer. xxv., the promise contained in *vv.* 11 f. being the 'word' of *v.* 24 here; the 7 weeks (=49 years) end with B.C. 558; the 62 weeks (434 years), reckoned, not as following the 7 weeks, but as beginning from the same point that they do, end correctly with 171, the year in which Onias was murdered; and the last week ends with 164, the year of Antiochus's death. The 7 weeks are thus included in the 62 weeks, and the entire number of weeks, reckoned consecutively, is not 70, but 63; it is, however, urged that the stress lies not upon the length of the period concerned in itself, but upon the events embraced in it, in so far as these depend upon a Divine decree; and so the sum of the years remains 70, even though the years do not follow consecutively. No doubt, it is not expressly stated either that the $7+62+1$ weeks of *vv.* 25—27 make up the 70 weeks of *v.* 24, or that the 62 weeks of *v.* 25 begin at the close of the 7 weeks mentioned in the same verse; nevertheless, it may be doubted whether an explanation which assumes the contrary is altogether natural. It might further be objected to this interpretation, (1) that a promise for the rebuilding of Jerusalem is not contained in Jer. xxv. 11 f., except, at most, implicitly; and (2) that for the first 7 'weeks' of the 62 (B.C. 606—558) no attempt whatever was made to 'rebuild' Jerusalem.

Van Lennep seeks to solve the difficulty by combining the historical with the symbolical interpretation: 60 weeks of years would have corresponded more exactly with the period from B.C. 588 to 164, but it would not have had the symbolical completeness of 70×7 (Gen. iv. 24; Matth. xviii. 22): the 7×7 years at the beginning, and the 7 years at the end, though both agree substantially with the actual periods (B.C. 588—538, and B.C. 171—164), are also primarily symbolical; 7×7 years is a jubile-period (Lev. xxv. 8 &c.), at the end of which Israel returns to Palestine, as the slave returns to his home; and the 7 years of trial are analogous to the 7 years of famine (Gen. xli. 30; 2 Sam. xxiv. 13; 2 Ki. viii. 1), or the seven 'times' of Nebuchadnezzar's madness, or the seven troubles of Job v. 19: the 62 intermediate weeks of years have thus no independent significance of their own, but are simply the residue which remains after the subtraction of $7+1$ from 70.

Specimens of other interpretations:—

(1) Wieseler (1846): *terminus a quo,* 4th year of Jehoiakim (Jer. xxv), B.C. 606[1]: 62 weeks thence end B.C. 172[1]; the last week is 172—165[1] (*vv.* 26—27). The '7 weeks' extend from 172 to the coming of Christ (the 'anointed one, the prince'), and represent a jubile-period (Is. lxi. 1, 2), to be understood in a spiritual sense, and not limited to 50 literal years.

(2) Delitzsch (1878): *terminus a quo,* Jehoiakim's fourth year, B.C. 605 (Jer. xxv.): 62 weeks thence end with 171 (the deposition and murder of Onias, *v.* 26); one week thence carries us to the death of Antiochus in 164 (*v.* 27). The '7 weeks' follow the 62+1: the 'anointed one, the prince' of *v.* 25 is the Messiah; as, however, the Advent of Christ did not take place 7 weeks (=49 years) after B.C. 164, Delitzsch owns the 'riddle' of the 7 weeks to be insoluble. The '70

---

[1] Different authorities vary by a year or so in the dates assigned by them to the same events.

weeks,' however, are 'quadratic sabbath-periods,' each consisting of $7 \times 7 = 49$ years; there are thus $49 \times 70 = 3430$ years from B.C. 605 to the Advent of Christ (the first and second advents being not distinguished). This result, it is added, is recommended by the fact that, as there were 3595 years from the Creation to Jehoiakim's fourth year, the entire duration of the world would be not appreciably in excess of 7000 years.

(3) Kranichfeld (1868)[1]: *terminus a quo*, c. 592 (Jer. xxix.) or 588 (destruction of Jerusalem). The 7 weeks end in 539 (the year of Daniel's vision). The 'anointed one, the prince' is Cyrus. The 62 weeks begin in 539, and end with the death of Christ (the 'anointed one' of *v.* 26). Certainly, in point of fact the 62 weeks end with B.C. 105, *vv.* 26 *b*, 27 referring to the time of Maccabees: there is thus a *lacuna* of 135 years (from B.C. 105 to A.D. 30), which Daniel, in accordance with the laws of 'perspective' prophecy, did not see.

(4) Von Orelli (1882)[2]: *terminus a quo*, B.C. 588: end of 7 weeks, B.C. 536; end of 62 weeks, A.D. 29 (the death of Christ, to whom the 'anointed one' in both *v.* 25 and *v.* 26 refers); 434 years from 536 is indeed only *c.* B.C. 100, but the 'weeks' are typical weeks, and are not to be taken as mere mathematical quantities. The 'redactor' of the Book of Daniel (who lived in the age of Antiochus Epiphanes) identified the last 'week' with his own time; and it seems to be Orelli's opinion that he modified the terms of *vv.* 26, 27 so as to introduce into them allusions to the events of B.C. 171—164.

(5) Nägelsbach (1858): *terminus a quo*, B.C. 536; end of 7 weeks, the dedication of the walls of Nehemiah (Neh. xii.), B.C. 434—2; end of 62 weeks thence, the birth of Christ; the last week, from birth of Christ to destruction of Jerusalem, A.D. 70. שָׁבוּעַ, 'week,' upon this theory may denote any 'heptad,' not one of 7 years only, but also one of any multiple of 7; in the first 7 weeks, it is of about 14 years; in the last week, of about 70 years.

(6) Kliefoth (1868), and Keil (1869): *terminus a quo*, the edict of Cyrus, B.C. 537; the weeks are to be understood symbolically, not of chronologically definite periods of time. The seven weeks extend from 537 to the advent of Christ; the 62 weeks from Christ to the appearance of Antichrist; during this time Jerusalem (in a spiritual sense, i.e. the Church) is built; the last week is the period of the great apostasy, ending with the second Coming of Christ. The words, 'an anointed one shall be cut off,' refer to the ruin of Christ's kingdom upon earth in the days of Antichrist (the 'prince that shall come'); *v.* 27 (the 70th week) relates throughout to the high-handed dealings of Antichrist; *v.* 24 to his final overthrow.

(7) Julius Africanus, the chronographer (*c.* 200 A.D.), *ap.* Jerome, *l.c.*: *terminus a quo*, the 20th year of Artaxerxes (B.C. 445); end of 70 weeks (reckoned as 490 *lunar* years of 354 days = (nearly) 475 solar years), death of Christ. This view has been revived recently, in a slightly modified form, by Dr Robert Anderson[3], according to whom the 'year'

---
[1] *Das Buch Daniel erklärt*, 1868.
[2] *O.T. Prophecy*, Engl. tr. (1885), p. 434 f.
[3] *The Coming Prince*, ed. 5 (1895), p. 123 ff.

of Daniel was the ancient luni-solar year of 360 days; reckoning, then, 483 years (= 69 'weeks'), of 360 days each, from 1 Nisan B.C. 445, the date of the edict of Artaxerxes, Dr Anderson arrives at the 10th of Nisan, in the 18th year of Tiberius Caesar, the day on which our Lord made His public entry into Jerusalem (Luke xix. 37 ff.). Upon this theory, however, even supposing the objections against B.C. 445 as the *terminus a quo* (see above) to be waived, the 70th week remains unexplained; for the 7 years following the Crucifixion are marked by no events tallying with the description given in *v.* 27.

It is impossible to regard any of these interpretations as satisfactory, or, in fact, as being anything else than a resort of desperation. Even of the interpretation adopted in this Commentary, it must be owned that, like the rival traditional interpretation, it is not free from objection. When, however, it is asked, which of these two interpretations labours under the most serious objection, it can hardly be denied that it is the traditional one. As has been shewn (p. 144 ff.), there are points of crucial significance, at which the supposed fulfilment does not tally at all with the terms of the prediction. On the other hand, a chronological error, which would be in principle inconsistent with a prediction given by direct supernatural revelation, is not a conclusive objection to an interpretation in which (*ex hyp.*) the prediction does not extend to the figures here in question, but is limited to the announcement of the approaching fall of Antiochus (*v.* 26 *b*, 27), and of the advent of the ideal age of righteousness which is then to commence (*v.* 24). The general parallelism of *vv.* 26 *b*, 27,—especially the suspension of the Temple services for 'half of the week,'—with other passages of the book where the persecutions of Antiochus are alluded to (as vii. 25, viii. 11, 13, xi. 31, xii. 7, 11), and the fact that elsewhere in c. vii.—xii. Antiochus is the prominent figure, and his age is that in which the prophecies culminate, are arguments which support the modern interpretation. The prophecy does not, upon this interpretation, cease to be a Messianic one: it promises an ideal end of the sin and trouble under which the people of God are at present suffering; and is thus Messianic in the broader sense of Is. iv. 3 f., and the other passages quoted in the note on 'everlasting righteousness,' *v.* 24. See further pp. lxxxvi f., lxxxix.; König, *Neue Kirchl. Ztschr.* 1900, pp. 1003—13, *Exp. Times*, xiii. 468—70.

Additional Note on the Expression 'The abomination of desolation.'

The following expressions occur in Daniel:—

1. viii. 13 הַפֶּשַׁע שֹׁמֵם; LXX. Theod. ἡ ἁμαρτία ἐρημώσεως.

2. ix. 27 שִׁקּוּצִים מְשֹׁמֵם; LXX. Theod. βδέλυγμα τῶν ἐρημώσεων.

3. xi. 31 הַשִּׁקּוּץ מְשֹׁמֵם; LXX. βδέλυγμα ἐρημώσεως (so 1 Macc. i. 54, of the heathen altar built by Antiochus on the altar of burnt-offering), Theod. βδέλυγμα ἠφανισμένον.

4. xii. 11 שִׁקּוּץ שֹׁמֵם; LXX. τὸ βδέλυγμα τῆς ἐρημώσεως (so Matth. xxiv. 15, Mk xiii. 14[1]), Theod. βδέλυγμα ἐρημώσεως.

[1] In the parallel in St Luke (xxi. 20) the expression is paraphrased ('when ye see *Jerusalem encompassed with armies*, then know that her *desolation* is at hand').

The explanation of these expressions is difficult. Neither שֹׁמֵם nor מְשֹׁמֵם can really mean 'desolation.' מְשֹׁמֵם might mean either *desolating* or *appalling*: שָׁמֵם (also ix. 27 *end*) would naturally mean either *desolated* or *appalled* (see on viii. 23), but neither of these renderings suits the subst. with which it is joined; it is, however, possible that, by an irregularity of form, of which there are a few examples (see *ibid.*), it might have an active force, *desolating* or *appalling*: but the absence of the art. before שֹׁמֵם in (1) and (3) is anomalous (Ges.-Kautzsch, § 126 *s*); and in (2) the plur. שִׁקּוּצִים (if this word is rightly connected with מְשֹׁמֵם) is impossible, though the correction שִׁקּוּץ מְשֹׁמֵם would here be an easy one. On the whole, the supposition that the ptcp. in each case means *appalling, horror-causing*, is the one that is least free from difficulty,—the word used being chosen possibly (as explained on xi. 31) for the sake of its assonance with שָׁמַיִם 'heaven.'

As regards the two passages in the N.T., three things may be observed. (1) In St Mark the best MSS. and editions (as Tisch., Westcott and Hort, and so R.V.) have the *masc. ἑστηκότα* (hence R.V. 'standing where *he* ought not'), and omit the words 'spoken of by Daniel the prophet' (which have been introduced from the parallel text of St Matthew, where they are contained in all MSS.). (2) The *interpretation* of the expressions in the N.T. is uncertain: the context, however, shews that it must refer to something—or rather (Mk.) to some *one*—standing in the Temple,—as is generally supposed, not long before its destruction by Titus (in which case the statue of a Roman emperor might, for instance, be intended[1]), though others suppose the reference to be to an expected future Antichrist (cf. 2 Thes. ii. 4)[2]. (3) As regards the bearing of our Lord's use of the expression upon the interpretation of it in the Book of Daniel, it is to be observed that in St Mark's Gospel, which has the presumption of presenting the 'synoptic tradition' in a more primitive and original form than the other Gospels, there is *no reference to Daniel at all*; hence, especially in view of the fondness of St Matthew for O.T. references, it becomes probable that even in the first Gospel the words, 'spoken of by Daniel the prophet,' are not part of our Lord's discourse, but are a comment added by the Evangelist. If this conclusion be accepted, it will follow that our Lord pronounces no judgement on the sense in which the expression is to be interpreted in Daniel: it is the expression alone which He borrows: His use of it by no means necessarily implies that He intends to denote by it the same object which it denotes in Daniel; and His authority cannot therefore be invoked against the interpretation of the expression, as used in Daniel, which has been adopted above.

[1] See for this and other cognate views the art. ABOMINATION OF DESOLATION in Hastings' *Dict. of the Bible*. A further discussion of the subject does not belong here.
[2] See ABOMINATION OF DESOLATION, and ANTICHRIST (§ 4), in the *Encyclopædia Biblica*; and cf. MAN OF SIN in Hastings' *Dict.* (§ iv.).

10 In the third year of Cyrus king of Persia a thing was revealed unto Daniel, whose name was called Belteshazzar; and the thing *was* true, but the time appointed *was* long: and he understood the thing, and had understanding of 2 the vision. In those days I Daniel was mourning three

CHAP. X.—XII. HISTORY OF THE SELEUCIDAE AND PTOLEMIES. REIGN OF ANTIOCHUS EPIPHANES, AND HIS TREATMENT OF THE JEWS. ADVENT OF THE KINGDOM OF GOD.

These three chapters form a whole, describing a vision of Daniel in the third year of Cyrus, by the Ḥiddeḳel (the Tigris), and (ch. xi., xii.) the revelations respecting the future which Daniel received in it from an angel. Daniel had fasted for 21 days, when he fell into a state of trance or vision, in which he saw a shining being standing before him, who told him that he had been sent in answer to his prayers, but that he had been prevented from reaching him before by the opposition of the 'prince' (i.e. the guardian-angel) of Persia; with the help of Michael, the 'prince,' or guardian-angel, of the Jews, he had at length been able to start on his mission, and he was now here in order to give Daniel a revelation concerning the future (x. 1—19). After a few introductory words (x. 20—xi. 1), the revelation follows in xi. 2—xii. 4 (there should be no break either at x. 21 or at xi. 45), a solemn concluding statement respecting the duration of the coming period of trial being given in the concluding dialogue, xii. 5—13.

This, the last vision contained in the Book, is also the most circumstantial; both the history of the Diadochi, and also the events of Antiochus Epiphanes' own reign, being described in much greater detail than had been given before (xi. 2—45), and the felicity to begin afterwards being more distinctly outlined (xii. 1—3).

(1) x. 1—xi. 1. Introductory. Daniel's vision, and his colloquy with the shining angel.

1. *king of Persia*] A title, not borne by the Persian kings while the Persian empire still lasted, though often given to them after it had passed away, as a mark of distinction from the Greek rulers who then followed[1].

a thing] or, *a* word: cf. ix. 23 *b*, and (Aram.) iv. 33.

Belteshazzar] See on i. 7; and cf. v. 12.

and the word (is) *true*, **and a great warfare**] The revelation is true (cf. viii. 26), and relates besides to a period of severe hardship and trial. 'Warfare' has the same figurative sense which it has in Is. xl. 2; Job vii. 1, xiv. 14 (A.V. in Job, as here, *appointed time*, following the interpretation of Kimchi; R.V. rightly *warfare*, figuratively of the hardships of life).

and he understood &c.] *and he* **gave heed unto** *the* **word**.

2. *was mourning*] or, *continued mourning*. The motive of Daniel's mourning is not stated; but it may be inferred from *v.* 12 (cf. ix. 3) to

---

[1] See the writer's *Introduction*, p. 511 f., with p. 512, *n.* 3 (ed. 6, p. 545, with p. 546, *n.* *; in ed. 8, 1909, revised and enlarged, pp. 545, 546, *n.* *, 554 *Add. Note*).

full weeks. I ate no pleasant bread, neither came flesh 3
nor wine in my mouth, neither did I anoint myself at all,
till three whole weeks were fulfilled. And in the four and 4
twentieth day of the first month, as I was by the side of
the great river, which *is* Hiddekel; then I lift up mine eyes, 5
and looked, and behold, a certain man clothed *in* linen,

have been grief for his people's sin (cf. Ezr. x. 6), and anxiety about its future (cf. Neh. i. 4).

three full weeks] **three weeks long.** Lit. *three weeks, days*—a pleonastic idiom, which occurs elsewhere (e.g. Gen. xli. 1; Deut. xxi. 13; 2 Sam. xiii. 23)[1]. 'Full' emphasizes the expression unduly.

3. *pleasant bread*] lit. *bread of desirablenesses* (ix. 23). Daniel did not fast absolutely; he only abstained from 'pleasant' food. *Flesh* and *wine* would, in the East, not be indulged in except at a festivity, or on other special occasions (e.g. Gen. xxvii. 25, 1 Sam. xxv. 11 [where LXX. followed by many moderns, has *wine* for *water*]; Is. xxii. 13).

neither did I anoint myself at all] The practice of anointing the body with oil or other unguents was common among the Jews, as among other ancient nations: it soothed and refreshed the skin, and was a protection against heat. It was customary after washing, especially in anticipation of a visit, a feast, &c. (Ruth iii. 3); and so to be anointed was a mark of contentment and joy (Is. lxi. 3, Eccl. ix. 8; cf. Matth. vi. 17), while, conversely, during mourning it was usual not to anoint oneself (2 Sam. xiv. 2; cf. xii. 20).

three whole weeks] The same expression which in *v.* 2 is rendered *full weeks.*

4. *the first month*] Abib (Ex. xxiii. 15), or (as it was called by the later Jews) Nisan (Neh. ii. 1),—the month in which the Passover (on the 14th day) and feast of Unleavened Cakes (15th—21st) were kept (Ex. xii. 1—13, 14—20). These sacred seasons thus fell within the period of Daniel's fast.

the great river] elsewhere the Euphrates (Gen. xv. 18; Josh. i. 4): here, of the *Ḥiddeḳel* (Gen. ii. 14), i.e. the Tigris (Ass. *Idiglat* or *Idiḳlat*): cf. the Syr. form *Deḳlath*. (*Tigris* is probably a Persian modification of the same name, suggested by the Old Pers. *tighri*, arrow [cf. *tighra*, pointed, sharp], on account of the swiftness of its stream: see Delitzsch, *Paradies*, p. 170 ff., who cites Strabo, xi. 14, 8, διὰ τὴν ὀξύτητα, ἀφ᾽ οὗ καὶ τοὔνομα, Μήδων τίγριν καλούντων τὸ τόξευμα.)

5—9. The dazzling being seen by Daniel in his vision, and the effects of the spectacle upon him. For a vision following a *fast*, cf. Apoc. of Baruch v. 7, ix. 2, xii. 5, xx. 5, 6, xxi. 1, xliii. 3, xlvii. 2; 2 Esdr. v. 13, 20, vi. 31, 35, ix. 24, 26, xii. 51: also Acts x. 10.

5. *lift up mine eyes*] in the vision: cf. viii. 3.

and saw] Daniel (*v.* 4) was on the side of the river; and it appears from xii. 6, 7, that the figure which he beheld was directly above the river itself, and consequently (x. 16) 'in front of' him. The description

---

[1] See Ges.-Kautzsch, § 131 d.

6 whose loins *were* girded with fine gold of Uphaz: his body also *was* like the beryl, and his face as the appearance of lightning, and his eyes as lamps of fire, and his arms and his feet like in colour to polished brass, and the voice of 7 his words like the voice of a multitude. And I Daniel

of the shining being which follows, contains many reminiscences of Ez. i. and ix.

a certain man] a man : the Hebrew idiom, as 1 Ki. xxii. 9, &c.

clothed in linen] The expression is suggested probably by Ez. ix. 2, 3, 11, x. 2, 6, 7. (White) linen garments were worn (on certain occasions) by priests or others performing sacred offices (Lev. vi. 10, xvi. 4; 1 Sam. ii. 18, xxii. 18; 2 Sam. vi. 14). Here, as in Ezek., the linen vesture indicates a celestial visitant: cf. Mark xvi. 5, Rev. xv. 6 (R.V. *marg.*).

whose loins, &c.] A girdle richly ornamented with gold was about his loins.

fine gold] Heb. *kéthem*, a choice, poetical word (e.g. Job xxviii. 19, xxxi. 24), the one generally used in the expression 'gold of Ophir' (Job xxviii. 16 ; Ps. xlv. 9; Is. xiii. 12).

Uphaz] only besides in Jer. x. 9, 'gold (*zāhāb*) from Uphaz.' No place Uphaz is, however, known; hence the reading in Jer. is probably corrupt, and we should read there 'from Ophir' (with Targ., Pesh., MSS. of LXX., and many moderns). Either the author of Daniel borrowed the expression from Jer. x. 9, after the text there had been corrupted; or we may suppose that *Uphaz* (אוּפָז) here is simply a scribal error for *Ophir* (אוֹפִר) : comp. the last note.

6. The dazzling appearance of his person.

His body] The word used in Ez. i. 11, 23.

the beryl] *the* chrysolith (as LXX. in Ex. and Ez. xxviii. 13)—said (see Smith, *D. B.*, s. v. BERYL) to be the topaz of the moderns—a flashing stone, described by Pliny as 'a transparent stone with a refulgence like that of gold.' Comp. Ex. xxviii. 20, and especially Ez. i. 16, x. 9, where the wheels of the chariot in Ez.'s vision are compared to the same stone. The Heb. is *tarshish*: it may be so called, as Pliny says of the chrysolith, on account of its having been brought from Spain (Tarshish, Tartessus).

as the appearance of lightning,...as torches *of fire*] cf. Ez. i. 13 (R.V. *marg.*), 'In the midst of the living creatures was an appearance like burning coals of fire, like the appearance of *torches*...and out of the fire went forth *lightning*.'

like the gleaming *of* burnished *brass*] from Ez. i. 7 (of the feet of the cherubic figures which supported the throne) 'and they sparkled *like the gleaming of burnished brass.*' *Gleaming* is lit. *eye*, fig. of something sparkling : so Ez. i. 4, 16, 22, 27, viii. 2, x. 9 ; Prov. xxiii. 31 (A.V. in all 'colour').

the voice of his words] or, *the* sound *of his words*: the words do not seem to become articulate until *v.* 11.

like the voice of a multitude] Is. xiii. 4 (the Heb. for 'voice,'

vv. 8—10.] DANIEL, X. 155

alone saw the vision: for the men that were with me saw
not the vision; but a great quaking fell upon them, so that
they fled to hide themselves. Therefore I was left alone, 8
and saw this great vision, and there remained no strength
in me: for my comeliness was turned in me into corruption,
and I retained no strength. Yet heard I the voice of his 9
words: and when I heard the voice of his words, then
was I in a deep sleep on my face, and my face toward the
ground. And behold, a hand touched me, which set me 10

'sound,' 'noise' is the same). But the expression is perhaps suggested
by Ez. i. 24 (R.V.) 'a noise of tumult' (where the Heb. for *tumult*
partly resembles that for *multitude* here). An impressive, but in-
articulate, sound seems to be what the comparison is intended to
suggest. With the last three clauses of this verse, comp. the description of the risen Christ in Rev. i. 14 *b*, 15.

7. Cf. Acts ix. 7, xxii. 9.

howbeit (*v.* 21) *a great quaking*] or *trembling*: the Heb. is the same
as in Gen. xxvii. 33 (lit. 'Isaac trembled with *a great trembling*').
They may have seen the effects of the vision upon Daniel (cf. *v.* 8).

8—9. Daniel was left alone, and fell motionless, as if stunned, upon
the earth.

8. **And I** (emph.) *was left alone, and saw this great vision*] 'great,'
on account of the majestic appearance of the angel.

and there **was left** (*v.* 17) *no strength in me*] Cf. 1 Sam. xxviii. 20.
The vision itself is more impressive than that of Gabriel in viii. 16—18,
and its effects upon Daniel are more marked. Comp. Rev. i. 17.

comeliness] The meaning is dignity of countenance. *Majesty*, *glory*,
is the idea of the word: cf. (of God) Ps. viii. 1, Hab. iii. 3; (of a
king), Ps. xlv. 3, Jer. xxii. 18 ('Ah lord! **or**, Ah his *glory*!'); of the
Israel of the future, compared to a nobly-spreading tree, Hos. xiv. 6
(where 'beauty,' A.V., R.V., is inadequate).

was turned **upon** *me into corruption*] i.e. disfigured, or destroyed, by
sudden pallor. The Hebrew word rendered 'corruption' is cognate
with that rendered 'marred' in Is. lii. 14 (also of the countenance).
For 'upon,' cf. v. 9, vii. 28; and see on ii. 1.

retained no strength] In the Heb., a late idiom, found otherwise only
v. 16, xi. 6; 1 Chr. xxix. 14; 2 Chr. ii. 5, xiii. 20, xxii. 9.

9. **And** *I heard the voice*, &c.] or, *the* **sound** (twice): see on *v.* 6.

then was I in, &c.] R.V. *then was I fallen into a deep sleep.*
The clause appears to describe, not the effect of the words which
Daniel heard, but the state in which he already was, when he heard
them. On the expression *a deep* (or *dead*) sleep, see on viii. 18.

on my face, **with** *my face*, &c.] cf. viii. 17, 18.

10—18. Daniel is gradually revived and reassured.

10. An invisible hand, touching him, reassured him, and partly
raised him up.

set me] lit. *caused me to move to and fro* or *totter* (see on Am. iv. 8),

11 upon my knees and *upon* the palms of my hands. And he said unto me, O Daniel, a man greatly beloved, understand the words that I speak unto thee, and stand upright: for unto thee am I now sent. And when he had spoken 12 this word unto me, I stood trembling. Then said he unto me, Fear not, Daniel: for from the first day that thou didst set thine heart to understand, and to chasten thyself before thy God, thy words were heard, and I am come 13 for thy words. But the prince of the kingdom of Persia

i.e. here, as the context shews, 'set me tottering upon my knees,' &c.: so R.V. *marg.* Cf. 2 Esdr. v. 15.

11. *And he said unto me*] The speaker is the dazzling being described in *vv.* 5, 6.

thou man greatly beloved] greatly desired, lit. *man of desirablenesses*: see on ix. 23.

stand upright] lit. *stand upon thy standing*, the idiom explained on viii. 18.

for now am I sent unto thee] now, i.e. (ix. 22) *at last*, after the delay described in *v.* 12.

trembling] that I should have been accosted by a being so august. The word, as Ezr. x. 9 (not as *v.* 7, above).

12. *set thine heart*] lit. *give thine heart*, i.e. apply thyself: a late idiom, found otherwise only in 1 Chr. xxii. 19; 2 Chr. xi. 16; Eccl. i. 13, 17, vii. 21, viii. 9, 16.

to understand] viz. the future destiny of Israel. Anxious questionings on the future of his people were the occasion of his prolonged mourning and abstinence (*vv.* 2, 3).

and to humble *thyself before thy God*] The verb, though it may be used more generally (Ps. cvii. 17), is applied here, as in Ezr. viii. 21 ('then I proclaimed a fast there, at the river Ahava, that we might *humble ourselves before our God*, to seek of him a straight way,' &c.), to the self-denial and mortification accompanying a *fast*. The more common (and technical) expression in the same sense is *to humble* (or [R.V.] *afflict*) *the soul*: see Lev. xvi. 29, 31; xxiii. 27, 29, 32; Num. xxix. 7 (all of the fast of the Day of Atonement); Is. lviii. 3, 5; Ps. xxxv. 13 ('I humbled my soul in fasting'); in a more general sense, Num. xxx. 13 (of a vow of self-denial). The corresponding subst. *ta'ănîth* has the same meaning in Ezr. **ix.** 5 (R.V. *marg.*); and regularly in post-Biblical Hebrew (the Mishnic treatise 'Ta'anith' deals with *fasting*).

and I am come because of *thy words*] i.e. the prayer implied in *vv.* 2, 3. 'I am come' is resumed at the beginning of *v.* 14, the explanation of the angel's delay in *v.* 13 being parenthetical.

13. The opposition, for 21 days (cf. *v.* 2), of the 'prince,' i.e. the patron-angel, of Persia, prevented the dazzling being from reaching Daniel sooner.

the prince of the kingdom of Persia] its patron- or guardian-angel.

withstood me one and twenty days: but lo, Michael, one

The doctrine of tutelary angels, presiding over the destinies of particular nations, though there appears a trace of the idea in Is. xxiv. 21, and according to some commentators, in Ps. lxxxii., is found for the first time distinctly in the O.T. in this prophecy of Dan. (x. 13, 20, 21, xi. 1, xii. 1). In the earlier books of the O.T. angels appear merely as the 'messengers' of Jehovah, with little or no personal character or distinctness of their own: in the later books of the O.T. grades and differences begin to be recognised among them; particular angels are appropriated to particular purposes or functions; and they begin to receive individual names (see below). The origin of the idea of patron-angels is matter of conjecture: even as applied to Israel, it evidently signifies more than is implied in such passages as Ex. xxiii. 20, 23, xxxii. 34, xxxiii. 2 (which speak of an angel leading Israel to its home in Canaan). According to some (see the art. ANGEL in the *Encycl. Biblica*, col. 108), they are the ancient 'gods of the nations,'—which, according to Deut. xxix. 26 (cf. iv. 19), are 'allotted' by Jehovah to the several peoples of the earth,—transformed into 'angels,' under the teachings of a more consistent monotheism, for the purpose of being more distinctly subordinated to Him; according to others (see the art. ANGEL in Hastings' *Dict. of the Bible*, p. 96 *b*), the idea is due to the tendencies which arose in later times, (1) of conceiving God as ruling the world by intermediate agencies, and (2) of personifying abstract conceptions, such as the 'spirit,' or genius, of a nation, and of locating such personified forces in the supersensible world, whence they ruled the destinies of men. Other passages in which the same idea is found are Ecclus. xvii. 17 ἑκάστῳ ἔθνει κατέστησεν ἡγούμενον); and Deut. xxxii. 8 LXX. ('he fixed the borders of the peoples according to the number *of the sons of God* [אל for ישראל],' a reading thought by some moderns to be the original). The later Jews developed the doctrine further, teaching, for instance, that each of the 70 nations mentioned in Gen. x. had its Angel-Prince, who defended its interests, and pleaded its cause with God (cf. the Targ. of Ps.-Jon. on Gen. xi. 7, 8 and Deut. xxxii. 8; and Weber, *System der Altsynag. Theol.*, p. 165 f.).

Michael] the patron-angel of the Jews (*v.* 21, xii. 1). The idea of the passage is that the fortunes of nations are determined by the angels representing them in heaven: the success or failure of these regulating the success or failure of the nations themselves. Cf. Is. xxiv. 21.

As was remarked in the last note but one, it is not till the later books of the O.T. that angels begin to receive names. The only angels mentioned by name in O.T. and N.T. are 'the Satan' (i.e. the unfriendly Opposer or Thwarter: see Davidson's note on Job i. 6), Job i.—ii., Zech. iii. 1, 2, 1 Ch. xxi. 1 [*altered* from the parallel, 2 Sam. xxiv. 1], and frequently in the N.T.; Michael, here and *v.* 21, xii. 1, Jude 9, Rev. xii. 7; and Gabriel, Daniel viii. 16, ix. 21, Luke i. 19, 26.

In the extra-canonical books other names of angels appear. Thus in the Book of Tobit, an angel Raphael is named, who, disguised as a man, performs various offices for Tobit and Tobias (iii. 17, *v.* 4, &c.); in xii. 15 (cf. *v.* 12), he is said to be 'one of the seven

of the chief princes, came to help me; and I remained

holy angels [cf. Enoch lxxxi. 5 'those seven holy ones,' xc. 21, 22] which present the prayers of the saints' to God. In 2 (4) Esdr. iv. 1, v. 20, x. 28, Uriel is mentioned; and in iv. 36 (R.V.) Jeremiel, the 'archangel.' In the book of Enoch many names of angels occur: in ix. 1 [see the Greek text, in Charles' ed., p. 333] and elsewhere, Michael, Uriel, Raphael, and Gabriel; in xx. 1—7 (p. 356 f., Charles) the names and offices of seven principal angels, or 'archangels,' are enumerated (Uriel, Raphael, Raguel, Michael, Sariel, Gabriel, and Remeiel); in xl. 2—10, those of four principal angels, called here 'presences' (cf. Is. lxiii. 9), Michael, Rufael (Raphael), Gabriel, and Phanuel (פנואל): the names of many fallen angels, who seduced the children of men (Gen. vi. 2, 5), are also given (vi. 7, viii. 1—3, lxix. 1—15, &c.). See, further, on the names and functions of angels in the later Jewish Angelology, Weber, *l.c.* p. 161 ff.; Edersheim, *Life and Times of Jesus*, ii. 745 ff.; and cf. A. B. Davidson's art. ANGEL in Hastings' *Dict. of the Bible.*

one of the chief princes] The reference is evidently to some group of superior angels, or (to adopt the later Greek expression) 'archangels.' In the book of Enoch, as has just been shewn, sometimes four angels (see esp. xl. 2—9), sometimes seven, are distinguished above the rest. Among the later Jews (Edersheim, *l.c.* p. 748 f.; *Midrash Rabba* on Numb. ii. 20) Michael, Gabriel, Uriel, and Raphael were usually regarded as the four principal angels, privileged to stand immediately about the throne of God; but seven are mentioned, not only in Enoch xx. 1—7, lxxxi. 5, xc. 21, but also in Tob. xii. 15 (see the last note), and Rev. viii. 2 ('the seven angels which stand before God'); and probably these seven are alluded to here. Cf. Jude 9, where Michael is called the 'archangel.'

Michael is the warrior-angel (cf. Rev. xii. 7), whose special office it is to protect the interests of Israel; in Enoch xx. 5 he is described as ὁ εἷς τῶν ἁγίων ἀγγέλων ὃς ἐπὶ τῶν τοῦ λαοῦ ἀγαθῶν τέτακται [καὶ] ἐπὶ τῷ λαῷ; in the Assumption of Moses x. 2 (ed. Charles, 1897) he appears to be the 'angel' who avenges Israel on their enemies at the end of the world; in the legend quoted in Jude 9 (see the patristic quotations, in Charles, *l. c.* p. 106 ff.), it is he who, as the angelic patron of Israel, defends the body of Moses against the devil (who claims it on the ground that Moses has been guilty of the murder of the Egyptians). For other extra-Biblical references to Michael, see Hastings' *Dict. of the Bible*, s. v.

remained there] properly, **was left over** *there* (the word used implying that others had departed, or been destroyed, Gen. xxxii. 24; 1 Sam. xxx. 9; 1 Ki. xix. 10; Am. vi. 9), though the meaning of the expression here is far from certain. According to some it is simply *I remained there*, which, however, does not do justice to the word used; according to v. Lengerke, Ges., and Keil, it is *I had the superiority*, i.e. obtained the victory (cf. Luther, *da behielt ich den Sieg*), the 'prince' of Persia having been, at least temporarily (see *v.* 20), disabled; according to

there with the kings of Persia. Now I am come to make 14 thee understand what shall befall thy people in the latter days: for yet the vision *is* for *many* days. And when he 15 had spoken such words unto me, I set my face toward the ground, and I became dumb. And behold, *one* like 16 the similitude of the sons of men touched my lips: then I

Ewald, it is *I was superfluous there*, i.e. (R.V. *marg.*) I was no longer needed. Meinh. and Behrm. follow LXX. and Theod. in reading *and I left him there* (הותרתיו for נותרתי); but this verb means not *to leave* simply, but *to leave over* or *remaining* (viz. from what has been taken elsewhere, Ez. xxxix. 28, or destroyed, Ex. x. 15, xvi. 19 *al.*): so that it is doubtful whether it would here be suitable. Perhaps, on the whole, we may acquiesce in the rend. *was left over* (viz. in the conflict): the 'prince of Persia,' for the time, succumbed; the angel, with Michael's aid, overcame his opposition, and so was able to come to Daniel.

beside (Neh. viii. 4) *the kings of Persia*] Both the plural, and also the statement itself that the angel, after his conflict, should have found himself 'beside' the kings of Persia, are strange. It is probable that we should read (with LXX., Meinh., Behrm.) 'beside *the prince of* the kings of Persia.'

14. And *I am come to make thee understand*, &c.] cf. viii. 16, ix. 22; also ix. 23 *b*.

what shall befall thy people **in the end of the** *days*] The sentence seems to be framed on the model of Gen. xlix. 1. On the 'end (a different word from that occurring in viii. 17, 19) of the days,' see on ii. 28. Here the expression denotes the age of Antiochus Epiphanes.

for **there is yet a** *vision for* **the** *days*] viz. the days just mentioned: a vision, relating to these, remains still to be told. Or, altering the point which indicates the article, *for the vision is yet for* (many) *days:* it relates to the 'end of the days,' not to the present; cf. viii. 17 *b*, 26 *b*.

15. In spite of the command not to fear (*v.* 12), and the encouraging nature of the words which followed (especially *v.* 12), Daniel does not recover his composure; and is only gradually reassured in the sequel (*vv.* 16—19).

I set..., and **was** *dumb*] As yet, he stood with his eyes fixed on the ground, dreading to look up and speechless.

16. A second touch restores Daniel's power of speech.

one *like* **the** *similitude*, &c.] not an actual man, but a figure or appearance resembling a man. The word rendered *similitude* is the one which in the visions of Ezekiel (i. 5, 10, 13, 16, 22, 26, 28, viii. 2, x. 1, 10, 21, 22) is rendered regularly by *likeness*: the variation here is presumably for the purpose of avoiding the juxtaposition of 'like' and 'likeness.'

touched my lips] cf.—though the expression is not quite the same, and the purpose is in each case different—Is. vi. 7 ('*made it*—the hot coal—*touch* my lips'), Jer. i. 9 ('*made it*—his hand—*touch* my mouth').

opened my mouth, and spake, and said unto him that
stood before me, O my lord, by the vision my sorrows
17 are turned upon me, and I have retained no strength. For
how can the servant of this my lord talk with this my
lord? for as for me, straightway there remained no strength
18 in me, neither is there breath left in me. Then there
came again and touched me *one* like the appearance of
19 a man, and he strengthened me, and said, O man greatly
beloved, fear not: peace *be* unto thee, be strong, yea,

The touch having restored Daniel's power of speech, he hastens to
excuse his confusion: the vision, he says, had overpowered him.

to him that stood **in front of** *me*] The dazzling being, whom Daniel
had seen in *vv.* 5, 6.

my lord] 1 Sam. i. 15, 26, xxii. 12, &c.; Zech. i. 9, iv. 4, 5, 13,
vi. 4.

by reason of *the vision my* **throes were** *turned upon me*] i.e. came
suddenly upon me. The word rendered *throes* is said properly of the
pains of a woman in travail (Is. xiii. 8); and the whole phrase occurs in
1 Sam. iv. 19 of the pains of labour suddenly seizing Ichabod's mother.
The figure is thus a strong one: it describes Daniel as being as prostrate
and helpless as a woman in the pains of labour. Cf. Is. xxi. 3, where
it is used similarly to describe the prostration produced by an alarming
vision.

and I **retained** *no strength*] *v.* 8, *end.*

17. *talk with this my lord*] with a being so glorious and terrible.

and *as for me, straightway* &c.] either *from now* (i.e. *from just now*)
there remaineth &c. (so most commentators); or (Keil) *from now* (i.e.
henceforth) *there will remain no strength in me,*—so paralysed, viz. am
I. The latter rendering is in accordance with the meaning of 'from
now' elsewhere; the former expresses a thought harmonizing better
with the clause which follows. 'Remain' is lit. *stand,* i.e. *maintain
itself:* cf. Eccl. ii. 9; and *kâm* in Josh. ii. 11.

neither is there breath, &c.] a hyperbole. Cf. (of actual death) 1 Ki.
xvii. 17; also, with 'spirit' for 'breath,' of the effects of fear, as here,
Josh. ii. 11; and of wonder, 1 Ki. x. 5.

18, 19. A third touch (see *vv.* 10, 16), followed by a second re-
assurance (see *vv.* 11—14) on the part of the dazzling being, restores
Daniel's composure entirely.

18. *one like the appearance of a man*] 'appearance,' as in viii. 15,
and often in the visions of Ezek. (i. 13, 14, 26, 27, 28, viii. 2, x. 1,
xlii. 11).

strengthened me] i.e. both restored my physical strength, and also
'encouraged' me, as the same word is rendered in Deut. i. 38, iii. 28.

19. *And* **he** *said*] The dazzling being described in *vv.* 5, 6, who
has been speaking in *vv.* 11 *a,* 12—14, and whom Daniel had addressed
in *vv.* 16 *b,* 17. Not the angel mentioned in *vv.* 16 *a,* 18.

Fear not (*v.* 12), *O man* **greatly desired**] *v.* 11.

be strong. And when he had spoken unto me, I was strengthened, and said, Let my lord speak; for thou hast strengthened me.

Then said he, Knowest thou wherefore I come unto 20 thee? and now will I return to fight with the prince of Persia: and when I am gone forth, lo, the prince of Grecia shall come. But I will shew thee that which is noted in the 21

be strong...was strengthened] as in *v*. 18. Cf. 2 Sam. x. 12, A.V., R.V. 'be of good courage, and let us play the man'; Heb., exactly as here, '*be strong*, and let us *strengthen ourselves* (or *be strengthened*)'; Ezr. vii. 28.

20—xi. 1. Before, however, the speaker proceeds to disclose the future to Daniel (xi. 2 ff.), in accordance with the promise of *v*. 14, he acquaints him with certain facts relating to the celestial world, calculated to inspire him with confidence: in himself, and Michael, the people of Israel have two champions able to defend them effectually against the assaults of heathen powers.

20. *Knowest thou*, &c.] A rhetorical question, designed to recall to Daniel what had been said in *vv*. 12, 14, and to indicate to him its importance.

and now will I return, &c.] to carry on and complete the successes begun in *v*. 13. 'Now' must mean, as soon as possible, as soon as I have given thee this revelation (xi. 2 ff.): I cannot tarry here longer than is necessary, as I have still to contend in heaven against the enemies of Israel.

and when I go forth (viz. from the contest with the 'prince' of Persia), *lo, the prince of* Greece (Heb. Javan, as viii. 21) **will come in**] As soon as the conflict with Persia is ended, one with Greece will begin: 'go forth' and 'come in,' as 2 Ki. xi. 5, 7. It would be more in accordance with the usual sense of *go forth* in such a connexion as the present, to understand it of *going forth to* the contest with the prince of Persia (cf. of going forth on a military expedition, with *to battle* expressed, Deut. xx. 1, xxi. 10; without it, Jud. ix. 29, 2 Sam. xi. 1, xviii. 2 (*end*), 3, 6, 2 Ki. ix. 21, &c.); but unless the future is greatly foreshortened, or 'go forth' **is** understood not of proceeding to, but of *continuing in*, the conflict (so Keil), this interpretation agrees hardly with the history; for the empire of Alexander and his successors did not arise till two centuries after the time of Cyrus.

21. Howbeit] 'but' is not strong enough: cf. *v*. 7. It is difficult to be sure what the thought tacitly opposed is: it may be, 'Howbeit (though I cannot stay long, *v*. 20 *a*), I can nevertheless tell thee this (xi. 2 ff.) about the future'; or 'Howbeit (though the contest, *v*. 20 *b*, may seem to be an endless one), I will tell thee about the future, for it contains, at least towards the end, an outlook of hope and consolation.'

I will **declare** (ii. 2) **unto** *thee that which is* **inscribed** *in the* **writing**

scripture of truth: and *there is* none that holdeth with me
11 in these *things*, but Michael your prince. Also I in the first year of Darius the Mede, *even* I, stood to confirm and to strengthen him.

of truth] i.e. the book in which God has inscribed beforehand, as truly as they will be fulfilled, the destinies of mankind: cf. Ps. cxxxix. 16. The figure is meant as a concrete expression of the truth that the future is *pre-determined* by God. The later apocalyptic writers often speak, in the same sense, of the 'heavenly tables,' in which the deeds and events of the future stand recorded; see e.g. Enoch lxxxi. 1, 2, xciii. 2, 3, ciii. 2, 3, cvi. 19, cvii. 1; and cf. the note in Charles' ed. p. 132 f.

inscribed] as in Aram. (v. 24, 25, vi. 8, 10) and New Hebrew. The word implies a more formal act than 'written.' *Noted* in Old Engl. has the force of *inscribed*: cf. *note* in Is. xxx. 8 for חקק, 'cut in,' 'engrave.'

and there is **not one** *that* **strengtheneth himself** *with me* **against** *these*, **except** *Michael your prince*] in my contest with the 'princes' of Persia and Greece (*v.* 20), only Michael supports me. The words seem to connect with the end of *v.* 20, rather than with the first part of *v.* 21, which is perhaps to be regarded as parenthetical.

strengtheneth himself *with me*] i.e. shews himself to be my valiant ally: cf. 1 Ch. xi. 10, 2 Ch. xvi. 9 (where 'in the behalf of' is lit. *with*, as here), xvii. 1.

xi. 1. And as for me, *in*...**I stood up to be a supporter** *and* **a stronghold unto him**] I myself, also, in the first year of Darius, came forward to support Michael. As soon as 'Darius the Mede' (v. 31, ix. 1) 'received the kingdom,' there was need for the defenders of Israel to co-operate on its behalf; and (it seems to be implied) it was through this angelic intervention that the natural hostility of Persia to Israel was turned to friendliness.

I stood up] The Heb. is peculiar, lit. *my standing (was)*. One or two parallels can be quoted (as Jud. xix. 9; Job ix. 27); but the addition of a letter would give the normal Hebrew for *I stood up* (עמדתי for עמדי).

a supporter] prop. *one holding strongly* or *firmly*: see Is. xli. 9, 13; Ez. xxx. 25.

stronghold] *vv.* 7, 10, 19, 31, 38, 39; Is. xxiii. 4, 11: here in a figurative sense, as often of Jehovah (e.g. Ps. xxvii. 1, xxviii. 1).

(2) **xi. 2—xii. 4. The revelation given to Daniel.**

This consists of a survey of the history from the beginning of the Persian period down to the time of Antiochus Epiphanes, followed by a description of the Messianic age, to begin afterwards. The description is brief and general in its earlier part, more detailed in the later parts. The angel first refers briefly to the doings of four Persian kings (*v.* 2), and of Alexander the Great (*v.* 3), with the division of his empire after his death (*v.* 4); then narrates more fully the leagues and conflicts between the kings of Antioch ('the kings of the north'), and of Egypt ('the kings of the south'), in the centuries following (*vv.* 5—20); and finally,

And now will I shew thee the truth. Behold, there *shall* 2 stand up yet three kings in Persia; and the fourth shall be far richer than *they* all: and by his strength through his riches he shall stir up all against the realm of Grecia.

most fully of all, describes the reign of Antiochus Epiphanes (*vv.* 21—45), including his conflicts with Egypt, and the persecution of the Jews (*vv.* 30 *b*—39). The death of Antiochus is followed by a resurrection (of Israelites), and the advent of the Messianic age (xii. 1—3). The revelation is intended to shew that the course of history is in God's hands, and that though it may bring with it a period of trial for His people, this will be followed, at the appointed time, by its deliverance. It is thus designed particularly for the encouragement of those living in the season of trial, i.e. under the persecution of Antiochus; it is accordingly to be 'sealed up' by Daniel until then (xii. 4).

As is usual in apocalyptic literature (Enoch, Baruch, 2 Esdras, &c.), no *names* are mentioned; the characters and events referred to being described in veiled language, which sometimes leaves the interpretation uncertain. The Commentary of Jerome is important in this chapter, on account of its preserving notices from writers no longer extant.

2. *And now will I* **declare truth unto** *thee*] something which will be verified by the event (cf. x. 21).

The four kings of Persia.

stand up] i.e. arise, as viii. 23, and below, *vv.* 3, 4, 7, 20, 21.

three kings] the three kings following Cyrus (x. 1) are Cambyses (B.C. 529—522), Gaumâta (Pseudo-Smerdis) 522 (for 7 months), and Darius Hystaspis (522—485). Gaumâta, however, might easily be disregarded by the writer: in this case, the third king would be Xerxes (485—465).

in Persia] **to, belonging to,** *Persia:* the construction, as Deut. xxiii. 2, 3 [3, 4]; Jer. xiii. 13 (see R.V. *marg.*); and frequently.

the fourth] the fourth, following the 'three'? or the fourth, including Cyrus (who is reigning at the time, x. 1), i.e. the last of the 'three'? The latter interpretation is the more probable one: otherwise, why was not '*four* kings shall stand up' said? In either case, the fourth king is Xerxes, Gaumâta being counted in the former case but not in the latter. On Xerxes' wealth and strength, see Hdt. vii. 20—99 (the account of the immense armament prepared by him against Greece).

and **when he is waxed strong**] The same expression (in the Heb.) as 2 Ch. xii. 1, xxvi. 16.

he shall stir up all (in conflict) **with,** &c.] he will set in motion (*v.* 25; Is. xiii. 17; Jer. l. 9) all the men and forces of his vast empire. The allusion is to the well-known expedition against Greece, to which Xerxes devoted all his treasures and all his energies, and which ended in the disastrous defeat at Salamis, B.C. 480. The description of Greece as a 'realm' or kingdom, is, of course, inexact: Greece, in the age of Xerxes, consisted of a number of independent states, democracies or oligarchies; a Greek 'kingdom' did not arise till the days of Philip and Alexander of Macedon.

11—2

3 And a mighty king shall stand up, that shall rule *with*
4 *great dominion*, and do according to his will. And when he shall stand up, his kingdom shall be broken, and shall be divided toward the four winds of heaven; and not to his posterity, nor according to his dominion which he ruled: for his kingdom shall be pluckt up, even for others besides those.

3. Alexander the Great (B.C. 336—323). The writer, passing over the intermediate Persian rulers, hastens to the period when the course of events begins to affect the Jews, limiting what he has to say respecting the whole of the Persian empire, and the founder of the Greek empire, to a single verse in each case.

a **warrior** *king*] The regular meaning of *gibbōr* ('mighty man') in Heb.: e.g. 2 Sam. i. 9, xxiii. 8, 1 Ki. i. 8, 10, Is. xlii. 13, &c.

do according to his will] carry out whatever he wishes: an expression implying the possession of irresistible and irresponsible power. Cf. Quintus Curtius x. 5, 35, 'Huius [fortunae] beneficio agere videbatur gentibus *quidquid placebat*.' Comp. on viii. 4; and below *vv*. 16, 36.

4. The disruption of Alexander's empire, after his death.

when he shall stand up] or, *at the time of his standing up.* The expression, if correct, will be intended to emphasize the short-lived duration of Alexander's empire (his reign extended from 336 to 323; his conquests in Asia from 334 to 323). But in view of viii. 8, Grätz's emendation, 'when he shall *become strong*' (וכעצמו for וכעמדו), is a probable one; the reference will then be to the manner in which Alexander was suddenly struck down in the midst of his successes.

be broken] The word is, no doubt, suggested by viii. 8, where it is used of the 'great horn,' which symbolizes Alexander.

toward the four winds of heaven] So also viii. 8. Alexander's empire, after his death, was broken up; and in the end the four kingdoms of Cassander, Lysimachus, Seleucus, and Ptolemy arose upon its ruins (see on viii. 8).

but (it shall) *not* (belong) *to his posterity*] Alexander, the conqueror's youthful son by Roxana, and Herakles, an illegitimate son, were both murdered in 310 or 309, the former by Cassander directly, the latter by Polysperchon at Cassander's persuasion (Diod. Sic. xix. 105, xx. 28).

nor (be) *according to his dominion*, **wherewith** *he ruled*] The divided kingdom would not, in any of its parts, retain the power and prestige which Alexander enjoyed. Cf. viii. 22, 'but not with his power.'

pluckt up] The figure is that of a tree: it is common in Jeremiah, as i. 10, xviii. 7, xxxi. 28.

and (it shall be) *for others besides* **these**] besides Alexander's generals,—with allusion to the independent petty dynasties which arose gradually in Cappadocia, Armenia, and other countries, during the century and a half that followed upon the death of Alexander (Jerome, von Leng., Bevan).

And the king of the south shall be strong, and *one* of 5
his princes; and he shall be strong above him, and have
dominion; his dominion *shall be* a great dominion. And 6

From this point onwards the author confines himself to the kingdoms of the north and of the south, i.e. of the Seleucidae (in Syria), and of the Ptolemies (in Egypt),—these being the two dynasties which during the period that elapsed from the death of Alexander to the time of Antiochus Epiphanes, successively dominated Palestine.

5. Ptolemy I. (Lagi), 305—285, and Seleucus I. (Nicator), 312—280.

the king of the south] The 'south' (Heb. *Negeb*), when applied to a particular region, means commonly in the O.T., the southern part of Judah (Gen. xii. 9, R.V. *marg.*); but in this chapter (as in viii. 9) it denotes regularly Egypt, as opposed to Antioch (or Syria), which is signified by the 'north.' Ptolemy, son of Lagus, a Macedonian, one of Alexander's most trusted and capable generals, who distinguished himself especially in his Indian campaigns, succeeded, in the partition of Alexander's empire which was arranged immediately after his death, in securing for himself Egypt, which he ruled as satrap from B.C. 322 to 305, when he assumed the title of king. He died B.C. 285.

and one *of his princes*] or **captains** (2 Ki. ix. 5, &c.). Seleucus, an officer of Alexander's 'companions' (ἑταῖροι), or distinguished corps of heavy cavalry, received at the convention of Triparadisus, in 321, the wealthy satrapy of Babylonia. Being in 316 taken to account for his administration by Antigonus (who had received in 323 Phrygia, Lycia, and Pamphylia, but increasing in power had presumed to control the provinces as he thought fit), he took refuge with Ptolemy in Egypt. Ptolemy appointed him his general; and he helped him to gain the battle of Gaza in 312. After this he induced Ptolemy to send him with a small force to recover Babylon. He was successful, and regained his satrapy; and the era of the Seleucidae (B.C. 312), by which in later times the Jews reckoned (1 Macc. i. 10), was fixed by the event.

and he (the latter, Seleucus) *shall be strong above him*[1] (the former, Ptolemy), *and have dominion: his dominion* shall be *a great dominion*] After the final defeat of Antigonus at Ipsus in 301 (which indeed was principally due to the large forces contributed by Seleucus), the empire ruled by Seleucus, reaching from Phrygia, Cappadocia, and Syria, on the W., almost to the Indus on the E., was much more extensive than that of Ptolemy, and commanded much larger resources. Seleucus is called by Arrian (*Exped. Alex.* vii. 22) the "greatest," as well as the most "princely-minded," of Alexander's successors; and he deserves, more than any of his brother generals, to be regarded as the heir of Alexander. Antioch was founded by him as his capital, B.C. 300.

---

[1] The reading 'but one of his captains shall be strong above him' (LXX., Theod., Meinh., Kamph., Prince) would improve this verse, without altering the sense.

in the end of years they shall join themselves together; for the king's daughter of the south shall come to the king of the north to make an agreement: but she shall not

In the distribution of provinces, an ambiguous position was taken by Cœle-Syria, with Phœnicia, and Palestine; and this intermediate region remained a bone of contention between the kings of Syria and Egypt, and in the century and a half which followed the death of Alexander, repeatedly changed hands. At Triparadisus, in 321, Syria was assigned to Laomedon; but Ptolemy got possession of it in 320, only to lose it again in 315 to Antigonus, to recover at least the S. part of it after the battle of Gaza in 312, and to relinquish it a second time to Antigonus in 311. After the battle of Ipsus in 301, Ptolemy, as a matter of fact, obtained Cœle-Syria and Phœnicia; but his right to these provinces became a subject of protracted dispute between the later Ptolemies and Seleucidae. On the one hand, it was alleged that after the victory it had been distinctly agreed that Seleucus should have 'the whole of Syria'; on the other, it was claimed that Ptolemy Lagi had only joined the coalition against Antigonus on the understanding that he should receive Cœle-Syria and Phœnicia (Polyb. v. 67; cf. also the quotation from Diodorus in Mahaffy, *Empire of the Ptolemies*, p. 66). Upon the whole, during the period here in question, Palestine remained, with short interruptions, in the hands of the Ptolemies till the battle of Paneion in 198, after which it was retained permanently by the kings of Syria.

6. Ptolemy II. (Philadelphus), 285—247, and Antiochus II. (Theos), 261—246.

Antiochus I. (Soter), B.C. 280—261, is passed by in the survey, as a ruler whose reign was of no importance to the Jews. The allusion in *v.* 6 is to what happened about B.C. 249. In order to terminate his long wars with Antiochus II. (Theos), Ptolemy Philadelphus gave him in marriage his daughter, Berenice, upon condition that he should divorce his legitimate wife, Laodice, and that his two sons, Seleucus and Antiochus, should renounce all claim to the throne of Syria: in the event of Antiochus and Berenice having issue, Ptolemy hoped in this way to secure Syria as an Egyptian province. After two years, however, Ptolemy died. Antiochus then took back Laodice, and divorced Berenice. Laodice, however, dreading her husband's fickleness ('ambiguum viri animum,' Jerome), and fearing lest he might again evince a preference for Berenice, before long procured his death by poison. She then persuaded her son, Seleucus, to secure the throne for himself by murdering both Berenice and her infant child (Jerome *ad loc.*; Appian, *Syr.* 65; Justin xxvii. 1).

at the end of (some) *years*] 31 years after the death of Seleucus Nicator.

join themselves together] by the matrimonial alliance just described.

and the daughter of the king *of the south*] Berenice.

come to] in marriage (cf. Josh. xv. 18; Jud. xii. 9).

to make an agreement] lit. *uprightness* (Ps. ix. 8), or *equity*

retain the power of the arm; neither shall he stand, nor his arm: but she shall be given up, and they that brought her, and he that begat her, and he that strengthened her in *these* times. But out of a branch of her roots shall one 7

(Ps. xcviii. 9), i.e. (here) the equitable adjustment of a dispute. Comp. *v.* 17.

but she shall not retain the power of the arm] fig. for, she will not be able to maintain herself against her rival, Laodice. As said above, she was first divorced by Antiochus in favour of Laodice, and afterwards murdered at her instigation.

neither shall he stand] Antiochus, who was murdered by Laodice.

nor his arm] his might will come to an end. Theod., Kamph., Prince, 'nor his *seed*' (זַרְעוֹ for זְרֹעוֹ), referring to Antiochus' issue by Berenice[1].

but she shall be given up] Berenice, put to death at the instigation of Laodice.

they that brought her] either into the marriage, or to Syria. The expression is a vague one. The reference may be (Ewald, Meinh.) to Berenice's attendants, who accompanied her to Antioch, and met there the same fate as their mistress; it may be (Hitz., Keil) simply to Antiochus (the plural being generic, without reference to the number of persons actually meant; cf. Gen. xxi. 7, Mt. ii. 20); it may even be, more generally, to the ministers of Ptolemy who supported the alliance, and who were 'given up,' in the sense of finding their expectations disappointed.

he that begat her and supported (*v.* 1) *her*] Ptolemy Philadelphus (so Ew., Hitz., Keil). Or, *he that begat her, and he that* obtained (*v.* 21) *her*; i.e. Ptolemy, and Antiochus (so von Leng., Zöckl., Meinh.).

in the times] at the time in question = *in* those *times* (R.V.).

7—9. Ptolemy III. (Euergetes I.), 247—222, and Seleucus II. (Callinicus), 246—226.

Ptolemy Euergetes I., Berenice's brother, an enterprising and energetic king, in revenge for his sister's murder, invaded the empire of Seleucus, seized Seleukeia (Polyb. v. 58 *end*), the fortified port of Antioch (Acts xiii. 4), and overran the greater part of Seleucus' Asiatic dominions as far as Babylon. The murder of Berenice had made Seleucus unpopular with his subjects; and had Ptolemy not been called home by an insurrection in Egypt, he would in all probability have made himself master of Seleucus' entire empire (Justin xxvii. 1). Ptolemy returned, bringing back with him an immense quantity of spoil (cf. Mahaffy, *The Empire of the Ptolemies*, pp. 196—200).

7. *But* **one of the shoots** (Is. xi. 1) *of her roots*] Ptolemy III., Berenice's brother.

---

[1] Bevan and Marti render the last three clauses, *but the arm* (fig. for the support afforded by Berenice) *shall not retain strength, neither shall his* (other) *arms* (supports) *abide* (prove effectual),—altering (with Hitz.) the division and punctuation of the last two words.

stand up *in* his estate, which shall come with an army, and
shall enter into the fortress of the king of the north, and
8 shall deal against them, and shall prevail: and shall also
carry captives *into* Egypt their gods, with their princes, *and*
with their precious vessels *of* silver and *of* gold; and he
9 shall continue *more* years than the king of the north. So
the king of the south shall come into *his* kingdom, and

shall stand up *in his* (Ptolemy II.'s) **place**] or *office, position*. So
Gen. xl. 13, xli. 13; and below, *vv.* 20, 21, 38.
and *shall come* **unto the** *army*] shall place himself at its head, with
the object, viz., of attacking Syria.
and *shall enter into the* **stronghold** *of the king of the north*]
Seleukeia.
and shall deal with *them*] viz. as he may find fit, in no friendly
manner; the pron. referring to the subjects of Seleucus: cf. Jer.
xviii. 23 'in the time of thine anger *deal thou with them.*'
and shall prevail] or *shew strength, shew himself strong.*
8. And also *their gods, with their* **molten images,** and *with their
precious vessels of silver and of gold, shall he* **bring into captivity** *into
Egypt*] The custom of carrying off the gods of a conquered nation was
common in antiquity: the capture of its gods implied naturally that the
nation's strongest support had passed into the hands of the victors.
Cf. Is. xlvi. 1, 2; Jer. xlviii. 7, xlix. 3. On the present occasion
Jerome, following Porphyry, states that Ptolemy brought back with
him 40,000 talents of silver and 2,500 precious vessels and images of
gods, among the latter being those which Cambyses had carried off
from Egypt 280 years before (cf. the Canopus decree, ll. 9—10:
Mahaffy, p. 230). In consequence of the recovery of these images,
it was said, the Egyptians conferred upon him the title of Euergetes
('Benefactor').
precious vessels] lit. *vessels of desire*: the same expression, 2 Chron.
xxxii. 27, xxxvi. 10; Hos. xiii. 15; Neh. ii. 9; Jer. xxv. 34.
and he shall **refrain** *some years from* (R.V.)] i.e. desist from attacking.
'Refrain' is lit. *stand*: cf. in the Heb. Gen. xxix. 35, 2 Ki. iv. 6.
**9. And he shall come into the kingdom of the king of the south,
but he** *shall*, &c.] After two years Seleucus Callinicus succeeded in
re-establishing his power in Asia (B.C. 242); but proceeding to march
against Ptolemy he was defeated, and obliged to retreat, accompanied
by only a few attendants, to Antioch (Justin xxvii. 2), B.C. 240.
10—19. Seleucus III. (Ceraunos), 226—223, and Antiochus III.
(the Great), 223—187: Ptolemy IV. (Philopator), 222—205, and
Ptolemy V. (Epiphanes), 205—181.
Seleucus Callinicus left two sons, Seleucus Ceraunos and Antiochus.
The former succeeded him, but was murdered, after two years, in the
course of an expedition in Asia Minor (Polyb. v. 40). Antiochus, who
then came to the throne, determined to resume the war with Egypt,
hoping, in view of Ptolemy Philopator's effeminacy and supineness,

shall return into his own land. But his sons shall be stirred 10

that an easy task lay before him (Polyb. v. 42)[1]. First, acting on the advice of his friend, the physician Apollophanes, he recovered the important fortress of Seleukeia (Polyb. v. 58—60, see above, on *v.* 7); then Theodotus, Ptolemy's præfect in Cœle-Syria (v. 40), invited him treacherously to take possession of that province, and enabled him further to secure Tyre, Ptolemais, and other neighbouring towns (v. 61). Meanwhile Ptolemy, roused from his lethargy by the loss of Cœle-Syria, had advanced his troops as far as Pelusium; and his ministers, wishing to gain time for further warlike preparations, succeeded in obtaining from Antiochus an armistice for four months. Antiochus accordingly retired for the winter to Seleukeia, leaving garrisons in Phœnicia and Cœle-Syria, which (being ignorant of Ptolemy's real intentions) he hoped he had now finally secured (v. 62—66). However, in the following spring (218), a large Egyptian army, which had meantime been organized, marched under Nicolaus through Palestine as far as a spot between Lebanon and the sea, where it was met by Antiochus and completely defeated (v. 68—69). After this Antiochus advanced into Palestine, takes Philoteria, Scythopolis (Beth-shean) and Atabyrium, as also Abila, Gadara, and Rabbath-Ammon, on the E. of Jordan, leaves a governor, with 8000 soldiers, in Samaria, and retires into winter-quarters at Ptolemais (v. 70—71).

In the next spring (217) Antiochus and Ptolemy both take the field, with armies of 60,000 or 70,000 men each (v. 79). Ptolemy, starting from Alexandria, advances to within 50 stadia of Raphia (the border-fortress of Palestine, in the direction of Egypt); Antiochus first marches to Gaza, then by slow stages, passing Raphia, to within five stadia of the spot on which the army of Ptolemy was encamped (v. 80). In the battle which ensued (v. 82—85), Antiochus was defeated (with the loss of 10,000 infantry, 300 cavalry, besides 4,000 prisoners), and fell back upon Gaza, retiring afterwards to Antioch (v. 86). He then sent to Ptolemy to ask terms of peace, which Ptolemy, satisfied with his victory, and with its natural consequence, the recovery of Cœle-Syria, granted for one year (v. 87).

The second part of *v.* 12 refers plainly to Ptolemy's victory at Raphia; but it is impossible to feel certain which of the events just described are referred to in *v.* 10*b*—12*a*. The sequence of events as described in these verses seems, in fact, not to agree with that of the narrative of Polybius.

10. *his sons*] Seleucus Ceraunos and Antiochus the Great, the two being grouped together, because (probably) the campaign of Seleucus in Asia Minor was the first stage in an organized plan of hostilities against Egypt.

shall **stir themselves** *up*] viz., as the word used implies, for war or combat (cf. ἐρεθίζω): so. *v.* 25; Deut. ii. 5, 9, 19, 24 [R.V. *contend*]; 2 Ki. xiv. 10 (properly, 'Why shouldest thou *stir thyself up* against—i.e. advance against, challenge—calamity?').

[1] The events summarized in *vv.* 10—12 are narrated at length in Polyb. v. 58—71, 79—87 (v. 62—68, 79—87, are translated in Mahaffy, *l.c.*, pp. 250—263).

up, and shall assemble a multitude of great forces: and *one* shall certainly come, and overflow, and pass through: then shall he return, and be stirred up, *even* to his fortress.
11 And the king of the south shall be moved with choler, and shall come forth and fight with him, *even* with the

and **he** (or **it**) *shall* **come on**] i.e. either Antiochus, or his army (the 'multitude' just spoken of). The attack upon Egypt, planned originally by the two brothers, was, after the death of Seleucus, carried out by Antiochus.

and **flood up** *and* **flow over**] viz. in the campaigns of 219 in Cœle-Syria, and of 218 in Palestine (as described above). The words are borrowed from Is. viii. 8: the advancing hosts of Antiochus (as in Is. those of the Assyrians) are compared to a flood of waters inundating a land. Cf. Jer. xlvii. 2.

and *he* (or *it*) *shall return*] Antiochus, after wintering in Ptolemais, 'returned' to the attack upon Egypt in 217.

and **they** (his forces) *shall* **stir themselves** *up* (advancing) **as far as** *his* **stronghold**] Probably Gaza, which was the most important fortress of Palestine on the south, and a play upon the name of which (עֻזָּה) is perhaps intended by the Heb. word here used (מָעֻזֹּה). The strength of Gaza may be estimated by the fact that it resisted Alexander the Great for two months.

11. *the king of the south*] Ptolemy Philopator.

shall be moved with choler (viii. 7), *and shall come forth*] to meet the advancing army of Antiochus (*v.* 10 *b*). In the narrative of Polybius, however, Ptolemy appears as the first in the field.

11 *b*—12 *a*. Very ambiguous. The two alternative explanations are :—

(1) *And he* (Ptolemy) will **raise a** great army, **and** it will be placed under his (Ptolemy's) command[1],—the fact being mentioned on account of Ptolemy's unwarlike nature and usual indifference,—(12) *and the multitude* (the army of Ptolemy) **shall lift itself up** (viz. to attack: cf. Is. xxxiii. 10 A.V.), *its*[2] (or *his*[2], i.e. Ptolemy's) *heart being* **exalted**, i.e. elated with the prospect of success (von Lengerke, Hitzig, Ewald, Meinhold); (2) *And he* (Antiochus) will **raise a** great army (cf. *v.* 13 *a*), **but** it will be given into his (Ptolemy's) hands, (12) *and the multitude* (the army of Antiochus) *shall be* **carried away** (R.V. *marg.* ; cf. for the rend. Is. viii. 4, xl. 24, xli. 16), **and**[3] *his* (Ptolemy's) *heart shall be* **exalted**, i.e. elated with the victory (Bev., Behrm., Keil for *v.* 11 *b*, Prince). There are objections to each of these interpretations, both on the score of Heb. usage, and relation to the context, and also on account (see above) of imperfect agreement with the history ; but, on the whole, the second is preferable. *To be exalted* (or *lifted up*), of the heart, as *ch.* v. 20; Deut. viii. 14, xvii. 20.

---

[1] 'Give into the hand,' as Gen. xxxii. 17, xxxix. 4, 2 Sam. x. 10.
[2] Heb. text (with no 'and').
[3] Heb. marg. (with 'and').

king of the north: and he shall set forth a great multitude; but the multitude shall be given into his hand. *And* when ¹² he hath taken away the multitude, his heart shall be lifted up; and he shall cast down *many* ten thousands: but he shall not be strengthened *by it*. For the king of the north ¹³ shall return, and shall set forth a multitude greater than the former, and shall certainly come after certain years with a great army and with much riches. And in those ¹⁴ times there shall many stand up against the king of the

set forth] lit. *cause to stand up*, i.e. **raise**; so *v.* 13.
and he (Ptolemy) *shall* **cause tens of thousands to fall**] at the battle of Raphia.
but he shall not **be strong**] he will gain no permanent advantage in consequence. Ptolemy by his victory recovered Cœle-Syria; but he did not pursue his success further; he again gave way to his natural indolence, and quickly resumed his dissolute life (Polyb. xiv. 12); so that when Antiochus sent to ask for terms of peace, he readily granted them. Justin (xxx. 1) writes of him, ' Spoliasset regno Antiochum, si fortunam virtute iuvisset.'

13. Twelve years after the battle of Raphia, in **205**, Ptolemy Philopator died, leaving a son aged 4 years, who succeeded him on the throne as Ptolemy V. (Epiphanes). Antiochus had meanwhile been gaining the series of successes in Persia, Bactria, Asia Minor, and even in India, which earned him the epithet of the ' Great.' Returning from the East, in the same year in which Philopator died, he concluded an alliance with Philip, king of Macedon, for a joint attack upon the infant king of Egypt, and partition of his foreign possessions between them (Polyb. xv. 20; cf. Jer. *ad loc.*). Details of the war are not known, the part of Polybius' history which described it being lost. We only learn from Justin (xxxi. 1) that he invaded Phœnicia and Syria; and from Polybius (xvi. 18, 40) that he captured Gaza, after a stout resistance.

shall return, &c.] *shall* **again raise** *a multitude, greater than the former*, with allusion to the forces by which he achieved his successes in Persia and the East. Jerome (quoting probably from Porphyry) speaks of the immense army which he brought back with him from the East.

and **he shall come on at the end of the times, (even of) years**] after 12 years, at the end of his conquests in Persia, Bactria, &c.

with much **substance**] the allusion is to the baggage, implements of war, &c., belonging to a well-appointed army. The word used (רכוש) denotes especially such possessions as stores, furniture, implements, &c.: see 1 Chr. xxvii. 31, 2 Chr. xx. 25 ('riches'—of an invading army), xxi. 14 (R.V.), 17; Ezr. i. 4, 6 ('goods').

14. *there shall many stand up*, &c.] Alluding to Antiochus, to Philip of Macedon, his ally, and also (according to Jerome) to rebellions which broke out in the provinces subject to Egypt, and

south: also the robbers of thy people shall exalt themselves
15 to establish the vision; but they shall fall. So the king

insurrections in Egypt itself, through dissatisfaction with the haughty and dissolute Agathocles, Ptolemy Philopator's chief minister and favourite (see Polyb. xv. 25—34 [Mahaffy, pp. 276—287], where a graphic account is given of the assassination of Agathocles in a popular tumult, immediately after the accession of the infant king, Ptolemy V.).

also the **children of the violent among** *thy people shall* **lift themselves up** *to establish* (the) *vision; but they shall* **be overthrown**] The allusion is apparently to a faction among the Jews, who, for the purpose of fulfilling certain prophecies, took the part of Antiochus against Ptolemy, but were unsuccessful.

Antiochus the Great, in the invasion referred to on *v.* 13, had, it seems, obtained possession of Palestine: shortly afterwards, however, in 200, the guardian of the young Ptolemy Epiphanes sent Scopas, an Aetolian mercenary, to recover it: he was successful, 'subdued the nation of the Jews' (Polyb. xvi. 39 *ap.* Jos. *l. c.*), and left a garrison in the citadel at Jerusalem. Within a year or two, as soon as his war with Attalus of Pergamum was over, Antiochus marched against Scopas, and defeated him with great loss at Paneion, by the sources of the Jordan (cf. Polyb. xvi. 18 f.), so that he was obliged to retreat, with 100,000 men, into Sidon, where Antiochus besieged him, and, though Ptolemy sent him assistance, compelled him to surrender (B.C. 198). After this Antiochus recovered Bataneea, Samaria, Abila and Gadara: he then entered Jerusalem, where the people received him gladly, provided his army with food, and assisted him to expel the garrison left in the citadel by Scopas; in return for this friendliness, Antiochus afterwards granted the Jews remission of many taxes, and contributed liberally to both the services and the repair of the Temple[1]. Only Gaza remained loyal to Ptolemy; and withstood a siege from Antiochus rather than join the Syrian side (Polyb. xvi. 40). We do not know particulars: but the allusion in this part of *v.* 14 can hardly be to anything except to a party in Jerusalem which (perhaps before the expedition of Scopas: notice Polybius' phrase 'subdued,' as though there had been some rebellion) supported Antiochus, and in some way was broken up.

violent] properly, *breakers down* (or *breakers through*): the word denotes a robber, Jer. vii. 11 ('a den of robbers'); Ez. vii. 22, xviii. 10; and is used of a destructive wild-beast, Is. xxxv. 9. The author chooses a strong term for the purpose of expressing his disapprobation of a party who were instrumental in bringing Judah under the rule of the Seleucidae, Antiochus the Great being the father of the hated Antiochus Epiphanes.

be overthrown] lit. *stumble*: see Prov. xxiv. 16.

15 a. **And** *the king of the north shall come, and* **throw up earthworks**, and *take* **a city of fortifications**] Sidon, in which Scopas was shut up, and which Antiochus took (see on *v.* 14).

[1] Jos. *Ant.* XII. iii. 3 (Mahaffy, p. 293 f.); Jerome on Dan. viii. 15: Ewald, *Hist.* v. 284.

of the north shall come, and cast up a mount, and take the most fenced cities: and the arms of the south shall not withstand, neither his chosen people, neither *shall there be any* strength to withstand. But he that cometh 16 against him shall do according to his own will, and none shall stand before him: and he shall stand in the glorious land, which by his hand shall be consumed. He shall 17 also set his face to enter with the strength of his whole kingdom, and upright ones with him; thus shall he do:

cast up a mount] i.e. throw up (lit. *pour out*, viz. from the baskets used for collecting the earth) earth-works, the expression often used in the O. T. of a besieging army (2 Sam. xx. 15; 2 Kin. xix. 32; Jer. vi. 6; Ez. iv. 2 *al.*). *Mount* is simply the old form of *mound*, the two words being really the same, though now differentiated in meaning. W. A. Wright (*Bible Word-Book*, s.v.) quotes from North's Plutarch (1595), *Alexander*, p. 748, 'all the army in their armour did cast up a *mount* of earth fashioned like a tombe.'

15 b—16. The final collapse of the Egyptian power in Syria.

15 b. *and the arms of the south shall not* **stand**] shall make no stand (*v.* 25; Am. ii. 15) against Antiochus. The *arm* (of the body) is often fig. for *strength* (Ps. lxxi. 18, lxxix. 11, lxxxiii. 8; Ezr. iv. 23; Judith ix. 7); here, the plur. is fig. for *forces*: cf. *vv.* 22, 31.

and as for *his chosen people* (i.e. his chosen warriors: cf. Ex. xv. 4; Jer. xlviii. 15), **there shall be no strength** (in them) **to stand**] so the Heb. accents. Scopas, and the three "duces inclyti" (Jerome) sent to assist him, could not resist the forces of Antiochus.

16. *But he* (Antiochus) *that cometh against him* (Ptolemy) *shall do according to his own will*] so greatly will he be superior to him: the phrase, as *v.* 3.

stand before him] viii. 4, **7.**

shall stand in the **beauteous** *land* (the land of Israel: see on viii. 9), **with destruction in** *his hand*] aimed, viz., against Egypt; possessed of Palestine (*v.* 14), he will 'stand' in it, menacing Egypt with ruin. Or (with a change of points), *with* **all of it** (the land) *in his hand* (power) (Bertholdt, Kamph., Prince).

17. *And he shall set his face*—i.e. purpose, plan (2 Kin. xii. 17; Jer. xlii. 15, 17; xliv. 12)—*to come with the strength*, &c.] to advance with all his force against Egypt. Livy (xxxiii. 19) describes how, in the spring of 197, *omnibus regni viribus connixus, quum ingentes copias terrestres maritimasque comparasset*, Antiochus himself set out with a fleet for the purpose of attacking all the cities on the coast of Cilicia, Lycia, and Caria, which were subject to Ptolemy. He did not actually invade Egypt, nor does the present verse say that he would do so.

and upright ones with him; thus shall he do] the words yield no sense: read, with very slight changes, **but shall make an agreement** (see *v.* 6) *with him*: so LXX. Theod. Vulg. (cf. R.V. *marg.*). He did not carry out his intention, but found it convenient to come to

and he shall give him the daughter of women, corrupting her: but she shall not stand *on his side*, neither be for him.
18 After this shall he turn his face unto the isles, and shall

terms with Ptolemy (φιλίαν καὶ σπονδὰς πρὸς τὸν Πτολεμαῖον ἐποιήσατο, Jos. *Ant.* XII. iv. 1). Antiochus had his eye on Asia Minor, and even on Europe: but being opposed by the Romans, he was glad to be on good terms with Egypt; he accordingly betrothed his daughter Cleopatra to Ptolemy Epiphanes, promising that she should receive as her dowry what was afterwards understood by the Egyptians to be the provinces of Cœle-Syria, Phœnicia, and Palestine, though this was denied before the Roman legates by Antiochus Epiphanes (Polyb. xxviii. 17, who appears to think that Antiochus Epiphanes was right)[1]. The marriage actually took place in the winter of 194—3, Antiochus taking his daughter to Raphia for the purpose (Livy xxxv. 13).

and he shall give him the daughter of women] his daughter Cleopatra.

corrupting her] a very improbable rendering: Cleopatra was not (as was the case with many of the queens of the Ptolemies) her husband's sister; and (Mahaffy, p. 330) she "bears an excellent character in Egyptian history." Keil renders *to destroy her*; but Cleopatra, so far as we know, lived happily in Egypt, and died a natural death. The only reasonable rendering is **to destroy it**,—the pronoun being referred *ad sensum* to Egypt. Antiochus was not really actuated by friendliness to Egypt; his true motives, no doubt, being (Hitz.) 'to protect himself against Roman interference, to gain a footing in Egypt, and, if the opportunity should offer, to secure the country for himself.' In 196, upon a false report of the death of Ptolemy reaching Lysimacheia (below, note), he actually started for the purpose of seizing Egypt (Livy xxxiii. 41).

but it shall not stand, neither be for **him** (emph.)] his plan will not succeed (cf. for the expression, Is. vii. 7, xiv. 24), nor turn out to his advantage, but (as is implied by the position of the pron., 'and not for him shall it be') to that of another. Jerome writes, 'Neque enim obtinere potuit Aegyptum: quia Ptolemaeus Epiphanes et duces eius, sentientes dolum, cautius se egerunt, et Cleopatra magis viri partes quam parentis fovit.' In point of fact, Ptolemy retained the friendship of the Romans, while Antiochus, to his cost (see on *v.* 18), lost it.

18. And *he shall turn his face to the isles* (or *coast-lands*), *and shall take many ; but a* **commander** *shall cause* **his** *reproach to cease* **to him** ; **nay, he shall even return his** *reproach* **unto him**] Antiochus cherished ambitious designs towards the West. In 196 most of the cities in Asia Minor submitted to him; in the same year he even crossed the

---

[1] The dowry seems in fact to have been not the provinces themselves, but their *revenues* (Wilcken [see p. 178 *n.*]; Mahaffy, p. 306).

Cleopatra's betrothal is alluded to in Polyb. xviii. 51 *end* (whence Livy xxxiii. 40): in reply to the Roman legates who were sent to him in 196 at Lysimacheia (in Thrace) to demand (among other things) that he should restore the cities taken from Ptolemy, Antiochus replied that he was on friendly terms with Ptolemy, 'et id agere se, *ut brevi etiam affinitas jungatur.*'

take many: but a prince for his own behalf shall cause the reproach offered by him to cease; without his own reproach he shall cause *it* to turn upon him. Then he shall 19 turn his face towards the fort of his own land: but he shall

Hellespont and seized the Thracian Chersonese, and in 195 set about organizing it as a satrapy for his son Seleucus. In 192 he landed in Greece, and occupied various places to the N. of the Isthmus of Corinth, but was defeated by the Romans in 191 at Thermopylae, and compelled to retire to Ephesus. The Romans next determined to expel Antiochus from Asia. Immense preparations were made on both sides: in the end, the decisive battle was fought in the autumn of 190, at Magnesia, near Smyrna, and Antiochus's huge army of 80,000 men was defeated, with enormous loss, by Lucius Cornelius Scipio (Livy xxxvii. 39—44). Antiochus was now obliged to renounce formally all claims to any part of Europe, or of Asia Minor, west of the Taurus, and to submit to other humiliating conditions of peace[1]. His ruin was complete: "never, perhaps," remarks Mommsen, "did a great power fall so rapidly, so thoroughly, so ignominiously, as the kingdom of the Seleucidae under this Antiochus the Great." These are the events alluded to in the present verse of Daniel.

turn his face] implying a change of purpose and direction: so *v.* 19.

isles (or *coast-lands*)] Heb. *'iyyîm*],—the word used regularly (e.g. Gen. x. 5; Is. xi. 11) of the islands and jutting promontories (for it includes both) of the Mediterranean Sea. Here it denotes in particular the coasts and islands of Asia Minor and Greece.

a commander] Lucius Cornelius Scipio, at the battle of Magnesia. The Heb. word (*ḳāẓîn*) means properly *a decider* (Arab. *ḳāḍi*), and is used of one who interposes, or acts, with authority: in Josh. x. 24, Jud. xi. 6, 11, of a military commander, as here; Is. iii. 6, 7, of a dictator, taking the lead in a civic emergency; of other authorities, civil or military, in Is. i. 10, xxii. 3; Mic. iii. 1, 9; Prov. vi. 7, xxv. 15 (all).

his *reproach*] implied in the defiant attitude adopted by him towards the Romans: not only had he, for instance, attacked many of their allies, but he told their legates at Lysimacheia that they had no more right to inquire what he was doing in Asia, than he had to inquire what they were doing in Italy (Liv. xxxiii. 40).

to him] a dative of reference,—though certainly redundant, after the pron. *his*; cf. (without a pron.) Jer. xlviii. 35; Ruth iv. 14.

return] hurl back, and at the same time requite,—viz. by the humiliating repulse at Magnesia, after which, in Appian's words (*Syr.* c. 37), men used to say, ἦν βασιλεὺς Ἀντίοχος ὁ μέγας. For the expression, which forms here a climax on 'make to cease,' see Hos. xii. 14; Neh. iv. 4 (Heb. iii. 36).

19. *Then he shall turn his face towards the* **strongholds** *of his own land; but he shall stumble,* &c.] The end of Antiochus (B.C. 187).

[1] See fuller particulars in Livy xxxvii. 39—45, 55; or in Mommsen's *Hist. of Rome*, Bk. III., chap. ix.

20 stumble and fall, and not be found. Then shall stand up in his estate a raiser of taxes *in* the glory of the kingdom:

After his discomfiture at Magnesia he was obliged to retire east of the Taurus, and confine himself to the 'strongholds of his own land.' To meet the heavy fine imposed upon him by the Romans[1] (Polyb. xxi. 14; Livy xxxvii. 45), he had to levy contributions where he could, and deemed sacrilege excusable under the circumstances. Having plundered for this purpose a wealthy temple of Bel in Elymais (Persia), he quickly met, says Diodorus (xxix. 15), τῆς προσηκούσης ἐκ θεῶν κολάσεως, being attacked by the inhabitants and slain (cf. Justin xxxii. 2). The last words of the verse allude to this disastrous enterprise, which brought his life to an end.

and not be found] implying complete disappearance: Ps. xxxvii. 36; Job xx. 8.

20. Seleucus IV. (Philopator), B.C. 187—175.

Antiochus the Great left two sons, Seleucus and Antiochus (Epiphanes), both of whom successively followed him on the throne.

And *in his* place (*v.* 7) *shall stand up* one that shall cause an exactor to pass through *the glory of the kingdom*] Seleucus IV. The words are generally considered to allude to an event from the reign of this monarch which affected the Jews. In 2 Macc. iii. we read, namely, how one Simon, guardian of the Temple, having quarrelled with the high-priest Onias, gave information to Apollonius, governor of Cœle-Syria and Phœnicia, of the treasures contained in the Temple, with the suggestion that they might prove useful to the king: Seleucus thereupon commissioned his chief minister (τὸν ἐπὶ τῶν πραγμάτων)[2], Heliodorus, to proceed to Jerusalem and appropriate them. Heliodorus accordingly visited Jerusalem for the purpose; but was prevented from carrying it out (according to the author of 2 Macc.) by a supernatural apparition, which appeared to him just as he was on the point of entering the treasury[3]. We are however imperfectly informed as to the events of Seleucus IV.'s reign; and it is possible that the allusion may be of a general kind: Seleucus (below, note) had to pay for nine years an annual sum of 1000 talents to the Romans, which he would naturally exact of his subject provinces; and perhaps the reference may be to the 'exactor' who visited Palestine regularly for the purpose[4].

an exactor] cf. the cognate verb in 2 Kin. xxiii. 35.

the glory of the kingdom] a prophet (Is. xiii. 19) had called Babylon 'the beauty of kingdoms'; and so here the land of Judah is called 'the glory of the kingdom' (viz. of the Seleucidae), their noblest and choicest province. The Heb. in this part of the verse is however unusual; and Bevan, transposing two words, would read, 'shall stand up an exactor (Seleucus IV. himself), who shall cause the glory of the

---

[1] 15,000 Eubœan talents; 500 at once, 2500 when the Romans ratified the peace, and 1000 yearly for 12 years.
[2] A title given to him also on an inscription (Niese, *op. cit.* [p. 140], p. 28 f.).
[3] Cf. Ewald v. 292; Stanley, *Jewish Church*, III. 287.
[4] Antiochus Epiphanes shortly afterwards sends into Judah an officer called ἄρχων φορολογίας (1 Macc. i. 29).

but within few days he shall be destroyed, neither in anger, nor in battle.

And in his estate shall stand up a vile person, to whom 21 they shall not give the honour of the kingdom: but he shall

kingdom (i.e. of his own kingdom) to pass away,'—with allusion to the inglorious reign of Seleucus IV.

but within few days (Gen. xxvii. 44, xxix. 20, Heb.) *he shall be* **broken, but not** *in anger, or in battle*] not by a passionate deed of violence, and not in open fight, but (it is implied) in some less honourable way: in point of fact, Seleucus, after an uneventful reign of 12 years, met his death, perhaps by poison, through a plot headed by his chief minister, Heliodorus (Appian, *Syr.* c. 45 ἐξ ἐπιβουλῆς Ἡλιοδώρου). The 'few days' may be reckoned either from the mission of Heliodorus, or perhaps from the inception of the plot: in either case the general meaning will be that he would come to a speedy and untimely end.

broken] i.e. ruined; of a person, as Prov. vi. 15, xxix. 1; *ch.* viii. 25. Cf. *v.* 26, below.

in anger] if this is the meaning, the Heb. is very unusual; Behrmann suggests, on the strength of Aramaic analogies (cf. P. S. col. 278, *bottom*), that the expression may perhaps mean **openly.**

21—45. Antiochus IV. (Epiphanes), 175—164.

21. Antiochus' accession. Antiochus was the younger brother of Seleucus Philopator; and, in accordance with the terms of the peace concluded by Antiochus the Great with the Romans (p. 175), he had been, for 14 years, one of the Syrian hostages at Rome[1]: Seleucus, in his 12th year had recalled him, sending, to take his place at Rome, his own son Demetrius (a boy aged 11 or 12); and it was while he was at Athens, on his way back to Antioch, that Seleucus was murdered by Heliodorus (above, on *v.* 20). Heliodorus aspired naturally to the throne, but was thwarted in his designs by Eumenes, king of Pergamum, and his brother, Attalus, who, as Antiochus was proceeding homewards, met him, unsolicited (ἀπαρακλήτως), with great friendliness, supplied him with money and troops, and so enabled him to secure the throne. An inscription has been recently discovered at Pergamum, recording a vote of thanks passed by the Council and people of Antioch to Eumenes and Attalus for the help thus given by them to Antiochus (see p. 205 f.).

And in his place shall stand up a **contemptible** *person*] Antiochus IV., called 'contemptible' (more lit. *despised*, Ps. xv. 4 (R.V.), cxix. 141) on account of his character (p. xxxviii f.), perhaps also in intentional opposition to the title 'Epiphanes.' In 1 Macc. i. 10 he is called a 'sinful root.'

upon *whom* **had** *not* **been conferred the majesty of the kingdom**]

---

[1] He had been well treated during these years, as he afterwards boasted in a message sent to the Senate (Livy xlii. 6), 'Ea merita in se senatus fuisse, quum Romae esset, eam comitatem iuventutis, ut pro rege, non pro obside, omnibus ordinibus fuerit.'

come in peaceably, and obtain the kingdom by flatteries.

The phrase, exactly as (in the Heb.) 1 Ch. xxix. 25 ('bestow,' lit. *put*), and Num. xxvii. 20 (A.V., R.V., weakly, 'honour'). The words, taken in conjunction with the two following clauses, imply that Antiochus had not been generally regarded as the heir to the throne, but that he gained it partly by a *coup d'état*, partly by address. His nephew, Demetrius, the son of Seleucus Philopator, was the lawful heir; but, as has been just said, he was a child, and also now a hostage at Rome.

but he shall come in (time of) security] i.e. unawares (*v.* 24, viii. 25).

by flatteries] or *smooth sayings*, i.e. plausible representations, the exact nature of which we do not know. Cf. viii. 23, which speaks of his mastery in dissimulation (מֵבִין חִידוֹת). The details are unknown to us: but it is quite possible that the support given to Antiochus by Eumenes and Attalus took the Antiochenes by surprise: it would be entirely in accordance with Antiochus' character that he should afterwards ingratiate himself with the people, and lead them to thank his two friends publicly for the part they had taken in securing him the kingdom. According to Jerome, there was a party in Syria, which supported the claims of his nephew (see on *v.* 17), the youthful son of Ptolemy Epiphanes and Cleopatra (afterwards Ptolemy Philometor), and refused to recognize Antiochus until he had disarmed their opposition *simulatione clementiae*.

Before proceeding further, it will be convenient to give a summary of the chief events of Antiochus Epiphanes' reign[1].

Antiochus' first expedition into Egypt (B.C. 170). The death, soon after Antiochus' accession, in 174 or 173, of his sister, Cleopatra, widow of Ptolemy Epiphanes, was the signal for fresh complications with Egypt. His nephew, Ptolemy Philometor, who was a boy of not more than 15 years old, fell now under the influence of his guardians, the eunuch Eulaeus and a Syrian named Lenaeus, who assured him that, if he would but make the attempt, he would easily recover for Egypt her Syrian possessions. Antiochus, learning through Apollonius, the governor of Cœle-Syria (whom he had sent to attend the enthronement of Philometor), Egyptian feeling towards himself, proceeded to act without further delay. First, with the intention, no doubt, of making himself popular with the Jews, he visited Jerusalem, and received there, at the instance of the Hellenizing high-priest Jason (above, on ix. 26), a magnificent welcome (2 Macc. iv. 21, 22). After this, he led his army into Phœnicia (*ibid.*). Both parties, now that

---

[1] The principal authorities are Polybius xxvi. 10, xxvii. 17, xxviii. 1, 16, 17, 18, 19, xxix. 1, 11, xxxi. 3, 4, 5, 11; Livy xli. 20, xlii. 6, 29, xliv. 19, xlv. 11, 12; Porphyry (as cited by Jerome on Dan. xi. 21 ff.), who states (see p. 622, ed. Bened.) that he follows various Greek authorities, including some now lost. Some uncertainty arises (especially as regards the 1st and 2nd Egyptian expeditions) from the fact that the records (in particular those of Polyb.) are incomplete. Among modern authorities, reference may be made in particular to J. F. Hoffmann, *Antiochus IV. Epiphanes*, 1873; and U. Wilcken's art. *Antiochus IV.*, in Pauly-Wissowa's *Real-Encyclopädie* (1894).

hostilities were actually beginning, sent embassies to Rome, each hoping to enlist the sympathies of the Senate, and each laying the blame of the war upon the other,—Antiochus declaring that he held the Syrian provinces by inheritance from his father Antiochus the Great, and that he was only defending rights which had been unjustly (παρὰ πάντα τὰ δίκαια) attacked, while Ptolemy contended that Antiochus the Great had taken advantage of the youth of his father, Ptolemy Epiphanes, to wrest these provinces from him. Nothing, however, of importance resulted from these embassies, and hostilities continued. In 170 B.C. Antiochus marched into Egypt with a considerable force (1 Macc. i. 17), defeated Ptolemy's troops between Pelusium and Mons Casius, and —by some dishonourable means which Polybius censures (xxviii. 7. 16) —obtained possession of the important border-fortress—the *claustra Aegypti*, as Livy calls it (xlv. 11)—of Pelusium. It was the clemency shewn by Antiochus in the battle near Pelusium—he rode about among his troops, and would not permit them to massacre the defeated Egyptians—that won for him the favour of the Egyptians, and facilitated considerably both his capture of Pelusium, and his subsequent conquest of Egypt (Diod. xxx. 14). After the fall of Pelusium, Eulaeus, it seems, persuaded Ptolemy to abandon his kingdom, and retire to Samothrace (Polyb. xxviii. 17ª); but,—apparently on the way thither,— he was intercepted, and fell into his uncle's hands. According to Jerome, Antiochus now, simulating friendship with his nephew, proceeded to Memphis, where *ex more Aegypti* he was crowned[1]; and pretending to be acting in Philometor's interests (*puerique rebus se providere dicens*), succeeded in occupying the whole of Egypt (cf. 1 Macc. i. 18—20), an act in which, Jerome adds, *tam callidus fuit, ut prudentes cogitationes eorum qui duces pueri erant, sua fraude subverteret*[2]. After this Antiochus prepared to return to Syria. Meanwhile, however, disturbances had arisen in Jerusalem. A rumour having been current of the death of Antiochus, Jason, the deposed and exiled high-priest (above, on ix. 26), thought the opportunity a favourable one for recovering his former position; so he attacked Jerusalem with 1000 men, and compelled Menelaus to take refuge in the citadel, but misusing his success for the purpose of slaughtering his own countrymen, was obliged to retire again to the country of the Ammonites (2 Macc. v. 5—10). Antiochus, hearing of these proceedings, thought Jerusalem was in revolt: so on his return from Egypt, he made a *détour* through Judaea, and entering the city with his army, massacred many of the inhabitants, penetrated into the sanctuary, and carried away all the sacred vessels, as well as all the other gold and silver that he could find there (1 Macc. i. 20—24; also, probably with some exaggeration, 2 Macc. v. 11—17, 21: cf. Jos. *B. J.* I. i. 1)[3]. In all this Antiochus was supported by Menelaus and his other Hellenizing

---

[1] Cf. the coin, No. 4, on the Plate, p. 192.

[2] Hoffmann thinks that the first campaign against Egypt ended at Pelusium, his occupation of Egypt, mentioned above, in Jerome's condensed account, belonging really to his second campaign.

[3] The statement in 2 Macc. v. 1 that these events took place on Antiochus's return from his *second* expedition into Egypt, appears to be erroneous.

friends among the Jews; indeed, according to Josephus (*Ant.* XII. v. 3) they opened the gates of Jerusalem to admit him.

Antiochus' second expedition into Egypt (B.C. 169). It was probably during Antiochus' absence from Egypt that Philometor's younger brother, Ptolemy Physcon (afterwards Euergetes II.), was proclaimed king in Alexandria. This led to Antiochus' *second* invasion of Egypt (B.C. 169), in which he gave out that he was acting from the honourable motive of restoring his nephew and ally, Philometor, to his lawful rights[1], while, of course, in reality he was simply playing off one brother against the other with the object of securing all for himself. Having defeated the Egyptian fleet in a naval battle near Pelusium, he marched to Memphis, and then sailed down the Nile towards Alexandria. A little S. of Naukratis he was met by an embassy of Achaeans and others, who came on behalf of Physcon to treat for peace. Antiochus received the envoys courteously, and listened to their arguments. They cast the whole blame for what had occurred upon Lenaeus; and referring to Ptolemy's youth, and his relationship to himself, entreated the king to lay aside his anger. Antiochus replied, stating at length the grounds on which he claimed Syria: it had been held by Antigonus, the founder of the Syrian empire, it had been afterwards ceded formally by the Macedonian kings to his son, Seleucus, and it had been conquered afresh by his own father, Antiochus the Great: the agreement, by which, as was alleged, it had been granted by Antiochus the Great to Cleopatra as a dowry (above, on *v.* 17) he entirely denied. Polybius adds that he convinced all who heard him of the justice of his contention (ὡς δίκαια λέγει). After this, Antiochus sailed on to Naukratis, where he treated the inhabitants graciously, giving to every Greek resident a gold coin. He then proceeded to lay siege to Alexandria. During the siege an embassy of Rhodians approached Antiochus with proposals for peace; but these envoys he cut short in their arguments by remarking that "the kingdom belonged to Ptolemy Philometor, that with him he had long been at peace [viz. since he fell into his hands, after the battle of Pelusium], and they were both friends; if therefore the Alexandrians were prepared to call Philometor back, he would not stand in their way." We do not know how long the siege of Alexandria continued; but the city must have suffered in it severely; Livy (xliv. 19) narrates how an embassy sent on behalf of Physcon to Rome, made a piteous appeal to the Senate, declaring that unless help were speedily forthcoming, the whole of Egypt would fall into the hands of Antiochus. C. Popillius Laenas, and two other envoys, were accordingly deputed by the Senate to terminate the war between the two kings, and to inform both that, whichever persisted in hostilities would not be regarded by the Romans as their friend or ally. However, before these envoys could reach Egypt, Antiochus, finding himself unable to take Alexandria, withdrew to Syria, leaving Philometor, *cui regnum quaeri suis viribus simulabat ut victorem mox aggrederetur*

---

[1] This was the *speciosus titulus* with the help of which, by means of letters and embassies, he sought to win the sympathy of all the cities of Asia and Greece (Liv. xlv. 11).

(Livy xlv. 11), as nominal king at Memphis, and stationing a strong garrison in Pelusium.

Antiochus' third expedition into Egypt (B.C. 168). The garrison left in Pelusium, the 'key of Egypt,' opened Philometor's eyes : it was evident that Antiochus wished to be in a position to return to Egypt with his army when he pleased, and also that the end of the war between the two brothers would be that the victor, whichever he was, would fall afterwards an easy prey to Antiochus. Accordingly Philometor made overtures of peace to Physcon, which, being seconded by Physcon's friends, and warmly supported by his sister, Cleopatra, were listened to favourably : before long a reconciliation was effected and Philometor was received into Alexandria (Livy xlv. 11). As Livy drily remarks, if Antiochus' real object had been to restore Philometor to his throne, he ought to have rejoiced at this reconciliation: in point of fact, however, he was so incensed at it, that he proceeded (B.C. 168) to attack the two brothers with far greater animosity (*multo acrius infestiusque*) than he had ever displayed towards the one. His fleet he sent on at once to Cyprus ; he himself, at the beginning of spring, marched by land through Cœle-Syria towards Egypt. At Rhinocolura, the border-stream of Egypt, he was met by the envoys of Philometor, who endeavoured to appease him by assuring him that their master gratefully recognized that it was by Antiochus' help that he had regained his kingdom, and that he hoped the king would still continue to be his friend. Antiochus replied that he would recall neither his army nor his fleet unless the whole of Cyprus were ceded to him, as well as Pelusium, and the country about the Pelusiac arm of the Nile; and appointed a day before which Philometor should declare whether he accepted these terms or not. As no answer came within the stipulated time, Antiochus advanced to Memphis, was well received by the people, 'partly from good-will, partly from fear,' and then proceeded by leisurely stages to Alexandria. At Eleusis, four miles from Alexandria, he was met by Popillius Laenas and the other Roman legates. He offered Popillius his hand. The Roman held out to him the ultimatum of the Senate, and bade him first read that. Antiochus, having read it, replied that he would consider with his friends what he would do. Popillius, *pro cetera asperitate animi* (cf. xlv. 10), drew with his staff a circle round the king ; and bade him give his answer to the Senate before leaving that circle. Antiochus was taken aback at this unexpected demand ; but, after a moment's hesitation, he replied, 'I will do what the Senate desires.' Then Popillius took his proffered hand. Antiochus was obliged to evacuate Egypt by a specified day ; the Roman legates then took measures to consolidate the peace between the two brothers, and sailing to Cyprus, obliged the forces of Antiochus (which had already obtained a victory over the Egyptian generals) to retire from the island. Both Philometor and Antiochus afterwards sent flattering and complimentary messages to the Senate (Livy xlv. 13). Thus ended Antiochus' *third* expedition into Egypt.

For the subsequent years of Antiochus' reign, see on xi. 40.

22 And *with* the arms of a flood shall they be overflown from before him, and shall be broken; yea also, the
23 prince of the covenant. And after the league *made* with him he shall work deceitfully: for he shall come up,
24 and shall become strong with a small people. He shall

22—24. General description of Antiochus' character and dealings. The verses have often (from Jerome onwards) been referred to Antiochus' first Egyptian campaign; but though occurrences in that campaign may be alluded to in them, they cannot, as a whole, be understood naturally as a description of it[1]. Observe also that the 'king of the south' is for the first time mentioned explicitly in *v.* 25.

22. *And the arms of the flood*] fig. for opposing forces. The metaphor is a mixed one: for 'arms,' cf. *v.* 15; for the fig. of the flood, *vv.* 10, 26, 40; Is. viii. 8, xxviii. 2, 15; Jer. xlvii. 2. The reference is ambiguous: it might of course be to the forces of Ptolemy Philometor; but more probably the domestic or other enemies who opposed Antiochus' rise to power are meant. According to Jerome there was a party in Syria which favoured the claims of Philometor.

shall be **flooded** (or **swept**) **away** *from before him*] he will prevail against them.

be broken] cf., of an army, 2 Ch. xiv. 12.

and also the prince of the covenant] most probably the high-priest, Onias III., who was deposed from his office by Antiochus in 175, and whose death was at least an indirect consequence of action taken by Antiochus (see above, on ix. 26). The words might, however, be also rendered *a confederate prince* (cf. Gen. xiv. 13; Ob. 7; Heb.): the reference would then be to Ptolemy Philometor; but it is an objection to this view that the king of Egypt is regularly throughout the chapter called the 'king of the south'; nor are the relations which (so far as we know) subsisted between Antiochus and Philometor such as would be described naturally as a 'covenant' or 'league.'

23. *And* **from the time when he** (or **any**) **joins himself unto** *him*—viz. in a league (2 Ch. xxx. 35, 37; cf. above, *v.* 6)—*he shall work* **deceit**] he will immediately scheme to overreach his ally. The reference is again ambiguous. The allusion might be specially to Antiochus' insincere friendship with Philometor, or to the manner in which he treated his allies in general.

and *he shall come up*] i.e., probably, rise to power (cf. Deut. xxviii. 43). The explanation 'go up (the Nile to Memphis)' (Jer. *ascendit Memphim*) is not natural. (The comma after *up* in A.V. should be transferred to follow *strong*.)

with a **little** (*v.* 34) **nation**] alluding apparently (Bevan) to the partisans of Antiochus, 'by whose help he was able to rise to power and overcome his rivals.'

[1] The terms in which Jerome (p. 713) describes the campaign (though the *facts*, he says, are derived from Porphyry) are manifestly coloured by the phraseology of these verses of Daniel.

enter peaceably even upon the fattest places of the province; and he shall do *that* which his fathers have not done, nor his fathers' fathers; he shall scatter among them the prey, and spoil, and riches: *yea*, and he shall forecast his devices against the strong holds, even for a time. And 25

24. In (time of) **security** (*v.* 21) **and** *upon the fattest places* (cf. Gen. xxvii. 28, Heb.) *of the province* **shall he come**] The Heb. is unusually harsh; though the fact in both A.V. and R.V. is most successfully concealed. 'In security' is probably accidentally out of place, and should follow 'come' (in the Heb. ובמשמני מדינה בשלוה יבוא for בשלוה ובמשמני מדינה יבוא). Cf. viii. 25 (also of Antiochus) 'and in (time of) security he shall destroy many.' Again, the allusion is uncertain: it may be to Antiochus' acquisition of power over Syria; it may be to his attacks upon Judah, or to his invasions of Egypt.

prey and spoil and substance *he shall scatter* **unto** *them*] to his followers, or it may be to his people generally (for the vague use of the pron., cf. *vv.* 7, 25). The allusion is, no doubt, to Antiochus' lavish prodigality, in which he differed from most of the previous Syrian kings ('his fathers,' and 'his fathers' fathers'), who were usually in lack of surplus money. Cf. 1 Macc. iii. 30, 'and he feared that he should not have enough as at other times for the charges and the gifts which he used to give aforetime with a liberal hand, and he abounded *above the kings which were before him*'; also his liberality at Naukratis (above, p. 180), and the anecdotes of his lavish gifts to boon-companions, and even to strangers, in Polyb. xxvi. 10. 9—10, and Athen. x. 52 (p. 438). He was also very munificent in gifts to cities and temples, and in public shows (Liv. xli. 20, who cites examples[1]). Naturally, the funds for such purposes were obtained largely from the 'prey' and 'spoil' of plundered provinces: cf. 1 Macc. i. 19, 'and he took the spoils of Egypt,' iii. 31; Polyb. xxxi. 4. 9 (the cost of the games given by him in rivalry with those of Aem. Paullus in 167, defrayed in part out of the plunder of Egypt).

against **fortresses, also,** *he shall* **devise** *his devices*] frame warlike plans,—whether successfully, as against Pelusium and the other places in Egypt which he secured (cf. 1 Macc. i. 19, of his first campaign in Egypt, 'and they took the strong cities in the land of Egypt'), or unsuccessfully, as against Alexandria (see p. 180): perhaps, more particularly, the latter ('devise,'—as though ineffectually).

and that, until *a time*] until the time fixed, in the counsels of God, as the limit of such enterprises: cf. *vv.* 27, 35.

---

[1] For instance, he promised and partly bore the cost of, a city-wall at Megalopolis in Arcadia: he contributed largely to the restoration of the temple of Zeus Olympios at Athens; he presented gold vessels to the Prytaneum at Cyzicus, and beautified Delos with altars and statues; and at home he not only made many improvements in his capital, but also, what in Syria was an innovation, gave frequent gladiatorial shows. The words 'spectaculorum quoque omnis generis magnificentia *superiores reges vicit*' (cf. Polyb. xxvi. 10. 11) illustrate especially 1 Macc. iii. 30, cited above.

he shall stir up his power and his courage against the king of the south with a great army; and the king of the south shall be stirred up to battle with a very great and mighty army; but he shall not stand: for they shall forecast devices 26 against him. Yea, they that feed of the portion of his meat shall destroy him, and his army shall overflow: and 27 many shall fall down slain. And both these kings' hearts *shall be* to do mischief, and they shall speak lies at one

25—28. Antiochus' first Egyptian expedition (B.C. 170).
25. *courage*] lit. *heart*: cf. Josh. ii. 11; Am. ii. 16; Ps. lxxvi. 5.
the king of the south] Ptolemy Philometor.
shall be stirred up] *shall* stir **himself** *up* (*v*. 10).
a great army...a very great and mighty army] We have no independent evidence as to the relative size of the armies of Antiochus and Philometor. There is however no reason to suppose that the author would not represent correctly what had taken place only two or three years before he wrote.
but he shall not stand, for they shall **devise** *devices against him*] In spite of his superior army, Philometor could not maintain the contest, owing to the treachery of his adherents. We cannot say more particularly what is referred to: it is possible that the fortress of Pelusium, and Philometor himself, both fell into Antiochus' hands by treachery.
26. **And** *they that* **eat** *of* **his delicacies** (i. 5) *shall* **break** *him*] some of his courtiers will be his ruin. For the expression, cf. 1 Kin. ii. 7, 'those that eat of thy table'; *break*, as *v*. 20. The allusion may be to Eulaeus and Lenaeus, at whose ill-advised suggestion it was that Philometor was first led to think of reconquering Syria, and the former of whom, after the battle of Pelusium, persuaded the king to abandon his country. Ptolemy Macron, also, the very capable (Polyb. xxvii. 12) governor of Cyprus (though this was perhaps later), deserted to Antiochus (2 Macc. x. 13).
and his army shall overflow] i.e. Antiochus' army. But the pronouns from *v*. 25 *b* refer all to Philometor: the verb should therefore probably be vocalized as a passive (יִשָּׁטֵף) *and his army* (Philometor's) **shall be flooded** (or **swept**) **away**; the word, as *v*. 22.
and many shall fall down slain] cf. 1 Macc. i. 18, 'and many fell down slain' (also of Antiochus' victories in Egypt), where the Greek (except in the tense) is exactly the same as in LXX. and Theod. here.
27. *And* **as for the two** *kings, their heart* (shall be) for *mischief; and* **at one table they shall speak lies**] Antiochus and Philometor, after the latter had fallen into his uncle's hands, were outwardly on friendly terms with one another; but their friendship was insincere, as is expressively shewn by the picture which the writer's words suggest: sitting and eating *at one table*, they both in fact *spoke lies*,—Antiochus, in professing disinterestedness, as though his only object were to gain Egypt for his nephew's benefit, (*cui regnum quaeri suis viribus simulabat*, Livy xlv. 11), and Philometor in feigning that he believed his uncle's assurances, and cherished for him gratitude and regard.

table; but it shall not prosper: for yet the end *shall be* at the time appointed. Then shall he return *into* his land 28 with great riches; and his heart *shall be* against the holy

but it shall not prosper] The common plan, on which they were supposed to be agreed, the conquest of Egypt, ostensibly for Philometor, in reality for Antiochus.

for the end (remaineth) *yet* for *the time appointed*] matters will not yet be settled in Egypt: the end of Antiochus' doings there belongs still to a time fixed in the future.

It must be admitted that some of the references in *vv.* 25—27 (esp. in *v.* 27) would be more pointed and significant, if they could be supposed to allude to events in the *second* Egyptian campaign of Antiochus, as well as to events in the *first*. Upon the chronology adopted above (which is that of most modern historians), this can only be, if the author, neglecting the strict chronological sequence, throws the first two Egyptian campaigns together, and then (*v.* 28) proceeds to describe the attack upon Jerusalem. We do not, however, possess any continuous narrative of the events of Antiochus' reign; nor does there seem to be any express statement that Antiochus *returned* to Syria, or even that he left Egypt, at the close of what is described above as his 'first' Egyptian expedition; hence it is possible that Mahaffy[1] is right in his contention that Antiochus' first two campaigns (as they are commonly called) were in reality only two stages in one campaign—the first stage ending at Pelusium, and the second embracing the conquest of Egypt, and both belonging to the year B.C. 170. If this view be adopted, the attack upon Jerusalem (*v.* 28; 1 Macc. i. 20—24) will come at the end of what is called above the 'second' Egyptian expedition (but thrown back now to B.C. 170)[2], and both that and the 'first' Egyptian expedition will be summarized in *vv.* 25—28 and 1 Macc. i. 16—19.

28. *Then*] **And.** A chronological sequence is not expressed in the Heb.; and is perhaps (see the beginning of the last note) not intended by the writer.

he shall *return* **to his own** *land*] in 170, at the close of his 'first' Egyptian campaign,—in whatever sense this may be understood (see on *v.* 27). The clause anticipates what really took place only after what is described in the two following clauses; and hence, it is repeated, in its proper place, at the end of the verse.

with great substance] the 'spoils of Egypt' (1 Macc. i. 19): the word, as *vv.* 13, 24. Cf. the allusion in *Orac. Sib.* iii. 614—5.

against the holy covenant] alluding to Antiochus' hostile visit to Jerusalem, in which he 'entered presumptuously into the sanctuary,' and carried away the golden vessels, and other treasures, belonging to the Temple, besides massacring many of the Jews (1 Macc. i. 20—24).

---

[1] *Empire of the Ptolemies*, p. 494 f., cf. pp. 333—337, 340. So Wellhausen, *Isr. und Jüd. Gesch.* (1894), p. 203 *n.* (ed. 3, 1897, p. 246 *n.*).
[2] An interval of two years between this attack upon Jerusalem, and the persecuting edict of B.C. 168 is required by the dates in 1 Macc. i. 20 and 1 Macc. i. 29, 54.

covenant; and he shall do *exploits*, and return to his own
29 land. At the time appointed he shall return, and come
toward the south; but it shall not be as the former, or as
30 the latter. For *the* ships of Chittim shall come against
him: therefore he shall be grieved, and return, and have
indignation against the holy covenant: so shall he do;
he shall even return, and have intelligence with them that

and he shall **do**] in the pregnant sense explained on viii. 12: R.V.
'*do* (his pleasure).'
and return to his own land] 1 Macc. i. 24; 2 Macc. v. 21.
29. Antiochus' 'third' Egyptian expedition (B.C. 168).
the time appointed] the time fixed in the counsels of God.
but it shall not be **in the latter time as in the former**] this expedition will not be as successful as the previous one.
30—39. Antiochus' retreat from Egypt, (*v.* 30*a*), and the measures adopted by him shortly afterwards against the Jews (*vv.* 30*b*—39).
30. *For* **Kitian ships** *shall come against him*] The allusion is to C. Popillius Laenas and the other Roman legates, who, as described above (p. 181), obliged Antiochus, when within sight of Alexandria, to withdraw his forces unconditionally from Egypt. *Kittim,* properly the *Kitians,* or people of *Kitti* (in Phœn. Inscriptions כתי), a well-known town in Cyprus, the Greek *Kition*; hence in the O.T. the name of the inhabitants of Cyprus, Gen. x. 4; Is. xxiii. 1, 12; somewhat more widely, in Jer. ii. 10; Ez. xxvii. 6, 'isles (or coast-lands) of the Kitians,' of the islands and coasts of the Mediterranean Sea. By the later Jews it was used still more generally for any western maritime people (cf. Jos. *Ant.* I. i. 1); thus in 1 Macc. i. 1, viii. 5 it denotes the Macedonians, and here 'Kitian ships' means *Roman* ships (so LXX. καὶ ἥξουσι Ῥωμαῖοι). The expression is suggested by the terms of Balaam's prophecy in Num. xxiv. 24 (where, however, it is not certain what exactly is denoted by it).

and *he shall be* **cowed**, *and return*] 'cowed' (a rare word: Ps. cix. 16, A.V., R.V., badly, '*broken* in heart'), viz. by the summary manner in which Popillius treated him[1]. Cf. the terms used by Polyb. (xxix. 11), 'Antiochus accordingly withdrew his forces to Syria, βαρυνόμενος καὶ στένων, εἴκων δὲ τοῖς καιροῖς κατὰ τὸ παρόν'; and Livy '*Obstupefactus* tam violento imperio' (the demand of Popillius).
have indignation &c.] a stronger expression than was used in *v.* 28; he will this time be incensed against it.
and he shall do] viz. his pleasure, as *v.* 28.
and *he shall return* (viz. home to Antioch), *ana have* **regard unto** (*v.* 37 Heb.) *them that* &c.] After his return home he will fix his attention upon the apostate Jews, and use them as his agents, for the purpose of carrying out his designs. Shortly before the time of Antiochus there had arisen a party among the Jews, whose object was to Hellenize their

---

[1] The word (נִכְאָה) might possibly, however, have here its Syriac sense of *rebuked*: cf. LXX. ἐμβριμήσονται αὐτῷ, a word which in Matth. ix. 30 is represented in the Pesh. by כאא.

forsake the holy covenant. And arms shall stand on his 31 part, and they shall pollute the sanctuary *of* strength, and shall take away the daily *sacrifice*, and they shall place

nation, and obliterate its distinctive characteristics (1 Macc. i. 11—15,— in *v.* 15 'and they made themselves uncircumcised, and *forsook the holy covenant*, and joined themselves to the Gentiles, and sold themselves to do evil'). Jason, the renegade high-priest (see on ix. 26), was one of the leaders of the movement; and he and others obtained Antiochus' sanction and authority to construct in Jerusalem a 'gymnasium,' or exercise-ground, after the Greek model, and introduce other Greek customs. The result was that Greek fashions became popular; even the priests, we read, neglected the services of the Temple for the purpose of amusing themselves in the palaestra. See 1 Macc. i. 11—15, 2 Macc. iv. 4—17.

31. *And arms*—i.e. forces (*vv.* 15, 22)—(coming) **from him** *shall* **stand up**] or (following the interpunction expressed by the Heb. accents), *shall* **stand up at his instance** (Is. xxx. 1, Heb.); 'stand up,' i.e. be set on foot, organized (cf. in the causative conj. *v.* 11). The 'arms' are the armed force sent by Antiochus to take possession of Jerusalem (see the next note).

and they shall pollute the sanctuary (even) **the stronghold**] The Temple at this time was fortified with high walls, which were broken down by the soldiers of Antiochus, but afterwards rebuilt (1 Macc. iv. 60, vi. 7): hence it is called a 'stronghold.' For the facts, see 1 Macc. i. 29 ff. Apollonius (2 Macc. v. 24), coming with an armed force, but lulling with friendly words the suspicions of the people, fell upon the city suddenly on a sabbath-day; and having obtained possession of it, took women and children prisoners, demolished many of the houses and fortifications, and strengthening the citadel (which overlooked the Temple), established in it a Syrian garrison. Cf. 1 Macc. i. 34, 36, 37, 'And they put there [in the citadel] a sinful nation [the Syrian garrison], transgressors of the law (ἄνδρας παρανόμους), and they strengthened themselves therein.... And it became a place to lie in wait in against the sanctuary (ἔνεδρον τῷ ἁγιάσματι), and an evil adversary unto Israel continually. And they shed innocent blood round about the sanctuary, and *defiled the sanctuary*' (comp. ii. 12).

and shall take away the **continual** (burnt-offering)] cf. viii. 11, where the expression is similar, and the reference is the same. Apollonius had not been long in possession of Jerusalem when Antiochus, wishing to unify his empire, and to assimilate as far as possible its different parts, determined to bring it all under the influence of Hellenic culture; and accordingly issued in Judah instructions to obliterate every trace of the ancient religion. All the Jewish sacrifices were to be abolished in the Temple; sabbaths and other festivals were to be disregarded; ceremonial observances (such as the prohibition to eat unclean food) were to be discontinued; the rite of circumcision was prohibited, under pain of death; books of the law were to be destroyed, and anyone found with them in his possession was to be punished with death.

32 the abomination that maketh desolate. And such as do wickedly against the covenant shall he corrupt by flatteries:

Special commissioners (ἐπίσκοποι) were appointed for the purpose of carrying out these directions. Not only, however, were Jewish institutions to be thrown aside, heathen ones were to take their place; the Temple was to be transformed into a sanctuary of Zeus Olympios (2 Macc. vi. 2), heathen altars and shrines were to be set up, swine's flesh and unclean beasts were to be sacrificed; and officers were appointed to see that all these injunctions were duly carried out (1 Macc. i. 41—53). The suspension of the Temple services (to which the words of the present verse allude) began in December, B.C. 168, and continued for rather more than three years (see p. 119).

and they shall set up *the abomination that* causeth appalment] i.e. the heathen altar erected on the altar of burnt-offering. See 1 Macc. i. 54, 'And on the 15th day of Chisleu [December] they builded an abomination of desolation (βδέλυγμα ἐρημώσεως,—the same expression which is used in the LXX. here) upon the altar,' and (v. 59) 'on the 25th day of the month they sacrificed upon the (idol-) altar (βωμόν), which was upon the altar (of God) (θυσιαστήριον)': cf. also vi. 7. A statue of Zeus Olympios was most probably associated with the altar[1]. On 'causeth appalment,' see on viii. 13; and cf. the parallel passages ix. 27, xii. 11.

In explanation of the somewhat peculiar expression used, an ingenious and probable suggestion has been made by Nestle (*ZATW.* 1884, p. 248; cf. Bevan, p. 193). The Heb. for 'that causeth appalment' is *shōmēm* (viii. 13, xii. 11), or *mĕshōmēm* (ix. 27, xi. 31); and according to Nestle, the 'abomination that causeth appalment' is a contemptuous allusion to בעל שמים *Baʻal shāmayim* ('Baal of heaven'), a title occurring often in Phœnician, and (with *shāmîn* for *shāmayim*) Aramaic inscriptions, and in the Syriac version of 2 Macc. vi. 2 found actually for the Ζεὺς Ὀλύμπιος of the Greek; the altar (with probably the accompanying statue of Zeus) erected by Antiochus upon the altar of burnt-offering being termed derisively by the Jews 'the abomination that causeth appalment,' the 'abomination' being the altar (and image?) of Zeus (Baal), and *shōmēm* being a punning variation of *shāmayim*[2].

32. *And such as do wickedly* (ix. 5, xii. 10) *against the covenant*] the disloyal Jews.

shall he make profane (Jer. xxiii. 11)] by abetting them in their designs, he will lead them from bad to worse. In Syr. the root here used acquired the special sense of *gentile* (e.g. Matth. vi. 7, xviii. 17, Pesh.), *apostate*, and represents, for instance, *Hellenic*, *Greek* (2 Macc.

---

[1] Cf. the tradition in the Mishna (*Taanith* iv. 6 העמיד צלם בהיכל), Euseb. (*ap.* Sync. 542, 21 καὶ τὸν ναὸν βεβηλοῖ Διὸς Ὀλυμπίου βδέλυγμα ἀναστηλώσας ἐν αὐτῷ), and Jerome (on Dan. xi. 31, 'Jovis Olympii simulacrum'), referred to by Grätz, *Gesch.* II. 2, p. 314 f.

[2] 'Abomination of desolation' (Greek versions of Dan., 1 Macc. i. 54) is not a possible rendering of the Heb. 'Abomination that maketh desolate' is possible; and, if correct, must imply that the heathen emblem standing in the court of the Temple was regarded as bringing with it the desertion and desolation of the sanctuary (cf. 1 Macc. iv. 38; and see also above, on viii. 13, and p. 151).

but the people that do know their God shall be strong, and do *exploits*. And they that understand among the 33 people shall instruct many: yet they shall fall by the

iv. 10, xi. 24, Pesh.); and possibly the word may have the definite sense of *make apostates* here (cf. R.V. *pervert*).

by flatteries] by specious representations, or promises, pointing out for example the advantages that would accrue to those who renounced their Judaism. Cf. the promises held out (1 Macc. ii. 18) to Mattathias ('thou and thy house shall be in the number of the king's friends, and thou and thy sons shall be honoured with silver and gold and many gifts'). Mattathias turned a deaf ear to such inducements; but the prospect of Antiochus' favour might easily influence men who were less staunch in their convictions.

but the people that do know their God shall **shew strength**] i.e. *exhibit firmness, constancy* (cf. Deut. xii. 23 'be *strong, firm*, not to eat the blood'; Josh. i. 7; 1 Ch. xxviii. 7), neither to yield to temptation nor to desert their religion for fear of the consequences. The decree of Antiochus led to numerous martyrdoms, many of the loyal Israelites submitting to death, even with torture, rather than renounce their faith. Cf. 1 Macc. i. 62 f. 'And many in Israel *were strong* (i.e. *firm*: the Greek word used stands for חזק in 1 Sam. xxx. 6; Ezr. x. 4, and elsewhere), and were fortified (like a strong city,—ὀχυρώθησαν) in themselves, not to eat unclean things (κοινά). And they chose to die, that they might not be defiled with the meats, nor profane the holy covenant; and they died.'

and **do**] they also will *do*, or *act*, in the pregnant sense of the word (cf. on viii. 12), in their cause, not less than the ambitious heathen king (viii. 12, 24, xi. 28, 30) in his.

33. *And they that* **be wise**] as the same word is rendered in A.V. of xii. 3, 10. The verb means properly *to shew understanding and discernment*, such as may lead a man to act judiciously and bring him success; hence it is sometimes rendered *prosper*, or *have good success*, &c. See examples of the word in Josh. i. 7, 8, 1 Sam. xviii. 5, Ps. ii. 10, Prov. x. 5, 19 'he that refraineth his lips *sheweth understanding*,' i.e. 'acts judiciously,' Is. lii. 13. Here it is used, as a term of approbation, to denote those who, in a time of severe trial, *shewed wisdom*, by choosing the right course, and strenuously refusing to give up their faith. The name given to the loyal party in the Maccabees is the *Hasidaeans*, i.e. *ḥasîdîm*, or 'godly': see 1 Macc. ii. 42, 'Then were gathered together unto them (i.e. unto Mattathias and his friends, who appear to have been the first to assume the aggressive against Antiochus' decree) a company of Hasidaeans (συναγωγὴ Ἀσιδαίων), mighty men out of Israel, every one that offered himself willingly (= מִתְנַדֵּב, Jud. v. 2; 2 Ch. xvii. 16; Neh. xi. 2) for the law. And all they that fled from the evils were added to them, and became a stay unto them'; 1 Macc. vii. 13; 2 Macc. xiv. 6.

shall **cause the** *many* **to understand**] The 'wise' (*maskîlîm*), the leaders of the patriotic party, will, by their influence and example, teach the masses, especially such as were halting between two opinions, to understand their duty.

sword, and by flame, by captivity, and by spoil, *many*
34 days. Now when they shall fall, they shall be holpen *with*
a little help: but many shall cleave to them with flatteries.
35 And *some* of them of understanding shall fall, to try them,
and to purge, and to make *them* white, *even* to the time
of the end: because *it is* yet for a time appointed.

yet they shall fall, &c.] alluding to the persecutions and martyrdoms
in which many of the loyal Jews perished; see 1 Macc. i. 60, 63, ii.
31—38; 2 Macc. vi. 10, 11, 18—31 (the aged scribe Eleazar), vii. (the
mother and her seven sons). 'Fall,' here and *vv.* 34, 35, is properly
stumble (*v.* 14).

many *days*] viz. till an effectual stand was made by the Maccabees.

34. In the midst of their trials a 'little help' will arise, to assist
them. The allusion is to the rising of the Maccabees. First of all,
Mattathias, either alone or assisted only by his sons, resisted openly
Antiochus' demands, and slew one of the officers sent to enforce them
(1 Macc. ii. 15—28): then others gradually joined themselves to him,
and carried the resistance further (*ib. vv.* 39—48): finally, after Mattathias' death, his son Judas Maccabaeus carried on the struggle. His first
victory was gained over Apollonius, who invaded Judah with a considerable
army; and shortly afterwards, Seron, commander of the host of Syria,
coming to avenge Apollonius' defeat, was routed with the loss of 800
men, by Judas at the head of a 'small company' ('Ιούδας...ὀλιγοστός),
1 Macc. iii. 10—24. After this, further successes were gained by Judas
over Antiochus' generals Lysias and Gorgias (*ib.* iii. 38—iv. 35), the
result of which was that, by the end of B.C. 165, the Jews recovered
possession of Mount Zion, and the Temple was re-dedicated (*ib.* iv.
36—61). The occasion was celebrated by a festival, lasting eight days
(*v.* 59), which was observed annually afterwards, and is referred to in
John x. 22 (τὰ ἐγκαίνια).

but many shall **join themselves** (Is. xiv. 1, lvi. 3) *unto them with
flatteries*] or *smooth sayings*, i.e. plausible, but insincere, protestations
of loyalty. In consequence of the severity shewn by Judas, and the
leaders of the patriotic party, many joined them from mere terror, and
were ready, if a favourable opportunity offered itself, to turn traitors.
On the severity of Judas and the patriots towards the Hellenizing
Jews, comp. allusions in 1 Macc. ii. 44, iii. 5*a*, 8, vi. 21—27, vii. 5—7,
24 (where Judas, it is said, 'took vengeance on the men that had deserted
from him'), ix. 23.

35. *And* some *of them that* **be wise** (*v.* 33) *shall fall, to* **refine** *among
them* (among the people at large), *and to* **cleanse,** *and to* **make white**]
The martyrdom of some of the godly leaders in the struggle would have
the effect of testing the faith of the people at large, and of confirming
and perfecting the character of those who were loyal. Cf. xii. 10.

to **refine**] the word means properly *to smelt* gold or silver ore (or alloy),
so as to free the noble metal from impurities; it is then often used
figuratively, sometimes of *testing*, sometimes of *purifying*, by severe

1. Silver Tetradrachm. Head of Antiochus, with diadem (in other coins of this type a *star* is seen distinctly on the forehead: Babelon, *Les Rois de Syrie*, XII. 3, 4).

Reverse: Apollo, seated on omphalos, holding arrow and bow. Inscription: **ΒΑΣΙΛΕΩΣ ΑΝΤΙΟΧΟΥ** ('Of King Antiochus').

 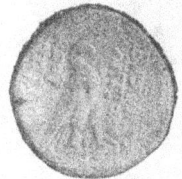

2. Silver Drachm. Head of Antiochus, radiate.

Reverse: Eagle, with closed wings, standing on thunderbolt. Inscription: **ΒΑΣΙΛΕΩΣ ΑΝΤΙΟΧΟΥ ΘΕΟΥ ΕΠΙΦΑΝΟΥΣ** ('Of King Antiochus, God Manifest').

3. Silver Tetradrachm. Head of Antiochus, as Zeus, with laurels.
Reverse: Zeus, wearing himation over shoulder, seated on throne: holds Nike (Victory), who crowns Inscription; and rests on sceptre. Inscription: ΒΑΣΙΛΕΩΣ ΑΝΤΙΟΧΟΥ ΘΕΟΥ ΕΠΙΦΑΝΟΥΣ ΝΙΚΗΦΟΡΟΥ ('Of King Antiochus, God Manifest, Victory-bearer').

4. Copper Pentechalcon. Head of Zeus-Serapis, wearing laurel-wreath, ending above in cap of Osiris.
Reverse: Eagle, with closed wings, standing on thunderbolt. Inscription: ΒΑΣΙΛΕΩΣ ΑΝΤΙΟΧΟΥ ΘΕΟΥ ΕΠΙΦΑΝΟΥΣ ('Of King Antiochus, God Manifest'). This coin was struck in Egypt, and illustrates Antiochus' conquest of that country (cf. Babelon, p. c).

(From casts taken from coins in the British Museum. The descriptions from Gardner's *Coins of the Seleucid Kings of Syria*, XI. 2, XII. 13, XI. 9, XII. 11.)

And the king shall do according to his will; and he 36 shall exalt himself, and magnify himself above every god,

discipline: cf. Is. i. 25, 'and *smelt away* as in a furnace (בְּכֹר) thy dross'; Jer. vi. 29, 'in vain *the smelter smelteth*, for the evil are not separated'; ix. 6 'Behold, I will *smelt* them, and try them'; Zech. xiii. 9.

until *the time of the end*] the fall of the *maskîlîm* will continue till the final end of the present order of things (viii. 17), which the author pictures as coinciding with the close of Antiochus' reign (*v.* 40).

for (it is) *yet for the time appointed*] the end has not come yet; it has still to wait for the moment fixed in the counsels of God: cf. *v.* 27 *end*.

36—39. The presumptuousness and impiety of Antiochus. Many of the older expositors supposed that at this point there was a transition from Antiochus to the future Antichrist, and that *vv.* 36—45 related exclusively to the latter; but whatever typical significance might be legitimately considered to attach to the character and career of Antiochus as a *whole*, it is contrary to all sound principles of exegesis to suppose that, in a *continuous* description, with no indication whatever of a change of subject, part should refer to one person, and part to another, and that 'the king' of *v.* 36, and 'the king of the south' of *v.* 45 should be a different king from the one whose doings are described in *vv.* 21—35. The fact that traits in the N.T. figure of Antichrist are suggested (apparently) by the description in *vv.* 36—39, does not authorize the inference that these verses themselves refer to Antichrist (cf. the Introd. p. xcvii).

36. *according to his will*] as viii. 4, xi. 3 (of Alexander); xi. 16 (of Antiochus the Great).

magnify himself] Is. x. 15. So *v.* 37.

above every god] Antiochus acquired a reputation for piety among the Greeks by his splendid presents to temples (cf. on *v.* 24); but by the manner in which he patronized, and selected for honour, particular deities (as Zeus Olympios, or Jupiter Capitolinus), he might be said, especially from an Israelitish point of view, to set himself above them all.

Antiochus, moreover, assumed divine honours. This is particularly evident, as Babelon has pointed out[1], on his coins. His best portraits appear to be those on the coins of his early years, which bear simply the inscription 'King Antiochus.' At a later period of his reign a star appears on his forehead, implying that he has assumed divine honours. Then in coins with the legend, 'King Antiochus, God' (or 'God Manifest' [Epiphanes]), the star disappears, but the portrait is idealized, the features approximating in type to those of Apollo. Other coins of the same type exhibit the head surrounded by a diadem with rays,— another mark of divine rank[2]. Lastly, on coins with the legend 'King Antiochus, God Manifest, Victory-bearer,' the head approximates even to that of Zeus Olympios, whose distinctive epithet Νικηφόρος ('Victory-bearer') the king himself assumes. See the accompanying Plate.

[1] In the instructive Introduction to *Les Rois de Syrie* (Catalogue of Coins in the National Library at Paris), 1891, p. xcii—iv.
[2] Babelon states that Antiochus Epiphanes is the first Seleucid king who is represented constantly on his coins with a crown of rays.

and shall speak marvellous *things* against the God of gods, and shall prosper till the indignation be accomplished: 37 for that that is determined shall be done. Neither shall he regard the God of his fathers, nor the desire of women,

and against the God of gods (the God of Israel: cf. ii. 47) *he shall speak marvellous things*] i.e. extraordinary impieties: cf. (also of Antiochus) vii. 8 'a mouth speaking great things,' 25 'shall speak words against the Most High.'

until indignation be accomplished] or, **be finished, exhausted**, i.e. until God's wrath on Israel has worked itself out. The words are borrowed from Is. x. 25. For 'accomplished,' see also Ez. v. 13, vi. 12, vii. 8, xiii. 15, xx. 8, 21.

for that that is determined shall be done] the Divine decree must take effect. The expression, as in ix. 27 (where see the note), from Is. x. 23.

37. And *the gods of his fathers* **he will not regard**] The honours paid by him to foreign deities implied a depreciation of the gods of his own country. He was particularly devoted to the cult of Jupiter Capitolinus, or Zeus Olympios. Even before he became king, while halting at Athens on his way home from Rome, he contributed largely to the restoration of the Olympieion in that city; afterwards, he built in Daphne, the suburb of Antioch, a temple to Zeus Olympios, with a colossal statue of the god, modelled on the famous one of Pheidias at Olympia, and began, though he did not live to complete it, a yet more magnificent temple to him in Antioch itself (Livy xli. 20). His coins also exhibit constantly (on the obverse) the head of either Zeus Olympios or Apollo; and, as was just remarked, in those belonging to the latter part of his reign the king himself bears the title Νικηφόρος,— an epithet belonging properly to Zeus.

and neither *the desire of women, nor any god,* **will he regard**] The 'desire of women' must, from the context, be the designation of some divinity—most probably (Ewald, Bevan) Tammuz, a celebrated Syrian and Phœnician deity, known to the Greeks as Adonis, whose rites were popular among women.

Adonis in the legend was a beautiful youth, the dearly loved spouse of Aphroditè, snatched from her by a cruel fate, and bitterly bewailed by her. The festival of Adonis consisted largely in an imitation of the mourning of Aphroditè, and hence was specially observed by *women*; cf. Ez. viii. 14 (where the prophet sees in vision, in the precincts of the Temple, 'the *women* weeping for Tammuz'); Jerome on Ez. *l. c.* 'plangitur a mulieribus quasi mortuus, et postea reviviscens canitur atque laudatur[1]'; Aristoph. *Lysistr.* 389 ff.; and Theocritus' Idyll

[1] Cf. Milton, *P. L.* i. 456 ff.:—

Tammuz came next behind,
Whose annual wound in Lebanon allured
The Syrian damsels to lament his fate
In amorous ditties all a summer's day;
While smooth Adonis from his native rock
Ran purple to the sea—supposed with blood
Of Tammuz yearly wounded. The love-tale
Infected Zion's daughters with like heat.

nor regard any god: for he shall magnify himself above all. But in his estate shall he honour the God of forces: 38 and a god whom his fathers knew not shall he honour with gold, and silver, and with precious stones, and pleasant things. Thus shall he do in the most strong holds with 39 a strange god, whom he shall acknowledge *and* increase *with* glory: and he shall cause them to rule over many,

(xv.) entitled Ἀδωνιάζουσαι, or 'Women keeping festival to Adonis.' According to Hippolytus, *Refut. Hær.* v. 9, the 'Assyrians' (? Syrians) called him the 'thrice-desired (τριπόθητος) Adonis': cf. Bion, in his Ἐπιτάφιος Ἀδώνιδος, ll. 24, 58.

nor any god] While there were some gods whom Antiochus honoured by erecting to them costly temples, he was ready enough, if in need of funds, to rob other temples of their treasures. Polybius (xxxi. 4. 10) expressly says that he plundered very many temples (ἱεροσυλήκει δὲ καὶ τὰ πλεῖστα τῶν ἱερῶν) in order to obtain money for his extravagances. He made an unsuccessful attempt to pillage a wealthy temple in Persia shortly before his death (*ib.* xxxi. 11; 1 Macc. vi. 1—4: see below).

38. *But in his* place *he will honour the god of* **strongholds**] it is not certain who is meant by the 'god of strongholds': possibly the reference is to some deity (? Mars) of whose worship by Antiochus we have no other notice; more probably, however, the name is simply an alternative designation of Jupiter Capitolinus.

and a god whom, &c.] No doubt, Zeus or Jupiter (cf. on *v.* 37). It is true, the first three Seleucidae, as their coins testify, recognized Zeus Olympios,—not, as Behrmann (misunderstanding a sentence of G. Hoffmann, *Einige Phön. Inschr.*, p. 29) states, Zeus Polieus,—as their patron; but Zeus was not, of course, a native Syrian deity.

pleasant things] better, **costly** *things*: lit. *things desired.* Cf. on *v.* 8 ('precious' cannot be used here; as the word is needed for *yĕḳārāh*, in 'precious stones').

39. And he will *do* **to the fortresses of strongholds** *with* (the help of) *a* **foreign** *god*] i.e. will conquer them by his aid. But the Heb. is strange; and the sense obtained connects badly with what follows. Hitz., Meinh., and Bevan, changing a point, render, 'And he shall procure for the fortresses of strongholds *the people of* a strange god,' supposing the reference to be to the heathen soldiers and colonists settled by Antiochus in the citadel in Jerusalem, and other parts of Judah (1 Macc. i. 33, iii. 36, 45). The rendering 'procure' for עשׂה is, however, not very probable here, 2 Sam. xv. 1, 1 Ki. i. 5, which are quoted in support of it, being hardly parallel. For *foreign god* (אלוה נכר), cf. Gen. xxxv. 4, Jer. v. 19 (אלהי), Ps. lxxxi. 9 (אל).

strange] i.e. (from Lat. 'extraneus') **foreign**, as regularly in A.V.

he whom *he* **recognizes, will increase glory**] his favourites will be loaded by him with honours. 'Recognize' (הִכִּיר), as Ruth ii. 10 ('take knowledge of'); Jer. xxiv. 5 ('regard').

shall cause them to rule over the *many, and shall divide* **land** *for a*

price] he will give them posts as governors, and grant them estates—seized, probably, from their rightful owners—for a bribe. An allusion to Antiochus' methods of government, and to the means by which he filled his empty treasuries; perhaps, also, in particular, to renegade Jews who had been thus rewarded for their apostasy. Jason, and after him Menelaus, both purchased the high-priesthood from Antiochus (2 Macc. iv. 8—10, 24); and Bacchides (*ib.* ix. 25) 'chose out the ungodly men, and made them lords over the country.' No doubt other similar instances were known to the author.

40—45. The end of Antiochus. Antiochus, being attacked by the king of Egypt, will again conduct an expedition into Egypt, passing through Judah on the way; he will gain great successes, till interrupted by rumours from the East and North; and starting from Egypt on a fresh career of conquest and destruction will perish on the way between Jerusalem and the sea-coast. How far the events here described correspond to the reality is a very doubtful point. Our principal authorities mention no expedition into Egypt after the one of B.C. 168. What we know from other sources of the closing events of Antiochus' life is as follows. In 167 B.C. he instituted at Daphne (near Antioch), in rivalry with those just celebrated by Aem. Paullus in Macedonia, a magnificent series of games, lasting 30 days. Soon after this, the Roman Senate, entertaining suspicions of his loyalty, sent Tiberius Gracchus to ascertain whether their suspicions were well-founded. Antiochus shewed himself quite master of the situation. He " received Tiberius so dexterously and amicably (οὕτως ἐπιδεξίως καὶ φιλοφρόνως) that the latter not only suspected no designs on his part, and could detect no trace of hostility on the score of what had happened at Alexandria, but even condemned those who made such allegations, on account of the extreme courtesy of his reception. For, besides other things, he gave up his palace, and almost even his crown, to the ambassadors, at least in appearance; for in reality, he was anything but prepared to make concessions to the Romans, and was, in fact, as hostile to them as possible " (Polyb. xxxi. 5). Although, however, Tiberius was satisfied of Antiochus' sincerity, the suspicions of the Senate were not allayed : for reports reached it from other quarters that he was conspiring secretly with Eumenes of Pergamum against the Romans (Polyb. xxxi. 4—6, 9). In 166 he started on the expedition, in the course of which he met his death. Leaving Lysias to take charge of his provinces between Egypt and the Euphrates and to carry on the contest with Judas Maccabaeus, he crossed the Euphrates in this year for the East (1 Macc. iii. 31—37),—according to *vv.* 28—31, because he was in need of funds, and intended 'to take the tributes of the countries, and to gather much money,' according to the condensed statement in Tac. *Hist.* v. 8 to war against the Parthians[1]. It was probably on this expedition that he subjugated Artaxias, king of Armenia, who had revolted (Diod. Sic. xxxi. 17 *a*, App. *Syr.* 45). While in Elymais (E. of Babylonia) he attempted unsuccessfully to pillage a temple; and soon afterwards died, after a short illness, at

---

[1] 'Rex Antiochus, demere superstitionem et mores Græcorum dare adnisus, quo minus teterrimam gentem in melius mutaret, Parthorum bello prohibitus est.'

Tabae in Persia (N. of Susa),—according to Polybius (xxxi. 11), 'becoming mad (δαιμονήσας), as some say,' in consequence of certain supernatural tokens of the anger of heaven on account of his attempted sacrilege, according to 1 Macc. vi. 5—16 through disappointment and grief at hearing of the successes of the Jews against Lysias (in 2 Macc. ix., the story of his death is told with legendary additions).

Porphyry, however, as reported by Jerome in his notes on these verses, does speak of a fourth Egyptian expedition of Antiochus. He says that Antiochus invaded Egypt in his 11th year, passing through Judaea on the way, but not molesting Edom, Moab, and the Ammonites, lest the delay should give Ptolemy time to strengthen his forces; that while fighting in Egypt he was recalled by reports of wars in the North and East; that he accordingly returned, captured Arvad (in Phoenicia), and ravaged Phoenicia, and afterwards proceeded to the East against Artaxias, that, having defeated him, he fixed his tent at a place called *Apedno*, between the Tigris and the Euphrates, and finally that, after his attempted sacrilege in Persia, he died of grief at Tabae (as stated above). It is true, our accounts of Antiochus' reign are incomplete, there being large gaps, especially in the parts of both Polybius and Livy which would naturally have contained particulars of his closing years. It is true also that, being, as Polybius tells us, unfriendly to the Romans, he might well have planned another campaign against their ally, Ptolemy[1]. But it is remarkable that no hint of any conquest (v. 43) of Egypt at this time has come down to us except through Jerome, the more so, since, as Prof. Bevan has remarked (p. 164), Egypt was now under Roman protection, so that an attack upon the country must at once have produced a war with Rome. The statement respecting the wealth of Antiochus in v. 43, also conflicts with what we know independently respecting his great financial difficulties at the time. And when the account given by Porphyry is examined more closely, it is seen (except in the particulars which we know already from other sources) to be strongly open to the suspicion of being derived from these verses of Daniel. Apart from the statements that it took place in his 11th year (which, as it must have been shortly before his death, was a date easy to fix), and that Arvad was captured by him, it contains nothing which could not have been inferred from the language of Daniel, and indeed is couched largely in the expressions used by Daniel. And the mention of Apedno as the place where he pitched his tent, is based obviously upon a misunderstanding of the Hebrew word found in v. 45. While, therefore, we are not in a position to deny categorically a fourth Egyptian campaign, the probabilities are certainly against it. Most likely the author draws here an imaginative picture of the end of the tyrant king, similar to the ideal one of the ruin of Sennacherib in Is. x. 28—32: he depicts him as successful where he had previously failed, viz. in Egypt; while reaping the spoils of his victories, he is called away by rumours from a distance; and then, just after he has set out on a further career of conquest and

---

[1] In Daniel, however, it is to be noted, it is the Egyptian king with whom the attack begins.

198   DANIEL, XI.   [vv. 40—42.

40 and shall divide the land for gain. And at the time of the end shall the king of the south push at him: and the king of the north shall come against him like a whirlwind, with chariots, and with horsemen, and with many ships; and he shall enter into the countries, and shall overflow 41 and pass over. He shall enter also into the glorious land, and many *countries* shall be overthrown: but these shall escape out of his hand, *even* Edom, and Moab, and the 42 chief of the children of Ammon. He shall stretch forth his hand also upon the countries: and the land of Egypt

plunder, as he is approaching with sinister purpose the Holy City, he meets his doom.

40. *at the time of the end*] The final close of Antiochus' reign. The expression denotes a period later than that of the persecutions described in *v.* 35, which are to last '*until* the time of the end.'

the king of the south] would still be Ptolemy Philometor.

butt with *him*] or, more exactly, *shew himself one that butts*, i.e. open a combat with him : the figure, as viii. 4.

and the king of the north, &c.] Antiochus will come against him like a whirlwind (for the figure, cf. Hab. iii. 14), with a vast armament.

and with many ships] Antiochus possessed a navy, which in his expeditions against Egypt of B.C. 170—168, he used with good effect (cf. p. 180).

enter into the countries] those viz. in his line of march.

overflow, and pass **through**] like a flood (as *v.* 10).

41. *the* **beauteous** *land*] the land of Israel, as *v.* 16.

shall be overthrown] lit. *shall stumble* (*vv.* 14, 19, 33, 35), i.e. be ruined : cf., for the expression, Is. iii. 8 'Jerusalem *hath stumbled*' (A.V., R.V., *is ruined*). The word for 'many' is fem.: hence 'countries' must be understood from *v.* 40, though it is, of course, their inhabitants who are really meant. Bevan, Behrmann, Marti, Kamph., and Prince (with the change of a point) read '*tens of thousands* shall be overthrown' (cf. *v.* 12).

Some countries will, however, escape ; in particular, three of Israel's ancient foes, of whom at least Edom and the Ammonites shewed hostility against the Jews at this time (cf. 1 Macc. iv. 61, v. 1—8). Jason, the renegade high-priest, twice found an asylum with the Ammonites (2 Macc. iv. 26, v. 7).

escape] *be delivered* (R.V.). (*Escape* is needed for a different Heb. word in *v.* 42.)

the chief of, &c.] i.e. the principal part of them. Cf., for the word, Num. xxiv. 20; Jer. xlix. 35; Am. vi. 1.

42. *stretch forth his hand*] viz. to seize them : see Ex. xxii. 8 ('put forth his hand upon'), where the verb in the Heb. is the same.

vv. 43—45.] DANIEL, XI. 199

shall not escape. But he shall have power over the treasures 43
of gold and of silver, and over all the precious *things* of
Egypt: and the Libyans and the Ethiopians *shall be* at
his steps. But tidings out of the east and out of the north 44
shall trouble him: therefore he shall go forth with great
fury to destroy, and utterly to make away many. And he 45
shall plant the tabernacles of his palace between the seas

shall not escape] i.e. shall have none to escape; lit. *shall not become an escaping body* (Gen. xxxii. 8 [9 Heb.]).
43. *have power*] lit. *rule*. He will secure great treasure from Egypt: cf. (in 170 or 169) 1 Macc. i. 19.
and the Libyans and the Ethiopians (shall be) *at his steps*] i.e. will follow in his train. The Libyans, on the W. of Egypt, and the Kushites (or Ethiopians) on the South, are both mentioned either as helping the Egyptians, or as serving in their army, in Nah. iii. 9, the Ethiopians also in Jer. xlvi. 9 (cf. Ez. xxx. 4, 5). Here they are represented as joining the army of the conqueror.
44. *But tidings*] or *rumours*, as the same word is rendered in 2 Ki. xix. 7 (= Is. xxxvii. 7), of the tidings which caused Sennacherib to withdraw. So Jer. li. 46; Ez. vii. 26. Lit. *something heard*. Here, probably, rumours of insurrections, or wars, in the E. and N. of his dominions.
trouble] **alarm.** See on iv. 5.
and he shall go forth] viz. out of Egypt.
to destroy and utterly to make away many] lit. 'and to **ban** (or **devote**) many.' The word, which means properly *to set apart, seclude*, is used primarily of the ban laid upon persons or objects hostile to Israel's religion (Ex. xxii. 20; Deut. ii. 34, vii. 2, 25, 26; Josh. vi. 17—19, &c.[1]): as this involved generally their destruction, it is often rendered in A.V. *utterly destroy* (so also in R.V., when applied to persons), though, of course, this rendering expresses only a secondary idea. In the present late passage, however, as in 2 Ch. xx. 23, it is simply a synonym for *destroy*.
45. *plant*] viz. as a tree: fig. for *fix*. A late usage: cf. Eccl. xii. 11; and see Levy, *NHWB.* iii. 380.
the tents of his palace] the large and sumptuous tent, or collection of tents, which would form naturally the headquarters of an oriental king[2]. The word for 'palace' (*appéden*) occurs only here in the O.T.: it is a Persian word, denoting properly a large hall or throne-room (see on viii. 1). From Persian it passed into Aramaic,—it is used in the Targ. of Jer. xliii. 10 of the 'royal pavilion' which Nebuchadnezzar was to erect in Egypt,—and occurs frequently in Syriac in the sense of 'palace.' The present passage shews that it passed similarly into late Hebrew.
between the seas **and** *the* **beauteous** *holy mountain*] between the

[1] See further the writer's Commentary on 1 Sam. xv. 33, or Deut. vii. 2.
[2] Polyaenus (*Strateg.* IV. iii. 24) describes the spacious and gorgeously decorated tent in which Alexander administered justice whilst in India.

in the glorious holy mountain; yet he shall come to his end, and none shall help him.

12 And at that time shall Michael stand up, the great prince which standeth for the children of thy people: and there shall be a time of trouble, such as never was since there was a nation *even* to that same time: and at that time thy people shall be delivered, every one that *shall*
2 be found written in the book. And many of them that

Mediterranean Sea (for the poet. plur., see Jud. v. 17, Deut. xxxiii. 19) and the hill of Zion; 'holy mountain,' as Ps. ii. 6, and frequently; 'beauteous' as *vv.* 16, 41.

and *he shall come to his end*] Antiochus died actually at Tabae in Persia. It is certainly not said here in so many words that he should meet his end at the spot on which his royal tent was to be pitched; but the connexion between the two parts of the verse naturally implies it: Antiochus is to meet his death in Palestine, the country in which he had committed his greatest crimes, and which he was even now threatening to invade and ravage again. Other prophets also represent the powers hostile to Israel as defeated in proximity to Jerusalem: cf. Ez. xxxix. 4, Joel iii. 2, 12 f., Zech. xiv. 2.

XII. **1—3.** There should be no break here: xii. 1—4 forms the concluding part of the angel's revelation to Daniel; and what is described in *vv.* 1—3 forms the immediate sequel of the fall of Antiochus. The overthrow of the world-power is pictured by the author as accompanied by a season of trial—perhaps political convulsions—out of which, however, the faithful among God's people are delivered; a resurrection of Israelites follows; and the age of bliss then begins for the righteous.

1. *Michael...the great prince*] i.e. the patron-angel of Israel (x. 13, 21).

stand up] as champion and defender (xi. 1; cf. x. 13). Hitherto the power of the 'prince' of Greece has been unchecked: now Michael interposes, for his people's final deliverance.

standeth for] i.e. protects (Est. viii. 11, ix. 16).

a time of trouble] The expression seems borrowed from Jer. xxx. 7 (where also Israel is spoken of as 'saved from it').

such as never was since, &c.] cf. Ex. ix. 18, 24, Joel ii. 2, Mark xiii. 19 (|| Matth. xxiv. 21).

shall be delivered] The period of deliverance here spoken of is the same as the period of redemption described in vii. 18, 26, 27, ix. 24.

written in the book] viz. of life, the register of the living: in Ps. lxix. 28 (cf. lxxxvii. 6, Ex. xxxii. 32) applied to the register of living members of the Theocratic community, which God is represented as keeping. Here, however, the expression is used, not of those living in the present life, but of those destined to share in the glorious life of the end; it is the 'register of the citizens of the Messianic kingdom' (Hitz.), including both those who enter it while yet living,

sleep in the dust of the earth shall awake, some to everlasting life, and some to shame *and* everlasting contempt.

and those (*v.* 2) who enter it after their resurrection. Cf. Is. iv. 3, where those who are worthy to survive the approaching judgement are described as 'written down *unto life* [i.e. a glorified, but still earthly life] in Jerusalem.' The same figure occurs in Enoch xlvii. 3 ('the books of the living were opened before Him'), cviii. 3 (the names of the wicked 'will be blotted out of the book of life, and out of the books of the holy ones'); and, applied in a Christian sense, in Phil. iv. 3, Rev. iii. 5, xiii. 8, xvii. 8, xx. 12, 15, xxi. 27; cf. Luke x. 20, Heb. xii. 23, Enoch civ. 1. See Charles on Enoch xlvii. 3; and Gebhardt and Harnack on Hermes, *Vis.* i. 3, 2.

2. **The resurrection.** The doctrine of a future life is not fully developed in the O.T.; it is *nascent*; and the stages in its growth are clearly distinguishable. The idea of a resurrection appears first, though in a national, not in an individual sense, in Hos. vi. 2: it appears next, also in a national sense (see Davidson's note, p. 267), in Ezekiel's famous vision of the Valley of dry bones (xxxvii. 1—14): the resurrection of individuals appears first in the post-exilic prophecy of Is. xxiv.—xxvii., viz. xxvi. 19 (see Skinner's note), though, as in Ezek. (xxxvii. 11), it is still expressly limited to Israel (it is denied, *v.* 14, of Israel's foes): in the present passage, a resurrection of the wicked, as well as of the righteous, is taught for the first time, and the doctrine of a different future reserved for each is also for the first time enunciated. See further the Introd. p. xcii.

many] The resurrection is still limited implicitly to Israel. It is not said who are to compose the 'many': perhaps the author thinks in particular of the martyrs, and apostates, respectively, who, on the one side or the other, had been prominent during the reign of Antiochus.

sleep] in death: cf. Jer. li. 39, 57; 1 Thess. iv. 14, v. 10.

in the **dusty ground**] lit. *the ground of dust.* The expression is peculiar, and occurs only here. 'Dust' is often said of the grave, as to 'lie down upon the dust' (Job xx. 11, xxi. 26), and 'they that go down to the dust' (Ps. xxii. 29).

shall awake] cf., in the same sense, Is. xxvi. 19; also (where it is denied) Job xiv. 12, and (of the Babylonians) Jer. li. 39, 57.

some to everlasting life] The expression occurs only here in the O.T., but it is frequent in post-Biblical Jewish writings: e.g. in Enoch (xxxvii. 4, xl. 9, lviii. 3, lxii. 14); Psalms of Sol. iii. 16 (cf. xiii. 9); 4 Macc. xv. 3 (cf. 2 Macc. vii. 9, 36); and in the Targums (in which passages of the O.T. relating really to the present life are often interpreted as referring to a future life)[1]. A more common synonym is 'the life of the age to come' (חיי העולם הבא), *Aboth* ii. 7, &c. (Dalman, *Die Worte Jesu*, p. 129).

some to **reproaches** (Ps. lxix. 9, 10 [Heb.]) and *everlasting* **abhorrence**] the last word (only once besides) from Is. lxvi. 24 'And they

---

[1] See examples in the writer's *Sermons on the O.T.* (1892), pp. 83, 88—91; Dalman, *Die Worte Jesu*, p. 128.

3 **And they that be wise shall shine as the brightness of the firmament; and they that turn many to righteousness as**
4 **the stars for ever and ever. But thou, O Daniel, shut up the words, and seal the book,** *even* **to the time of the end: many shall run to and fro, and knowledge shall be increased.**

[the carcases of the transgressors, slain outside Jerusalem] shall be an *abhorring* unto all flesh.' Cf. in the N.T., Matt. xxv. 46; John v. 29.

3. Those who in the time of trial had by example and precept preserved many in righteousness and faith, will then receive their reward.

they that be wise] The words do not mean the 'wise' generally, but those mentioned in xi. 33, 35 (the word being the same which is there used), men like Mattathias (1 Macc. ii.), the staunch and firm leaders of the loyal Jews, during Antiochus' persecutions. These "are distinguished from the rest of the faithful Israelites—they not only live for ever, but are eternally glorified" (Bevan). Cf. Enoch civ. 2 ('Be hopeful: for aforetime ye were put to shame through ills and affliction; but soon ye will shine as the stars of heaven, ye will shine and ye will be seen, and the portals of heaven will be opened to you'); Matt. xiii. 43.

as the brightness of the firmament] cf. Ex. xxiv. 10.

and they that **make the** *many* **righteous**] The expression, as Is. liii. 11, 'by his knowledge shall my righteous servant *make the many righteous.*' In neither case is the verb to be understood in the later technical sense of 'justify': the meaning, in both cases, is *to lead to righteousness* by teaching—in Is. liii. by instruction in the ways and will of God ('by his *knowledge*'), here by warning, exhortation, and example of constancy (cf. xi. 33 'shall make the many to understand').

4. The closing injunction to Daniel.

shut up, &c.] The injunction is similar to that in viii. 26.

until *the time of the end*] i.e. (viii. 17) the time of Antiochus' persecution, regarded from the standpoint of Daniel himself. The words are meant to explain why the visions in the book, though communicated to Daniel, were not made generally known until the time of the persecution. Cf. on viii. 26; and contrast Rev. xxii. 10.

many shall run to and fro, and knowledge shall be increased] A famous passage, prefixed by Bacon in its Latin form (*Multi pertransibunt, et multiplex erit scientia*) to the first edition of his *Novum Organum*, and interpreted by him (I. 93) as signifying that the complete exploration of the world (pertransitus mundi), which seemed to him to be then on the point of accomplishment, would coincide with great discoveries in science (augmenta scientiarum). This explanation of the words is, however, unhappily, too foreign to their context to be probable. But it must be admitted that the words are enigmatic. The verb rendered *run to and fro* occurs elsewhere, Jer. v. 1, Am. viii. 12 (of literal movement hither and thither); Zech. iv. 10, 2 Ch. xvi. 9 (of Jehovah's eyes, present in every part of the earth);

vv. 5—7.]   DANIEL, XII.   203

Then I Daniel looked, and behold, there stood other 5
two, the one on this side of the bank of the river, and the
other on that side of the bank of the river. And *one* said 6
to the man clothed in linen, which *was* upon the waters
of the river, How long *shall it be to* the end of *these*
wonders? And I heard the man clothed in linen, which 7
was upon the waters of the river, when he held up his

and the sense generally given to the passage is that *many will* then
run to and fro in the book, i.e. diligently explore and study it, *and*
so the *knowledge* of God's providential purposes, to be obtained from it,
—how, for instance, He tries, but at the same time rewards, His own
faithful servants, and how the course of human history leads ultimately
to the establishment of His kingdom,—*will be increased.*

The text, it must be owned, is open to suspicion. Prof. Bevan
making a slight change (הרעה for הדעת), in a sense suggested by the
LXX., obtains the rendering 'many shall run to and fro (viz. in distraction), and *evils* (calamities) shall be increased,' i.e. the revelation is to
remain concealed, because there is to ensue a long period of commotion
and distress. For the thought of the emended clause, he compares
1 Macc. i. 9 (of the wars and other troubles brought upon the world by
the Seleucidae and the Ptolemies) 'and they *multiplied evils* in the earth.'

(3) xii. **5—13.** Conclusion. The revelation (xi. 2—xii. 4) is ended;
but nothing has been said about the *duration* of the troubles foretold in
it. And yet, to those living in the midst of them, this was a question of
vital interest. Daniel accordingly asks, and receives, specific information on this point (*v.* 6 ff.).

5. *other two*] i.e. (as we should now say) *two others*, in addition, viz.
to the glorious being, whom Daniel saw (x. 5, 6), and who had been
speaking to him since (x. 11—14, 19, x. 20—xii. 4).

river (twice)] Heb. *yĕʾōr*, an Egyptian word, elsewhere in the O.T.
the regular name of the Nile (Ex. ii. 3, &c.), but here and in *vv.* 6, 7,
denoting the Tigris (see x. 4). The proper force of the word must have
been forgotten; and it must be used in the general sense of *stream*.

6. *And* one] i.e. one of the angels just mentioned, whom Daniel
hears speaking (cf. viii. 13).

the man clothed in linen] The glorious figure described more fully
in x. 5, 6.

upon] **above,** i.e. hovering in the air, above the stream; cf. viii. 16.

the *wonders*] or *extraordinary things*, viz. the extraordinary trials
and sufferings described in xi. 31—36 (cf. the same expression, with
regard to the deeds, or words, of Antiochus, in viii. 24 and xi. 36).

7. The answer to the inquiry, given with solemn emphasis, and
overheard by Daniel.

upon] **above,** as *v.* 6.

and *he* **lifted** *up*, &c.] The lifting up of the (right) hand implied
an appeal to heaven, and is frequently mentioned as a gesture
accompanying an oath: Gen. xiv. 22; and (with another Heb. word

right hand and his left hand unto heaven, and sware by him that liveth for ever that *it shall be* for a time, times, and a half; and when *he* shall have accomplished to scatter the power of the holy people, all these *things* shall 8 be finished. And I heard, but I understood not: then said I, O my lord, what *shall be* the end of these *things?* 9 And he said, Go thy way, Daniel: for the words *are* closed

for *lift up*) Ex. vi. 8, Deut. xxxii. 40, Ez. xx. 5 *al.* Of an angel, as here, Rev. x. 5.

and his left hand] *both* hands, as the more complete guarantee of the truth of what is about to be affirmed.

by him that liveth for ever] cf. Rev. x. 6. The usual form of oath in the O.T. is '(As) Jehovah liveth' (e.g. Jud. viii. 19), or (in God's mouth) '(As) I live,'—once (Deut. xxxii. 40) '(As) I live for ever.' The formula here used seems to be based upon the last-cited passage: comp. also 'him that liveth for ever' in Dan. iv. 34.

for a time, times, and a half] i.e. 3½ years, to be reckoned, probably, as was explained on vii. 25 (where the same expression occurs), from the mission of Apollonius in the middle of B.C. 168 to the re-dedication of the Temple in Dec. 165.

and **as they finish shattering** (Ps. ii. 9, Jer. li. 20—23 [A.V. 'dash or break in pieces']) *the power of the holy people*] alluding to the persecution of Antiochus.

'Power' is lit. *hand*, figurative of *power to act, strength*: cf. Deut. xxxii. 36, 'for he saw that *power* (lit. *hand*) was gone'; Is. xxxvii. 27, 'their inhabitants were of small *power*' (lit. *short of hand*), &c. To *shatter the hand* is an obvious figure for reducing to helplessness.

all these things *shall be finished*] The end of what has been foretold (*vv.* 31—36) will coincide with the end of the persecution.

The Heb. of the last clause but one is however unusual: and the definition given of the end of the persecution seems almost tautologous. Hence Bevan and Marti, transposing two words, and changing the punctuation, read, 'and as the power of the shatterer of the holy people cometh to an end [or, 'as the hand (cf. vii. 25)...faileth (Ps. lxxi. 9)'], all these things shall be finished,' i.e. Antiochus is to be the last oppressor of all, when *his* power has ceased, the sufferings of the holy people will be ended for ever.

8—13. The answer was far from explicit, so that Daniel did not understand it: he accordingly asked for more definite particulars.

8. *O my lord*] x. 16.

what shall be *the* **closing stage** *of these* things?] i.e. what will be the closing stage of the 'wonders,' or extraordinary sufferings, of *v.* 6, which may serve as a sign that the actual 'end' is not far off? 'End' here is in the Heb. אחרית, a different word from 'end' in *v.* 6 (קץ), and means not the absolute *close* of a thing, but the *closing* or *latter part* of it: see Job viii. 7, xlii. 12 ('latter end').

9. Go, *Daniel,* &c.] i.e. do not inquire further: *for the words are*

vv. 10—12.] DANIEL, XII. 205

up and sealed till the time of the end. Many shall be 10
purified, and made white, and tried; but the wicked shall
do wickedly: and none of the wicked shall understand;
but the wise shall understand. And from the time *that* 11
the daily *sacrifice* shall be taken away, and the abomination
that maketh desolate set up, *there shall be* a thousand two
hundred and ninety days. Blessed *is* he that waiteth, and 12
cometh to the thousand three hundred *and* five and thirty

shut up *and sealed* (*v.* 4) *till the time of the end:* if Daniel does
not understand them, it does not signify; they are not intended for him,
but for readers in a distant future, viz. in the age of Antiochus
Epiphanes, when they will first be divulged.

10. The 'time of the end' characterized: it will be an age of
trial and probation, in which many will come out purified and
ennobled, while others will only have their wickedness confirmed.

Many shall **cleanse themselves,** *and* **make themselves white,** *and*
be refined] by their sufferings, and their constancy under temptation,
their characters will be ennobled and refined (cf. xi. 35). The two
reflexives are not to be pressed unduly; but they imply that the
martyrs, by their deliberate acceptance of suffering, are, to a certain
degree, the agents in the purification of their characters.

but the wicked shall do wickedly] The trial will have no effect
upon them, beyond giving them further opportunities of doing
wickedly, and so confirming them in their wickedness.

none of the wicked shall understand—i.e. act with understanding—
but **they that be wise** *shall understand*] shall act with understanding.
The wicked act blindly, not perceiving the consequences of their
wickedness; the 'wise,' the religious teachers of the nation (the same
word as in *v.* 3, xi. 33, 35), shew insight into the ways and providence
of God. For 'understand,' cf. Ps. xlix. 20, lxxxii. 5, Hos. iv. 14.

11, 12. The duration of the persecution defined.

that *the* **continual** (burnt-offering) *shall be taken away*] as xi. 31;
cf. viii. 11.

and the abomination that **appalleth** *set up*] also as xi. 31 (cf.
viii. 13, ix. 27): see the notes on these passages.

a thousand two hundred and ninety days] the *terminus a quo* is
15 Chisleu [Dec.], B.C. 168 (1 Macc. i. 54); and 1290 days, reckoned
from this date, would end in June—according to Cornill, *Siebzig
Wochen*, p. 29, on June 6—B.C. 164. The death of Antiochus took
place in the course of B.C. 164: the exact date of it is not known;
but it is not improbable that it is pictured by the writer as syn-
chronizing with the end of the 1290 days.

12. Happy is *he that waiteth, and* **attaineth** *to* **a** *thousand three
hundred* and *five and thirty days*] Happy is he who waits (cf. Is.
xxx. 18, 'happy are all they that *wait* for him,' lxiv. 4), not giving
up his trust in Jehovah, for 45 days ($=1\frac{1}{2}$ month) beyond the 1290
days mentioned in *v.* 11. Why this further limit is assigned, it is

13 days. But go thou thy way till the end *be*: for thou shalt rest, and stand in thy lot at the end of the days.

impossible to say with any certainty. All that can be said is that the turning-point (whatever it may have been), marked by the close of the 1290 days, was not pictured by the author as introducing at once the period of complete blessedness—this he did not conceive as beginning for 45 days afterwards. What he imagined as the cause of the postponement must remain matter of speculation: if the 1290 days are rightly interpreted as ending with the death of Antiochus, he may have thought, for instance, that its full effects would not appear at once, and that true rest would not begin for the Jews till after a short interval more.[1]

13. After indicating (*vv.* 11, 12) the duration of the persecution, the angel turns to Daniel; and the book closes with a word of consolation addressed to him personally. He is to await the 'end' in the grave, from which, in the resurrection spoken of in *v.* 2, he will arise to take his appointed place, beside the other saints.

But **thou, go thou to the end**] i.e. depart to await the end. (As in *v.* 9, there is nothing in the Heb. corresponding to 'thy way.')

and *thou shalt rest* (in the grave, Is. lvii. 2), *and* **stand up to** *thy lot*] to thy appointed portion or place: 'lot' being used in a figurative sense, as in Jud. i. 3, Ps. cxxv. 3, and in the N.T. Acts xxvi. 18, Col. i. 12 (in both which passages 'inheritance' is properly 'lot' [κλῆρος]').

at the end of the days] the extreme end of the present period,—i.e., reckoned from Daniel's standpoint, the period ending with the fall of Antiochus,—when the resurrection of *v.* 2 will take place, and the age of never-ending blessedness (*v.* 3) will begin.

---

[1] The period of 1335 days is the source of the Apocryphal 'Ascension of Isaiah,' iv. 12: see the note *ad loc.* in Charles' edition (1900).

APPENDIX.

The Inscription recording the Vote of Thanks to Eumenes and Attalus passed by the Council and people of Antioch[1].

As this inscription, which was discovered inscribed on a marble stele, on the site of the ancient Pergamum in Aug. 1885, is of some interest, and has never, so far as the present writer is aware, been published in England, it may be worth quoting here. Its purport, it will be seen, is to describe how Eumenes, king of Pergamum, came forward, with great readiness and liberality, to assist Antiochus with money and forces to gain his throne, how his brother Attalus co-operated with him, and how two other brothers, Philetaerus and Athenaeus, also shewed goodwill at the same time. The Council of Antioch agreed therefore to propose to the people to honour with golden crowns not only Eumenes and his brothers, for the benefits they had conferred upon the state, but also their deceased father Attalus, and the queen-mother Apollonis, for having educated their children in such virtuous ways. The bestowal of these honours was to be announced both in Daphne, the pleasure-suburb of Antioch, and in Pergamum, at the public games; and stone tablets, with the decree engraved upon them, were to be set up in Antioch itself, in Daphne, and in Pergamum. The inscription confirms, and fills out, the brief statement of Appian (*Syr.* 45) that Eumenes and Attalus τὸν Ἀντίοχον ἐς αὐτὴν [τὴν Συρίαν] κατάγουσιν, ἑταιριζόμενοι τὸν ἄνδρα. The opening lines are imperfect.

6 ....ὡς εἰς σύσστασιν[2] ἦι θε[λ-
........καὶ ἀδελφοῦ πέμπτου[3] τὰ ε...
......μετ]αλλάξαντος Σελεύκου [καὶ
τῆς συμφορ]ᾶς παρακαλούσης θεωροῦντες
10 πόρον τ]ὸγ καιρὸμ παραδιδόντα πρὸς τὸ κατα-
θέσθαι χάριγ καὶ εὐεργεσίαν, πάντα πάρεργα
τ]ἆλλα ποιησάμενοι καὶ ἑαυτοὺς ἐπέχρησαν[4] καὶ
μέχρι τῶν ὁρίων τῆς ἰδίας βασιλείας συμπρο-
ελθόντες καὶ χρήμασι χορηγήσαντες καὶ

---

[1] From Fränkel, *Die Inschriften von Pergamon* (1890), I. No. 160.
[2] The conspiracy of Heliodorus.
[3] In all probability, Antiochus Epiphanes, who is known to have had both four brothers and four sisters.
[4] Risked their lives.

APPENDIX.

15 δυνάμεις παρασκευάσαντες καὶ τῶι διαδήματι
μετὰ τῆς ἄλλης κατασκευῆς κοσμήσαντες
ὡς καθῆκεν καὶ βο[υθ]υτήσαντες καὶ πίστεις
ποιησάμενοι πρὸς ἀλλήλους μετὰ πάσης εὐνοίας
καὶ φιλοστοργίας ἀξιολόγως συγκατέστησαν ἐπὶ τὴ[μ
20 πατρώιαν ἀρχὴν τὸμ βασιλέα Ἀντίοχον. Ὅπως ἂν οὗ[ν
ὁ δῆμος ἐγ χάριτος ἀποδόσει φαίνηται πρωτεύω[ν
καὶ τοὺς ἑαυτὸν καὶ τοὺς φίλους εὐεργετοῦντα[ς
ἀπαρακλήτως φανερὸς εἶ τιμῶν καὶ τὰ καλὰ τῶ[ν
ἔργων εἰς ἀίδιομ μνήμην ἀνάγων καὶ νῦν καθάπε[ρ
25 καὶ πρότερον· ἀγαθεῖ τύχηι δεδόχθαι τεῖ βουλεῖ
τοὺς λαχόντας προέδρους εἰς τὴν ἐπιοῦσαν ἐκκλησίαν
χρηματίσαι περὶ τούτων, γνώμην δὲ ξυμβάλλεσθαι
τῆς βουλῆς εἰς τὸν δῆμον ὅτι δοκεῖ τεῖ βουλεῖ
ἐπαινέσαι τὸμ βασιλέα Εὐμένη βασιλέως Ἀττά[λου
30 καὶ βασιλίσσης Ἀπολλωνίδος καὶ στεφανῶσαι χρυσ[ῶι
στεφάνωι ἀριστέωι κατὰ τὸν νόμον ἀρετῆς ἕνεκεν
καὶ εὐνοίας καὶ καλοκαγαθίας ἣν ἀπεδείξατο
πᾶσιν ἀνθρώποις σπεύσας ὑπὲρ τοῦ βασιλέως Ἀντιόχου
καὶ συγκαταστήσας αὐτὸν εἰς τὴν τῶμ προγόνων [ἀ]ρ[χήν.
35 Κατὰ ταὐτὰ δὲ στεφανῶσαι καὶ Ἄτταλον, ὅτι μετὰ τοῦ
ἀδελφοῦ Εὐμένους πάντα συνέπραξεν ἀόκνως
καὶ φιλοκινδύνως. Ἐπαινέσαι δὲ καὶ τοὺς ἀδελφοὺς
αὐτῶν Φιλέταιρον καὶ Ἀθηναῖον καὶ στεφανῶσαι χρυσῶι
στεφάνωι ἑκάτερον αὐτῶν εὐνοίας ἕνεκεν καὶ
40 φιλοτιμίας, ἣμ παρέσχοντο κατὰ τὴγ κάθοδον τοῦ
βασιλέως Ἀντιόχου. Ἐπαινέσαι δὲ καὶ τοὺς γονεῖς
αὐτῶν, τόν τε βασιλέα Ἄτταλον καὶ τὴμ βασίλισσαν
Ἀπολλωνίδα[1], καὶ στεφανῶσαι χρυσῶι στεφάνωι
ἀριστείωι ἀρετῆς ἕνεκεν καὶ καλοκαγαθίας,
45 ἣμ περιεποίησαν τοῖς υἱοῖς προστάντες τῆς παιδείας
αὐτῶν καλῶς καὶ σωφρόνως. Ἀναγορεῦσαι δὲ τοὺς
στεφάνους τούτους ἔν τε τοῖς ἀγῶσιν οἷς......,
ὡσαύτως δὲ καὶ ἐν οἷς ὁ βασιλεὺς Εὐμένης μετά τε τῶν
ἀδελφῶν καὶ τοῦ δήμου τοῦ Περγαμηνῶν, κατὰ ταὐτὰ δὲ
50 καὶ ἐν οἷς ὁ βασιλεὺς Ἀντίοχος ἐπὶ Δάφνει [θ]ήσει, καθάπερ
αὐτοῖς ἔθος ἦν. Ἵνα δὲ καὶ τὸ ὑπόμνημα διαμένει συμ[φ]α[νὲς
εἰς τὸν αἰώνιογ χρόνον, ἀναγράψαι τόδε τὸ ψήφισμα εἰς στήλας
λιθίνας καὶ στῆσαι τὴμ μὲν ἐν ἀγορᾶι παρὰ τὰς εἰκόνας τὰς
τοῦ βασιλέως Ἀντιόχου, τὴν δὲ ἐν τῶι ἱερῶι τῆς Νικηφόρου
55 Ἀθηνᾶς[2], τὴν δὲ ἐν τῶι ἐπὶ Δάφνει, τοῦ Ἀπόλλωνος ἱερῶι.
Τῆς δὲ διαποστολῆς αὐτοῦ πρός τε τὸμ βασιλέα[3] καὶ τὴ[μ
μητέρα καὶ τοὺς ἀδελφοὺς ἐπιμεληθῆναι τοὺς στρατηγ[ούς,
ὅπως ἐπιμελῶς γένηται καὶ τὴν ταχίστην.

[1] Attalus I. (now dead), and Apollonis, the mother of Eumenes, who was still living.
[2] At Pergamum,—no doubt the same stele on which the inscription was found.
[3] Eumenes.

INDEX.

Abed-nego, 7 f.
'abomination' (שִׁקּוּץ), 142, 150
'abomination of desolation,' xliv, lxxiii, 150, 151, 188
'abomination that maketh desolate,' 188, 205, cf. 118, 142, 151
Adonis, 194 f.
Ahasuerus, lii, liv, 127
Alexander the Great, xxxiii f.; conquests of, 113 f., 164; division of empire after death of, xxxiv f., 29, 115, 122, 164
Amêl-Marduk (Evil-Merodach), xxvii, li
Amesha-Spentas, xciv f.
'ancient of days,' 85
angels, assembly of, surrounding God, 51, 86; interpreting visions, lxxviii, 89; winged, 134; called 'wakeful ones' (עִירִין), 49 f.; names and ranks of, 157 f.; patron-angels, 156 f.; doctrine of in Dan., lxiv, xciii—xcvi
'Annalistic tablet' of Cyrus, xxviii—xxxi, 65 n.
anoint, to (מָשַׁח), as a religious rite, 137; to anoint (סוּךְ) the person, 153
'anointed one,' an, 138, 139 f.
Anshan (or Anzan), the home of Cyrus, 111
'answer,' to (peculiar sense of), 23 f., 40, 43
Antichrist, xcvii f., 95, 97, 151, 193
Antiochus I. (Soter), 166
—— II. (Theos), 166 f.
—— III. (the Great), xxxvi—xxxviii, 168—176
—— IV. (Epiphanes), meaning of 'Epiphanes,' xxxviii n.; outline of reign, xxxviii—xlvi; accession of, 177 f., 207 f.; character of, xxxviii f., 123 f., 182 f.; power of dissimulation, 123, 178, 184, 196; munificence and prodigality, xxxix, 183; presumptuousness and impiety, 61, 84, 87, 92, 116, 124, 193—5; assumption of divine honours by, 193; expeditions against Egypt, xxxix f., 178—181, 184—6; attack on Jerusalem in B.C. 170, xliii, 84, 185; endeavour to Hellenize the Jews and suppress their religion, xl—xlvi, lxxxvi, 91, 92 f., 99 f., 110, 115—120, 121 f., 123 f., 140—2, 186—194; last years of, 196 f.; death, 27 (cf. 30), 124, 197, 200; coins of, 193; central figure in book of Dan., lxv f., cf. civ, 99 f., 150; type of Antichrist, xcvii f.
apadâna, 111, 126, 199
'Apedno,' 197
apocalyptic literature, lxxvii—lxxxv, 163
Apollonius, xliv, 124, 187
aposiopesis, 41
Aramaic, 19; Aramaic of Dan., lix—lx, civ
archaisms in the Authorized Version—
  astonied, 43
  base, 51 f.
  brass, 27
  commune, 11
  cunning, 5
  demand, 25, 51
  excellent, 27, 32—34, 57, 65
  favour (=face), 5
  Grecia, 122, 161, 163
  Jewry, 66
  meat, 49
  mount (=mound), 173

INDEX.

archaisms in the Authorized Version—
  note, noted, 162
  of certainty, 20
  or ever, 78
  ordain, 25
  other (=others), 203
  people (=peoples), 38
  prefer, preferred, 72
  require, 21
  saint (=angel), 118
  science, 5
  set (=seated), 86
  shew (=tell), 18 f., 47
  strange (=foreign), 195
  well favoured, 5
  whiles, 62
  worse liking, 9
  would (=desired to), 90
archangels, xciv, xcv f., 158
Arioch, 22
arm, fig. of strength, 167 ; arms, fig. of forces, 173, 182, 187
army (or host) of heaven, 56, 116
Ashpenaz, 4
Asmodeus, xcv
Assumption of Moses (apocryphal book), lxxxiii, xcvii n., 158
Astyages, xxviii, xxx, liii
asyndetic construction common in Aram. of Dan., 76

Baal of heaven (בעל שמים), 188
Babylon, conquest of, by Cyrus, xxix—xxxii, 60 f., 70
Bacon, motto of his *Novum Organum*, 202
bagpipe (סומפניה), 39
banquets in Babylonia and Persia, 61, 62
Barnabas, so-called Epistle of, 95
Baruch, Apocalypse of, lxxxi f., 153
Baruch, prayer in book of, compared with Dan. ix., lxxiv—lxxv, 128 ff.
'Bath-Ḳol,' 55
bear, 82
'beauteous land,' 115, 173, 198, cf. 199 f.
'before' a superior, to speak, &c., 21, 75
Behistun inscription, 71 n.
Bel (lord), title of Marduk, xx, 31, 48, 61

Bel and the Dragon, xx f.
Belshazzar, xxviii, xxix, l—lii, lxviii, 60, 61, 80
Belteshazzar, lv, 7, 48
Berenice (daughter of Ptolemy Philadelphus, married to Antiochus II., Dan. xi. 6), 166 f.
Berosus, xxiv, xxv n., xxvii, xxxii, 2, 59 n., al.
beryl, 154
book of life, the, 200 f.
books containing the destinies of men, 162
books recording the deeds of men, 86
'books, the' (of Scripture), 127
burnt-offering, the daily, 116, 187, 205

Cambyses, xxxii, liii f.
Canon of the O. T., xlvii f.
'captain of the guard' (רב טבחיא), 22 f.
Carchemish, battle of (B.C. 605), xlix, 2
chain of gold, 64
'Chaldaeans,' in ethnic sense, 12, 13 n., in sense of astrologers, xlix f., 6, 12—14, 15
'chief princes' (=archangels), 158
Chisian MS. (of LXX. of Dan.), c, ci
Chittim (Kitians), 186
'choler, to be moved with,' 114
chronology, incorrect, 146, 147
Cleopatra (daughter of Antiochus the Great, sister to Antiochus Epiphanes, married to Ptolemy Epiphanes, Dan. xi. 17), xxxvii f., 101, 174
'coats,' 42 f.
Coele-Syria and Palestine, a bone of contention between Syria and Egypt, xxxiv—xxxviii, 166
'come up upon the heart,' to, 26
Commentaries on Daniel, cii f., civ
'compassion,' 'to give to compassion before...,' 130
'consort' (ישגל), 62
Cyaxares, 28
'Cylinder-inscription' of Cyrus, xxxi, 59 n.
Cyrus, xxviii—xxxii 12, 79, 138, 152

INDEX.

Daniel, the name, xviii *n.*, 7; whether alluded to by Ezekiel, xvii f.; apocryphal stories of, in Susanna, xviii f. (allusion to in Shakespeare, xix); in Bel and the Dragon, xx f.; in later Jewish writings, xxi; so-called Tomb of, at Susa, xxi

Daniel, the book of:—contents of, ix—xvi; aim of, xvi f., lxix, lxxiii; written partly in Heb., partly in Aram., xxii f., 19; allusions to, in Sibylline Oracles, lxxii; in 1 Macc., lxxiii f.; in N. T., lxxiv, 109, 151; Greek versions of, xviii, xcviii ff.; history embraced in, xxiii—xlvii; authorship and date of, xlvii—lxxvi, civ f.; literary character of, lxxvi—lxxxv; whether of composite authorship, cv; characteristic doctrines of, lxiii f., lxxxv ff.; the future as pictured in, lxxxvi; expressions in N. T. borrowed from, or suggested by, lxxxv, xcvii f., 151, 200

Daphne (suburb of Antioch), 194, 196, 207

Darius Hystaspis, liv, 70, 71, 72

Darius the Mede, lii—liv, 70, 71, 127, 162

'determiners (of fates)' (גָּזְרִין), 15, 25

Deuteronomy, reminiscences of, 127 ff.

'devote' (or 'ban'), to (הַחֲרִים), 199

Diadochi (successors of Alexander the Great), rule of the, 123, 152, 162 ff.

didactic aim of Dan. i—vi, xvi—xvii, lxix, 1, 17, 35, 46, 61, 71

'do,' to (used absolutely), 117 f., 133, 189

dreams, 17 f., 49

dulcimer, 39

Dura, 36

eagle (נֶשֶׁר, properly 'griffon-vulture'), 81

'earth, the whole (*or* all the),' expression used hyperbolically, 29, 46, 92

Ecclesiasticus, xlviii, lxii

Elam, 110, 111

'enchanters' (אַשָּׁפִים), 12, 15, 18

'end, time of the,' 121, 122, 193, 198, 202, 205

Enoch, the book of, lxxix—lxxxi, lxxxv; cited in illustration of parts of Dan., 44, 49 f., 85, 86, 87, 89, 105—107, 125, 158, 162, 201, 202

eschatology of Dan., 202—204, lxxxvi, cf. lxxxvii f., xcii f.

Esdras (Ezra), second (fourth) book of, lxxxii f., 95, 99 *n.*, 107 f.

Ethiopians (Kushites), 199

Eumenes, king of Pergamum, 101, 177, 207 f.

eunuchs, 4

everlasting life, 201

Evil-Merodach, *see* Amêl-Marduk

Ezekiel, reminiscences of, lxii f., 115, 120, 121, 125, 154, 155, 159, 160

'family above,' the, 51

family of criminal punished with him, 78

fast predisposing to a vision, lxxxv, 153

fire, symbolizing the Deity, 85

foods, unclean, 8

four empires of Daniel, 94—102

Gabriel, 120

'gate' of the king, 32

'God of gods,' 31

'God of heaven,' 23

'governor' (*peḥāh*), xxix, xxxiii, 36

Greek words in Dan., lviii f., 38, 39

Gubaru (Gobryas), xxix, xxx, xxxi, liv, 60 f.

hand, fig. of power, 204

'hand, to lift up the' (in oath), 203 f.

'hard (*or* dark) sentences' (חִידוֹת), 65

'hard' (of the spirit), 67

Ḥasidaeans (חֲסִידִים), xlv, 189

heart (=intellect), 51, 81

'heaven' (expression of reverence for 'God'), 53 f.

heavenly tables, the, 162

Hebrew style of Dan., lx—lxiii

Heliodorus, 101 f., 176, 177, 207

Hellenizing party in Judah, xl ff., 141, 186 f., 188 f., 190

Ḥiddekel, the, 153

'holy gods,' the, 48

holy one (=angel), 50, 118

INDEX.

holy ones (ideal designation of Israelites), 90, 124
horn, the great (Alexander), 113, 114, 122
horn, the little, 84, 91, 92, 94 f., 98 f., 100; 115
horns, symbolical sense of, 84
horns, the ten (in Dan. vii.), 84, 91, 92, 94 f., 96, 98—102
host of heaven, 116, cf. 56
'hour,' 39, 52
'house of God' (late expression for 'house of Jehovah'), 3
'humble oneself,' to (said of one fasting), 156
hyperbole, 46, 92, 160

images erected by the Ass. kings, 35 f.
imaginative narratives, didactic value of, lxx, lxxi; in vogue among the Jews, lxxii
'India House Inscription' of Nebuchadnezzar, xxiv f., 46, 55
'intreat the favour of,' to, 130 f.

Jason, high-priest, xlii, xliii, 139, 187, 198
Jeremiah, prophecy of restoration after 70 years, 126, 127; reminiscences of in Dan. ix., 128 ff.
Jerome, on the LXX. version of Dan., xcviii f.; his Comm. on Daniel, ciii; referred to or quoted, ciii *n.*, 143, 163—197 (*passim*)
Judas Maccabaeus, xlv f., 120, 190
'judgements' (=ordinances), 128
Jupiter Capitolinus, 193, 194, 195

'king of kings,' title of Bab. and Persian kings, 28
kingdom of God, the, lxiv, lxxxv—lxxxix, 16, 17, 30, 88, 92 f., 200—202

'latter days,' the, 26, 159
leopard, 83
Libyans, 199
linen apparel, 154
living God, the, 77

lord of lords, title of Marduk, 31
lot, fig. of portion, inheritance, 206
lycanthropy, 58 f.

Maccabees, rise of the, xlv f., 189, 190
Macedonian empire, 29
magic, Assyrian and Babylonian, 12—16
'magicians' (חרטמים), 11, 15, 18
Magnesia, battle of (B.C. 190), xxxviii, 175
Marduk (Merodach), xxiv, xxvi, xxvii, xxxi f., 3, 31
Median empire, liii, 28, 70; as represented in Dan., 29, 70, 82, 95, 100 f., 112
Melzar, 9
měně, 68 f.
Meshach, 7
Messiah, the, 102, 104 f., 106—8, 139, 144
Messianic age, lxxxix, 136, 200. *See* kingdom of God
Michael, 157, 158, 161, 162, 200
'midrash,' midrashic, lxxi *n.*, lxxii
Mishael, 7
'Most High,' 44, 90
'most holy,' a, 137

Nabopolassar, xxiii f., 2
Nabu-balâṭsu-iḳbi, father of Belshazzar, xxvii, l, li, 62
Nabu-na'id (Nabonnēdus, Nabonidus), the last native king of Babylon, xxvii—xxxii, li, 18, 60 f., 65 *n.*
'name, to make a,' 131; a name to be 'called over,' 132 f.
names, change of, 7
Nebuchadnezzar, orthography and meaning of name, 3; reign and character of, xxiv—xxvi, 46; buildings of, xxiv f., cf. 55; represented as a typical despot, 46; madness of, 58—60
Nergal-shar-uẓur (Neriglissar), xxvii, li

Onias III. (high-priest), xlii, 139 f., 182

Paneion (*or* Panias, Paneas), battle of (B.C. 198), xxxvii, 166, 172

INDEX. 213

pĕrĕs, 69
'Persia, king of' (late title), 152
Persian empire, xxxii f., 29, 95, 100 f., 112, 113, 163
Persian words in Daniel, list of, lvi f.
Pharisees (פרושים), xlv n.
Popillius Laenas, Q., 181, 186
Porphyry, ciii, 182 n., 197
post-dating, 17
'praefect' (sāgān), 32, 36
prayer towards Jerusalem, 74 ; thrice a day, 75
predictions of prophets, lxvi, lxvii
pride, Biblical teaching on, 46, 57 f.
'prince' (נגיד), 138
'Prince of princes' (שׂר שׂרים), 124
prophets, their ideal pictures of the future, lxxxviii—xc, 197 *bottom*
psaltery, 38 f.
Ptolemies, 31, 165
Ptolemy I. (Lagi), xxxiv f., 30, 165, 166
—— II. (Philadelphus), xxxvi, 166 f.
—— III. (Euergetes I.), 167 f.
—— IV. (Philopator), 168—171
—— V. (Epiphanes), 171—174, 178
—— VII. (Philometor), nephew of Antiochus Epiphanes, 101 f., 178—181, 184, 198
—— Physcon (afterwards Euergetes II.), 180 f.
purple, a royal colour, 64

Raphia, battle of (B.C. 217), xxxvii, 169, 170 f.
resurrection, the, xc—xciii, 200—202, 206
Revelation, book of, imagery or expressions in, suggested by Daniel, lxxxv, xcvii f.
'riddles,' 65 f., 123
'righteous, to make,' 202
'righteousness,' in later Heb.=alms, 54
Roman empire, whether represented in Dan., 95—98
roof-chamber, 74

sackbut, 38
'saint,' of Israel, 90; =angel, 118
satraps, 36, 71, 72

Scipio, Luc. Cornelius (Dan. xi. 18), 190
'scripture of truth,' the, 162
'seal,' to, fig. uses of, 136, 202, 205
seals, use of in antiquity, 76
Seleucidae, the, 30, 31, 165
Seleucus I. (Nicator), xxxv, 165, 166
—— II. (Callinicus), 167 f.
—— III. (Ceraunos), 168, 169 f.
—— IV. (Philopator), xxxviii, 101 f., 176 f.
Septuagint version of Dan., xviii, lxxvi, xcviii—cii
seventy weeks, prophecy of the, 126 f., 135 ff., 143—150
Shadrach, 7
'sheath' (said of the body), 89
Shinar, 3
Shushan, 111
Sibylline oracles, the so-called, lxxiii, lxxxiii f.; quoted, 98 f.
'signs and wonders,' 47
'son of the gods,' a, 44
'son of man' (בר אנש), 88, 102—110; (בן אדם), 121
Song of the Three Children, the, xviii, 44
'sorcerers' (מכשפים), 15, 18
'stand before,' to (=to attend upon), 7, 11, 32
stars, symbolizing Israelites, 116, 202
Susa, xxi, 111, 125 f.
Susanna, History of, xviii—xix
symbolic imagery, lxxvi f., lxxviii, 16 f., 18, 49, 80 (cf. cv f.), 104, 112, 113
symphonia, 39
Syriack, 19
Syro-Hexaplar version of Dan., xviii n., ci

Tammuz, 194
tĕkēl, 68 f.
temple, desecration of by Antiochus Epiphanes, xliv, 116—120, 187 f.
—— suspension of worship in for three years, 116, 119, 141 f., 187 f., 205
—— re-dedication of (B.C. 165), xlvi, 190
Theodotion's Greek version of Dan., xviii, xcviii—c

INDEX.

third pers. plur., with indef. subj. (periphr. for passive), 9 f., 53, 55, 68, 82, 88 (*bis*)
three-and-a-half years of trouble, the, 93, 204; cf. 119, 205, 206
'times,' 51
'treasurer,' 37
trigon (סבכא), 38
'troubled,' to be, inadequate rendering of various Heb. and Aram. words, 18, 48 (*bis*), 52, 63, 64, 65, 89, 94
'truth,' in objective sense, of the true religion, 117

Ulai, the river, 112
unclean foods, 8
upharsin, 68 f.
Uphaz, 154
'upon,' idiom. uses of, 18, 64, 77, 94, 155
upper chamber, 74

'watcher' (עיר), 19 f., 51
wild ass, 68
'wise men' of Babylon (חכמים), 15, 16, 22
'wise, they that be' (המשכילים), 189, 190, 202, 205
'without hand(s),' 27, 124

Xerxes, 163

Zeus Olympios, honoured by Antiochus Epiphanes, xlix, 188, 193, 194, 195
Zoroastrianism, xciv—xcvi

אדרגזר, *counsel-giver*, 37
אהה, *ah!* 128
אזדא, *certain, sure*, 20
אחשדרפן, *satrap*, 36
אכל קרצי, *to eat the pieces of*, fig. to *accuse*, 40
אמר = *to appoint*, 11
אסר, *interdict*, 73
אפדן, *palace*, 199
ארוכה, *fresh flesh, healing*, 55
אשפין, אשפים, *enchanters*, 12, 15
אשר למה, *for why? = lest*, 9

בירה, *citadel, acropolis*, 111
בלה, *to wear away*, 92
בר אנש, *son of man*, 88, 103

גבור, *mighty man, warrior*, 164
גדבר, *treasurer* (?), 37
גזרין, *determiners* (of fates), 15, 25
גיל, *age, generation*, 9
[גרה] התגרה, *to stir oneself up* (against), 169

דחון........(?), 77
דת, *law*, 21, 72
דתבר, *law-bearer, justice*, 37

הדבר, *minister*, 43
הדם, *limb*, 20
הוד, *majesty*, 155
היה (or הוא), *to be*, with the partic., 10, 88; נהיה, *to be done with* (prob.), 18, 125
המניך, *necklace*, 64
הרהרין, *imaginings*, 47

זיו, *brightness*, 57, 63
זן, *kind*, lvi

החזיק, חזק, התחזק, חזק, *to be strong, strengthen*, &c., 160, 161, 162, 189
חמודות, *desirablenesses*, 134 f.
[חנף] החניף, *to make profane*, 188 f.
[חצף] מהחצפה, *harsh*, 23
חריץ, *moat* (?), 139
[חרץ] נחרצה, נחרצת, *that which is determined*, 141, 142
חרטמים, *magicians*, 11, 15

טעם, *discretion*, 22; = *decree*, 45

יאר, *stream* (properly, the *Nile*), 203
יון, *Javan* (Greeks, Greece), 122
יקיר, *difficult*, 21
[יתר] נותר, *to be left over*, 158 f.

[כאה] נכאה, *to be cowed*, 186

INDEX.

כָּפֵר, to cancel, condone, 136
כרבל, hat (prob.), 43
כתם, gold, 154
שׂם על לב, נתן לב ל = to give heed, 8; = to apply oneself to, 156

מדע, knowledge, 5
מועד, stated (or appointed) time, 92, 121
מזון, food, 49
מחא ביד, to strike the hand of (=to arrest), 56 f.
מכון, place, 117
מלצר .... (?), 9
מנחה, oblation (also meal-offering), 31, 141 f.
מִשְׁרוּקִיתָא, pipe, 38

נבזבה, reward, 20
נגיד, leader, ruler, prince, 138
נדן, receptacle, sheath, 89
ניחוחין, tranquillizings, contentments, 31

סבכא, trigon, 38
סגן, praefect, 32
סומפניה (συμφωνία), bagpipe, lviii, 39
סרבל, mantle (prob.), 42 f.
סרך, president, 71 f.

עז פנים = defiant, 123
עִיר, wakeful one (of an angel), 49 f.
עמד (late for קום), to stand up, 122
עֹמֶד, a standing, 121
עציב, pained, 77
עצר כח, to retain strength, 155

פחה, governor, xxix, xxxiii, 36
פטיש .... (?), 43
פלאים, נפלאות, wonderful, extraordinary things, 123, 194, 203

פסנתרין (ψαλτήριον), psaltery, lviii, 38
פריץ, a breaker through, violent one, robber, 172
פרק, to tear away, break off, liberate, redeem, 54
פרתמים, foremost men, nobles, 5
פתבג, offering (of choice food), delicacy, 6
פתגם, message, word, lvi

צבא, host, warfare, 117, 152
צדא .... (?), 41
צדקה, righteousness, in late Heb. = alms, 54
צירים, throes, 160
צפיר, he-goat, 122
צרף, to smelt, fig. to refine, 190 f., 205

קטרין, knots, 66
קים, subsistent, (ever-)enduring, 79
קיתרס (κίθαρις), lyre, lviii, 38
קצין, dictator, commander, 175

[רגשׁ] הרגש, to throng, 73
רז, secret, lvi
רחב, broad place, 139
רכושׁ, substance, 171
רענן, flourishing, 47
רשׁם, to inscribe, 162

שׁאלתא, question, matter, 51
שׁלוה, tranquillity, security, 124, 183
[שׁמם] אשׁתּומם, to be appalled, 52; שׁמֵם, מְשׁמֵם, causing appalment, 118, 142, 150 f.
שׁעה, hour, 39 f., 52

תלתא, a third part, 64
תמיד, continuance (of the daily burnt-offering), 116
תפתיא .... (?), 37

www.ingramcontent.com/pod-product-compliance
Lightning Source LLC
Chambersburg PA
CBHW070232230426
43664CB00014B/2270